GPU Pro 360

Guide to Lighting

GPU Pro 360

Guide to Lighting

Edited by Wolfgang Engel

CRC Press
Taylor & Francis Group
Boca Raton London New York

CRC Press is an imprint of the
Taylor & Francis Group, an **informa** business
AN A K PETERS BOOK

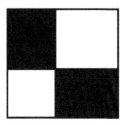

Introduction

This book describes rendering techniques of global illumination effects suited for direct rendering applications in real time.

Chris Wyman, Greg Nichols, and Jeremy Shopf describe an interactive instant radiosity method, i.e., the indirect illumination in a scene is represented with a set of virtual point light sources, which significantly reduces fill-rate compared to previous work. They use a multiresolution splatting approach and demonstrate an efficient implementation using the stencil buffer. This technique does not require geometry shaders and thus fully utilizes GPU rasterization power. The hierarchical stencil culling ensures that illumination is rendered efficiently at appropriate resolutions.

In the "Screen-Space Directional Occlusion" chapter, Thorsten Grosch and Tobias Ritschel introduce their improvement on image space ambient occlusion techniques. With only little overhead, they sample environment light and visibility (in contrast to pure ambient occlusion, where both are computed separately). Their method displays oriented and colored shadows, and additionally computes one indirect bounce of light. As other image space methods, it is independent of the scene complexity and does not require precomputation.

Péter Dancsik and László Szécsi present their GPU real-time ray-tracing technique for rendering reflective and refractive objects, and their caustics. It exploits a representation of the geometry using geometry imposters, such as distance textures, height maps, and geometry images. This allows a fast intersection computation, and the separation of static and dynamic objects make interactive speed possible.

In "Temporal Screen-Space Ambient Occlusion," Oliver Mattausch, Daniel Scherzer, and Michael Wimmer adapt temporal coherence for improving the performance of *screen-space ambient occlusion* (SSAO) techniques. Their algorithm reuses *ambient occlusion* (AO) sample information from previous frames if available, and adaptively generates more AO samples as needed. Spatial filtering is applied only to regions where the AO computation does not yet converge. This improves the overall quality as well as performance of SSAO.

In "Level-of-Detail and Streaming Optimized Irradiance Normal Mapping," Ralf Habel, Anders Nilsson, and Michael Wimmer describe a clever technique for irradiance normal mapping, which has been successfully used in various games. They introduce a modified hemispherical basis (hierarchical, in the spirit of spherical harmonics) to represent low-frequency directional irradiance. The key to this basis is that it contains the traditional light map as one of its coefficients, and further basis functions provide additional directional information. This enables shader *level-of-detail* (LOD) (in which the light map is the lowest LOD), and streaming of irradiance textures.

"Real-Time One-Bounce Indirect Illumination and Indirect Shadows Using Ray Tracing," by Holger Gruen, describes an easy-to-implement technique to achieve one-bounce indirect illumination, including shadowing of indirect light, in real time, which is often neglected for fully dynamic scenes. His method consists of three phases: rendering of indirect light with *reflective shadow maps* (RSMs), creating a three-dimensional grid as acceleration structure for ray-triangle intersection using the capabilities of Direct3D 11 hardware, and, finally, computing the blocked light using RSMs and ray casting, which is then subtracted from the result of the first phase.

In their chapter, "Real-Time Approximation of Light Transport in Translucent Homogenous Media," Colin Barré-Brisebois and Marc Bouchard describe an amazingly simple method to render plausible translucency effects for a wide range of objects made of homogenous materials. Their technique combines precomputed, screen-space thickness of objects with local surface variation into a shader requiring only very few instructions and running in real time on a PC and console hardware. The authors also discuss scalability issues and the artist friendliness of their shading technique.

"Diffuse Global Illumination with Temporally Coherent Light Propagation Volumes," by Anton Kaplanyan, Wolfgang Engel, and Carsten Dachsbacher, describes the global-illumination approach used in the game *Crysis 2*. The technique consists of four stages: in the first stage all lit surfaces of the scene are rendered into RSMs. Then a sparse three-dimensional grid of radiance distribution is initialized with the generated *surfels* from the first stage. In the next step, the authors propagate the light in this grid using an iterative propagation scheme and, in the last stage, the resulting grid is used to illuminate the scene similarly to the irradiance volumes technique described by Natalya Tatarchuk in the technical report "Irradiance Volumes for Games" (ATI Research, 2004).

The next chapter is "Ray-Traced Approximate Reflections Using a Grid of Oriented Splats," by Holger Gruen. In this chapter, Gruen exploits the features of DX11-class hardware to render approximate ray-traced reflections in dynamic scene elements. His method creates a 3D grid containing a surface splat representation on-the-fly and then ray marches the grid to render reflections in real time. Gruen also outlines further improvements, for example, using hierarchical grids, for future hardware.

Our next chapter is "Screen-Space Bent Cones: A Practical Approach," by Oliver Klehm, Tobias Ritschel, Elmar Eisemann, and Hans-Peter Seidel. Ambient occlusion computed in screen space is a widely used approach to add realism to real-time rendered scenes at constant and low cost. Oliver Klehm and his coauthors describe a simple solution to computing bent normals as a byproduct of screen-space ambient occlusion. This recovers some directional information of the otherwise fully decoupled occlusion and lighting computation. The authors further extend bent normals to bent cones, which not only store the average direction of incident light, but also the opening angle. When preconvolving distant lighting, this results in physically more plausible lighting at the speed and simplicity of ambient occlusion.

The chapter "Physically Based Area Lights," by Michal Drobot, discusses the lighting approach used in the Playstation 4 exclusive launch title *Killzone: Shadow Fall* from Guerrilla Games. The author went beyond the energy preserving model implementation and focused on accurate area light representation needed, for example, for realistic specular reflections of the Sun. Area lights are almost a necessity for effective work with the new energy preserving lighting models, as these don't allow artists to fake bright and wide specular lobes any more.

"High Performance Outdoor Light Scattering Using Epipolar Sampling," by Egor Yusov, describes the efficient solution for rendering large scale Sun-lit atmospheres. The author uses epipolar sampling and 1D min-max shadow maps to accelerate the rendering process.

The next chapter, "Hi-Z Screen-Space Cone-Traced Reflections," by Yasin Uludag, describes the fast screen-space real-time reflections system used in the game *Mirror's Edge*. Uludag uses ideas from cone tracing to produce plausible reflections for any surface roughness as well as hierarchical Z-buffers to accelerate the ray marching pass.

"TressFX: Advanced Real-Time Hair Rendering," by Timothy Martin, Wolfgang Engel, Nicolas Thibieroz, Jason Yang, and Jason Lacroix, discusses techniques used for hair rendering in the *Tomb Raider*. The authors cover individual conservative hair rasterization and antialiasing, transparency sorting using linked lists, as well as lighting and shadowing of the hair volume.

"Wire Antialiasing," by Emil Persson, focuses on the very specific problem of antialiasing and lighting of wire meshes (such as telephone cables).

The chapter "Real-Time Lighting via Light Linked List," by Abdul Bezrati, discusses an extension to the deferred lighting approach used at Insomniac Games. The algorithm allows us to properly shade both opaque and translucent surfaces of a scene in an uniform way. The algorithm manages linked lists of lights affecting each pixel on screen. Each shaded pixel then can read this list and compute the appropriate lighting and shadows.

The next two chapters describe techniques used in *Assassin's Creed IV: Black Flag* from Ubisoft. "Deferred Normalized Irradiance Probes," by John Huelin, Benjamin Rouveyrol, and Bartłomiej Wroński, describes the global illumination with day–night cycle support. The authors take time to talk about various tools and runtime optimizations that allowed them to achieve very quick turnaround time during the development.

"Volumetric Fog and Lighting," by Bartłomiej Wroński, focuses on volumetric fog and scattering rendering. The chapter goes beyond screen-space ray marching and describes a fully volumetric solution running on compute shaders and offers various practical quality and performance optimizations.

The next chapter, "Physically Based Light Probe Generation on GPU" by Ivan Spogreev, shows several performance optimizations that allowed the generation of specular light probes in *FIFA 15*. The algorithm relies on importance sampling in order to minimize the amount of image samples required to correctly approximate the specular reflection probes.

"Real-Time Global Illumination Using Slices," by Hugh Malan, describes a novel way of computing single-bounce indirect lighting. The technique uses slices, a set of 2D images aligned to scene surfaces, that store the scene radiance to compute and propagate the indirect lighting in real time.

The next three chapters try to solve a particular set of performance or quality issues in tiled forward or deferred rendering techniques. The last chapter brings new ideas to cloud rendering and lighting and goes beyond the usual ray marching through several layers of Perlin noise.

"Clustered Shading: Assigning Lights Using Conservative Rasterization in DirectX 12," by Kevin Örtegren and Emil Persson, discusses an interesting improvement and simplification of clustered shading by utilizing conservative rasterization available in DirectX 12. Tiled shading partitions screen into a set of 2D tiles and for each tile finds all lights that intersect it. Geometry rendering then reads the light information from the corresponding tile and performs actual shading. Clustered shading uses 3D cells instead of 2D tiles and reduces the amount of lights that can potentially affect a given pixel.

"Fine Pruned Tiled Light Lists," by Morten S. Mikkelsen, describes a novel tiled rendering optimization used in *Rise of the Tomb Raider*. Assignment of lights to tiles happens in two steps. The first step computes a simple bounding volume intersection with the 2D tile. The second step actually determines whether any pixel in the tile intersects with the light shape in three dimensions and excludes all lights that do not affect the visible pixels. The second step is more costly but greatly reduces the amount of lights per tile. This chapter also utilizes asynchronous compute to utilize spare GPU cycles during shadow map rendering, effectively making this computation almost free.

"Deferred Attribute Interpolation Shading," by Christoph Schied and Carsten Dachsbacher, presents an exciting take on classical deferred shading. Instead of storing material properties in the G-buffer, the authors chose to store triangle information for each pixel and evaluate the material at a later stage of the rendering. This approach greatly reduces the bandwidth requirements of deferred rendering and allows for much easier support of multi-sample antialiasing techniques.

"Real-Time Volumetric Cloudscapes," by Andrew Schneider, describes the cloud rendering solution used in *Horizon: Zero Dawn* by Guerrilla Games. The author focuses on two important aspects of cloud rendering. First, he describes a novel way of combining Worley and Perlin noises and flow maps to approximate shapes of various cloud types. Second, he focuses on challenges of correct approximation of various lighting phenomena in the clouds.

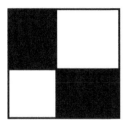

Web Materials

Example programs and source code to accompany some of the chapters are available on the CRC Press website: go to https://www.crcpress.com/9780815385523 and click on the "Downloads" tab.

The directory structure follows the book structure by using the chapter numbers as the name of the subdirectory.

General System Requirements

The material presented in this book was originally published between 2010 and 2016, and the most recent developments have the following system requirements:

- The DirectX June 2010 SDK (the latest SDK is installed with Visual Studio 2012).

- DirectX 11 or DirectX 12 capable GPUs are required to run the examples. The chapter will mention the exact requirement.

- The OS should be Microsoft Windows 10, following the requirement of DirectX 11 or 12 capable GPUs.

- Visual Studio C++ 2012 (some examples might require older versions).

- 2GB RAM or more.

- The latest GPU driver.

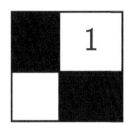

Fast, Stencil-Based Multiresolution Splatting for Indirect Illumination
Chris Wyman, Greg Nichols, and Jeremy Shopf

1.1 Introduction

Realism has long been an important goal for both offline and interactive renderers. Global illumination provides visual richness not achievable with direct illumination models and plays a vital role in perceived realism. Unfortunately the cost of global effects generally precludes use in interactive applications and has led to the development of numerous approximations, including screen-space approximations [Ritschel et al. 09], fast ray tracing via intelligent shooting of select rays [McGuire and Luebke 09], and instant radiosity solutions [Dachsbacher and Stamminger 06].

Recent work significantly improves quality and speed, but important trade-offs must still be considered when selecting an interactive global illumination algorithm. Screen-space approximations, while easy to implement, generally achieve interactions only between adjacent geometry and exhibit problems near image discontinuities. Ray-tracing techniques have difficulties in fully dynamic scenes and require many rays to avoid undersampling. Instant radiosity solutions, typically based on reflective shadow maps [Dachsbacher and Stamminger 05], stress GPU fill-rate and scale linearly with the number of virtual point lights used to approximate lighting.

This chapter presents improvements to interactive instant radiosity solutions that significantly reduce fill rate by using *multiresolution* splats and demonstrates an efficient implementation using the stencil buffer. Unlike initial multiresolution splatting [Nichols and Wyman 09], this implementation does not perform amplification via geometry shaders and thus remains on the GPU fast path. Instead, we utilize the GPU's hierarchical stencil culling to efficiently render illumination at appropriate resolutions.

We first review the concepts of instant radiosity and reflective shadow maps before introducing multiresolution splatting and prior implementation techniques. Section 1.5 then describes our stencil-based splatting approach, provides pseudocode for the rendering algorithms, and details the mathematics of our splat refinement metrics.

1.2   Quick Review: Instant Radiosity

One way to quickly render complex lighting is *instant radiosity* [Keller 97], which is actually a bit of a misnomer. Instant radiosity can be thought of as a variant of bidirectional path tracing [Lafortune and Willems 93], where paths are traced from both the light source and the viewpoint and then combined to reduce variance in the computed illumination. Figure 1.1 depicts how instant radiosity's bidirectional approach works. First photons are emitted from the light. These photons may bounce a number of times, and each photon-surface intersection becomes a *virtual point light* (or VPL). In the second stage, paths from the eye are emitted and each intersection along the path gathers direct light from both the VPLs and original lights.

Graphics hardware can accelerate instant radiosity by rendering one shadow map per VPL and performing per-pixel shading computations using standard hardware lights to represent the VPLs. However, path emission usually occurs on the CPU and high quality illumination in dynamic scenes requires thousands of VPLs (and their shadow maps) each frame.

Figure 1.1. Instant radiosity emits photons probabilistically (left) and path intersections are stored as virtual point lights (VPLs). Each VPL acts as a point light (right), directly illuminating all unoccluded pixels. Combining direct light from the original source and the VPLs approximates a global illumination solution.

1.3   Quick Review: Reflective Shadow Maps

Reflective shadow maps improve instant radiosity's performance by adding assumptions that allow an efficient implementation entirely on the GPU. In particular, global illumination is limited to a single bounce. Additionally VPL visibility is ignored, allowing VPLs to illuminate all pixels despite occluders (see Figure 1.2). The basic algorithm [Dachsbacher and Stamminger 06] works as follows:

1. Render a shadow map augmented by position, normal, and color.

2. Select VPLs from this shadow map.

3. Render from the eye using only direct light.

4. For each VPL:

    (a) Draw a "splat" centered on the VPL in eye-space.

    (b) Each splat fragment illuminates one pixel from a single VPL.

    (c) Blend the fragments into the direct illumination buffer.

For a full solution each VPL must affect every pixel, requiring a full-screen splat for each VPL. Unfortunately, this consumes a lot of fillrate and quickly reduces performance with increasing resolution or VPL sampling (see Figure 1.3). Reducing the buffer resolution used during splatting improves performance at the cost of blurring illumination over discontinuities and high-frequency normal variations. Alternatively, smaller focused splats can be rendered around each VPL, but since every VPL cannot affect each pixel, the results can appear unnaturally dark.

Figure 1.2. Reflective shadow maps select VPLs directly from the light's shadow map (left), limiting indirect light to a single bounce. Each VPL acts as a point light (right) that contributes direct illumination. Unlike instant radiosity, VPL visibility is ignored, allowing indirect illumination to travel through occluders.

Figure 1.3. Splatting illumination from each VPL onto the entire screen (left) consumes enormous fillrate. Reducing render buffer resolution (center) reduces fillrate in exchange for blurring illumination across discontinuities and normal variations. Focusing splats around their corresponding VPLs (right) artificially darkens illumination as only a subset of VPLs contribute to each pixel.

1.4 Multiresolution Splatting

Multiresolution splatting [Nichols and Wyman 09] addresses the fillrate problem by rendering splats into multiple buffers of varying resolution. This allows a full-screen splat for each VPL but allows adaptive selection of the splat resolution to reduce fill rate where illumination varies slowly. Where blurring is unacceptable, splats are rendered at high resolution. Elsewhere, splat resolution varies depending on the acceptable level amount of blur.

Using naive splatting techniques, each full-screen splat covers a million fragments (at 1024^2). Multiresolution splatting reduces this to around 60,000 multiresolution fragments, even in reasonably complex scenes such as in Figure 1.4. This fillrate reduction compares to naively splatting into a reduced resolution (256^2) buffer, without the resulting blur.

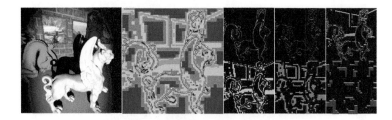

Figure 1.4. Multiresolution illumination splatting starts with a rendering of direct illumination (left). Each VPL spawns a full-screen splat, allowing each VPL to contribute light to every pixel. However, these splats are rendered at multiple resolutions depending on the speed of local illumination variations. A pseudocolor full-screen splat (center) shows the areas of varying resolution, which are rendered into distinct buffers (right).

1.4.1 Implementing Multiresolution Splatting

Implementing this multiresolution approach is quite similar to the prior technique from Section 1.3:

1. Render a shadow map augmented by position, normal, and color.

2. Select VPLs from this shadow map.

3. Render from the eye using only direct light.

4. For each VPL:

    (a) Draw a full-screen "splat."

    (b) Each splat fragment illuminates one texel (in one of the multiresolution buffers in Figure 1.4) from a single VPL, though this texel may ultimately affect multiple pixels.

    (c) Blend each fragment into the appropriate multiresolution buffer.

5. Combine, upsample and interpolate the multiresolution buffers.

6. Combine the interpolated illumination with the direct light.

This has two key algorithmic differences: splats are split into clusters of different resolution fragments (in step 4b) and the multiresolution buffer needs upsampling to final resolution (in step 6) prior to blending with the direct light. These are discussed in Sections 1.4.2 and 1.4.3.

1.4.2 Iterative Splat Refinement

Splitting splats into clusters of fragments at various resolutions proves quite time-consuming. Our prior work used the iterative refinement is depicted in Figure 1.5.

For each VPL, this iterative approach spawns a full-screen splat at the coarsest possible illumination buffer resolution. At each fragment we determine if this coarse sampling blurs the illumination unacceptably, due to discontinuities inside the fragment (see Section 1.5.2 for details on discontinuity detection). Unacceptable blur results in a refinement of the fragment into four, finer resolution fragments. Otherwise the coarse sample is left alone. This process is repeated iteratively until no unacceptable blur remains or we refine to the final image resolution (see Listing 1.1).

Our implementation uses a cheap preprocess to perform an initial coarse 16^2 sampling, stored into a small vertex buffer. The outer `for` loop is managed by the CPU, with each loop cycle invoking a render pass. A geometry shader processes

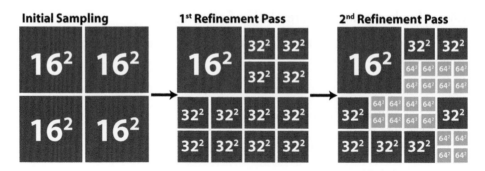

Figure 1.5. Iterative refinement of multiresolution splats starts with a uniform, coarse image sampling (e.g., 16^2 samples). Coarse fragments are processed, identifying those needing further refinement and creating four finer resolution fragments. Further iterations further refine fragments until some threshold is achieved, such as a maximal refinement level or exceeding a specified fragment count.

each patch, checks for any image discontinuities, and selectively outputs either the original input patch or four refined patches. The output list of patches is either iteratively refined or rendered, as follows, as multiresolution fragments (see Listing 1.2).

Here, multiresolution fragments are rendered once per VPL. We found reversing the order of the loops, rendering the multiresolution splat just once, and gathering illumination from all VPLs generally gives better performance. Additionally, iterative patch refinement can either happen once per splat or once per frame. The second method leads to higher performance, in exchange for less flexible refinement metrics.

```
patches ← CoarseImageSampling();
for  (i=1 to numRefinementPasses)  do
  for all  (p ∈ patches)  do
    if  ( NoDiscontinuity( p ) )  then
      continue;
    end if
    patches ← (patches − {p});
    patches ← (patches ∪ SubdivideIntoFour( p ) );
  end for
end for
```

Listing 1.1. Setting acceptable blur.

```
patches ← IterativelyRefinedPatches();
vpls ← SampledVirtualPointLights();
for all  ( v ∈ vpls )  do
  for all  ( p ∈ patches )  do
    TransformToFragmentInMultiresBuffer( p ); // In vertex shader
    IlluminateFragmentFromPointLight( p, v ); // In fragment shader
    BlendFragmentIntoMultiresBufferIllumination( p );
  end for
end for
```

Listing 1.2. Gathering illumination from VPLs for splatting.

1.4.3 Upsampling Multiresolution Illumination Buffers

Since our multiresolution illumination buffer contains fragments at various resolutions as well as large, empty regions, we need an upsampling stage to recreate a fully populated, high resolution buffer (see Listing 1.3). This upsampling basically uses a "pull" step from "push-pull" gap-filling algorithms (e.g., [Grossman and Dally 98]). The coarsest resolution buffer is upsampled by a factor of two with bilinear interpolation occurring only between valid texels (i.e., those covered by coarse splat fragments). Interpolated results are combined with the next finer resolution buffer and the upsample, interpolate, and combine process is iteratively

```
coarserImage ← CoarseBlackImage();
for all  ( buffer resolutions j from coarse to fine )  do
  finerImage ← MultresBuffer( level j );
  for all  ( pixels p ∈ finerImage )  do
    if  ( InvalidTexel( p, coarserImage ) )  then
      continue; // Nothing to blend from lower resolution!
    end if
    p₁, p₂, p₃, p₄ ← FourNearestCoarseTexels( p, coarserImage );
    ω₁, ω₂, ω₃, ω₄ ← BilinearInterpolationWeights( p, p₁, p₂, p₃,
    p₄ );
    for all  ( i ∈ [1..4] )  do
      ωᵢ = InvalidTexel( pᵢ, coarserImage ) ) ?  0 :  ωᵢ;
    end for
    finerImage[p]  += (ω₁p₁ + ω₂p₂ + ω₃p₃ + ω₄p₄)/(ω₁ + ω₂ + ω₃ + ω₄)
  end for
  coarserImage ← finerImage;
end for
```

Listing 1.3. Unsampling the multiresolution illumination buffer.

repeated until a complete, full-resolution indirect illumination buffer is achieved. Note that one ω_i must be nonzero (otherwise `InvalidTexel( p, coarserImage )` would be true).

1.5   Fast Stencil-Based Multiresolution Splatting

Sadly, splat refinement via iteratively applying a geometry shader causes most GPUs to fall off their "fast track," as the number of multiresolution fragments generated is not known in advance. This degrades performance significantly. It also initiates passes on the CPU, introducing synchronization points. Additionally, both a vertex *and* fragment shader process each multiresolution fragment.

We now introduce a significantly faster approach for multiresolution splatting that avoids these bottlenecks. Two key observations allow us to transform the problem. First, the iterative refinement steps have no dependencies (and can thus be parallelized) for most classes of discontinuity detectors. Second, we reformulate multiresolution splatting as a hierarchical culling problem utilizing the GPU's built-in hierarchical stencil culling.

1.5.1   Parallel Splat Refinement into a Stencil Buffer

Consider the depiction of a multiresolution splat shown in Figure 1.6. For a given fragment **F**, we can determine whether **F** belongs in the multiresolution splat by evaluating a discontinuity detector at **F** and the corresponding coarser fragment **F***. This suffices as long as a discontinuity in **F** implies that **F*** also contains a discontinuity. Given that most discontinuity detectors, including those outlined

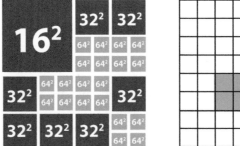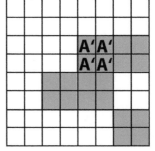

Figure 1.6. The multiresolution splat (left) depicted in Figure 1.5 can be computed in parallel rather than iteratively. All fragments in the multiresolution buffers (right) are processed in parallel. Fragment A still contains discontinuities, and is thus invalid (fragments A' are used instead). Fragment B is valid; it contains no discontinuities but fragment B^* does. Fragment C needs no refinement, but since C^* also has no discontinuities fragment C is unnecessary.

```
for all  (fragments f ∈ image)  do
  if  ( ∄j such that f ∈ MIPMAPLEVEL( j ) )  then
    continue; // Fragment not actually in multires buffer
  end if
  j ← GETMIPMAPLEVEL( f );
  if  ( ISDISCONTINUITY( f, j ) )  then
    continue; // Fragment needs further subdivision
  end if
  if  ( NODISCONTINUITY( f, j + 1 ) )  then
    continue; // Coarser fragment did not need subdivision
  end if
  SETSTENCIL( f );
end for
```

Listing 1.4. Parallel splat refinement.

in Section 1.5.2, satisfy this criteria, we can evaluate fragments in all levels of the multiresolution buffer in parallel (see Listing 1.4).

Note this refinement algorithm only has a single loop, instantiated by drawing a full-screen quad over the multiresolution buffer depicted in Figure 1.7. This multiresolution illumination buffer is actually stored as a single buffer containing all resolution buffers. Loop internals are performed in the fragment shader, simultaneously for all fragments.

Effectively, the shader splits fragments into four categories: those not in the multiresolution buffer (i.e., from the gray area of Figure 1.7), those that need additional refinement, those where a coarser fragment already suffices, and those

Figure 1.7. Conceptually, multiresolution rendering uses a "render-to-mipmap" approach (left). Our new stencil-based approach requires a flattened multiresolution buffer to instantiate a parallel refinement pass that sets fragment stencil bits (right).

that belong to the multiresolution splat. In the first three cases, the fragment is discarded. In the last case, we set a stencil bit to allow quick identification of appropriate fragments during splatting.

1.5.2 Discontinuity Detection

Discontinuity detection plays an important role in both performance and quality. Splatting relies on the observation that low resolution illumination suffices in smoothly changing areas, but finer resolution is necessary near discontinuities. Poor discontinuity detection either misses edges or refines excessively. Missing edges introduce blurring and excessive refinement requires additional splat fragments that add to the rendering cost.

We use a two-phase discontinuity detection. Most importantly, depth discontinuities around object silhouettes must be identified to avoid blur between background and foreground geometry. Secondly, large normal variations such as the creases on a cube also introduce high frequencies into the indirect illumination. While not necessarily apparent when combining with direct and indirect illumination, blur across large normal variations stands out in shadowed regions where only indirect light contributes.

Other factors may also influence the discontinuity detector. For instance, illumination discontinuities due to reflected Phong highlights may call for additional refinement. Similarly, the use of multiresolution splatting for screen space ambient occlusion may necessitate not only edge detection, but also proximity detection. However, for diffuse global illumination we found depth and normal tests suffice.

Detecting depth discontinuities. Silhouette edges exhibit large depth changes from one pixel to the next. The most space-efficient way to identify such discontinuities relies on a maximum mipmap, where each mipmap texel stores the maximal one-pixel depth discontinuity inside its screen-space area. We compute this max-mipmap by first applying a 3×3 filter to a linear-depth image. This filter computes a per-pixel derivative $\Delta \mathbf{D}_{x,y}$ as

$$\Delta \mathbf{D}_{x,y} = \frac{\max_{\forall s,t}(\mathbf{D}_{s,t}) - \min_{\forall s,t}(\mathbf{D}_{s,t})}{\mathbf{D}_{x,y}}.$$

Here $\mathbf{D}_{s,t}$ is the linear depth of the pixel (s,t), for $s \in [x-1...x+1]$ and $t \in [y-1...y+1]$. We then create a maximum mipmap, with each texel at level j storing the maximum of its four children at level $j-1$.

Computing $\Delta \mathbf{D}_{x,y}$ via a 3×3 filter (instead of in a 2×2 mipmap cluster) is vital to finding discontinuities occurring over power-of-two pixel boundaries.

The normalization by $\mathbf{D}_{x,y}$ chooses slightly smaller discontinuities nearer the viewer over larger, distant discontinuities. Blurring nearby edges is typically more noticeable than on smaller distant objects.

The function $\texttt{IsDiscontinuity}(\,\mathbf{D}_{x,y}, j\,)$ looks up $\Delta\mathbf{D}_{x,y}$ from mipmap level j and determines if it is larger than a specified depth threshold $\mathbb{T}_{depth}$. Larger values of $\mathbb{T}_{depth}$ results in fewer refined fragments, in exchange for additional blur across depth discontinuities. We found varying $\mathbb{T}_{depth}$ with mipmap level j can be helpful, starting with a lower value at coarse resolutions and increasing for finer levels. This avoids coarse splat fragments suddenly splitting into very fine fragments with small camera motions.

Detecting normal discontinuities. Strong illumination variations inside object silhouettes typically arise due to variations in surface orientation. To properly refine our multiresolution splats in these areas, we need a mipmap that identifies large normal variations. Ideally, we would create a normal cone for each mipmap texel and subdivide if the cone angle exceeds some threshold.

Unfortunately, we know no efficient approach for creating an image-space mipmap of normal cones. Instead we use a conservative approximation that gives similar results. Given a set of n unit length normals $\vec{\mathbf{N}}_0$, $\vec{\mathbf{N}}_1$, ..., $\vec{\mathbf{N}}_n$, we compute maximum and minimum vectors $\vec{\mathbf{N}}_{\max}$ and $\vec{\mathbf{N}}_{\min}$:

$$\vec{\mathbf{N}}_{\max} = \begin{pmatrix} \max_{s\in[0..n]}(\vec{\mathbf{N}}_s.x) \\ \max_{s\in[0..n]}(\vec{\mathbf{N}}_s.y) \\ \max_{s\in[0..n]}(\vec{\mathbf{N}}_s.z) \end{pmatrix}, \quad \vec{\mathbf{N}}_{\min} = \begin{pmatrix} \min_{s\in[0..n]}(\vec{\mathbf{N}}_s.x) \\ \min_{s\in[0..n]}(\vec{\mathbf{N}}_s.y) \\ \min_{s\in[0..n]}(\vec{\mathbf{N}}_s.z) \end{pmatrix}.$$

The angle between $\vec{\mathbf{N}}_{\max}$ and $\vec{\mathbf{N}}_{\min}$ then conservatively bounds the angle of a corresponding normal cone. Furthermore, these max and min operations can be efficiently performed during creation of a min-max mipmap (e.g., [Carr et al. 06]).

Simplifying further, we avoid computing the angle between $\vec{\mathbf{N}}_{\max}$ and $\vec{\mathbf{N}}_{\min}$ and instead compute $\Delta\vec{\mathbf{N}} = \vec{\mathbf{N}}_{\max} - \vec{\mathbf{N}}_{\min}$. Components of $\Delta\vec{\mathbf{N}}$ range from 0 for similar orientations to 2 for widely varying normals. We introduce a threshold $\mathbb{T}_{normal} \in [0..2]$ and detect a normal discontinuity whenever any component of $\Delta\vec{\mathbf{N}}$ exceeds $\mathbb{T}_{normal}$.

As image-space normals lie in a single z-hemisphere, we only store x-and y-components of $\vec{\mathbf{N}}_{\max}$ and $\vec{\mathbf{N}}_{\min}$ in a single, four-component mipmap. Our function $\texttt{IsDiscontinuity}(\,\vec{\mathbf{N}}_{x,y}, j\,)$ looks up the two-component vectors in the jth mipmap level and performs two threshold comparisons.

1.5.3 Rendering with Stenciled Multiresolution Splatting

After creating a stencil buffer containing the locations of our splat's multiresolution fragments, we must define how to render a splat. Standard splatting approaches render a single screen aligned quad per splat. However since many of our multiresolution fragments do not belong in our splats, we cannot expect good performance this way.

Instead, our approach relies on modern GPUs' hierarchical stencil and z culling. Naively drawing a full-screen multiresolution splat consumes significant fill rate. However, enabling the stencil test to draw only appropriate fragments (e.g., those shown in Figure 1.7) allows early stencil culling to cheaply eliminate nearly all extraneous fragments. Algorithmically, this works as shown in Listing 1.5.

```
pixels ←FullScreenQuad();
vpls ← SampledVirtualPointLights();
for all ( v ∈ vpls ) do
  for all ( p ∈ pixels )  do
    if ( FailsEarlyStencilTest( p ) ) then
       continue; // Not part of multiresolution splat
    end if
    IlluminatePatchFromPointLight( p, v );
  end for
end for
```

Listing 1.5. Rendering.

Since this culling utilizes hierarchical rasterization hardware, it processes roughly the same number of splat fragments as the earlier implementation (from Section 1.4.2) without the overhead of running each fragment though an unnecessary vertex shader.

Stenciled splatting generates a multiresolution buffer *identical* to the slower implementation from Section 1.4.2. As before, this must be upsampled to a single full resolution buffer before combining indirect and direct illumination.

1.6 Results and Analysis

We implemented both the iterative and stencil refinement techniques in OpenGL using GLSL. Table 1.1 compares performance of the two techniques in four scenes of varying complexity. Timings were obtained on a dual-core 3GHz Pentium 4 with a GeForce GTX 280, with all results rendered at 1024^2. Both refinement and splatting techniques generate identical images, compared in Figure 1.8 to renderings without indirect illumination.

Rendering Steps for Iterative Refinement (Section 1.4)	Cornell Box	Feline Scene	Sponza Atrium	Indoor Garden
1) Render Direct Light	1.8 ms	5.8 ms	2.8 ms	2.8 ms
2) Render RSM	0.9 ms	2.3 ms	1.4 ms	1.6 ms
3) Create Min-Max Mipmap	0.7 ms	0.7 ms	0.7 ms	0.7 ms
4) Iterated Refinement	1.3 ms	1.7 ms	1.3 ms	1.6 ms
5) Splat All Fragments	45.8 ms	67.0 ms	58.1 ms	130.0 ms
6) Upsample Illumination	1.6 ms	1.7 ms	1.3 ms	1.3 ms
Total	52.1 ms	79.2 ms	65.6 ms	138.0 ms

Rendering Steps for Stenciled Refinement (Section 1.5)	Cornell Box	Feline Scene	Sponza Atrium	Indoor Garden
1) Render Direct Light	1.8 ms	5.8 ms	2.8 ms	2.8 ms
2) Render RSM	0.9 ms	2.3 ms	1.4 ms	1.6 ms
3) Create Min-Max Mipmap	0.7 ms	0.7 ms	0.7 ms	0.7 ms
4) Stenciled Refinement	0.7 ms	0.7 ms	0.7 ms	0.7 ms
5) Stencil Splatting	2.5 ms	3.5 ms	3.0 ms	6.6 ms
6) Upsample Illumination	1.6 ms	1.7 ms	1.3 ms	1.3 ms
Total	8.2 ms	14.7 ms	9.9 ms	13.7 ms

	Cornell Box	Feline Scene	Sponza Atrium	Indoor Garden
Total Frame Speedup	6.4×	5.4×	6.6×	10.1×
Step 4 and 5 Speedup	14.7×	16.4×	16.1×	18.0×

Table 1.1. Rendering costs for iterative refinement and splatting (discussed in Section 1.4) compared to stencil refinement and splatting (described in Section 1.5) for various scenes. Our fast stencil approach reduces per-frame rendering times 5–10×. Refinement and splatting costs alone decrease by more than 15×.

Key points to notice include that the variable cost iterative refinement is replaced by a constant cost stenciled refinement that does not depend on scene complexity. Costs for iterative refinement depend on the number of multiresolution fragments generated whereas costs for stenciled refinement depend only on image resolution. Additionally, stenciled refinement does not require Shader Model 3 hardware, allowing multiresolution splatting to run on older hardware.

The clear win with stenciled refinement, though, occurs during splatting. Each multiresolution fragment no longer needs to be instantiated as an individual point, properly positioned by a vertex shader, and rasterized into a single fragment. Instead a single full-screen quad eliminates all these extraneous vertex and rasterization steps and renders all fragments in parallel, utilizing hierarchical hardware culling to eliminate excess fragments.

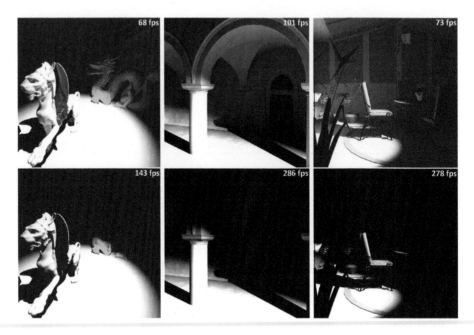

Figure 1.8. (Top) Renderings of the feline scene, Sponza atrium, and indoor garden using multiresolution splatting. (Bottom) The same renderings without one-bounce indirect lighting.

1.7   Conclusion

This chapter explored a new stencil-based formulation of multiresolution splatting. Multiresolution splatting significantly reduces the fillrate consumption used by GPU-based instant radiosity techniques for interactive diffuse global illumination. Our stenciled approach reduces the cost of approximate one-bounce indirect lighting to only a few milliseconds without introducing blur.

While presented in the context of interactive global illumination, we believe our stencil-based multiresolution technique applies to a variety of other problems. In particular, any problem decomposable into multiple independent frequencies may benefit from a similar approach.

1.8   Demo and Source

Available at http://www.cs.uiowa.edu/~cwyman/.

Bibliography

[Carr et al. 06] Nathan A. Carr, Jared Hoberock, Keenan Crane, and John C. Hart. "Fast GPU Ray Tracing of Dynamic Meshes Using Geometry Images." In *Graphics Interface*, 137, 137, pp. 203–209, 2006.

[Dachsbacher and Stamminger 05] Carsten Dachsbacher and Marc Stamminger. "Reflective Shadow Maps." In *Symposium on Interactive 3D Graphics and Games*, pp. 203–208, 2005.

[Dachsbacher and Stamminger 06] Carsten Dachsbacher and Marc Stamminger. "Splatting Indirect Illumination." In *Symposium on Interactive 3D Graphics and Games*, pp. 93–100, 2006.

[Grossman and Dally 98] J. Grossman and William Dally. "Point Sample Rendering." In *Eurographics Workshop on Rendering*, pp. 181–192, 1998.

[Keller 97] Alexander Keller. "Instant Radiosity." In *Proceedings of SIGGRAPH*, pp. 49–54, 1997.

[Lafortune and Willems 93] Eric Lafortune and Yves Willems. "Bi-Directional Path Tracing." In *Compugraphics*, pp. 145–153, 1993.

[McGuire and Luebke 09] Morgan McGuire and David Luebke. "Hardware-Accelerated Global Illumination by Image Space Photon Mapping." In *High Performance Graphics*, pp. 77–89, 2009.

[Nichols and Wyman 09] Greg Nichols and Chris Wyman. "Multiresolution Splatting for Indirect Illumination." In *Symposium on Interactive 3D Graphics and Games*, pp. 83–90, 2009.

[Ritschel et al. 09] Tobias Ritschel, Thorsten Grosch, and Hans-Peter Seidel. "Approximating Dynamic Global Illumination in Image Space." In *Symposium on Interactive 3D Graphics and Games*, pp. 75–82, 2009.

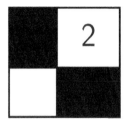

2

Screen-Space Directional Occlusion
Thorsten Grosch and Tobias Ritschel

2.1 Introduction

Real-time global illumination is still an unsolved problem for large and dynamic scenes. Currently, real-time frame rates are only achieved through approximations. One such approximation is *ambient occlusion* (AO), which is often used in feature films and computer games, because of its good visual quality and simple implementation [Landis 02]. The basic idea is to pre-compute average visibility values at several places on the surface of the mesh. These values are then multiplied at runtime with the unoccluded illumination provided by the graphics hardware (see Figure 2.1). Typically, the visibility values are pre-computed and

Figure 2.1. Ambient occlusion can be used to combine separately computed visibility values with the unoccluded illumination from the GPU. The left image shows the unoccluded illumination, the center image shows the ambient occlusion that darkens the cavities and contact regions only. If both are multiplied, a more realistic appearance can be obtained, as shown on the right.

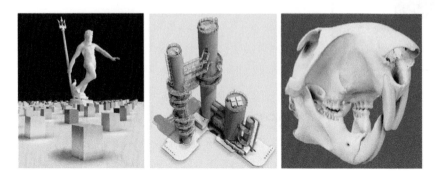

Figure 2.2. Screen-space directional occlusion examples.

stored for each vertex or texel of the mesh. The average visibility is computed by shooting some rays in the upper hemisphere of the surface point and counting the number of blocked rays. Due to this separation of visibility and illumination, ambient occlusion is only a coarse approximation of the actual illumination, but the results are often visually plausible. In this chapter, we present an extension of ambient occlusion that displays *oriented* and *colored* shadows correctly and additionally computes one *indirect bounce* of light [Ritschel et al. 09] (see Figure 2.2). Since our method works in image space, it is independent of the scene complexity and any kind of dynamic scenes can be illuminated at real-time frame rates without any pre-computation.

2.2 Screen-Space Ambient Occlusion

One drawback of ambient occlusion is that it works only for static scenes. If visibility values are pre-computed for each vertex or texel, these values become invalid if the mesh is deformed. Some first ideas for dynamic scenes were presented by [Bunnell 06] and [Hoberock and Jia 07] by approximating the geometry with a hierarchy of discs. The easiest way to deal with dynamic scenes is to compute ambient occlusion based on the information in the frame buffer, so-called *screen-space ambient occlusion* (SSAO). Here the depth buffer is used to compute the average visibility values *on-the-fly* instead of a pre-computation. As shown in [Mittring 07], the computational power of recent GPUs is sufficient to compute SSAO in real time. Moreover, this approach does not require any special geometric representation of the scene, since only the information in the frame buffer is used to compute the occlusion values. It is not even necessary to use a three-dimensional model that consists of polygons, since we can compute occlusion from any rendering that produces a depth buffer.

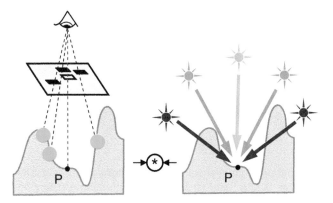

Figure 2.3. Screen-space ambient occlusion: for each pixel in the frame buffer, a set of neighboring pixels is inspected and a small sphere is placed at the corresponding three-dimensional position. An occlusion value is computed for each sphere and all these values are accumulated into one ambient occlusion value. Finally, this value is multiplied with the unoccluded illumination from all directions.

To explain the differences of our method (see Figure 2.3), let us have a look at the computation of standard SSAO [Shanmugam and Arikan 07] first: for each pixel in the frame buffer, we inspect some neighboring pixels and read their depth values. This allows us to compute the corresponding three-dimensional position and we can place a small sphere with a user-defined radius there. Now an occlusion value is computed for each sphere, which depends on the solid angle of the sphere with regard to the receiver point. These occlusion values are all accumulated into a single ambient occlusion value. Finally, the unoccluded illumination from all directions (e.g., from a set of point lights extracted from an environment map) is computed with the standard GPU pipeline and the AO value is multiplied with this unoccluded illumination.

2.2.1 SSAO Problems

Ambient occlusion typically displays darkening of cavities and contact shadows, but all *directional* information of the incoming light is ignored. This happens because only the geometry is used to compute ambient occlusion while the actual illumination is ignored. A typical problem case is shown in Figure 2.4: in case of directionally-varying incoming light, ambient occlusion will display a wrong color. Therefore we extend recent developments in screen-space AO towards a more realistic illumination we call *screen-space directional occlusion* (SSDO). Since we loop through a number of neighboring pixels in the fragment program, we can

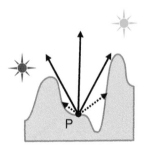

Figure 2.4. A typical problem case for ambient occlusion with a red and a green light. Since the red light is blocked and the green light illuminates the point **P**, we expect to see a green shadow here. But ambient occlusion computes the illumination from all directions first, so the point **P** is initially yellow and then scaled by some average occlusion value, resulting in a brown color.

compute an *individual* visibility value for each of them instead of collapsing all the information into a single AO value. So the basic idea is to use the visibility information for the incoming light from each direction and illuminate *only* from the *visible* directions, resulting in a directional illumination. For the further description of SSDO we assume that we have a deep frame buffer that contains positions, normals, and reflectance values for each pixel.

2.3   Screen-Space Directional Occlusion

Since we can not directly shoot rays to test the visibility for a given direction, we need some kind of approximation for the visibility. Here we assume the local geometry around each point to be a height field. The test for visibility therefore reduces to a test whether a sample point is below or above the surface. All sampling points below the surface are treated as occluders while sampling points above the surface are classified as visible. Our algorithm is visualized in Figure 2.5 and can be summarized as follows: first, we place a hemisphere around the three-dimensional point of the pixel, which is oriented along the surface normal. The radius r_{max} of this hemisphere is a user parameter and determines the size of the local neighborhood where we search for blockers. Then, some three-dimensional sampling points are uniformly distributed inside the hemisphere. Again, the number of sampling points N is a user parameter for time-quality trade-off. Now we test if the illumination from each sampling direction is blocked or visible. Therefore, we back-project each sampling point into the deep frame buffer. At the pixel position we can read the three-dimensional position on the surface, and move each point onto the surface. If the sampling point moves towards the viewer,

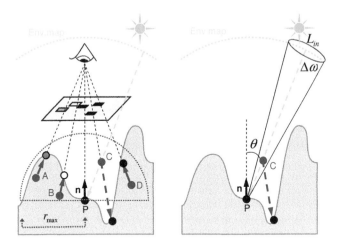

Figure 2.5. Screen-space directional occlusion. Left image: to compute the Directional Occlusion at point P, we create some uniformly distributed sampling points in a hemi-sphere and back-project them into the deep frame buffer. Each point which is (initially) below the surface is treated as an occluder. Right image: the illumination is only computed from the visible points. Here we assume a solid angle for each sampling direction and use the incoming radiance from a blurred environment map.

it was initially below the surface and it is classified as blocked. If it moves away from the viewer, it was initially above the surface and it is classified as visible. In the example in Figure 2.5, the points **A**, **B** and **D** are below the surface and classified as blockers. Only sample **C** is visible, because it is above the surface. Consequently, the illumination is computed from direction **C** only. We found this to be a good approximation for the visibility. For details about misclassifications see [Ritschel et al. 09].

2.3.1 Direct Illumination

For natural illumination we use an environment map. Since we try to keep the number of samples low, we blur the environment map in a preprocess. The filter kernel is thereby adjusted to the solid angle of one sample. In this way we compute the average radiance over the solid angle of one sampling direction and we avoid flickering artifacts, e.g., when the environment map is rotated. Figure 2.6 shows an example of an environment map and the blurred version. Since the solid angle is different for each pixel in the environment map, a spatially-varying filter would be required. However, we found the visible error to be small and use a Gaussian filter with a fixed kernel size. Finally, the direct illumination

Figure 2.6. We use a blurred environment map for illumination since the number of samples is low; this image already contains the average of the incoming radiance inside the solid angle for each incoming direction. In this example we use a Lat/Long representation of the Kitchen Environment Map by Paul Debevec.

can be computed as follows:

$$L_{\text{dir}}(P) = \sum_{i=1}^{N} \frac{\rho}{\pi} \cdot L_{\text{in}}(\omega_i) \cdot V(\omega_i) \cdot \cos\theta_i \cdot \Delta\omega,$$

where L_{in} is the blurred radiance from the environment map in direction ω, V is our approximated visibility and $\frac{\rho}{\pi}$ is the diffuse BRDF of the surface. The $\Delta\omega$ is the solid angle for each direction and can be computed as $\Delta\omega = \frac{2\pi}{N}$. For a given resolution $w \times h$ of the environment map, the pixel width of the filter kernel can be approximated as $\sqrt{(w \cdot h/2)/N}$

Note that the environment map that we use in Figure 2.6 contains two main sources of light: an orange lamp on the ceiling and the light blue illumination which is coming in through the windows. Ambient occlusion does not correctly display the resulting shadows since the incoming illumination is ignored and only average visibility values are used. So the resulting ambient occlusion basically consists of static, grey contact shadows. But in fact, this illumination results in two colored, oriented shadows which are correctly reproduced with directional occlusion. Figure 2.7 shows the visual difference between directional occlusion and ambient occlusion, rendered at similar frame rates.

Listing 2.1 shows the main part of the GLSL fragment program that computes SSDO. We use a deep frame buffer that contains the position and normal in world coordinates for each pixel (**positionTexture** and **normalTexture**). Furthermore, we use pre-computed, random sampling points which are uniformly distributed in a unit hemisphere. These sampling points are stored in a two-dimensional texture (**seedTexture**), where each line contains N different sampling points. Each pixel then selects a different line, depending on the pixel position (see Section 2.4). Then, a local frame around the pixel normal is computed and

Figure 2.7. Difference between ambient occlusion and directional occlusion. Note how ambient occlusion just displays grey contact shadows whereas directional occlusion can reconstruct the correct orientation and color for shadows of small-scale details.

the sampling points are scaled by the hemisphere radius (`sampleRadius`) and rotated into the local frame. This world-space sample position is then projected into the current frame buffer and the corresponding texture coordinate is computed (`occluderTexCoord`). Next, we read the position buffer at this texture coordinate and compute the z-coordinate in camera coordinates of both the world space sample position and the position in the position buffer (`depth` and `sampleDepth`). Since we look along the negative z-axis, all depth values will be negative. If `-sampleDepth` is smaller that `-depth`, the sampling point moved towards the viewer and we found an occluder. For practical reasons, we ignore all occluders with a projected sample position which is outside the hemisphere (`distanceTerm`). Otherwise, the silhouette edges of all objects would be darkened. Instead of using 0 and 1 for visibility, we add another user-controlled parameter to adjust the SSDO strength (`strength`). Therefore, the sum of radiances `directRadianceSum` might become negative and we have to clamp to zero after the loop.

```
// Read position and normal of the pixel from deep framebuffer.
vec4 position = texelFetch2D(positionTexture,
                ivec2(gl_FragCoord.xy), 0);
vec3 normal = texelFetch2D(normalTexture,
                ivec2(gl_FragCoord.xy), 0);

// Skip pixels without geometry.
if(position.a > 0.0) {
```

```
vec3 directRadianceSum = vec3(0.0);
vec3 occluderRadianceSum = vec3(0.0);
vec3 ambientRadianceSum = vec3(0.0);
float ambientOcclusion = 0.0;

// Compute a matrix that transform from the unit hemisphere.
// along z = -1 to the local frame along this normal
mat3 localMatrix = computeTripodMatrix(normal);

// Compute the index of the current pattern.
// We use one out of patternSize * patternSize
// pre-defined unit hemisphere patterns (seedTexture).
// The i'th pixel in every sub-rectangle uses always
// the same i'th sub-pattern.
int patternIndex = int(gl_FragCoord.x) % patternSize +
                   (int(gl_FragCoord.y) % patternSize) *
                   patternSize;

// Loop over all samples from the current pattern.
for(int i = 0; i < sampleCount; i++) {

    // Get the i'th sample direction from the row at
    // patternIndex and transfrom it to local space.
    vec3 sample = localMatrix * texelFetch2D(seedTexture,
                ivec2(i, patternIndex), 0).rgb;
    vec3 normalizedSample = normalize(sample);

    // Go sample-radius steps along the sample direction,
    // starting at the current pixel world space location.
    vec4 worldSampleOccluderPosition = position +
    sampleRadius * vec4(sample.x, sample.y, sample.z, 0);

    // Project this world occluder position in the current
    // eye space using the modelview-projection matrix.
    // Due to the deferred shading, the standard OpenGL
    // matrix can not be used.
    vec4 occluderSamplePosition = (projectionMatrix *
    modelviewMatrix) * worldSampleOccluderPosition;

    // Compute the pixel position of the occluder:
    // Do a division by w first (perspective projection),
    // then scale/bias by 0.5 to transform [-1,1] -> [0,1].
    // Finally scale by the texture resolution.
    vec2 occluderTexCoord = textureSize2D(positionTexture,0)
    * (vec2(0.5) + 0.5 * (occluderSamplePosition.xy /
    occluderSamplePosition.w));

    // Read the occluder position and the occluder normal
    // at the occluder texture coordinate.
    vec4 occluderPosition = texelFetch2D(positionTexture,
                        ivec2(occluderTexCoord), 0);
    vec3 occluderNormal = texelFetch2D(normalTexture,
                        ivec2(occluderTexCoord), 0);
```

```
// Compute depth of current sample pos. in eye space.
float depth = (modelviewMatrix *
worldSampleOccluderPosition).z;

// Compute depth of corresponding (proj.) pixel position.
float sampleDepth = (modelviewMatrix *
occluderPosition).z + depthBias;

// Ignore samples that move more than a
// certain distance due to the projection
// (typically singularity is set to hemisphere radius).
float distanceTerm = abs(depth - sampleDepth) <
singularity ? 1.0 : 0.0;

// Compute visibility when sample moves towards viewer.
// We look along the -z axis, so sampleDepth is
// larger than depth in this case.
float visibility = 1.0 - strength *
(sampleDepth > depth ? 1.0 : 0.0) * distanceTerm;

// Geometric term of the current pixel towards the
// current sample direction
float receiverGeometricTerm = max(0.0,
dot(normalizedSample, normal));

// Compute spherical coordinates (theta, phi)
// of current sample direction.
float theta = acos(normalizedSample.y);
float phi = atan(normalizedSample.z,normalizedSample.x);
if (phi < 0) phi += 2*PI;

// Get environment radiance of this direction from
// blurred lat/long environment map.
vec3 senderRadiance = texture2D(envmapTexture,
vec2( phi / (2.0*PI), 1.0 - theta / PI ) ).rgb;

// Compute radiance as the usual triple product
// of visibility, radiance, and BRDF.
// For practical reasons, we post-multiply
// with the diffuse reflectance color.
vec3 radiance = visibility * receiverGeometricTerm *
                senderRadiance;

// Accumulate the radiance from all samples.
directRadianceSum += radiance;

// Indirect light can be computed here
// (see Indirect Light Listing)
// The sum of the indirect light is stored
// in occluderRadianceSum
}

// In case of a large value of-strength, the summed
// radiance can become negative, so we clamp to zero here.
```

```
        directRadianceSum = max(vec3(0), directRadianceSum);
        occluderRadianceSum = max(vec3(0), occluderRadianceSum);

        // Add direct and indirect radiance.
        vec3 radianceSum = directRadianceSum + occluderRadianceSum;

        // Multiply by solid angle and output result.
        radianceSum *= 2.0 * PI / sampleCount;
        gl_FragColor = vec4(radianceSum, 1.0);

    } else {

        // In case we came across an invalid deferred pixel
        gl_FragColor = vec4(0.0);
    }
```

Listing 2.1. SSDO source code.

2.3.2   Indirect Bounces of Light

SSDO can correctly handle directionally varying, incoming light. However, up to now we have described only direct light, which is arriving from an environment map. Additionally, some light is reflected from the surface, resulting in indirect light. Several offline techniques, like Radiosity or Path Tracing can compute such indirect light, but not at real-time frame rates for dynamic scenes. In contrast to this, we work in image space again and use the direct light stored in the frame buffer as a source of indirect light. The work by Mendez et al. [Mendez et al. 06] already mentions such an option: here, an average reflectance color is used to approximate the color bleeding. In contrast to this, we can include the *sender direction* and the actual *sender radiance*. In the previous section, we already classified each sampling point as visible or occluded. If a sampling point is occluded, we assumed that no light is arriving from this direction. But in fact, it is only the direct light which is blocked. Instead, some indirect light is reflected from the blocker position towards the receiver point. To compute this indirect light, we use the pixel color L_{pixel} of each sampling point which was classified as occluded and place a small, colored patch on the surface (an example is shown in Figure 2.8). The pixel normal is used to orient the patch on the surface. Now we compute the fraction of light that is arriving from this sender patch to our receiver point $\mathbf{P}$ using a *form factor*.

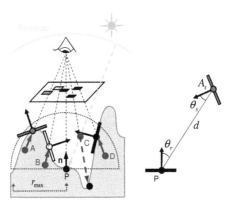

Figure 2.8. For indirect light, a small patch is placed on the surface for each occluder and the direct light stored in the frame buffer is used as sender radiance. To compute the fraction of light arriving at the receiver, we use a simple form factor approximation.

Finally, the indirect light at point $\mathbf{P}$ can be approximated as

$$L_{\text{ind}}(P) = \sum_{i=1}^{N} \frac{\rho}{\pi} \cdot L_{\text{pixel,i}}(\omega_i) \cdot (1 - V(\omega_i)) \cdot F_{rs},$$

where

$$F_{rs} = \frac{A_s \cdot \cos\theta_{s,i} \cdot \cos\theta_{r,i}}{\pi \cdot d_i^2}$$

is a simple form factor approximation that computes the fraction of light, which is transferred from sender s to receiver r. Angles $\theta_{s,i}$ and $\theta_{r,i}$ are the angles between the transmission direction and the sender / receiver normal, and d_i is the distance between sender and receiver. This distance should be clamped to avoid singularity problems. Alternatively, a constant can be added in the denominator. The area of the sender patch is A_s. Since we take the information from a single pixel, we do not know the actual shape of the sender, so we set this value to $A_s = \pi \cdot r_{\text{max}}^2/N$. If we assume a flat, circular area around $\mathbf{P}$ and use N uniformly distributed samples, each sample will cover this area. Depending on the slope distribution inside the hemisphere, the actual value for can be higher, so we can use this parameter to control the strength of the color bleeding manually. In the example in Figure 2.8, no indirect light is calculated for patch $\mathbf{A}$, because it is back-facing. Patch $\mathbf{C}$ is in the negative half-space of $\mathbf{P}$, so it does not contribute, too. Patches $\mathbf{B}$ and $\mathbf{D}$ are both senders of indirect light. Figure 2.9 shows the visual effect if indirect light is included. Listing 2.2 shows an excerpt of the fragment program that computes the indirect light.

Figure 2.9. Difference between SSAO and SSDO with an additional indirect bounce. Note how the colored cubes reflect colored light onto the ground if they are directly illuminated.

```
// Read the (sender) radiance of the occluder.
vec3 directRadiance = texelFetch2D(directRadianceTexture,
                           ivec2(occluderTexCoord), 0);

// At this point we already know the occluder position and
// normal from the SSDO computation. Now we compute the distance
// vector between sender and receiver.
vec3 delta = position.xyz - occluderPosition.xyz;
vec3 normalizedDelta = normalize(delta);

// Compute the geometric term (the formfactor).
float unclampedBounceGeometricTerm =
      max(0.0, dot(normalizedDelta, -normal)) *
      max(0.0, dot(normalizedDelta, occluderNormal)) /
      dot(delta, delta);

// Clamp geometric term to avoid problems with close occluders.
float bounceGeometricTerm = min(unclampedBounceGeometricTerm,
                           bounceSingularity);

// Compute the radiance at the receiver.
vec3 occluderRadiance = bounceStrength * directRadiance *
                           bounceGeometricTerm;

// Finally, add the indirect light to the sum of indirect light.
occluderRadianceSum += occluderRadiance;
```

Listing 2.2. Source code for indirect light computation. At this point the pixel position and the occluder position / texture coordinate are known from the SSDO computation. This code can be included at the end of the loop in Listing 2.1.

2.4   Interleaved Sampling

To reduce the number of samples per pixel we use *interleaved sampling*, as suggested by [Segovia et al. 06] and already used for ambient occlusion, e.g. in [Mittring 07]. Therefore, we pre-compute $M \times M$ sets of N low-discrepancy samples. At runtime, each pixel inside a block of $M \times M$ pixels selects one of the sets. The low-discrepancy sampling ensures that each set contains well-distributed, uniform samples, without a preferred direction. Consequently, a similar illumination is computed for each pixel. However, since we use a quite low number of samples, the repeating $M \times M$ pattern is often visible in the image, and the whole image looks noisy. To remove this noise, a geometry-sensitive blur is finally used. Figure 2.10 shows the original and the blurred image. For the geometry-aware blur, a kernel size of approximately $M \times M$ removes most of the noise. The filter we use inspects all values inside the filter kernel, but the average is computed only for those pixels with a position and normal which is similar to the position and normal of the center pixel. To avoid blurring over material edges, we apply this filter to irradiance values and multiply with the (colored) pixel reflectance after blurring. To further improve the rendering speed, a separated filter can be used: first, a vertical filter $(1 \times M)$ is used and then the output is passed to a horizontal filter $(M \times 1)$. Although this concatenation of two one-dimensional filters is not perfectly identical to the original two-dimensional filter [Pham and van Vliet 05], this is a useful approximation in many practical cases. Please have a look at the demo, available in the book's web materials, to see the strong similarity of both filters and the difference in rendering speed.

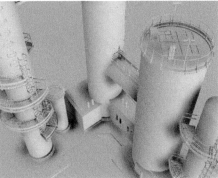

Figure 2.10. Interleaved sampling. By using a different set of sampling points for each pixel, the original image looks noisy and the repeating $M \times M$ pattern is visible (left). This noise can be removed with a geometry-sensitive blur filter of approximately the pattern size (right).

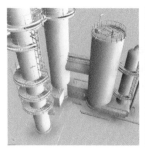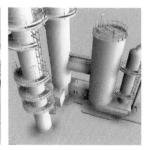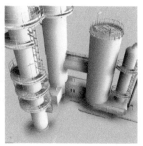

Figure 2.11. Varying the number of samples per pixel (from left to right: 4, 8, 16, and 32).

2.5 Discussion

Our method is an approximation of global illumination that correctly displays oriented and colored shadows as well as approximated indirect light, which is entirely computed in image space. The time and quality depends on several parameters: first of all, the number of samples N determines the quality of the resulting shadows, as shown in Figure 2.11. The corresponding timings are listed in Table 2.1. When increasing the search radius, more blockers can be found, but the sampling density is reduced if N is kept fixed. Figure 2.12 shows the effect of this. Increasing the radius of the hemisphere results in larger shadows, but shadows of small details start to disappear. A higher number of samples can be used to bring these shadows back.

Although we achieve plausible illumination, such an approach has several limitations. First of all, we can only simulate occlusion or indirect light which is visible in the frame buffer. If a blocker is not visible it will never throw a shadow.

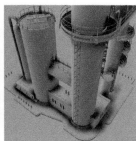

Figure 2.12. When varying the radius of the hemisphere, different types of shadows become visible. Using a small radius shows the shadows of the ladder and the small sticks on the ground. When increasing the radius (and keeping the number of samples fixed), these shadows disappear; shadows of larger structures, like the contact shadows of the tower, start to appear. Further increasing the radius results in larger shadows.

Resolution	N	SSDO	Indirect Light
512×512	4	2.1	1.0
512×512	8	3.4	3.8
512×512	16	9.4	5.0
512×512	32	16.4	8.9
1024×1024	4	9.2	2.9
1024×1024	8	18.2	8.4
1024×1024	16	32.1	17.9
1024×1024	32	60.2	37.0

Table 2.1. SSDO and indirect light timing values for different frame buffer resolutions and varying number of samples. All timing values are in milliseconds, measured on a NVIDIA GeForce GTX 280 graphics card.

This can happen for two reasons: the blocker is occluded by some other object from the current viewpoint or the blocker is outside the viewing frustum. For a moving camera, this can result in shadows that disappear and reappear later. The same can happen for sources of indirect light: anything which is not visible in the camera image will not create indirect light. Both cases can be solved by depth peeling and additional cameras, as shown in [Ritschel et al. 09]. However, the frame rate drops since we have to render the scene several times from several viewpoints. The use of a voxel model seems to be a promising alternative, as recently shown by [Reinbothe et al. 09].

2.6 Conclusion

In this chapter, we presented screen-space directional occlusion (SSDO). This technique is an improvement over ambient occlusion and allows fast computation of directional occlusion and indirect light, both entirely computed in image space. Due to the plausible results we think that SSDO can make its way into upcoming computer games for approximate real-time global illumination of large and dynamic scenes.

Bibliography

[Bunnell 06] M Bunnell. "Dynamic Ambient Occlusion and Indirect Lighting." In *GPU Gems 2*, edited by W. Engel, pp. 223–233. Addison-Wesley, 2006.

[Hoberock and Jia 07] Jared Hoberock and Yuntao Jia. "High-Quality Ambient Occlusion." In *GPU Gems 3*, Chapter 12. Reading, MA: Addison-Wesley, 2007.

[Landis 02] H. Landis. "RenderMan in Production." In *ACM SIGGRAPH 2002 Course 16*, 2002.

[Mendez et al. 06] A. Mendez, M. Sbert, J. Cata, N. Sunyer, and S. Funtane. "Realtime Obscurances with Color Bleeding." In *ShaderX4: Advanced Rendering Techniques*, pp. 121–133. Charles River Media, 2006.

[Mittring 07] Martin Mittring. "Finding Next-Gen: CryEngine 2." In *SIGGRAPH '07: ACM SIGGRAPH 2007 courses*, pp. 97–121. New York: ACM, 2007.

[Pham and van Vliet 05] T.Q. Pham and L.J. van Vliet. "Separable Bilateral Filtering for Fast Video Preprocessing." *IEEE International Conference on Multimedia and Expo*.

[Reinbothe et al. 09] Christoph Reinbothe, Tamy Boubekeur, and Marc Alexa. "Hybrid Ambient Occlusion." *EUROGRAPHICS 2009 Areas Papers*.

[Ritschel et al. 09] Tobias Ritschel, Thorsten Grosch, and Hans-Peter Seidel. "Approximating Dynamic Global Illumination in Image Space." In *Proceedings ACM SIGGRAPH Symposium on Interactive 3D Graphics and Games (I3D) 2009*, pp. 75–82, 2009.

[Segovia et al. 06] Benjamin Segovia, Jean-Claude Iehl, Richard Mitanchey, and Bernard Péroche. "Non-interleaved Deferred Shading of Interleaved Sample Patterns." In *SIGGRAPH/Eurographics Graphics Hardware*, 2006.

[Shanmugam and Arikan 07] Perumaal Shanmugam and Okan Arikan. "Hardware Accelerated Ambient Occlusion Techniques on GPUs." In *Proceedings of the ACM SIGGRAPH Symposium on Interactive 3D Graphics and Games*, pp. 73–80. ACM, 2007.

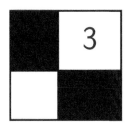

3

Real-Time Multi-Bounce Ray-Tracing with Geometry Impostors
Péter Dancsik and László Szécsi

3.1 Introduction

Rendering reflective and refractive objects or their caustics is a challenging problem in real-time applications. It requires non-local shading, which is intricate with the incremental rendering pipeline, where a fragment shader can only work with local, interpolated vertex data and textures to find the color of a surface point. The above effects are usually associated with ray-tracing, which does not offer the same performance as incremental rendering. Typically, ray-tracing effects are added into real-time scenes using specialized tricks based on texturing. These usually assume that there is only one reflective or refractive object in the scene, and that it is enough to consider only one or two bounces of light. In this chapter, we follow a similar practical philosophy, but remove these limitations in order to be able to render scenes like a complete chessboard full of glass pieces, or even refractive objects submerged into animated liquids.

We extend previous approximate ray-tracing techniques that were based on environment distance impostors [Szirmay-Kalos et al. 05] in order to handle scenes with multiple reflective and refractive objects in real time. There are two key ideas that allow this. First we turn around the distance impostor approach not to intersect internal rays with enclosing environmental geometry, but external rays with an object. We show how the secondary reflected and refracted rays can be traced efficiently. We also examine how other types of geometry impostors—namely geometry images [Carr et al. 06] and height fields [Oliveira et al. 00, Policarpo et al. 05]—can be adapted to the same task.

The second idea is the separation of static and dynamic objects. Classic distance impostors can be used for the static environment, and only the environment impostors of moving objects need to be updated in every frame. Light paths passing through moving objects can be found by searching their geometry impostors.

The proposed rendering method maintains impostors of object meshes as well as impostors for the environment of reflective or refractive objects. When such an object is rendered, the shader uses both the environment impostor and impostors of other objects to find intersections of secondary rays. In the following chapter we first examine what impostor representations we can use and how they can be used for intersection. We then deal with strategies to organize static and dynamic geometry into the environment and object impostors to facilitate real-time rendering.

3.2   Geometry Impostors

Ray-tracing requires the intersection of a light ray with scene geometry. In order to make this feasible in real-time applications, instead of intersecting a ray with actual geometry primitives, approximate representations are used. Typically, the scene is rendered into a texture from a cleverly selected reference point, and this texture is queried for intersections. When the origin of the ray is not the same as the reference point, then finding the intersection becomes a search process using consecutive dependant texture fetches. There are several approaches on how to render the geometry into textures, and how to search for the intersections using these representations. All of them use a texture as a stand-in for the actual geometry. We refer to these textures as geometry impostors.

When a ray intersects the geometry, the next step is shading the intersected surface point, meaning that we have to find the radiance emitted towards the ray origin. Therefore, a texel of an impostor has to store shading information in addition to the location of the surface point. Typically, this means that the radiance emitted towards the reference point is evaluated and stored when creating the impostor, hoping that the ray origin will not be very far from the reference point, or that the surfaces are diffuse, and the direction we look at them from does not matter. In case of highly specular surfaces, however, we need to store the surface normal vector so that we can evaluate the shading formula exactly.

In case of mirror-like or glassy objects, the color of the surface is usually uniform and does not need to be stored in every texel, but the surface normal is important as it is necessary for the computation of secondary rays.

3.2.1   Distance Impostors

Distance impostors are very much like environment maps, but they also contain the distance between a reference point and the surface points visible in the texels.

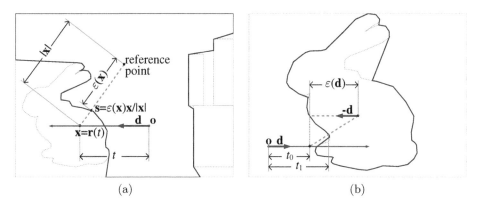

(a)   (b)

Figure 3.1. (a) Environment distance impostor nomenclature. (b) Object distance impostor with the first two steps of projection search.

This can be stored in the alpha channel conveniently. They are usually cube maps, addressable with the direction from the reference point. In case of reflective and refractive objects, the cube map contains the distance and the surface normal, and is called a *distance-normal impostor*.

If not all points of the geometry are visible from the reference point, the nonvisible parts will be missing in the impostor. Therefore, this representation works best with star-convex objects.

In this chapter, we use two distinct types of distance impostors. One of them is the *environment distance impostor* (Figure 3.1(a)). This is a cube map that contains the surrounding geometry of an object, and thus typically has multiple objects rendered onto it. We can assume that all ray origins are inside the environment, but the bounding box of included geometry is unknown. The other type of distance impostor contains a single object (Figure 3.1(b)). Rays to be traced might arrive from the outside, and the bounding box of the object is known. The objects handled this way are typically mirror or glass objects, which means these are usually distance-normal impostors.

3.2.2   Height Maps

Height maps are a classic and straightforward way of encoding 2.5-dimensional geometry in two-dimensional texture maps. The most prominent example is bump mapping, used mostly to add detail to triangle mesh models. To get a height map, the geometry is rendered onto a reference plane using an orthogonal projection, and every texel contains the distance of the surface point from the plane. There are numerous displacement mapping techniques [Szirmay-Kalos and Umenhoffer 08], ranging from bump mapping to relaxed cone tracing, that solve the ray–height map intersection problem with varying accuracy. Out of those, binary search is a simple-to-implement, solid and effective technique, even though it does not guarantee to find the first intersection.

Typically two height maps, storing displacements on the two sides of the reference plane, are needed to approximate a solid object. This representation requires a dimension along which the depth structure of the solid is simple, but arbitrary concavities are allowed in the other two dimensions.

If the solid is symmetric to the reference plane, a single height map is enough. If it has some rotational symmetry, then the reference plane can be rotated around the axis of symmetry without changing the geometry or the height map. When searching for an intersection, we can rotate the plane like a billboard to get optimal results. All intersection search algorithms perform best when the incoming rays arrive perpendicular to the reference plane.

3.2.3   Geometry Images

Geometry images [Carr et al. 06] also map surface points to a texture, but do so without projection to an image plane, using the classic UV-mapping instead. Thus finding an intersection with a ray cannot be done using a search that exploits the relation of texel coordinates and surface point locations. Instead, a bounding-volume hierarchy is built over the texels and stored in mipmap levels. The intersection algorithm is thus similar to that of ray-tracing with bounding volume hierarchies. The upside is that geometry of any complexity can be stored, but the intersection is more expensive to compute.

3.3   Intersection Computation with an Environment Distance Impostor

We can think of the environment visible from the reference point as the surface of a single, manifold object, as shown in Figure 3.1. To handle directions where nothing is visible, we can assume a skybox at a large but finite distance. The ray origin is always within the environment surface, and there always is an intersection. The ray equation is $\mathbf{r}(t) = \mathbf{o} + t\mathbf{d}$, where $\mathbf{o}$ is the ray origin, $\mathbf{d}$ is the ray direction, and t is the ray parameter. Let us use a coordinate system that has the reference point at its origin. Querying the environment with a point $\mathbf{x}$ returns $\varepsilon(\mathbf{x})$, which is the distance of the environment surface point $\mathbf{s}$ that is visible towards $\mathbf{x}$. We can compute $\mathbf{s}$ as $\varepsilon(\mathbf{x})\mathbf{x}/|\mathbf{x}|$.

At the intersection point, $\varepsilon(\mathbf{x}) = |\mathbf{x}|$, and the ratio $|\mathbf{x}|/\varepsilon(\mathbf{x})$ is one. Let $\delta(t)$ be $|\mathbf{r}(t)|/\varepsilon(\mathbf{r}(t))$, a function that computes this ratio for a point at a given ray parameter t. We call a ray parameter t' an undershooting if $\delta(t') < 1$, and an overshooting if $\delta(t') > 1$.

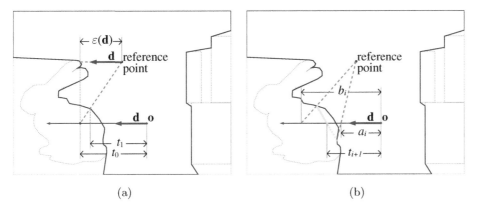

Figure 3.2. Projection and false position search in environment impostors.

We have to find the ray parameter $t^\star$ of the intersection. We use the iterative process proposed by Szirmay-Kalos [Szirmay-Kalos et al. 05], constructing a sequence of values $t_0, t_1, \ldots$ that converges to $t^\star$. Figure 3.2 shows how the values are generated. We start the first phase, which we call projection search, with classic environment mapping, querying the distance map for the ray direction, yielding distance $\varepsilon(\mathbf{d})$. This gives us an environment surface point at $\mathbf{d}\varepsilon(\mathbf{d})$. We look for the point on the ray which is the closest to this surface point. Its ray parameter t_0 can be computed as

$$t_0 = \varepsilon(\mathbf{d}) - \mathbf{o} \cdot \mathbf{d}.$$

The ray point can again be used to query the environment distance map, restarting the process. In general, the iteration can be written as

$$t_{i+1} = t_i + \varepsilon(\mathbf{d})(1 - \delta(t_i)).$$

Note that this sequence is not mathematically guaranteed to converge to the intersection, but it is easy to compute and works for practical scenes. A case that we still need to avoid is that the sequence oscillates and does not converge to the actual solution. Therefore we keep track of the largest undershooting (a_i denotes its value at the ith iteration) and the smallest overshooting (b_i at the ith iteration). As soon as we have one of both, we can switch to the false position root-finding method, depicted in Figure 3.2. We get the new guess for the ray parameter as

$$t_{i+1} = \frac{[\delta(b_i) - 1]\, a_i - [\delta(a_i) - 1]\, b_i}{\delta(b_i) - \delta(a_i)}.$$

We also update the undershooting or the overshooting value

$$a_{i+1} = \begin{cases} a_i & \text{if } \delta(t_{i+1}) > 1, \\ t_{i+1} & \text{if } \delta(t_{i+1}) < 1, \end{cases}$$

$$b_{i+1} = \begin{cases} t_{i+1} & \text{if } \delta(t_{i+1}) > 1, \\ b_i & \text{if } \delta(t_{i+1}) < 1. \end{cases}$$

Note that it is possible to use the false position root-finding method exclusively, with $a_0 = 0$, which is always an undershooting, and a sufficiently large b_0 to guarantee an overshooting.

3.4 Ray-Object Intersection Using Distance Impostors

First we calculate the intersections with the bounding box of the object. If there are none, then neither will there be any intersection with the object.

The most important difference between the ray–environment intersection and the ray–object intersection is that the ray origin is not within the surface, and an intersection is not guaranteed. However, if there is an intersection, then we can compute it as the intersection of a new ray started along the original one, from within the object, and in the opposing direction. The resulting search process is depicted in Figure 3.1. If there is no intersection, the algorithm returns a bogus result, but it is easy to check whether the δ value is near one, which holds true only for real intersections.

3.5 Ray-Object Intersection Using Height Maps

The two halves of the object are approximated by two height map impostors. When looking for an intersection with a ray, we call them the near half and the far half, depending on the ray direction and irrespective of the actual position of the ray origin. The solution of the ray–height map intersection problem is very similar to the search we performed in distance impostors. Let $z(\mathbf{x})$ be the distance of point $\mathbf{x}$ from the reference plane, and $h(\mathbf{x})$ the geometry height at the orthogonal projection of $\mathbf{x}$ onto the plane. We call a ray parameter a an undershooting if $z(\mathbf{r}(a)) > h(\mathbf{r}(a))$, and call b an overshooting if $z(\mathbf{r}(b)) < h(\mathbf{r}(b))$. Starting with an initial search range of (a_0, b_0), we iterate to get a convergent sequence just like we did with the false position method. However, now we use binary search (see [Oliveira et al. 00], [Policarpo et al. 05]). The next element is always computed as

$$t_{i+1} = \frac{a_i + b_i}{2}.$$

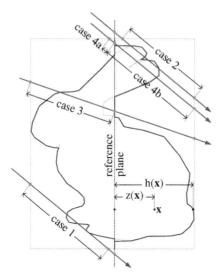

Figure 3.3. Height impostor.

The undershooting or the overshooting value is updated just like in the false position method. Note that binary search does not actually require us to query $h(a_0)$ or $h(b_0)$. Thus, if an adequate search range has already been obtained, it is preferable to the false position method. Furthermore, if both endpoints of the search range happen to be undershootings, binary search still has a decent chance to hit an actual overshooting, delivering a correct result. The false position method would instantly step out of the search range in such a situation.

With binary search, we need to identify the initial search ranges in the near and far height maps. First, we calculate the intersection ray parameters with the reference plane and with the bounding box of the object (see Figure 3.3). The ray crosses the plane at t_{plane}, enters the bounding box at t_{enter}, and leaves at t_{exit}. If the ray does not intersect the bounding box, then there will be no intersection with the object either. If $t_{\mathrm{exit}} < t_{\mathrm{plane}}$ (case 1 in Figure 3.3), we only need to search the height map of the near half between t_{enter} and t_{exit}. Likewise, if $t_{\mathrm{plane}} < t_{\mathrm{enter}}$ (case 2), we only have to search the height map of the far half between the entrance and exit points. Otherwise we first search the height map of the near half between t_{enter} and t_{plane} (case 3 and 4a). If no intersection has been found, we also search the far half between t_{plane} and t_{exit} (case 4b).

Note that binary search is not guaranteed to find the first intersection, and in cases 1 and 2 it can happen that both endpoints of the search range are undershootings. However, a tightly fitting bounding box minimizes those cases, and binary search often performs flawlessly in practice.

3.6   Tracing Multiple Refractions within a Single Object

Using any of the above impostors—or even geometry images—we can store surface normals and use the surface normal at the found intersection point to spawn refraction or reflection rays. Tracing these against the geometry can again be done with the previously discussed methods, continuing up to an arbitrary number of bounces. Two refractions within an object are typically sufficient to get plausible results. When objects are rendered incrementally, we still can use the impostor to trace secondary rays in the pixel shader.

3.7   Multiple Ray Bounces with Object Impostors Only

Rigid bodies like glass objects can have their impostors computed only once, when loading the model geometry, and the impostors of dynamic geometries like fluids must be rendered in every frame. Identical objects can share impostors. It is straightforward to construct a ray tracer once all the objects in the scene have their own object impostors. Simply, all objects must be intersected with all rays, always keeping the smallest positive intersection. Exceptions can be made for rays started within objects, where it is sufficient to only search the impostor of the containing object itself. The first intersection with the eye rays can easily be found by rasterization, and then the pixel shader operating on these first bounce points can perform the rest of the ray-tracing.

However, for a reasonably populated scene, this approach is prohibitively expensive. One way to attack the problem would be to use spatial subdivision schemes like regular grids or bounding volume hierarchies to decrease the number of intersection computations. We found that maintaining and traversing these structures carries an overhead that is in a higher order of magnitude than intersection searches themselves. Thus, they start to pay off at high object counts, and less so in typical real-time rendering scenes. That said, a complete ray-tracing solution could be built on impostors and bounding volume hierarchies, without the need to make assumptions on the dynamism of objects in the scene. In this chapter, we discard this option in favor of real-time rendering of more typical scenes.

3.8   Multiple Ray Bounces with Environment Distance Impostors Only

Every reflective or refractive object in the scene can have its own environment distance impostor, storing the incoming radiance in every pixel. If there is any kind of dynamism in the scene, then the environment impostors have to be re-rendered in every frame. In the final to-screen pass, diffuse objects can be rendered normally. The pixel shader of refractive or reflective objects has to perform a simple intersection search with the environment to obtain reflected colors.

Note that we can use the very same rendering algorithm also when creating the environment impostors, meaning that proper reflections will appear in the environment map itself. Of course, in the very first frame, the environment maps will only contain the diffuse color information. In the second frame, we can use the maps of the first frame when creating the new impostors, which will already contain reflections of a single bounce. In later frames, impostors will contain more and more bounces, even if somewhat delayed. Thus, multi-bounce rendering is fairly automatic. However, updating all cube maps requires a large number of rendering passes, which is not feasible in every frame. Applications mostly get around this by allowing only a single reflective object or by reflecting a static environment only.

3.9   Combination of Environment and Object Impostors

The object impostor method works great as long as we only have few objects, and environment impostors are effective if the environment is static. In a typical scene, only few objects are moving. Thus, it is possible to use environment impostors that do not need to be updated in every frame for the static environment, and add the moving objects back by using object impostors.

First, every refractive or reflective object should have an impostor of its own static environment, and only these have to be updated regularly (though not necessarily in every frame that belongs to moving objects). We also need object impostors for all meshes used by specular objects, for both multiple refraction and intersection with external rays.

Whenever a reflective or refractive object is rendered, the secondary rays are traced against the static environment using the environment impostor of the rendered object, and against all of the moving objects using their object impostors; this keeps the nearest result. The rendered object itself—if it happens to be a moving object—is excluded from intersections with the secondary rays. Figure 3.4 illustrates this process. At the shaded surface point (1), the reflection and refraction rays are generated, and the refraction ray is tested against the object impostor to get the exit point (2) and the second refraction. Then both exiting rays are tested against the environment (3 and 4) and the object impostors of moving objects. In the depicted example, the reflection ray hits such an object (5). There the process starts from the beginning, using the object impostor (6) and environment impostor (7 and 8) of the moving object. However, we do not test the exiting reflection and refraction rays for intersection with other moving objects anymore, as those would be hardly noticeable in the rendered image.

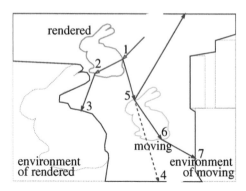

Figure 3.4. Combination of environment and object impostors.

3.10   Caustics and Shadows

As described by Wyman [Wyman and Davis 06], caustics can be rendered effectively using approximate geometry representations by tracing light paths from light sources. The geometry impostors can also be used this way. We render the scene placing a camera at the light source, with a shader that outputs the texture coordinates of diffuse surfaces hit after multiple bounces. Then these photon hits are splatted into the caustic light maps as small billboards, as described in [Szirmay-Kalos et al. 05]. The caustic light maps are used to modulate the diffuse color when rendering the objects. To add shadows, we used conventional shadow mapping.

Caustics or shadows due to moving objects can cause changing lighting conditions on static objects as well. This would invalidate the environment impostors of static objects, forcing us to update them in every frame, jeopardizing real-time performance and undermining the concept of separation of static and moving objects. There are two solutions to this problem. First, if we can identify potential caustics and shadow receivers, we can handle them as moving objects when tracing reflection and refraction rays. These objects are diffuse, so we can stop the process depicted in Figure 3.4 at hit 5. Second, we can avoid invalidating the static environment impostors by storing the texture coordinates instead of diffuse colors. When an intersection with the environment is found, the diffuse texture and the caustics light map can be accessed to determine the surface color. This requires a uniformly addressable texture mapping covering the complete static geometry, which can be a single UV-atlas or a texture array of individual UV-atlases, where supported.

3.11 Example Application: Glass Chess

A diffuse chessboard with a complete set of glass pieces—only one of them moving at any time—is an ideal scenario for the presented method. There are only seven meshes used (the board and the six chess piece types); thus only seven object impostors are required. All objects are symmetrical, accurately represented by height maps. Apart from the knight, all pieces exhibit cylindrical symmetry, allowing us to rotate the reference plane freely around the vertical axis. The chessboard itself is diffuse, and it is the only caustics and shadow receiver. It is handled as a moving object because of its dynamic lighting.

In every frame the shadow map, the caustics light map, and the environment impostor of the moving piece are updated. The object impostors and the environment impostors of stationary pieces remain unchanged. When rendering an object, the pixel shader intersects the reflected and refracted rays with the environment impostor, the chessboard, and the moving piece. When a new piece starts moving, the previously moving piece becomes stationary. All environment impostors must be updated to exclude the new moving piece and include the old one.

The chessboard scene with 33 glass pieces (a full chess set plus a sphere of glass) was rendered at a 640×480 resolution (see Figure 3.5 for screenshots). The height map impostors had 512×512 resolution, while the environment and object impostors had $6 \times 256 \times 256$ and $6 \times 512 \times 512$ texels, respectively. We

Figure 3.5. Left: the whole test scene. Right: double refraction using height map impostors.

	Height Map	Distance Impostor
No moving objects	102	188
Classic	2.5	3.5
Combined	22	35

Table 3.1. Frames per second rates achieved with different rendering algorithms and impostor representations.

used an NVIDIA GeForce 8800GTX graphics card for measurements. Table 3.1 summarizes the results. We compared three algorithms. In the first case, no objects were moving, and therefore it was not necessary to update any of the impostors in any frame. In the second case, we used the classic method described in Section 3.8, where environment impostors have to be updated in every frame. The last line of the table shows frame rates for our proposed method combining environment and object impostors. All cases were measured with both height map and distance cube map object impostors. As these impostors are used in all three algorithms for computing multiple refractions within objects, this choice impacts frame rates in all the three cases. The proposed method was ten times faster than the classic approach with both impostor representations.

3.12   Example Application: Alien Pool

The second application demonstrates how dynamic surfaces and intersecting refractive objects can be handled by placing an ice object into a pool of fluid. The static but caustics-receiving environment consists of the diffuse walls of the room. The container walls themselves form a reflective, transparent cylinder. Within the container, the liquid and the floating object are reflective and refractive moving objects.

The motion of the liquid is synthetized using ripple height maps, and the resulting surface can also be represented by a height map impostor. The floating object is star-convex and well approximated by an object distance impostor.

Even though the static environment is a caustics receiver, we avoid re-rendering the static environment impostor in every frame by storing the texture coordinates instead of diffuse colors, as described in Section 3.10. This map has a resolution of $6 \times 512 \times 512$ texels. Otherwise the settings were identical to those listed in Section 3.11. Figure 3.6 shows reflected and refracted light forming dynamic caustics patterns in the test scene. We measured 50 frames per second using both a geometry image for the floating solid and a distance object impostor.

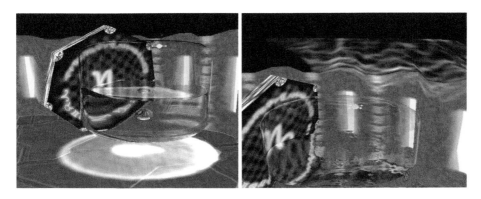

Figure 3.6. Left: refracted caustics under the pool. Right: reflected caustics above the pool.

3.13 Conclusion

With the use of geometry impostors, we can render convincing, complex ray-tracing effects in real-time applications. The two key points are: choosing a good representation for our geometry that avoids losing detail, but allows for fast intersection tests; and separating the static and dynamic aspects of the scene, so that we have to update only a few impostors in every frame. In our experience, cube map distance impostors are good approximations for even strongly concave environment geometries, with the relatively high construction cost amortized if we store only the static environment in such maps. Height map impostors proved to be surprisingly versatile and also well applicable to animated meshes. Finally, the separation of moving objects and handling them with object impostors made it possible to render multi-bounce effects in real time, in scenes densely populated with mirror-like and glass objects.

Bibliography

[Carr et al. 06] N.A. Carr, J. Hoberock, K. Crane, and J.C. Hart. "Fast GPU Ray Tracing of Dynamic Meshes Using Geometry Images." In *Proceedings of Graphics Interface 2006*, pp. 203–209. Toronto: Canadian Information Processing Society, 2006.

[Oliveira et al. 00] Manuel M. Oliveira, Gary Bishop, and David McAllister. "Relief Texture Mapping." *Proceedings of SIGGRAPH 2000.*

[Policarpo et al. 05] Fabio Policarpo, Manuel M. Oliveira, and J. L. D. Comba. "Real-Time Relief Mapping on Arbitrary Poligonal Surfaces." *ACM SIGGRAPH 2005 Symposium on Interactice 3D Graphics and Games.*

[Szirmay-Kalos and Umenhoffer 08] L. Szirmay-Kalos and T. Umenhoffer. "Displacement Mapping on the GPU-State of the Art." In *Computer Graphics Forum*, 27, 27, pp. 1567–1592. Citeseer, 2008.

[Szirmay-Kalos et al. 05] Laszlo Szirmay-Kalos, Barnabas Aszodi, Istvan Lazanyi, and Matyas Premecz. "Approximate Ray-Tracing on the GPU with Distance Impostors." *Computer Graphics Forum 24.*

[Wyman and Davis 06] Chris Wyman and Scott Davis. "Interactive Image-Space Techniques for Approximating Caustics." In *I3D '06: Proceedings of the 2006 Symposium on Interactive 3D Graphics and Games*, pp. 153–160. New York: ACM, 2006.

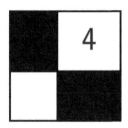

Temporal Screen-Space Ambient Occlusion
Oliver Mattausch, Daniel Scherzer, and Michael Wimmer

4.1 Introduction

Ambient occlusion (AO) is a shading technique that computes how much of the hemisphere around a surface point is blocked, and modulates the surface color accordingly. It is heavily used in production and real-time rendering, because it produces plausible global-illumination effects with relatively low computational cost. Recently it became feasible to compute AO in real time, mostly in the form of *screen-space ambient occlusion* (SSAO). SSAO techniques use the depth buffer as a discrete scene approximation, thus have a constant overhead and are simple to implement.

However, to keep the computation feasible in real time, concessions have to be made regarding the quality of the SSAO solution, and the SSAO evaluation has to be restricted to a relatively low number of samples. Therefore, the generated AO is usually prone to surface noise, which can be reduced in a post-processing step with a discontinuity filter. Depending on the chosen filter settings, we can either keep sharp features and accept some noise, or get a smooth but blurry solution due to filtering over the edges (as can be seen in Figure 4.1). Also, for dynamically moving objects, the noise patterns will sometimes appear to float on the surfaces, which is a rather distracting effect. To get a solution that is neither noisy nor blurry, many more samples have to be used. This is where *temporal coherence* comes into play.

4.1.1 Exploiting Temporal Coherence

The *reverse reprojection* technique [Scherzer et al. 07, Nehab et al. 07] allows us to reuse pixels from previous frames and refine them over time. This allows keeping

Figure 4.1. SSAO without temporal coherence (23 FPS) with 32 samples per pixel, with (a) a weak blur, (b) a strong blur. (c) TSSAO (45 FPS), using 8–32 samples per pixel (initially 32, 8 in a converged state). (d) Reference solution using 480 samples per frame (2.5 FPS). All images at 1024×768 resolution and using 32-bit precision render targets. The scene has 7 M vertices and runs at 62 FPS without SSAO.

the number of samples that are computed in a single frame low, while effectively accumulating hundreds of samples in a short amount of time. Note that ambient occlusion has many beneficial properties that make it well suited for temporal coherence: there is no directional dependence on the light source or the viewer, AO techniques consider only the geometry in a local neighborhood, and only the SSAO in a *pixel neighborhood* is affected by a change in the scene configuration.

In this article, we focus specifically on how to use reverse reprojection to improve the quality of SSAO techniques in a deferred shading pipeline. In particular, we show how to detect and handle changes to the SSAO caused by moving entities, animated characters, and deformable objects. We demonstrate that these cases, which are notoriously difficult for temporal coherence methods, can be significantly improved as well. A comparison of our *temporal SSAO* (TSSAO) technique with conventional SSAO and a reference solution in a static scene configuration can be seen in Figure 4.1.

Note that this algorithm is complementary to the method described in the "Fast Soft Shadows With Temporal Coherence" chapter of this book, which also provides code fragments that describe the reprojection process.

4.2   Ambient Occlusion

From a physical point of view, AO can be seen as the diffuse illumination due to the sky [Landis 02]. AO of a surface point p with normal n_p is computed as [Cook and Torrance 82]:

Figure 4.2. This figure compares rendering without (left) and with (right) AO, and shows that AO allows much better depth perception and feature recognition, without requiring any additional lighting.

$$\text{ao}(p, n_p) = \frac{1}{\pi} \int_\Omega V(p, \omega) D(|p - \xi|) n_p \cdot \omega d\omega, \qquad (4.1)$$

where ω denotes all directions on the hemisphere and V is the (inverse) binary visibility function, with $V(p, \omega) = 1$ if the visibility in this direction is blocked by an obstacle, 0 otherwise. D is a monotonic decreasing function between 1 and 0 of the distance from p to ξ, the intersection point with the nearest surface. In the simplest case, D is a step function, considering obstacles within a certain sampling radius only, although a smooth falloff provides better results, (e.g., as given by an $exp(.)$ function).

Figure 4.2 demonstrates the visual impact of SSAO for the depth perception of a scene.

4.2.1 Screen Space Ambient Occlusion

SSAO methods attempt to approximate the original AO integral in screen space. Several versions of SSAO with different assumptions and trade-offs have been described. Note that our algorithm can be seen as a general strategy to improve an underlying SSAO method.

We assume that any SSAO method can be written as an average over contributions C which depend on a series of samples s_i:

$$AO_n(p) = \frac{1}{n} \sum_{i=1}^{n} C(p, s_i). \qquad (4.2)$$

In order to approximate Equation (4.1) using the Monte Carlo integration, the contribution function for SSAO is often chosen as [Ritschel et al. 09]:

$$C(p, s_i) = V(p, s_i) D(|s_i - p|) \max(\cos(s_i - p, n_p), 0). \qquad (4.3)$$

In contrast to Equation (4.1), directions have been substituted by actual sample points around p, and thus $V(p, s_i)$ is now a binary visibility function that gives 0 if s_i is visible from p, and 1 otherwise. The method is called "screen-space" ambient occlusion because V is evaluated by checking whether s_i is visible in screen space with respect to the current z-buffer. Note that some SSAO methods omit the depth test, and the contribution of s_i depends on distance and incident angle [Fox and Compton 08].

We assume that the samples s_i have been precomputed and stored in a texture, for example, a set of three-dimensional points uniformly distributed in the hemisphere, which are transformed into the tangent space of p for the evaluation of C. If this step is omitted and samples on the whole sphere are taken, then the sample contribution has to be doubled to account for wasted samples that are not on the upper hemisphere. $D(.)$ is a function of the distance to the sample point that can be used to modulate the falloff.

4.3   Reverse Reprojection

Reverse reprojection associates image pixels from the current frame with the pixels from the previous frame that represent the same world-space position. The technique allows the reuse of pixel content from previous frames for the current frame. The technique was shown to be useful for a variety of applications, like shadow mapping, antialiasing, or even motion blur [Rosado 07].

Reprojection techniques use two render targets in ping-pong fashion, one for the current frame and one representing the cached information from the previous frames. In our context we cache AO values and therefore denote this buffer as the *ambient-occlusion buffer*.

For static geometry, reprojection is constant for the whole frame, and can be carried out in the pixel shader or in a separate shading pass (in the case of deferred shading), using the view (V) and projection (P) matrices from the previous frame $f - 1$ and the current frame f, where t denotes the post-perspective position of a pixel [Scherzer et al. 07]:

$$t_{f-1} = P_{f-1}V_{f-1}V_f^{-1}P_f^{-1}t_f. \tag{4.4}$$

In our deferred shading pipeline, we store *eye-linear* depth values for the current frame and the previous frame, and use them to reconstruct the world-space positions p. In our implementation, because we already store the world-space positions, we have only to transform the current world-space position p_f with the previous view-projection matrix $P_{f-1}V_{f-1}$ to get t_{f-1}. From t_{f-1} we calculate the correct lookup coordinates tex_{f-1} into the AO buffer by applying the perspective division and scaling the result to the range [0..1] (i.e., $tex_{f-1} = \frac{t_{f-1}+1}{2}$.).

4.3.1 Dynamic Objects

For dynamic scenes, the simple Equation (4.4) does not work, because reprojection depends on the transformations of moving objects. Therefore, it was proposed to apply the complete vertex transformation twice, once using the current transformation parameters (modeling matrix, skinning, etc.), and once using the parameters of the previous frame [Nehab et al. 07].

In a deferred shading pipeline, the previous position p_f needs to be accessed in a separate shading pass, where information about transformation parameters is already lost. Therefore, we store the *3D optical flow* $p_{f-1} - p_f$ in the frame buffer as another shading parameter (alongside normal, material, etc.), using a lower precision for these offset values than for the absolute depth values (16 bit instead of 32 bit).

4.4 Our Algorithm

In this section, we first describe the SSAO sample accumulation, then the detection and handling of pixels that carry invalid information, and last, some optimizations to our algorithm.

4.4.1 Refining the SSAO Solution Over Time

The main concept of our algorithm is to spread the computation of AO (Equation (4.2)) over several frames by using reprojection. Whenever possible, we take the solution from a previous frame that corresponds to an image pixel and refine it with the contribution of new samples computed in the current frame. In frame f, we calculate a new contribution C_f from k new samples:

$$C_f(p) = \frac{1}{k} \sum_{i=j_f(p)+1}^{j_f(p)+k} C(p, s_i), \qquad (4.5)$$

where $j_f(p)$ counts the number of unique samples that have already been used in this solution. We combine the new solution with the previously computed solution:

$$AO_f(p) = \frac{w_{f-1}(p_{f-1})AO_{f-1}(p_{f-1}) + kC_f(p)}{w_{f-1}(p) + k},$$

$$w_f(p) = \min(w_{f-1}(p_{f-1}) + k, w_{\max}), \qquad (4.6)$$

where the weight w_{f-1} is the number of samples that have already been accumulated in the solution, or a predefined maximum after convergence has been reached.

Theoretically, this approach can use arbitrarily many samples. In practice, however, this is not advisable: since reprojection is not exact and requires bilinear filtering for reconstruction, each reprojection step introduces an error that exacerbates over time. This error is noticeable as an increasing amount of blur. Furthermore, the influence of newly computed samples becomes close to zero, and previously computed samples never get replaced. Therefore we clamp w_f to a user-defined threshold w_{max}, which causes the influence of older contributions to decay over time. Thus,

$$\text{conv}(p) = w_f(p)/w_{\max} \qquad (4.7)$$

is an indicator of the state of convergence. Note that for $w_{max} \to \infty$, accumulating contributions from Equation (4.5) correspond to $n \to \infty$ in Equation (4.2) and would thus converge to the correct value of the desired integration, except for the blurring discussed above.

Implementation notes. The value w_{f-1} is stored in a separate channel in the ambient occlusion buffer. In order to achieve fast convergence, we use a Halton sequence, which is known for its low discrepancy [Wang and Hickernell 00], for sample generation. As a starting index into this sample set, we use j_f, which we also store in the AO-buffer. In summary, the RGBA target of an AO-buffer stores the following parameters:

- the SSAO solution $C_{f-1}(p)$

- the weight of the previous solution w_{f-1}

- the starting index j_{f-1}

- the eye-linear depth d_{f-1}.

The current index position is propagated to the next frame by means of reverse reprojection as with the SSAO values. In order to prevent the index position from being interpolated by the hardware and introducing a bias into the sequence, it is important to always fetch the index value from the nearest pixel center in the AO-buffer. The pixel center can be found using the formula in Equation (4.8), given the reprojected coordinates tex_{f-1}:

$$\text{pixelcenter} = \frac{\lfloor \text{tex}_{f-1}\text{res}_{x,y} \rfloor + 0.5}{\text{res}_{x,y}}, \qquad (4.8)$$

where $\text{res}_{x,y}$ is the current frame buffer resolution in x and y.

4.4.2   Detecting and Dealing with Invalid Pixels

When reprojecting a fragment, we need to check whether the pixel looked up in the previous frame actually corresponds to the current pixel, i.e., whether the cached AO value is valid. If it became invalid, we have to invalidate the previous solution accordingly. In order to detect such invalid pixels, we check if any one of the following three conditions has occurred: 1.) a disocclusion of the current fragment [Scherzer et al. 07], 2.) changes in the *sample neighborhood* of the fragment, and 3.) a fragment that was previously outside the frame buffer. Following, we discuss these cases.

Detecting disocclusions. We check for disocclusions by comparing the current depth of the fragment d_f to the depth of the cached value at the reprojected fragment position d_{f-1}. In particular, we compare the *relative* depth differences of the eye-linear depth values:

$$|1 - \frac{d_f}{d_{f-1}}| < \epsilon. \tag{4.9}$$

Equation (4.9) gives stable results for large scenes with a wide depth range, which are not oversensitive at the near plane and are sufficiently sensitive when approaching the far-plane regions. In case of a disocclusion, we always discard the previous solution by resetting w_{f-1} to 0 and we compute a completely new AO solution.

Detecting changes in the neighborhood. Testing for disocclusions may be sufficient for avoiding most temporal-coherence artifacts for methods that affect only the current pixel, like super sampling, or for SSAO in a purely static scene. However, shading methods like SSAO gather information from neighboring pixels using a spatial sampling kernel. Hence, in dynamic environments, we have to take into account that the shading of the current pixel can be affected by nearby moving objects, even if no disocclusion of the pixel itself has happened. Consider, for

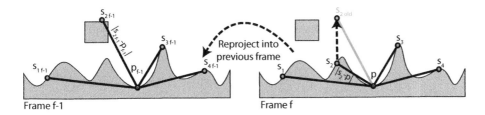

Figure 4.3. The distance of p to sample point s_2 in the current frame (right) differs significantly from the distance of p_{f-1} to s_{2f-1} in the previous frame (left), so we assume that a local change of geometry occurred, which affects the shading of P.

example, a scenario wherein a box is lifted from the floor. The SSAO values of pixels in the contact-shadow area surrounding the box change, even if there is no disocclusion of the pixel itself.

The size of the neighborhood to be checked is equivalent to the size of the sampling kernel used for SSAO. Checking the complete neighborhood of a pixel would be prohibitively expensive, and therefore we use sampling. Actually, it turns out that we already have a set of samples, namely the ones used for AO generation. That means that we effectively use our AO sampling kernel for two purposes: for computing the current contribution $C_f(p)$, and to test for validity.

Our invalidation scheme is visualized in Figure 4.3. The validity of a sample s_i for shading a pixel p can be estimated by computing the change in relative positions of sample and pixel:

$$\delta(s_i) = ||s_i - p| - |s_{if-1} - p_{f-1}||. \tag{4.10}$$

The reprojected position s_{if-1} is computed from the offset vector stored for s_i (recall that the first rendering pass stores the offset vectors for all pixels in the frame buffer for later access by the SSAO-shading pass). Note that, for the neighborhood test, we use only those samples that lie in front of the tangent plane of p, since only those samples actually modify the shadow term.

Theoretically we could also check if the angle between surface normal and vector to the sample point has changed by a significant amount from one frame to the next, and practical cases are imaginable when the vector length is not enough. However, this would require more information to be stored (the surface normal of every pixel in the previous frame), and in all our tests we found it sufficient to evaluate Equation (4.10).

Note that in order to avoid one costly texture lookup when fetching p_f, the required values for this test and for the AO computation should be stored in a single render target.

Smooth invalidation. It makes perfect sense to use a binary threshold to detect disocclusions. In this spirit, for the neighborhood check of a pixel we could evaluate $\delta(s_i) < \epsilon$ for all samples and discard the previous solution for this pixel if this condition is violated for any of the samples. However, consider, for example, a slowly deforming surface, where the AO will also change slowly. In such a case it is not necessary to fully discard the previous solution. Instead we introduce a new continuous definition of invalidation that takes a measure of change into account. This measure of change is given by $\delta(s_i)$ at validation sample position s_i, as defined in Equation (4.10). In particular, we compute a *confidence* value $\mathrm{conf}(s_i)$ between 0 and 1. It expresses the degree to which the previous SSAO solution is still valid:

$$\mathrm{conf}(s_i) = 1 - \frac{1}{1 + S\delta(s_i)}.$$

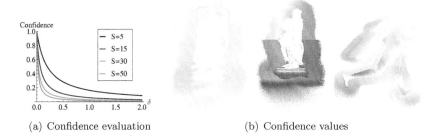

(a) Confidence evaluation   (b) Confidence values

Figure 4.4. (a) Confidence function depending on the distance difference δ for smoothing factor $S = 5, 15, 30, 50$. (b) Visualization of the confidence values computed by our smooth invalidation technique, showing a rotation (left), a translation (middle), and an animated (walking) character (right). We use a continuous scale from red (confidence=0) to white (confidence=1).

The parameter S controls the smoothness of the invalidation, and is set to a value ($15 \leq S \leq 30$) in our current implementation. As can be seen in Figure 4.4, for different values of S, the confidence is 1 if the relative distance has not changed ($\delta(x) = 0$), and approaches 0 for large values of $\delta(s_i)$. The overall confidence of the previous AO solution is given by

$$\mathrm{conf}(p) = \min(\mathrm{conf}(s_0), .., \mathrm{conf}(s_k)).$$

We multiply it with w_t to modify the weight of the old solution in Equation (4.6). Also, in order to prevent flickering artifacts in regions with large changes, we do not increase the index into the array of samples if the convergence is smaller than a threshold (e.g., for $\mathrm{conv}(p) < 0.5$) to reuse the same samples.

Figure 4.5 shows the effect of our novel invalidation scheme on a scene with a translational movement. Checking only disocclusions causes artifacts visible

Figure 4.5. Rotating dragon model using different values for smooth invalidation factor S. (left) $S = 0$ (i.e., no invalidation), (middle) $S = 100$, (right) $S = 15$. Note that no invalidation causes a wrong shadow (left), while a too high value causes unwanted noise in the shadow (middle).

as wrong contact shadows (left). Additionally, checking the pixel neighborhood for changes in the AO using our smooth invalidation technique allows for correct shadows (middle and right). Choosing a too high value for S will remove the temporal-coherence artifacts, but produces too much noise (middle). On the other hand, there is much less noise at the transitions between the silhouettes of moving objects and the background when choosing a proper value for S (right).

Handling of frame-buffer borders. Samples that fall outside of the frame buffer carry incorrect information that should not be propagated. Hence we check for each pixel if one or more of the samples have been outside the frame buffer in the *previous frame*. In this case, we do not use smooth invalidation, but discard the previous values completely since they are undefined. In the same spirit, we do not use samples that fall outside of the frame buffer to compute our confidence values.

4.4.3   Adaptive Convergence-Aware Spatial Filter

SSAO methods usually apply a spatial-filtering pass after shading computations in order to prevent noise artifacts caused by insufficient sampling rates. We also apply spatial filtering, but only as long as the temporal coherence is not sufficient. Variants of the cross bilateral filter [Eisemann and Durand 04] are typically used, where filtering over edges is avoided by taking the depth differences into account. Although this filter is not formally separable, in a real-time setting it is usually applied separately in x and y directions to make evaluation feasible.

In contrast to previous approaches, we have additional information for this filter which can greatly reduce noise (i.e., the convergence $\mathrm{conv}(p)$ of our AO values in pixel p (Equation 4.7)). Recently disoccluded pixels (e.g., in a thin silhouette region) can gather more information from nearby converged pixels than from other unreliable pixels. Furthermore, we apply the filter kernel directly to world-space distances. This application automatically takes depth differences into account, and can detect discontinuities in cases of high depth differences:

$$AO_{\mathrm{filt}}(p) = \frac{1}{K(p)} \sum_{x \in F} g(|p - x|)\mathrm{conv}(x)AO(x),$$

$$K(p) = \sum_{x \in F} g(|p - x|)\mathrm{conv}(x),$$

where x is the individual filter samples in the screen-space support F of the filter (e.g., a 9×9 pixel region), $K(p)$ is the normalization factor, and g is a spatial-filter kernel (e.g., a Gaussian). As a pixel becomes more converged, we shrink the screen-space filter support smoothly, using the shrinking factor s:

$$s(p) = \frac{\max(c_{\mathrm{adaptive}} - \mathrm{conv}(p), 0)}{c_{\mathrm{adaptive}}},$$

Figure 4.6. Rotating dragon, closeups of the marked region are shown. TSSAO without filter (middle) and with our filter (right). Note that the filter is applied only in the noisy regions, while the rest stays crisp.

so that when convergence has reached c_{adaptive}, we turn off spatial filtering completely. We found the setting of c_{adaptive} to be perceptually uncritical (e.g., a value of 0.2 leads to unnoticeable transitions).

The influence of the adaptive convergence-aware filter on the quality of the TSSAO solution is shown in Figure 4.6.

Adaptive sampling. Though spatial filtering can reduce noise, it is more effective to provide additional input samples in undersampled regions. Or, to put it differently, once the AO has reached sufficient convergence, we can just reuse the computed solution, thus using fewer samples in regions that are not undersampled. We adapt the number k of new AO samples per frame as a function of convergence. Note that these AO samples are completely unrelated to the screen-space samples used for spatial filtering in the previous section, where the kernel size is adapted instead of changing the number of samples.

It is necessary to generate at least a minimum number of samples for the same reasons that we clamp $w_f(p)$ in Equation (4.6) (i.e., to avoid blurring artifacts introduced by bilinear filtering). Furthermore, a certain number of samples is required for detecting invalid pixels due to changing neighborhoods (Section 4.4.2). In order to introduce a minimum amount of branching, we chose a simple two-

Parameter name	Value
Initial samples k_1	32
Converged samples k_2	8–16
Threshold c_{adaptive}	0.2
Threshold c_{spatial}	0.3
Threshold c_{rot}	0.5
Smooth invalidation factor S	15–30
Maximum weight w_{max}	500–1500
Filter width F	5x5

Table 4.1. Recommended parameters for the TSSAO algorithm.

stage scheme, with k_1 samples if $\text{conv}(p) < c_{\text{spatial}}$ and k_2 samples otherwise (refer to Table 4.1 for a list of parameters actually used in our implementation).

This requires a variable number of iterations of the AO loop in the shader. Since disoccluded regions are often spatially coherent (as can be seen in Figure 4.4(b)), the dynamic branching operations in the shader are quite efficient on today's graphics hardware.

4.4.4 Optimizations

These optimizations of the core algorithm allow for faster frame rates and better image quality due to greater precision.

Random noise. As in most AO approaches, we rotate the sampling pattern by a different random vector for each input pixel. This rotation trades banding artifacts due to undersampling for noise. However, this leads to a surprisingly large performance hit, supposedly due to texture-cache thrashing [Smedberg and Wright 09]. Therefore we turn off the rotation once convergence has reached a certain threshold c_{rot}. Note that this optimization works well in most cases, but can sometimes cause problems for the neighborhood invalidation, resulting in some noticeable artifacts.

Local space. In order to avoid precision errors in large scenes, we store our position values in a local space that is centered at the current view point. These values can be easily transformed into world-space values by passing the previous and the current view point as parameters to the shader.

4.5 SSAO Implementation

We implemented and tested our algorithm using the methods of Fox and Compton [Fox and Compton 08] and Ritschel et al. [Ritschel et al. 09], but it is also possible to implement one of the many alternatives [Bavoil et al. 08, Mittring 07]. In this section we outline the first two algorithms and give some implementation hints based on our experience.

Algorithm of Ritschel et al. The SSAO method of Ritschel et al. uses a 3D sampling kernel, and a depth test to query the sample visibility, thus implementing the contribution function in Equation (4.3). This is in contrast to the original Crytek implementation [Mittring 07], which does not use the incident angle to weight the sample. In order to get a linear SSAO falloff, we use a sample distribution that is linear in the sampling-sphere radius. Note that we use a constant falloff function $D(x) = 1$, in this case—the falloff is caused only by the distribution of the sample points. The differences to the ray-traced AO are mainly caused by the screen-space discretization of the scene.

Algorithm of Fox and Compton. The algorithm of Fox and Compton samples the depth buffer around the pixel to be shaded and interprets these samples as small patches, similar to radiosity. While not physically accurate, it often gives a pleasing visual result because it preserves more small details when using large kernels for capturing low-frequency AO. On the downside, this method is prone to reveal the underlying tessellation. As a remedy, we do not count samples at grazing angles of the hemisphere (i.e., where the cosine is smaller than a given ϵ). We used Equation (4.11) to implement the algorithm:

$$C(p, s_i) = \frac{\max(\cos(s_i - p, n_p), 0)}{\max(\epsilon, |s_i - p|)}. \tag{4.11}$$

The main difference from other SSAO methods is that each sample is constructed on a visible surface, and interpreted as a patch, whereas in Equation (4.11)), samples are used to evaluate the visibility function. The denominator represents a linear falloff function $D(.)$, where we also guard against zero sample distance.

The screen-space sampling radius is defined by projecting a user-specified world-space sampling radius onto the screen, so that samples always cover roughly similar regions in world space. When the user adjusts the world-space radius, the intensity of each sample needs to be scaled accordingly in order to maintain a consistent brightness.

Sample generation. In order to obtain the samples used for SSAO, we first compute a number of random samples ζ in the range $[0 \ldots 1]$ using a Halton sequence. For the method of Fox and Compton, we use 2D (screen-space) samples uniformly distributed on a disc of user-specified size. These samples are then projected from screen space into world space by intersecting the corresponding viewing rays with the depth buffer and computing their world space position. We generate the screen-space samples s_i from 2D Halton samples $\zeta_{x,y}$ using Equation (4.12):

$$\begin{aligned} \alpha &= 2\pi\zeta_x, \\ r &= \sqrt{\zeta_y}, \\ s_i &= (r\cos(\alpha), r\sin(\alpha)). \end{aligned} \tag{4.12}$$

For the method of Ritschel et al., we use 3D hemispherical samples generated in the tangent space of a surface point. From 3D Halton samples $\zeta_{x,y,z}$, hemispherical samples s_i are created using

$$\begin{aligned} \alpha &= 2\pi\zeta_x, \\ r &= \zeta_y, \\ s_i &= (r\cos(\alpha)\sqrt{1 - \zeta_z}, r\sin(\alpha)\sqrt{1 - \zeta_z}, r\sqrt{\zeta_z}). \end{aligned} \tag{4.13}$$

This formula uses the variables ζ_x and ζ_z to compute a point on the unit sphere (i.e., a random direction), and ζ_y to set the sample distance r. Note that in order to use variance-reducing *importance sampling* (rather than uniform sampling), this formula creates a distribution proportional to the cosine-weighted solid angle. Furthermore, Szirmay-Kalos et al. [Szirmay-Kalos et al. 10] have shown that a uniform distribution of samples along the distance r corresponds to a linear falloff function $D(.)$ (refer to Equation (4.1)) of the occluder influence with respect to r. Using this importance sampling scheme, we simply have to count the numbers of samples that pass the depth test during SSAO shading.

Maximum allowed sample distance. If the distance from the pixel center to the intersection point with the depth buffer is too large, a sample is very likely to cause wrong occlusion (refer to Figure 4.7(a)). However, introducing a *maximum allowed sample radius* and setting it to a too small value can cause samples where valid occlusion is missed (refer to Figure 4.7(b)). This is because they are projected to a location outside the allowed sample radius. We set the maximum

(a) If the allowed sample distance is unrestricted, shadows are cast from disconnected objects (1). If it is set equal to the sampling radius, some valid samples are not counted, resulting in overbright SSAO (2). Allowing 2 times the radius (3) is a good trade-off and closest to a ray-traced solution (REF).

(b) 2D illustration of the issue arising when setting the maximum allowed sample distance (shown in blue, sampling radius shown in red) too small. While the samples (shown in black) which are projected to the disconnected surface are correctly rejected (left), this configuration also rejects valid samples (right).

Figure 4.7. The effect of the maximum allowed sample distance (from the shaded pixel to the depth buffer intersection).

allowed sample radius to reject those samples where the distance is more than two times larger than the sampling radius of the SSAO kernel. This trade-off largely prevents incorrect shadowing of distant and disconnected surfaces caused by objects in the foreground, while still accounting for correct occlusion in the vicinity of the current pixel.

Frame buffer borders. A problem inherent in SSAO is the handling of samples that fall outside the frame buffer borders (requested by fragments near the border). The simplest solution is to settle for reusing the values at the border by using clamp-to-edge. To avoid artifacts on the edges of the screen due to the missing depth information, we can optionally compute a slightly larger image than we finally display on the screen. It is sufficient to extend about 5–10% on each side of the screen depending on the size of the SSAO kernel and the near plane.

4.6 Results

We implemented the proposed algorithm in OpenGL using the Cg shading language. As test scenes, we used two models of different characteristics (shown in Figure 4.8): (a) the Sibenik cathedral and (b) the Vienna city model. Both scenes were populated with several dynamic objects. The walk-through sequences taken for the performance experiments are shown in the accompanying videos. Note that most SSAO artifacts caused by image noise are more distracting in animated sequences, hence we point interested readers to these videos which can be downloaded from http://www.cg.tuwien.ac.at/~matt/tssao/. For all of our tests we used an Intel Core 2 processor at 2.66 GHZ (using 1 core) and an NVIDIA GeForce 280GTX graphics board. To achieve sufficient accuracy in large-scale scenes like Vienna, we use 32-bit depth precision. Both the ambient occlusion buffer and the SSAO texture are 32-bit RGBA render targets.

Generally TSSAO provides finer details and fewer noise artifacts. This can be seen in Figure 4.1 for a static scene (using the method of Fox and Compton),

| (a) | (b) | (c) |

Figure 4.8. Used test scenes: (a) Sibenik cathedral (7,013,932 vertices) and (b) Vienna (21,934,980 vertices) in the streets and (c) from above.

Figure 4.9. Close-up of a distant dragon in Sibenik cathedral at 1600×1200 resolution: SSAO using 32 samples at 12 FPS (left close-up); TSSAO using 8–32 samples per frame at 26 FPS (right close-up).

where we compare TSSAO to SSAO with a weak and a strong blur filter, which gives a high or low weight, respectively, to discontinuities. Furthermore, we compare TSSAO to a reference solution using 480 samples per frame, which was the highest number of samples our shader could compute in a single frame. Notice that the TSSAO method is visually very close to the reference solution, to which it converges after a short time.

Figure 4.9 shows that the method also works for high-resolution images. The TSSAO algorithm provides good quality even for fine details in the background. Figure 4.10 shows a capture of a deforming cloak of an animated character. Although deforming objects are difficult to handle with temporal coherence, it can be seen that TSSAO significantly reduces the surface noise. We used the method of Fox and Compton for Figure 4.9, and the method of Ritschel et al. for Figure 4.10.

In terms of visual image-quality, TSSAO performs better than SSAO in all our tests. It corresponds to at least a 32-sample SSAO solution (since 32 samples are always used for disocclusions), while the converged state takes up to several hundred samples into account. Note that a similar quality SSAO solution would

Figure 4.10. Close-up of a deforming cloak: SSAO using 32 samples (middle) and TSSAO using 8–32 samples (right). Notice that the surface noise (causing severe flickering artifacts when animated) is reduced with TSSAO.

resolution	Vienna (fps)			Sibenik cathedral (fps)		
	SSAO	TSSAO	Deferred	SSAO	TSSAO	Deferred
1600x1200	14	29	73	10	12	38
1024x768	30	51	97	21	25	65
800x600	42	63	102	29	34	67
800x600 h	65	77		47	49	

Table 4.2. Average timings for the two walk-through sequences shown in the videos for 32-bit precision render targets using full and half resolution. We compare standard SSAO, our method (TSSAO), and deferred shading without SSAO as a baseline. For SSAO we used 32 samples in all scenes. For TSSAO we used 8 (16)–32 samples in Vienna (Sibenik cathedral).

be prohibitively slow. In terms of correctness, however, we have to keep in mind that using a smooth invalidation causes the algorithm to deviate from a correct solution for the benefit of a better visual impression.

Timings. Table 4.2 shows average timings of our walk-throughs, comparing our method (TSSAO) with SSAO without temporal coherence and the performance-baseline method, deferred shading without SSAO. TSSAO uses 8 06 16 samples, respectively, when converged and 32 otherwise for Vienna and for Sibenik cathedral, whereas SSAO always uses 32 samples. In our tests TSSAO was always faster than SSAO, for full and for half-resolution SSAO computation. Note that, after convergence has been reached, TSSAO neither applies spatial filtering nor the random rotations of the sampling-filter kernel (refer to Section 4.4.4).

Figure 4.11 shows the frame time variations for both walk-throughs. Note that online occlusion culling [Mattausch et al. 08] is enabled for the large-scale Vienna model, and thus the frame rate for the baseline deferred shading is quite high for such a complex model. The frame-rate variations for TSSAO stem from the fact that the method generates adaptively more samples for recently dis-

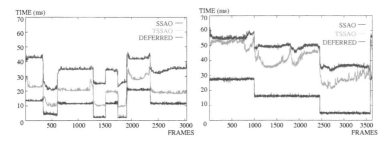

Figure 4.11. Frame times of the Vienna (left) and the Sibenik cathedral walk-through (right) at resolution 1024 × 768, using 32-bit precision render targets.

occluded regions. The frame times of TSSAO are similar to SSAO for frames where dynamic objects are large in screen space. For more static parts of the walk-throughs, TSSAO is significantly faster.

4.7 Discussion and Limitations

In the case of deforming objects, most of the visual improvements compared to conventional SSAO come from the smooth invalidation (refer to the close-up of the cloak in Figure 4.10). Carefully adjusting the smooth invalidation factor is quite important here, and using this optimization too loosely can result in artifacts such as a noticeable dark trail following moving objects.

There is definitely a limit to exploiting temporal coherence once the objects are moving or deforming too quickly. In such a case, our algorithm will deteriorate to the quality of conventional SSAO. Also, invalidation may fail in cases of thin (with respect to the SSAO kernel size), quickly moving structures, which are missed by the invalidation algorithm. Likewise, a very large kernel size can also cause problems with the invalidation, because the sampling could just miss events that cause changes to the AO.

The main targets of this algorithm are real-time visualization and games. The adaptive sampling optimization cannot guarantee constantly better frame times than conventional SSAO, and disturbing fluctuations in the frame time can happen. However, we have to keep in mind that games usually undergo extensive play-testing in order to avoid annoying frame rate drops. Faster SSAO in most frames is useful, because more time for other effects is available.

Also, note that adaptive sampling, which is responsible for frame rate variations, is a feature of the algorithm that can be disabled, thus falling back to the speed of conventional SSAO, but still obtaining significantly improved image quality. Furthermore, the major purpose of this algorithm is to speed up the standard case of moderate dynamic movements.

4.8 Conclusions

We have presented a screen-space ambient-occlusion algorithm that utilizes reprojection and temporal coherence to produce high-quality ambient occlusion for dynamic scenes. Our algorithm reuses available sample information from previous frames if available, while adaptively generating more samples and applying spatial filtering only in the regions where insufficient samples have been accumulated. We have shown an efficient new pixel validity test for shading algorithms that access only the affected pixel neighborhood. Using our method, such shading methods can benefit from temporal reprojection also in dynamic scenes with animated objects.

Bibliography

[Bavoil et al. 08] Louis Bavoil, Miguel Sainz, and Rouslan Dimitrov. "Image-Space Horizon-Based Ambient Occlusion." In *ACM SIGGRAPH 2008 Talks, SIGGRAPH '08*, pp. 22:1–22:1. New York: ACM, 2008.

[Cook and Torrance 82] Robert L. Cook and Kenneth E. Torrance. "A Reflectance Model for Computer Graphics." *ACM Trans. Graph.* 1 (1982), 7–24.

[Eisemann and Durand 04] Elmar Eisemann and Frédo Durand. "Flash Photography Enhancement via Intrinsic Relighting." *ACM Trans. Graph.* 23 (2004), 673–678.

[Fox and Compton 08] Megan Fox and Stuart Compton. "Ambient Occlusive Crease Shading." *Game Developer Magazine*, 2008.

[Landis 02] Hayden Landis. "Production-Ready Global Illumination." In *Siggraph Course Notes, Vol. 16.* New York: ACM, 2002.

[Mattausch et al. 08] Oliver Mattausch, Jiří Bittner, and Michael Wimmer. "CHC++: Coherent Hierarchical Culling Revisited." *Computer Graphics Forum (Proceedings of Eurographics 2008)* 27:2 (2008), 221–230.

[Mittring 07] M. Mittring. "Finding Next Gen - CryEngine 2." In *ACM SIGGRAPH 2007 courses, SIGGRAPH '07*, pp. 97–121. New York: ACM, 2007.

[Nehab et al. 07] Diego Nehab, Pedro V. Sander, Jason Lawrence, Natalya Tatarchuk, and John R. Isidoro. "Accelerating real-time shading with reverse reprojection caching." In *Proceedings of the Eurographics Symposium on Graphics Hardware 2007*, pp. 25–35. Aire-la-Ville, Switzerland: Eurographics Association, 2007.

[Ritschel et al. 09] Tobias Ritschel, Thorsten Grosch, and Hans-Peter Seidel. "Approximating Dynamic Global Illumination in Image Space." In *Proceedings of the 2009 Symposium on Interactive 3D Graphics and Games*, pp. 75–82. New York: ACM, 2009.

[Rosado 07] Gilberto Rosado. "Motion Blur as a Post-Processing Effect." In *GPU Gems 3*, pp. 575–576. Reading, MA: Addison Wesley, 2007.

[Scherzer et al. 07] Daniel Scherzer, Stefan Jeschke, and Michael Wimmer. "Pixel-Correct Shadow Maps with Temporal Reprojection and Shadow Test Confidence." In *Proceedings of the Eurographics Symposium on Rendering 2007*, pp. 45–50. Aire-la-ville, Switzerland: Eurographics Association, 2007.

[Smedberg and Wright 09] Niklas Smedberg and Daniel Wright. "Rendering Techniques in Gears of War 2." In *Proceedings of the Game Developers Conference '09*, 2009.

[Szirmay-Kalos et al. 10] Laszlo Szirmay-Kalos, Tamas Umenhoffer, Balazs Toth, Laszlo Szecsi, and Mateu Sbert. "Volumetric Ambient Occlusion for Real-Time Rendering and Games." *IEEE Computer Graphics and Applications* 30 (2010), 70–79.

[Wang and Hickernell 00] Xiaoqun Wang and Fred J. Hickernell. "Randomized Halton Sequences." *Mathematical and Computer Modelling* 32 (2000), 887–899.

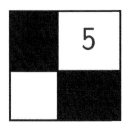

Level-of-Detail and Streaming Optimized Irradiance Normal Mapping

Ralf Habel, Anders Nilsson, and Michael Wimmer

5.1 Introduction

Light mapping and normal mapping are the most successful shading techniques used in commercial games and applications today, because they require few resources and result in a significant increase in the quality of the rendered image. While light mapping stores global, low-frequency illumination at sparsely sampled points in a scene, normal maps provide local, high-frequency shading variation at a far higher resolution (see Figure 5.1).

The problem with combining the two methods is that light maps store irradiance information for only one normal direction—the geometric surface normal—and therefore cannot be evaluated using the normals stored in a normal map. To overcome this problem, the irradiance (i.e., the incoming radiance integrated over the hemisphere) has to be precalculated for all possible normal map directions at every sample point. At runtime, this (sparse) *directional irradiance* signal can be reconstructed at the (dense) sampling positions of the normal map through interpolation. The final irradiance is calculated by evaluating the interpolated directional irradiance using the normal vector from the normal map.

Because such a (hemispherical) directional irradiance signal is low-frequency in its directionality, it can be well represented by smooth lower-order basis functions. Several bases have been successfully used in games such as spherical harmonics in *Halo 3* [Chen and Liu 08], or the hemispherical *Half-Life 2* basis [McTaggart 04]. It has been shown [Habel and Wimmer 10] that the hemispherical $\mathcal{H}$-basis provides the overall best representation compared to all other bases

67

Figure 5.1. A scene without albedo maps showing the difference between light mapping (left) and irradiance normal mapping (right).

because it is directly constructed to carry hemispherical directional irradiance signals and incorporates the same advantages that spherical harmonics have.

However, none of the options to represent the directional irradiance signal provides an efficient and resource-optimal way to define increments of detail for shader level-of-detail (LOD) or for streaming of textures. To eliminate those drawbacks, we introduce a modification to the $\mathcal{H}$-basis that maintains its high accuracy and fast evaluation. In contrast to any other known basis representation, the modified $\mathcal{H}$-basis explicitly contains the traditional light map as one of its coefficients and is therefore an extension of light mapping rather than a replacement, providing the light map as the lowest shader LOD.

To apply the optimized irradiance normal mapping, we first derive all necessary equations and calculations, after which we discuss implementation issues such as correct tangent space, color spaces, or compression.

5.2 Calculating Directional Irradiance

The directional irradiance of a surface point $\vec{x}$ is defined as

$$E(\vec{x}, \vec{n}) = \int_{\Omega^+} L(\vec{x}, \vec{\omega}) \max(0, \vec{n} \cdot \vec{\omega}) d\vec{\omega} \qquad (5.1)$$

and covers all possible surface normals $\vec{n}$ in the upper hemisphere Ω_+, with L being the incoming radiance. Because we do not want to keep track of the orientation of the hemispheres at every point, the hemispheres are defined in tangent space, (i.e., around the interpolated surface normal and (bi)tangent), which is also the space where the normal maps are defined.

To determine the incoming directional irradiance, we need to calculate the radiance $L(\vec{x}, \omega)$ in a precomputation step similar to traditional light mapping. Any method that creates a radiance estimate such as shadow mapping, standard ray tracing, photon mapping [Jensen 96], final gathering, or path tracing [Kajiya 86] can be used, and existing renderers or baking software can be applied.

Given the radiance $L(\vec{x}, \omega)$, calculating $E(\vec{x}, \vec{n})$ (Equation (5.1)) for a point $\vec{x}$ corresponds to filtering L with a diffuse (cut cosine) kernel. Doing this in Euclidean or spherical coordinates is prohibitively expensive, because we have to filter a large number of surface points. Instead, we use spherical harmonics as an intermediate basis in which the filtering can be done much more efficiently. Spherical harmonics are orthonormal basis functions that can approximate any spherical function. A comprehensive discussion of spherical harmonics can be found in [Green 03] and [Sloan 08]. Unfortunately, different definitions exist; to avoid confusion, we use the definition without the Condon-Shortley phase, as shown in Appendix A for our calculations.

As shown by [Ramamoorthi and Hanrahan 01], a spherical directional irradiance signal is faithfully represented with three spherical harmonics bands (nine coefficients per color channel). Therefore, we need only to use spherical harmonics up to the quadratic band.

First, we rotate the sampled radiance of a surface point into the tangent space and expand it into spherical harmonics coefficients s_m^l by integrating against the spherical harmonics basis functions Y_m^l over the upper hemisphere Ω_+:

$$s_m^l = \int_{\Omega_+} L(\vec{\omega}) Y_m^l(\vec{\omega}) d\vec{\omega}.$$

In almost all cases, the coefficients are calculated using Monte Carlo Integration [Szirmay-Kalos]:

$$s_m^l \approx \frac{2\pi}{N} \sum_{i=1}^{N} L(\vec{\omega_i}) Y_m^l(\vec{\omega_i}),$$

where N is the number of hemispherical, equally distributed, radiance samples $L(\vec{\omega_i})$. More advanced methods, such as importance sampling, can be applied, as long as a radiance estimate represented in spherical harmonics is calculated. The diffuse convolution reduces to an almost trivial step in this representation. Following [Ramamoorthi and Hanrahan 01], applying the Funk-Hecke-Theorem, integrating with a cut cosine kernel corresponds to multiplying the coefficients of each band with a corresponding factor a^l:

$$a^0 = 1 \quad a^1 = \frac{2}{3} \quad a^2 = \frac{1}{4},$$

to arrive at the final directional irradiance signal represented in spherical harmonics:

$$E_{\mathrm{SH}}(\vec{n}) = \sum_{l,m} s_m^l Y_m^l(\vec{n}). \tag{5.2}$$

We have built the necessary division by π for the exitant radiance into the diffuse kernel so we do not have to perform a division at runtime.

By storing nine coefficients (respectively, 27 in the trichromatic case) at each surface point, in either textures or vertex colors, we can calculate the final result at runtime by looking up the normal from the normal map and we can calculate the final irradiance by evaluating Equation (5.2). However, we are not making the most efficient use of the coefficients since the functions are evaluated only on the upper hemisphere Ω_+, and not the full sphere. The created directional irradiance signals can be better represented in a hemispherical basis.

5.3 $\mathcal{H}$-Basis

The $\mathcal{H}$-basis was introduced in [Habel and Wimmer 10] and forms an orthonormal hemispherical basis. Compared to all other orthonormal hemispherical bases, such as [Gautron et al. 04] or [Koenderink et al. 96], the $\mathcal{H}$-basis consist of only polynomial basis functions up to a quadratic degree and therefore shares many properties with spherical harmonics. Some of the basis functions are actually the same basis functions as those used in spherical harmonics, but re-normalized on the hemisphere, which is why the $\mathcal{H}$-basis can be seen as the counterpart of spherical harmonics on the hemisphere up to the quadratic band.

The basis is explicitly constructed to carry hemispherical directional irradiance signals and can provide a similar accuracy with only six basis functions compared to nine needed by spherical harmonics, and a higher accuracy than any other hemispherical basis [Habel and Wimmer 10]. These basis functions are:

$$\begin{aligned}
H^1 &= \frac{1}{\sqrt{2\pi}}, \\[2mm]
H^2 &= \sqrt{\frac{3}{2\pi}}\sin\phi\sin\theta = \sqrt{\frac{3}{2\pi}}y, \\[2mm]
H^3 &= \sqrt{\frac{3}{2\pi}}(2\cos\theta - 1) = \sqrt{\frac{3}{2\pi}}(2z - 1), \\[2mm]
H^4 &= \sqrt{\frac{3}{2\pi}}\cos\phi\sin\theta = \sqrt{\frac{3}{2\pi}}x,
\end{aligned}$$

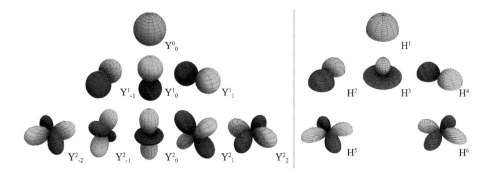

Figure 5.2. Spherical Harmonics basis functions (left) compared to the $\mathcal{H}$-basis functions (right). Green are positive and red are negative values.

$$H^5 = \frac{1}{2}\sqrt{\frac{15}{2\pi}}\sin 2\phi \sin^2\theta = \sqrt{\frac{15}{2\pi}}xy,$$

$$H^6 = \frac{1}{2}\sqrt{\frac{15}{2\pi}}\cos 2\phi \sin^2\theta = \frac{1}{2}\sqrt{\frac{15}{2\pi}}(x^2 - y^2).$$

Please note that compared to [Habel and Wimmer 10], the negative signs caused by the Condon-Shortley phase have been removed in the basis functions H^2 and H^4 for simplicity and for consistency with the spherical harmonics definitions. A visual comparison of the spherical harmonics basis functions to the $\mathcal{H}$-basis can be seen in Figure 5.2.

5.3.1 Modified $\mathcal{H}$-Basis

The band structure of the $\mathcal{H}$-basis (similar to spherical harmonics) provides a natural way for controlling the level of approximation of the directional irradiance signal. For example, given a normal from the normal map, we can use only the first four coefficients (corresponding to the constant and all linear basis functions) to calculate the irradiance. If a higher accuracy is demanded, we can simply use the two quadratic functions H^5 and H^6 in addition to the other four basis functions.

Another level of detail that is very important, especially for objects that are far away, is to not use a normal map at all, but to use a standard light map in order to avoid the loading or streaming of both the used normal map as well as coefficients for the $\mathcal{H}$-basis. A light map corresponds to irradiance values calculated for the geometric normal, which is defined in tangent space as $\vec{n}_g = (0,0,1)$ ($\theta = 0$ in spherical coordinates), so the light map value is actually $E(\vec{n}_g)$. If E is represented in the $\mathcal{H}$-basis, we can see that only H^1 and H^3 evaluate to a nonzero value $\vec{n}_g$, so only the corresponding two coefficients

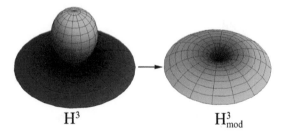

$$H^3 \qquad\qquad\qquad H^3_{\mathrm{mod}}$$

Figure 5.3. The original basis function H^3 (left), and its replacement H^3_{mod} (right). In contrast to H^3, H^3_{mod} is always 0 for $\vec{n}_g = (0, 0, 1)$.

are required. But this is still less efficient than standard light mapping, which requires only one coefficient (i.e., texture). Thus, using the $\mathcal{H}$-basis, we have to load twice the amount of data in order to arrive at the same result we would achieve with light mapping. The question arises, can we combine both light mapping and irradiance normal mapping in one framework?

First, we note that while the $\mathcal{H}$-basis is an orthonormal basis, orthonormality is not required for representing directional irradiance. Thus we can sacrifice this property for the sake of another advantage. As we have seen, all but two of the basis functions always evaluate to 0 when evaluated in the direction of $\vec{n}_g$, but the optimal case would be to have only one contributing function in this case. We can achieve this goal by redefining the basis function H^3 as

$$H^3_{\mathrm{mod}} = \sqrt{\frac{3}{2\pi}}(1 - \cos\theta) = \sqrt{\frac{3}{2\pi}}(1 - z),$$

which is a function that is still linearly independent of the other basis functions, and depends only on z ($\cos\theta$ in spherical coordinates) like H^3. However, this function also evaluates to 0 in the direction of the geometric normal $\vec{n}_g$ (see Figure 5.3). Through this modification, the constant basis function H^1 now represents the traditional light map, while we still maintain the high accuracy of the original $\mathcal{H}$-basis when using all coefficients. Therefore we have constructed a set of basis functions that extends the standard light map approach rather than replacing it.

5.3.2 Expansion into the Modified $\mathcal{H}$-Basis

In Section 5.2, we precomputed the directional irradiance in the spherical harmonics basis as E_{SH} (Equation (5.2)). Transforming E_{SH} into the more efficient, modified $\mathcal{H}$-basis requires another precomputation step. We calculate a transformation matrix by projecting the spherical harmonics basis functions into the modified $\mathcal{H}$-basis [Sloan 08], resulting in

$$T_{\mathcal{H}\mathrm{mod}} = \begin{pmatrix} \frac{1}{\sqrt{2}} & 0 & \sqrt{\frac{3}{2}} & 0 & 0 & 0 & \frac{3}{4}\sqrt{\frac{5}{2}} & 0 & 0 \\ 0 & \frac{1}{\sqrt{2}} & 0 & 0 & 0 & \frac{3\sqrt{\frac{5}{2}}}{8} & 0 & 0 & 0 \\ 0 & 0 & -\frac{1}{\sqrt{2}} & 0 & 0 & 0 & -\frac{1}{2}\sqrt{\frac{15}{2}} & 0 & 0 \\ 0 & 0 & 0 & \frac{1}{\sqrt{2}} & 0 & 0 & 0 & \frac{3\sqrt{\frac{5}{2}}}{8} & 0 \\ 0 & 0 & 0 & 0 & \frac{1}{\sqrt{2}} & 0 & 0 & 0 & 0 \\ 0 & 0 & 0 & 0 & 0 & 0 & 0 & 0 & \frac{1}{\sqrt{2}} \end{pmatrix} \quad (5.3)$$

We arrive at the coefficient vector for the modified $\mathcal{H}$-basis $\vec{h} = (h_1, h_2, .., h_6)$ by multiplying the serialized spherical harmonics coefficient vector $\vec{s} = (s_0^0, s_{-1}^1, s_0^1, .., s_2^2)$ with the matrix $T_{\mathcal{H}\mathrm{mod}}$. This matrix multiplication also automatically extracts the light map into the coefficient for the constant basis function h_1.

5.3.3 Runtime Evaluation

Up to now, we have precomputed the directional irradiance at different surface points and represented it in the modified $\mathcal{H}$-basis defined in the tangent space of the surface points. The necessary coefficients are transported either on a per-vertex basis or using coefficient texture maps. In the trichromatic case, this results in one color per vertex or one texture per coefficient. As the normal map is also defined in tangent space, we simply need to evaluate the basis functions in the direction of the normal map normal ($\vec{n}$) and weight them by the interpolated coefficients

$$E_{\mathcal{H}\mathrm{mod}}(\vec{n}) = \sum_{i=1}^{n} h_i H_{\mathrm{mod}}^i(\vec{n})$$

for every surface point $\vec{x}$. Please note that $H_{\mathrm{mod}}^i(\vec{n}) = H^i(\vec{n})$ except for the modified basis function H_{mod}^3. Similar to light mapping, the result can be modulated by a lookup from an albedo texture and combined with additional shading effects, such as specular lighting.

5.4 Implementation

In the previous sections, we derived all necessary expressions and equations to precompute the data and evaluate it at runtime. In the following sections, we will discuss practical issues that occur in an application of irradiance normal mapping, such as proper generation, representation, and compression of the data. In general, more sophisticated methods can be applied to compress and distribute the coefficient maps [Chen and Liu 08, Sloan et al. 03], but this usually requires the use of proprietary formats that are beyond this discussion.

5.4.1   Precomputing Directional Irradiance

Solving the radiance distribution in a full scene is a complex task in itself and is usually done using commercial renderers or game-engine-native baking software. In our case, we use the Maya-based [Autodesk 10] rendering and baking plug-in, Turtle 5.1 [Illuminate Labs 10]. Turtle can be customized to bake into any basis through LUA scripting. A script implementing the discussed methods is included in the demo and can also be executed with the trial version of Turtle 5.1.

Because we construct a physically correct representation of the directional irradiance, we need to take into account that all calculations are performed in linear color space. Therefore, irradiance normal mapping lends itself to be used in a linear rendering pipeline using sRGB texture lookups and frame buffers, or gamma-correct high dynamic range (HDR) tone mapping where necessary. If a non-gamma-correct pipeline is used, the result simply needs to be exponentiated with $1/2.2$.

Concerning resolutions of coefficient textures, the exact same principles used in standard light mapping apply, and the chosen resolution directly reflects the spatial resolution of the lighting that can be represented.

5.4.2   Directional Irradiance Tangent Space

In almost all practical cases that use texture maps, a second set of texture coordinates that create an unambiguous mapping of the surfaces is used to define the light map, or in our case, coefficient textures. If the unambiguous texture coordinates are used only for a light map, the orientation of the corresponding tangent spaces spanned by the different texture coordinate sets is irrelevant for the light map evaluation. This changes with irradiance normal mapping because it may happen that both tangent spaces have different orientations, and the normal map resides in a different tangent space than the directional irradiance.

Fortunately, both texture coordinate sets share the same vertices and geometric normals, as well as interpolation in the rendering pipeline. By simply using the tangent and bitangent of the normal map tangent space in the directional irradiance texture coordinates during the precomputation, a tangent space for the directional irradiance texture coordinates is constructed that is correctly oriented with the normal- and albedo-map tangent space.

Effectively, the directional irradiance texture coordinate set is used only to define the surface points where it is calculated and stored, while the normal map tangent space defines the tangent and bitangent for both spaces, resulting in a correctly aligned irradiance signal relative to the normal map. Turtle provides the option to use the (bi)tangent of another texture coordinate set in its baking menu.

Since both tangent spaces are aligned, when evaluating the directional irradiance at runtime, we need neither the normals nor the (bi)tangents of any tangent space but solely the texture coordinate sets to define the texture lookups.

5.4.3   Texture Normalization and Range Compression

The output of the precomputations are floating point values which, similar to spherical harmonics, can also be negative. Though we could use floating point texture formats to represent the sign and full dynamic range of the directional irradiance, this option is prohibitively expensive in most cases, though it leads to the best possible output.

To transport the coefficient textures efficiently, we treat the map containing h_1, which is also the light map, differently, because it can never get negative, in contrast to the other coefficients. Compared to standard light mapping, we cannot allow h_1 and the other coefficient maps to oversaturate, since this would lead to color-shifting artifacts. To avoid oversaturation, we can simply choose the lighting so that h_1 stays within the range $[0..1]$, or clamp the calculated radiance to this range before the spherical harmonics expansion in order to transport h_1 with an 8-bit texture.

Additionally, because h_1 is a light map, we change the color space from linear to sRGB by exponentiation with $1/2.2$ to avoid quantization artifacts associated with an 8-bit linear representation. As with standard texture maps, we have to interpret the texture as sRGB data when evaluating it at runtime.

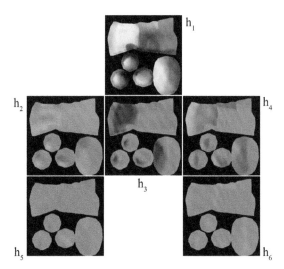

Figure 5.4. A set of coefficient textures. The coefficient h_1 is the standard light map.

```
for each surface point do {

  color SHc[9] //3 bands Spherical Harmonics coefficients

  //Monte-Carlo-Integration in tangent space over
  //the hemisphere to project into SH[] basis functions
  for each radiance sample L(direction) in N do {
    for each SHc do {
      SHc[]   +=  L(direction)*SH[](direction)
    }
  }
  SHc[] = (2*PI/N)*SHc[]

  //Diffuse convolution
  SHc[0] = SHc[0]
  SHc[1,2,3] = 2.0/3.0*SHc[2,3,4]
  SHc[4,5,6,7,8] = 1.0/4.0*SHc[4,5,6,7,8]

  //Projection into modified H-basis
  color modHc[6] // modified H-basis coefficients

  //Transform matrix
  for each color in modHc[] do {
    modHc[0] =  0.70711*SHc[0]+1.2247*SHc[2]+1.1859*SHc[6]
    modHc[1] =  0.70711*SHc[1]+0.59293*SHc[5]
    modHc[2] = -0.70711*SHc[2]-1.3693*SHc[6]
    modHc[3] =  0.70711*SHc[3]+0.59293*SHc[7]
    modHc[4] =  0.70711*SHc[4]
    modHc[5] =  0.70711*SHc[8]
  }

  //Convert first coefficient to sRGB
  modHc[0] = pow(modHc[0],1/2.2)

  //Range compress rest with global factor of 0.75
  for each modHc[] except modHc[0] do {
    modHc[] = modHc[]+0.75/(2*0.75)
  }

  write modHc[]
}
```

Listing 5.1. Pseudo-code for calculating the coefficients for the modified $\mathcal{H}$-basis including the texture optimizations.

Because the coefficients $h_{2..6}$ can be negative, we perform a similar range compression as done with normal maps, keeping them in linear color space. For a data-independent range compression, if h_1 is in the range $[0..1]$, a rule of thumb is that the other coefficients do not exceed the range of $[-\frac{3}{4}..\frac{3}{4}]$, resulting in a range compression

$$h'_{2..6} = \frac{h_{2..6} + \frac{3}{4}}{2 \cdot \frac{3}{4}}.$$

The range compression factor of $\frac{3}{4}$ may be changed according to the scene and lighting conditions to further increase the accuracy of the coefficient representation over a range compression of $[-1..1]$, as used in normal mapping. Figure 5.4 shows a set of coefficient textures resulting from the calculations shown. Pseudocode showing all precomputation calculations, including the described optimizations, is given in Listing 5.1.

Optimal range compression. A much better way to represent the coefficients is to perform a range compression on a per-shape, per-texture, or even per-channel basis. Calculating both the minimum and maximum value (with negative minima for $h_{2...6}$) or the maximum absolute range (to replace the previously chosen $\frac{3}{4}$) and normalizing the data can increase the quality of the representation significantly. This allows irradiance normal mapping within both standard and HDR frameworks, using just 8-bit textures. Because directional irradiance is a convolved signal, it does not have the extreme values of radiance signals such as HDR environment maps, so this optimized 8-bit representation may be sufficient. Besides the exposition of the minimum/maximum or maximum absolute-range value to the shader, there is almost no overhead since most of the coefficients need to be transported range compressed anyway.

5.4.4   Texture Compression

In a manner similar to that used for light maps, the coefficient maps can be compressed using DXT texture formats. Since we do not need any alpha information, DXT1 compression can deliver a compression rate of $6 : 1$. Because we have six coefficient maps, a set of compressed maps therefore requires the same amount of memory as an uncompressed light map. Since we effectively add up several DXT compressed textures, compression artifacts may also add up to an intolerable level. These artifacts can be counteracted by choosing a higher-coefficient map resolution or by modulating the result with an albedo map to obfuscate the color shifts.

5.4.5   Levels of Detail and Streaming

As discussed in Section 5.3.1, the lowest LOD is formed by evaluating only the constant term $h_1 H^1_{\mathrm{mod}}(\vec{n})$. As a mid-range LOD, only the first four coefficients,

Figure 5.5. Detail of a game scene without albedo texturing using four coefficients (left) and for more accuracy six coefficients (right). The differences can be marginal, though six coefficients show more detail where the normal map normal is perpendicular to the geometric normal.

consisting of the constant and the linear basis functions, can be used. This LOD uses the normal map, so the appearance of a material compared with the lowest LOD may cause popping artifacts. A small distance-based region where the middle LOD is blended with the lowest can suppress those artifacts, as can be seen in the demo.

As highest LOD, a full evaluation using all six coefficient maps can be applied, though the difference between using four or six coefficients can be marginal, and four coefficients may already deliver a perceptually accurate result (see Figure 5.5). Depending on the available resources, the highest LOD can therefore be skipped if the quality of the middle LOD is sufficient. The reason for this behavior is that the quadratic basis functions H^5_{mod} and H^6_{mod} mostly contribute if the normal map normal is perpendicular to the geometric normal.

All levels of details are cumulative, so if textures are streamed, the next higher LOD uses the same textures as the lower one. Also, due to the linearity of the basis functions, the coefficient textures can be used simultaneously even if they are available at different resolutions, switching to an appropriate LOD as soon as some mip-level of a coefficient texture is available. The HLSL code for evaluating the modified $\mathcal{H}$-basis is given in Listing 5.2, including range decompression, gamma-correct color-space lookups, and levels of detail.

```
float3 n = 2*tex2D(normal,texUV)-1; //tangent space normal map

float3 irr =
  0.39894*tex2D(h1,lightUV) //is sRGB lookup ( x^2.2 )
  //stop here for lowest LOD (lightmap)
  +(2*0.75*tex2D(h2,lightUV)-0.75)*0.69099*n.y //not sRGB lookup
  +(2*0.75*tex2D(h3,lightUV)-0.75)*0.69099*(1-n.z)
  +(2*0.75*tex2D(h4,lightUV)-0.75)*0.69099*n.x
```

```
//stop here for middle LOD
+(2*0.75*tex2D(h5,lightUV)-0.75)*1.54509*n.x*n.y
+(2*0.75*tex2D(h6,lightUV)-0.75)*0.77255*(n.x*n.x-n.y*n.y);
//full evaluation

color = irr*tex2D(albedo,texUV) //is sRGB lookup ( x^2.2 );

//write color to sRGB frame buffer ( x^(1/2.2) )
```

Listing 5.2. HLSL code for evaluating the modified $\mathcal{H}$-basis, including a modulation with an albedo map. The different levels of detail are created by stopping the irradiance calculation at the shown points.

5.5 Results

We have implemented the described approach in the graphics engine OGRE 1.6.5 [OGRE 10]. The accompanying web materials contain the binaries as well as the full source code of the demo and the Turtle script to bake out coefficient maps with the described optimizations. All levels of detail and texture formats can be directly compared and viewed in both low-dynamic as well as high-dynamic range rendering pipelines with or without albedo textures (see Figure 5.6).

This can act as a reference implementation since any game engine or application that supports light mapping and shaders can be easily modified to support irradiance normal mapping. Besides the precomputation, only several additional textures need to be exposed to the shader compared to a single texture when using light mapping. The shader calculations consist only of a few multiply-adds for range decompression of the textures and to add up the contributions of the basis functions. Both the data as well as the evaluation are lightweight and simple, and are therefore also applicable to devices and platforms that have only a limited set of resources and calculation power.

5.6 Conclusion

We have derived a modification of the $\mathcal{H}$-basis that allows formulating irradiance normal mapping as an extension of light mapping rather than as a replacement by containing the light map of the basis function coefficients. We discussed the efficient calculation and representation of directional irradiance signals in the modified $\mathcal{H}$-basis using spherical harmonics as an intermediate representation for efficient filtering. A description of the accompanying implementation was given, showing the different levels of detail and optimizations for 8-bit textures, such as optimal color spaces and range compression.

Figure 5.6. A full scene without (top) and with (bottom) albedo mapping.

5.7 Appendix A: Spherical Harmonics Basis Functions without Condon-Shortley Phase

$$Y_0^0 = \frac{1}{2}\sqrt{\frac{1}{\pi}}$$

$$Y_{-1}^1 = \frac{1}{2}\sqrt{\frac{3}{\pi}}\sin\phi\sin\theta = \frac{1}{2}\sqrt{\frac{3}{\pi}}y$$

$$Y_0^1 = \frac{1}{2}\sqrt{\frac{3}{\pi}}\cos\theta = \frac{1}{2}\sqrt{\frac{3}{\pi}}z$$

$$Y_1^1 = \frac{1}{2}\sqrt{\frac{3}{\pi}}\cos\phi\sin\theta = \frac{1}{2}\sqrt{\frac{3}{\pi}}x$$

$$Y_{-2}^2 = \frac{1}{2}\sqrt{\frac{15}{\pi}}\sin 2\phi\sin^2\theta = \frac{1}{2}\sqrt{\frac{15}{\pi}}xy$$

$$Y_{-1}^2 = \frac{1}{2}\sqrt{\frac{15}{\pi}}\sin\phi\cos\theta\sin\theta = \frac{1}{2}\sqrt{\frac{15}{\pi}}yz$$

$$Y_0^2 = \frac{1}{4}\sqrt{\frac{5}{\pi}}(3\cos^2\theta - 1) = \frac{1}{4}\sqrt{\frac{5}{\pi}}(3z^2 - 1)$$

$$Y_1^2 = \frac{1}{2}\sqrt{\frac{15}{\pi}}\cos\phi\cos\theta\sin\theta = \frac{1}{2}\sqrt{\frac{15}{\pi}}zx$$

$$Y_2^2 = \frac{1}{4}\sqrt{\frac{15}{\pi}}\cos 2\phi\sin^2\theta = \frac{1}{4}\sqrt{\frac{15}{\pi}}(x^2 - y^2)$$

Bibliography

[Autodesk 10] Autodesk. "Maya. Maya is a registered trademark or trademark of Autodesk, Inc. in the USA and other countries." Available at http://www.autodesk.com, 2010.

[Chen and Liu 08] Hao Chen and Xinguo Liu. "Lighting and Material of Halo 3." In *SIGGRAPH '08: ACM SIGGRAPH 2008 Classes*, pp. 1–22. New York: ACM, 2008.

[Gautron et al. 04] Pascal Gautron, Jaroslav Krivánek, Sumanta N. Pattanaik, and Kadi Bouatouch. "A Novel Hemispherical Basis for Accurate and Efficient Rendering." In *Rendering Techniques*, pp. 321–330. Aire-la-Ville, Switzerland: Eurographics Association, 2004.

[Green 03] Robin Green. "Spherical Harmonic Lighting: The Gritty Details." Available at http://citeseer.ist.psu.edu/contextsummary/2474973/0, 2003.

[Habel and Wimmer 10] Ralf Habel and Michael Wimmer. "Efficient Irradiance Normal Mapping." In *I3D '10: Proceedings of the 2010 ACM SIGGRAPH Symposium on Interactive 3D Graphics and Games*, pp. 189–195. New York: ACM, 2010.

[Illuminate Labs 10] Illuminate Labs. "Turtle for Maya." Available at http://www. illuminatelabs.com, 2010.

[Jensen 96] Henrik Wann Jensen. "Global Illumination using Photon Maps." In *Proceedings of the Eurographics Workshop on Rendering Techniques '96*, pp. 21–30. London: Springer-Verlag, 1996.

[Kajiya 86] James T. Kajiya. "The Rendering Equation." In *SIGGRAPH '86: Proceedings of the 13th Annual Conference on Computer Graphics and Interactive Techniques*, pp. 143–150. New York: ACM, 1986.

[Koenderink et al. 96] Jan J. Koenderink, Andrea J. van Doorn, and Marigo Stavridi. "Bidirectional Reflection Distribution Function Expressed in Terms of Surface Scattering Modes." In *ECCV '96: Proceedings of the 4th European Conference on Computer Vision-Volume II*, pp. 28–39. London, UK: Springer-Verlag, 1996.

[McTaggart 04] G. McTaggart. "Half-Life 2/Valve Source Shading." Technical report, Valve Corporation, 2004.

[OGRE 10] OGRE. "OGRE Graphics Engine." Available at http://www.ogre3d.org, 2010.

[Ramamoorthi and Hanrahan 01] Ravi Ramamoorthi and Pat Hanrahan. "An Efficient Representation for Irradiance Environment Maps." In *SIGGRAPH '01: Proceedings of the 28th Annual Conference on Computer Graphics and Interactive Techniques*, pp. 497–500. New York: ACM, 2001.

[Sloan et al. 03] Peter-Pike Sloan, Jesse Hall, John Hart, and John Snyder. "Clustered Principal Components for Precomputed Radiance Transfer." *ACM Trans. Graph.* 22:3 (2003), 382–391.

[Sloan 08] Pete-Pike Sloan. "Stupid Spherical Harmonics (SH) Tricks." Available at http://www.ppsloan.org/publications/StupidSH36.pdf, 2008.

[Szirmay-Kalos] Laszlo Szirmay-Kalos. *Monte Carlo Methods in Global Illumination - Photo-Realistic Rendering with Randomization*. Saarbrücken, Germany: VDM Verlag Dr. Mueller e.K.

Real-Time One-Bounce Indirect Illumination and Shadows Using Ray Tracing
Holger Gruen

6.1 Overview

This chapter presents an easily implemented technique for real-time, one-bounce indirect illumination with support for indirect shadows. Determining if dynamic scene elements occlude some indirect light and thus cast indirect shadows is a hard problem to solve. It amounts to being able to answer many point-to-point or region-to-region visibility queries in real time. The method described in this chapter separates the computation of the full one-bounce indirect illumination solution into three phases. The first phase is based on *reflective shadow maps* (RSM) [Dachsbacher and Stamminger 05] and is fully Direct3D 9 compliant. It generates the one-bounce indirect lighting from a kernel of RSM texels without considering blockers of indirect light. The second phase requires Direct3D 11–capable hardware and dynamically creates a three-dimensional grid that contains lists of triangles of the geometry that should act as blockers of indirect light. The third phase traverses the 3D grid built in phase 2, tracing rays to calculate an approximation of the indirect light from RSM texels that are blocked by geometry. Finally, the result of the third phase is subtracted from the result of the first phase to produce the full indirect illumination approximation.

6.2 Introduction

Real-time indirect illumination techniques for fully dynamic scenes are an active research topic. There are a number of publications (e.g., [Ritschel et al. 09a, Wyman and Nichols 09, Kapalanyan 09, Dachsbacher and Stamminger 06, Dachsbacher and Stamminger 05]) that describe methods for indirect one-bounce illumination for fully dynamic scenes, but they do not account for indirect shadows. Only a handful of methods for indirect illumination have been described to date that also include support for indirect shadows in the context of fully dynamic scenes and interactive frame rates (e.g., [Ritschel et al. 08, Ritschel et al. 09a, Ritschel et al. 09b, Kapalanyan and Dachsbacher 10, Yang et al. 09, Thibieroz and Gruen 10]).

Direct3D 11-capable GPUs allow the concurrent construction of linked lists using scattering writes and atomic operations (see [Yang et al. 09]). This capability is used as the basic building block for the solution to real-time indirect shadowing described in this chapter. Linked lists open the door for a new class of real-time algorithms to compute indirect shadows for fully dynamic scenes using ray-triangle intersections. The basic idea behind these techniques is to dynamically build data structures on the GPU that contain lists of triangles that represent low *level-of-detail* (LOD) versions of potential blockers of indirect light. Most game engines already rely on having low LOD versions of game objects for rendering or simulation purposes. These low LOD objects can readily be used as the approximate blockers of indirect light, as long as the LOD is good enough to capture the full topology of objects for proper self-shadowing.

The data structures containing lists of triangles are traversed using ray tracing to detect if some amount of the indirect light is blocked. Although this approach could probably be used to implement ray tracing of dynamic scenes in general, the following discussion considers only the application of linked lists in the context of the computation of indirect shadows and for low LOD-blocker geometry.

[Thibieroz and Gruen 10] discuss some of the implementation details of a proof-of-concept application for the indirect shadowing technique presented in [Yang et al. 09]. However, the scene used to test the indirect illumination solver did not contain any dynamic objects. Tests with more complicated dynamic scenes and rapidly changing lighting conditions revealed flickering artifacts that are not acceptable for high-quality interactive applications. The algorithms presented below address these issues and are able to deliver real-time frame rates for more complicated dynamic scenes that include moving objects and changing lighting conditions.

As described in the overview, the techniques explained below separate the process of computing indirect illumination into three phases. The reason for specifically separating the computation of indirect light and blocked indirect light is that it makes it easier to generate the blocked indirect light at a different fidelity or even at a different resolution than the indirect light. Furthermore, game developers will find it easier to add just the indirect light part of the technique if they can't rely on Direct3D 11-capable hardware for indirect shadowing. The three phases for computing the full one-bounce illumination approximation are explained in detail in the following sections.

6.3 Phase 1: Computing Indirect Illumination without Indirect Shadows

The approach for one-bounce indirect illumination described in this chapter is based on "Reflective Shadow Maps" [Dachsbacher and Stamminger 05].

One starts by rendering a G-buffer as seen from the eye and a reflective shadow map (RSM) as seen from the light. RSMs use the observation that one-bounce indirect illumination from a light source is caused by surfaces that are visible from the light's viewpoint.

As a RSM is also essentially a G-buffer of the scene as seen from the light, each texel of the RSM can be treated as a *virtual point light* source (VPL). So for each screen pixel of the camera-view G-buffer, one accumulates indirect light from a kernel of RSM texels as shown in Figure 6.1.

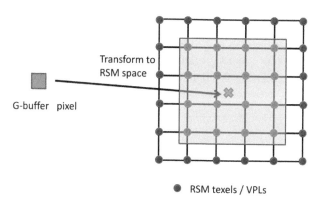

Figure 6.1. Accumulating light from a kernel of RSM texels.

The contribution of each VPL is computed as shown in Figure 6.2. If possible the approximate surface area that each RSM pixel represents should be rendered to the RSM as well.

[Thibieroz and Gruen 10] use a well-known trick to achieve good quality and real-time frame rates for a 20×20 kernel of VPLs. They employ a form of bilinear filtering. This works nicely for a static scene and a low-resolution RSM. It turns out though, that for dynamic scenes a much higher-resolution RSM ($\geq 512 \times 512$) and also a much bigger kernel of RSM pixels ($\geq 80 \times 80$) are needed. For dynamic scenes, the techniques described in [Thibieroz and Gruen 10] do not provide real-time frame rates.

One way to reach good performance for a VPL kernel of, for example, 81×81 pixels is to not use a full kernel of VPLs at each screen pixel, but to use a dithered pattern of VPLs that considers only one out of $N \times N$ VPLs. The samples for each screen pixel are then offset by its 2D pixel position modulo N. This is

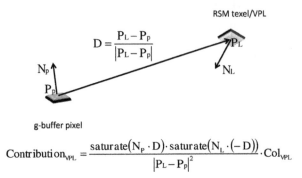

Figure 6.2. Computing the contribution of a VPL.

similar in spirit to [Segovia et al. 09] but does not actually split the G-buffer into sub-buffers for better memory coherence.

The shader in Listing 6.1 demonstrates how this can be implemented for a pattern that only uses one out of 6×6 VPLs.

```
// this function evaluates the weighting factor
// of a vpl
float evaluateVPLWeightingFac(RSM_data d, // data for VPL
                              float3 f3CPos, // pos of pix
                              float3 f4CN, // normal of pix
                              )
{
    // compute indirect light contribution weight
    float3 f3D = d.f3Pos.xyz - f3CPos.xyz;
    float fLen = length( f3D );
    float fInvLen = rcp( fLen );
    float fDot1 = dot( f3CN, f3D );
    float fDot2 = dot( d.f3N, -f3D );

    return  saturate( fInvLen * fInvLen ) *
            saturate( fDot1 * fInvLen ) *
            saturate( fDot2 * fInvLen );
}

// this function computes the indirect light from a kernel of
// VPLs inside the RSM.A repetitive screen space pattern is used
// to do interleaved shading to reduce the number
// of samples to look at
float3 computeIndirectLight(
                            float2 tc, // RSM cords of g-bug pix
                            int2 i2Off,// kernel start offset
```

```
                            float3 f3CPos, // g-buf pix pos
                            float3 f3CN // g-buf pix normal )
{
    float3 f3IL = (0.0f).xxx; // init indirect illumination

    // loop over VPL kernel
    for( float row = -LFS; row <= LFS; row += 6.0f )
    {
        for( float col = -LFS; col <= LFS; col += 6.0f )
        {
            // unpack RSM g-buffer data for VPL
            RSM_data d = LoadRSMData( tc, i2Off, row, col );

            // accumulate weighted indirect light
            f3IL += d.f3Col *
                    evaluateVPLWeightingFac( d, f3CPos, f3CN ) *
                    d.PixelArea;
        }
    }

    return f3IL;
}

// indirect light is computed for a half width/ half height
// image
float4 PS_RenderIndirectLight( PS_SIMPLE_INPUT I ) : SV_TARGET
{
    // compute screen pos for RT that is 2*w, 2*h
    int3 tc = int3( int2( I.vPos.xy ) << 1, 0 );

    // start offset of the VPL kernel repeats every 6x6 pixels
    int2 i2Off = ( int2( I.vPos.xy ) % (0x5).xx );

    // load gbuffer data at the current pixel
    GBuf_data d = LoadGBufData( tc );

    // transform world space pos to rsm texture space
    float2 rtc = transform2RSMSpace( d.f3CPos );

    // compute indirect light
    float3 f3IL = computeIndirectLight( rtc, i2Off,
                                        d.f3CPos, d.f3CN );

    return float4( f3IL, 0.0f );
}
```

Listing 6.1. Accumulating indirect light over a dithered kernel of VPLs.

Note that the shader assumes that the indirect light is computed at a resolution that is half as high and half as wide as the screen resolution.

Figure 6.3. Demo scene without indirect illumination.

Figure 6.4. Demo scene with indirect illumination.

As the dithered result from Listing 6.1 is not smooth, a bilateral blurring step (see e.g., [Tomasi and Manduchi 98]) is performed and then the image is sampled up to the full-screen resolution using *bilateral upsampling* [Sloan et al. 09]. Both bilateral filter operations use the differences in normal and light space-depth between a central G-buffer pixel and samples in the filter footprint.

Figures 6.3 and 6.4 show screenshots of a demo implementing the algorithm described above. The demo uses a 512×512 RSM and a dithered 81×81 kernel of VPLs. The frame rate of the demo is usually above 250 frames per seconds on an AMD HD5970 at 1280×800, which shows that the technique works fast enough to be used in interactive applications and computer games.

6.4   Phase 2: Constructing a 3D Grid of Blockers

In order to compute indirect shadows in the context of the RSM-based indirect illumination described above, one ideally needs to find a way to detect which VPLs can really be seen from a point in space and which are occluded by blocker geometry. Conceptually, the most straightforward way to detect occluding geometry is to trace rays from the position of a G-buffer pixel to the VPLs in the RSM.

As this has to work for arbitrary and ideally dynamic scenes a method needs to be found to quickly build a data structure that allows for fast ray tracing of these scenes. A simple solution to this problem is to dynamically update a 3D grid with the relevant blocker geometry (see e.g., [Thibieroz and Gruen 10]). Similar in spirit, a 3D grid containing a list of blocker triangles per cell can be constructed on Direct3D 11 hardware using a scattering compute shader. [Yang et al. 09] describes how to concurrently build linked lists on a GPU, and the exact same principles are used to generate a 3D grid with a list of triangles in each grid cell. Please note that only the triangles of a very low LOD representation of blocker objects need to be added to the 3D grid. Usually even complex blocker objects can be approximated sufficiently with only a few hundred triangles in order to generate reasonable indirect shadows.

A compute shader is used to directly pull triangle data from the index and vertex buffers of the blocker objects and to perform a rough and conservative 3D rasterization of several hundred blocker triangles in parallel. Each triangle is added to the list of triangles of each grid cell it touches. This process is depicted in Figure 6.5 and is run every frame to captures any change in position, orientation, or animation pose of the blocker geometry.

The simplest rasterization loop that can be implemented is to add a blocker triangle to all cells its bounding box touches. As intersection tests do carry out full ray-triangle intersections, this overly conservative rasterization doesn't create any false occlusion and will work well if the blocker triangles are not a lot larger than a cell of the 3D grid. As soon as triangles get more than twice as

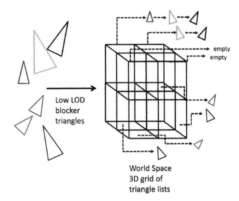

Figure 6.5. Rasterizing blocker triangles into a 3D grid.

big as the grid cells, this form of rasterization becomes inefficient. Similarly, the effectiveness of the grid for reducing the number of ray-triangle intersections is reduced if blocker triangles are a lot smaller than the cells of the grid.

The following compute shader implements the simple rasterization just described.

```
//
// Add triangles defined by an index and a vertex buffer into
// the linked list of each 3D grid cell they touch
//
// Note: This is a simplified 3D rasterization loop as it
// touches all grid cells that are touched by the bounding box
// of the triangle and adds the triangle to the list of all
// these grid cells
//
[numthreads( GROUPSIZE, 1, 1 )]
void CS_AddTrisToGrid(   uint3 Gid : SV_GroupID,
                         uint3 GTid : SV_GroupThreadID,
                         uint GI : SV_GroupIndex )
{
    // compute offset into index buffer from the thread and
    // group ids
    uint uOffset = GROUPSIZE * Gid.y + GTid.x;
    uint3 indices;
    LinkedTriangle t;
    uint3 start, stop;

    // only process valid indices
    if( uOffset < g_IndexCount ) {
        // add startindex to the offset
        uOffset += g_StartIndexLocation;
```

```
// fetch three indices for triangle
Indices = fetchIndices( uOffset );

// add base vertex location
indices += g_BaseVertexLocation.xxx;

// compute offset for vertices into the vertex buffer
uint3 voffset = indices * g_VertexStride.xxx +
                g_VertexStart.xxx;

// load vertex data of triangle--prepare triangle
float3 v0 = g_bufVertices.Load( voffset.x ).xyz;
float3 v1 = g_bufVertices.Load( voffset.y ).xyz;
float3 v2 = g_bufVertices.Load( voffset.z ).xyz;

// now call e.g., skinning code for the vertices
// if the vertices belong to a skinned object

t.v0 = v0;
t.edge1 = v1 - t.v0;
t.edge2 = v2 - t.v0;

// compute bounding box of tri and start and
// stop address for rasterization
computeStartStop( start, stop, v0, v1, v2 );

// iterate over cells
for( uint zi = start.z; zi <= stop.z; ++zi ) {
    for( uint yi = start.y; yi <= stop.y; ++yi ) {
        for( uint xi = start.x; xi <= stop.x; ++xi ) {
            // alloc new offset
            uint newOffset = LinkedTriGridBuffer.
                                IncrementCounter();
            uint oldOffset;

            // update grid offset buffer
            StartOffsetBuffer.
            InterlockedExchange( 4 * ( xi + yi *
                                CELLS_XYZ + zi *
                                CELLS_XYZ * CELLS_XYZ ),
                                newOffset, oldOffset );

            // store old offset
            lt.prev = oldOffset;

            // add triangle to the grid
            LinkedTriGridBuffer[ newOffset ] = t;
} } } } }
```

Listing 6.2. Rasterizing blocker triangles into a 3D grid of lists.

6.5 Phase 3: Computing the Blocked Portion of Indirect Light

Now that the grid has been created, it can be used to detect which VPLs are occluded and which are not occluded. In a separate rendering pass, the light from all blocked VPLs is accumulated. The reason for not interleaving this pass with phase 1 is that this pass generates more flexibility in terms of how many rays are shot for detecting blocked indirect light. Shooting rays is still a costly operation and one typically wants to shoot only few.

Listing 6.3 shows the shader code for accumulating blocked indirect light for a half-width, half-height buffer and a dithered 13×13 kernel of indirect light. As an optimization, rays are shot only if there is some amount of indirect light at the current pixel.

Note that the demo implementation uses an adapted version of the fast ray-triangle intersection algorithm presented in [Möller and Trumbore 97].

```
//
// This function walks the 3D grid to check for intersections of
// triangles and the given edge
//
float traceRayLinkedTris( float3 f3OrgP, float3 f3D )
{
        float fIntersection = (0.0f), fI, fLen;
        float3 f3Inc, f3P;

        // setup the march along the ray trough the grid cells
        setupRay( fLen, f3P, f3Inc );

        // do the march
        for( fI = 0.0f;
             fI <= fLen;
             fI += 1.0f, f3P += f3Inc )
        {
            // check_for_intersection walks through the list
            // of tris in the current grid cell and computes
            // ray triangles intersections
            if( check_for_intersection( int3( f3P ), f3P,
                            f3OrgP, f3D ) != 0.0f ) {
                fIntersection = 1.0f;
                break;
            }
        }
    return fIntersection;
}

float3 computeBlockedIndirectLight( float2 tc, float2 fc,
                        int2 i2Off, float3 f3CPos,
                        float3 f3CN )
```

```
{
    float3 f3IL = (0.0f).xxx;

    // loop over VPL kernel
    for( float row = -SFS; row <= SFS; row += 6.0f) {
        for( float col = -SFS; col <= SFS; col += 6.0f ) {
            // unpack RSM g-buffer data for VPL
            RSM_data d = LoadRSMData( adr );

            // compute weighting factor for VPL
            float f = evaluateVPLWeightingFac( d,f3CPos, f3CN );

            if( f > 0.0f ) {
                f3IL += traceRayLinkedTris(f3CPos.xyz, f3D )*
                    * d.f3Col * f;
            }
        }
    }

    // amplify the accumulated blocked indirect light a bit
    // to make indirect shadows more prominent
    return 16.0f * f3IL;
}

// renders the accumulated color of blocked light using a 3D
// grid of triangle lists to detect occluded VPLs
float4
PS_RenderBlockedIndirectLightLinkedTris( PS_SIMPLE_INPUT I ) :
SV_TARGET
{
    int3 tc = int3( int2( I.vPos.xy ) << 1, 0 );
    int2 i2Off = ( int2( I.vPos.xy ) % (0x5).xx );
    Gbuf_data d = LoadGBufData( tc );

    // transform world space pos to rsm texture space
    float2 rtc = transform2RSMSpace( d.f3CPos );

    float3 f3IS = 0.0f;
    float3 f3IL = g_txIndirectLight.SampleLevel(
                g_SamplePointClamp, I.vTex.xy, 0 ).xyz;

    // is any indirect light (phase 1) reaching this pixel
    [branch]if( dot( f3IL, f3IL ) > 0.0f )
        f3IS = computeBlockedIndirectLight( rtc, i2Off,
                                            d.f3CPos, d.f3CN );

    return float4( f3IS, 0.0f );
}
```

Listing 6.3. Accumulating blocked indirect light.

Figure 6.6. Demo scene with indirect illumination and indirect shadows.

Again, the dithered, blocked indirect light is blurred and upsampled using a bilateral filter. After that, the blocked indirect light is subtracted from the indirect light, and the result is clamped to make sure that indirect illumination doesn't become negative. This generates the full indirect illumination approximation with indirect shadowing. Finally, indirect illumination is combined with direct illumination and shadowing to produce the final image as shown in Figure 6.6.

The performance for rendering the full one-bounce indirect illumination, including indirect shadows with tracing nine rays per pixel is at 70–110 fps for a $32 \times 32 \times 32$ grid and a resolution of 1280×800 on an AMD HD5970. The number of blocker triangles that get inserted into the 3D grid in every frame is in the order of 6000.

6.6 Future Work

There are several future directions for improving the techniques described in this chapter.

1. The use of a hierarchical grid for speeding up ray-triangle intersections.

2. The insertion of references to a hierarchical structure, for example., a kd-tree (encoded in a buffer) into the lists of each grid cell. This would allow for faster ray-tracing of rigid or static scene elements.

3. The use of a binary 3D grid that could be generated by a scattering pixel shader and the use of the SM5 instruction for an atomic binary or operation (`InterlockeOr()`). Early experiments show that this is feasible and fast, but the resulting blocked indirect light is not stable for low enough resolutions of the binary 3D grid.

4. Instead of computing the accumulated contribution of blocked VPLs for each pixel, it would be possible to compute a spherical harmonics projection of the blocked indirect light of a distribution of VPLs at the center of each cell of the 3D grid. For a given screen pixel one could reconstruct a smooth approximation of the blocked indirect light from the tri-linear interpolation of eight sets of the spherical harmonics coefficient of the eight relevant grid cells.

Bibliography

[Dachsbacher and Stamminger 05] Carsten Dachsbacher and Marc Stamminger. "Reflective Shadow Maps. " In *Proceedings of the 2005 Symposium on Interactive 3D Graphics and Games*, I3D '05, pp.203–231. New York, ACM, 2005.

[Dachsbacher and Stamminger 06] Carsten Dachsbacher and Marc Stamminger. "Splatting Indirect Illumination." In *Proceedings of the 2006 Symposium on Interactive 3D Graphics and Games*, I3D '06, pp. 93–100. New York, ACM, 2006.

[Eisemann and Décoret 06] Elmar Eisemann and Xavier Décoret. "Fast Scene Voxelization and Applications." In *Proceedings of the 2006 Symposium on Interactive 3D Graphics and Games*, I3D '06, pp. 71–78. New York, ACM, 2006.

[Kapalanyan 09] Anton Kapalanyan. "Light Propagation Volumes in CryEngine 3." In *Advances in Real-Time Rendering in 3D Graphics and Games Course - SIGGRAPH 2009*. Available online http://www.crytek.com/cryengine/cryengine3/presentations/light-propagation-volumes-in-cryengine-3, 2009.

[Kapalanyan and Dachsbacher 10] Anton Kaplanyan and Carsten Dachsbacher. "Cascaded Light Propagation Volumes for Real-Time Indirect Illumination," In *Proceedings of the 2010 ACM SIGGRAPH Symposium on Interactive 3D Graphics and Games*, I3D '10, pp. 99–107. New York: ACM, 2010.

[Möller and Trumbore 97] Thomas Möller and Ben Trumbore. "Fast, Minimum Storage Ray/Triangle Intersection," *journal of graphics tool* 2:1 (1997), 21–28.

[Ritschel et al. 08] T. Ritschel, T. Grosch, T. M. H. Kim, H.-P. Seidel, C. Dachsbacher, and J. Kautz. "Imperfect Shadow Maps for Efficient Computation of Indirect Illumination." *ACM Trans. Graph.* 27:5 (2008), 129:1–129:8. .

[Ritschel et al. 09a] T. Ritschel, T. Grosch, and H.-P. Seidel. "Approximating Dynamic Global Illumination in Image Space." In *I3D '09: Proceedings of the 2009 Symposium on Interactive 3D Graphics and Games*, I3D '09, pp. 75–82. New York, ACM, 2009.

[Ritschel et al. 09b] T. Ritschel, T. Engelhardt, T. Grosch, H.-P. Seidel, J. Kautz, and C. Dachsbacher. "Micro-Rendering for Scalable, Parallel Final Gathering." *ACM Transactions on Graphics (Proc. SIGGRAPH Asia 2009)* 28:5 (2009), 132:1–132:8.

[Sloan et al. 09] P.-P Sloan, N. Govindaraju, D. Nowrouzezahrai and J. Snyder. "Image-Based Proxy Accumulation for Real-Time Soft Global Illumination." In *Proceedings of the 15th Pacific Conference on Computer Graphics*, pp. 97–105. Washington, DC: IEEE Computer Society, 2009.

[Segovia et al. 09] B. Segovia, J.C. Iehl R. Mitanchey and B. Péroche. "Non-Interleaved Deferred Shading of Interleaved Sample Patterns." in *Proceedings of the 21st ACM SIGGRAPH/EUROGRAPHICS Symposium on Graphics Hardware*, pp. 53–60. Aire-la-Ville, Switzerland, Eurographics Asociation, 2009.

[Tomasi and Manduchi 98] C. Tomasi and R. Manduchi. "Bilateral Filtering for Gray and Color Images." In *Proceedings of the Sixth International Conference on Computer Vision*, pp. 839–846. Washington, DC: IEEE Computer Society, 1998.

[Thibieroz and Gruen 10] N. Thibieroz and H. Gruen. "'OIT and Indirect Illumination Using DX11 Linked Lists." In *Proceedings of Game Developers Conference*, 2010.

[Wald et al. 09] I. Wald. T. Ize, A. Kensler, A. Knoll, and S¿ G¿ Parker. "Ray Tracing Animated Scenes Using Coherent Grid Traversal." *ACM Transanction on Graphics (Proc. SIGGRAPH ASIA)* 25:3 (2006), 485–493.

[Wyman and Nichols 09] C. Wyman and G. Nichols. "Multiresolution Splatting for Indirect Illumination." In *I3D '09: Proceedings of the 2009 Symposium on Interactive 3D Graphics and Games*, pp. 83–90. News York: ACM, 2009.

[Yang et al. 09] J. Yang, J. Hensley, H. Gruen, and N. Thibieroz. "Dynamic Construction of Concurrent Linked-Lists for Real-Time Rendering." *Computer Graphics Forum (Eurographics Symposium on Rendering 2010)*29:4 (2010), 1297–1304.

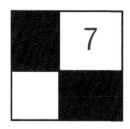

Real-Time Approximation of Light Transport in Translucent Homogenous Media

Colin Barré-Brisebois and Marc Bouchard

7.1 Introduction

When reproducing visual elements found in nature, it is crucial to have a mathematical theory that models real-world light transport. In real-time graphics, the interaction of light and matter is often reduced to local reflection described by *bidirectional reflectance distribution functions* (BRDFs), for example, describing reflectance at the surface of opaque objects [Kurt 09]. In nature, however, many

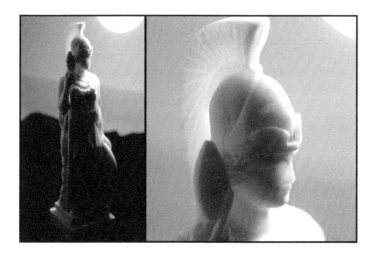

Figure 7.1. A partially translucent statue of Athena.

Figure 7.2. The final result.

objects are (partly) translucent: light transport also happens within the surface (as shown in Figure 7.1).

To simulate light transport inside objects in real time, developers rely on various complex shading models and algorithms, (e.g., to replicate the intricate subsurface scattering found in human skin [d'Eon 09, Hable 09].) Conversely, this chapter presents a fast real-time approximation of light transport in translucent homogenous media, which can be easily implemented on programmable graphics hardware (PC, as well as video game consoles). In addition, the technique scales well on fixed and semi-fixed pipeline systems, it is artist friendly, and it provides results that fool the eyes of most users of real-time graphics products. This technique's simplicity also permits fast iterations, a key criteria for achieving visual success and quality in the competitive video game industry. We discuss the developmental challenge, its origins, and how it was resolved through an initial and basic implementation. We then present several scalable variations, or improvements to the original technique, all of which enhance the final result (see Figure 7.2).

7.2   In Search of Translucency

First and foremost, the technique we present was originally implemented in the graphics research pursued for EA Montréal's *Spore Hero* video game. In this game, we wanted to create simple-yet-eerie, translucent, mushroom-like worlds. Our materials were inspired by the statue in Figure 7.1 and had to demonstrate convincing diffuse translucency, whereby the amount of light that traveled inside

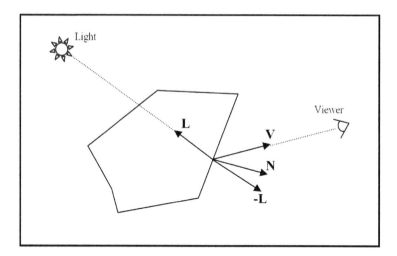

Figure 7.3. Lighting vectors.

the shape was influenced by the varying thickness of that same shape. In mathematical terms, this means that the amount of light that penetrates the surface of the shape (but also the amount of light exiting at the opposite hemisphere to the BRDF) can be defined with a *bidirectional transmittance distribution function* (BTDF). Our current method attempts to phenomenologically replicate inner-surface diffusion, in which light traveling inside the object is scattered based on material properties. This phenomena can be described using a *bidirectional surface scattering reflectance distribution function* (BSSRDF) [Jensen 01]. With this technique, we wanted to approximate the BSSRDF using minimal available GPU resources. After careful analysis, we discovered that using distance-attenuated regular diffuse lighting, combined with the distance-attenuated dot product of the view vector and an inverted light vector, would simulate basic light transport inside an object (see Figure 7.3).

Through this research, executed in prototype levels not included with the final product, we discovered that the technique worked well for numerous simple shapes. However, the technique did not take thickness into account and we had to return to the drawing board, seeking a solution that was more effective and complete.

7.3   The Technique: The Way out Is Through

Using the aforementioned math, it is possible to create a rough simulation of highly scattering material that works well for very simple objects, such as spheres and cubes, since most lights used at runtime show radial diffusion properties. In

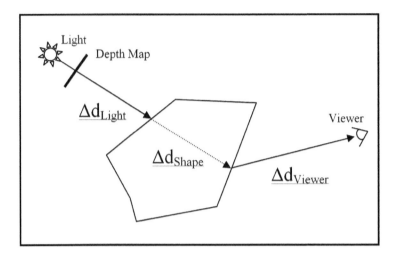

Figure 7.4. Local thickness for Hebe.

cases with more complex models, it is necessary to be aware of the thickness, or rather, the distance traveled by the light inside the shape, in order to properly compute light transport inside that same shape. As seen in [Dachsbacher 03, Green 04, Ki 09], this thickness can be computed using depth maps. The referential, as determined by the depth map, allows us to easily compute the distance traveled by the light from the light source Δd_{Light}, through the shape Δd_{Shape}, and to the pixel Δd_{Viewer} (see Figure 7.4).

Despite the fact that this method provides quite convincing results, successfully creating a technique that achieves a similar effect on current gaming platforms, without relying on depth maps would be beneficial. It would eliminate the need for an additional depth rendering pass, wherein the geometry is submitted a second time (and possibly a third time, in cases where it was already submitted to a global shadowing solution). The method is acceptable in cases where the object rendered with translucency uses its own depth map for shadows because its memory and performance cost are already amortized. Our team wanted to expand upon this idea to find an alternative, seeking a technique that would scale well on a variety of programmable and semifixed pipeline graphics hardware without relying on depth maps. In doing so, we wanted to test the limits and avoid detrimental changes to the runtime. To accomplish this task, our team needed to find the means to establish object thickness, or rather, areas on the object that should be translucent or opaque: we define this information as *local thickness*.

7.3.1 Variation 1: Computing Local Thickness

As seen in [Sousa 08], it is possible for artists to define a texture in which the values are approximately representative of the mesh's thickness; with dark values for opaque, and bright values for translucent. Effectively demonstrated in *Crysis*, this method works well for semiflat surfaces such as tree leaves. Unfortunately, in cases where the environment has numerous translucent objects, shaped in various forms, the process of defining which areas on the shape are translucent is a tedious manual process.

To streamline this process we rely on a normal-inverted and color-inverted computation of *ambient occlusion* (AO), which can be done offline and stored in a texture using your favorite modeling software. Since ambient occlusion determines how much environmental light arrives at a surface point, we use this information for the inside of the shape. Through inverting the surface normal during the computation, it is possible to find an approximate result that tells us how much light traveling inside the homogenous media would become occluded at the point where it exits the shape.

The result is a texture with inverted colors that depict two types of area, translucent areas in white and opaque areas in black (see Figure 7.5). Conversely, in cases where you have a good level of tessellation, it is possible to store this information in the vertex color. Finally, we can use this information to improve the computation of light transport, where the final result lies between real

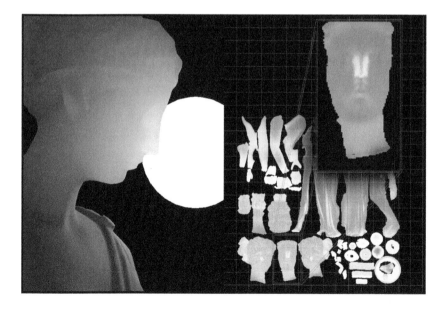

Figure 7.5. Local thickness for Hebe.

subsurface scattering and distance-based attenuation. The inverted AO gives a feeling of scattering, (i.e., collecting light), while using a single distance value for distance-based attenuation.

```
// fLightAttenuation == Light attenuation from direct lighting
// cBRDF              == Computed color for BRDF lighting
// cDiffuse           == Light Diffuse Color
// cTranslucent       == Light Translucency Color

// Compute the BSSRDF
float fLTDot = pow(saturate(dot(vCamera, vLight)), fLTPower);
float fLT = fLightAttenuation * tex2D(texInvAO, input.vUV);
fLT += fLTDot * fLightAttenuation * fLTScale;

// Compute the final color for the BSSRDF (translucency)
float3 cBSSRDF = lerp(cDiffuse, cTranslucent, fLT) * fLT;

// The final result
return float4(cBRDF + cBSSRDF, 1.0f);
```

Listing 7.1. The light transfer in HLSL.

7.3.2 Variation 2: Screen-Space Thickness

In cases where you can afford the extra computation, and still be below the cost of using depth maps, an alternative improvement provided by this new technique relies on a screen-space representation of thickness. As seen in [Oat 08], per-pixel thickness can be easily approximated in an additional pass using a blend-mode trick. Once this alternative to local thickness is computed, it is possible to scale the simplified light-transport result based on the angle of the camera to the light source.

This alternative must be used wisely because it is not valid for every scenario. Given that the information originates from the camera, rather than from the light, it is possible to know only how thick the foreground surface is. Nonetheless, this added information allows us to improve the final result and can be used in conjunction with the local thickness.

There might be game scenarios in which you could use screen-space thickness as the sole means of achieving convincing translucency, and in which there is no need for precomputed local thickness. For example, one could imagine a scenario in which there is a light far in the distance (i.e., in a tunnel) and there are numerous objects that rotate and flow toward the viewer. This scenario is one example where screen-space thickness can provide positive results, especially when applied to arbitrary and animated shapes. As shown in Figure 7.6, screen-space thickness is also effective in cases where there is a bright hemispheric light

Figure 7.6. Using screen-space thickness only.

surrounding the objects. Unfortunately, a still image does not do this variation justice, therefore we recommend viewing the demo in the web materials.

7.3.3 Variation 3: Improving Local Surface Variation

As a further enhancement, one can distort the inverted light vector (see Figure 7.3) based on the surface normal to improve the final result by showing local surface variation. This improvement can also be made using an additional noisy normal map that is customized for the surface type. A single sample is enough, however, if more samples are provided, the final result will be improved. This approach also works quite well if the object's surface is porous (as shown in Figure 7.2).

An example of the aforementioned variation is provided on the accompanying CD. Obviously, it is a quick alternative which does not measure up to the methods of [d'Eon 09, Hable 09] when simulating realistic human skin. However, it can certainly be used as a ready substitute for fast subsurface scattering on objects such as the ears and nose, various animated and static environmental shapes, and even cartoon/nonhuman characters. Further, the image shown in Figure 7.7 relies only on the distortion, not on precomputed local thickness. Combined, both variations significantly increase the quality of the final result (see Figure 7.9).

7.4 Performance

The performance numbers for all techniques illustrated in this paper are given in Table 7.1. Timings are given in *frames-per-second* (FPS) and the complex-

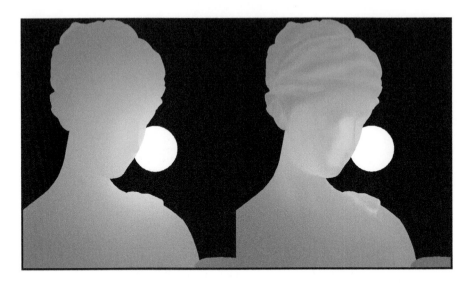

Figure 7.7. Without (left) and with (right) normal distortion.

ity is presented in terms of added *arithmetic logic unit* (ALU) and *texture unit* (TEX) shader instructions. These benchmarks were established using an NVIDIA GeForce GTX260, at a resolution of 1280 × 720, in a scene comprised of several instances of our Hebe statue, with approximately 200,000 triangles.

Overall, these numbers illustrate that our technique approximates light transport inside translucent homogenous media at a very reasonable cost. This method also provides significant benefits in cases when developers want a quick impression of subsurface scattering. In fact, the technique requires only 17 additional instructions to achieve a significant and convincing effect. Finally, if the option is financially viable, adding screen-space thickness to the computation will further improve the final result. The cost of this computation can be managed through the use of a quarter-sized buffer, with filtering in order to prevent artifacts at the boundaries. Realistically, one could rely on a lightweight separable-Gaussian

Technique	FPS	Instructions (ALU+TEX)
Without Translucency	1100	-
Variation 1: Translucency + Local Thickness	1030	17 (16 + 1)
Variation 2: Translucency + Screen-Space Thickness	740	20 (17 + 3)
Variation 3: Translucency + Normal Distortion	1030	19 (18 + 1)

Table 7.1. Performance numbers.

blur, and even use a bilateral filter when up-sampling. A blurred result would definitely complement our diffuse computation.

7.5 Discussion

In the following section we discuss various elements and potential concerns that were not forgotten but were put aside during the development of this technique and its variations. These concerns will now be addressed.

7.5.1 Caveat? Best-Case Scenario?

Because this technique is an approximation, some specific instances will not yield optimal results. Figure 7.8 shows an example in which light travels in and out of the concave hull at point **A**, casting a shadow on point **B**. Though it is possible to generate local thickness that is aware of the concavity (by changing the parameters used for the ambient occlusion computation in Section 7.3.1), this has to be minimized when demonstrating visually convincing examples of diffuse translucency, as is effectively represented in Figure 7.5 and Figure 7.9. Our technique works more effectively with convex hulls or hulls with minimal concavity.

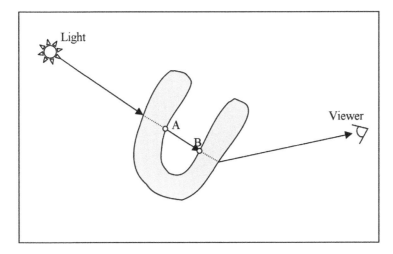

Figure 7.8. Concave hull.

7.5.2 Deferred Rendering?

Rendering engines are evolving toward a deferred shading model. Thus, this technique must be adapted accordingly. Given that deferred implementations differ from one project to the next, it is pertinent to provide general hints regarding the adaptation of the technique within a deferred context. These hints are an adequate starting point, leaving clear room for improvement. An example implementation is provided in the web materials.

The implementation is dependent on available space on the G-buffer. In cases where a single channel is available, the local thickness can be stored as a grayscale value: this is done in the same way that it is stored for specular maps. Subsequently, the light and view-dependent part of the BSSRDF computation can be processed at the same time as the deferred lighting pass. The final result can then be combined with the scene at the same time that the diffuse lighting is computed. In cases where there is no space left for storing the local thickness, this technique will have to be treated in an additional pass and the translucent objects will have to be rendered once again. Fortunately, the z-buffer will already be full and this minimizes the number of affected pixels.

7.6   Conclusion

This chapter illustrates an artist-friendly, fast and scalable real-time approximation of light transport in translucent homogenous media. Our technique allows developers to improve their games' visuals by simulating translucency with reasonable and scalable impact on the runtime. Providing such convincing results

Figure 7.9. The final result, with Hebe.

through simple means is essential in the development of triple-A games. We hope that this technique will inspire developers in the continuous effort to improve games by promoting the development of new techniques that carefully blend art and technology. In the end, our objective is not to focus upon mathematical perfection, but to create convincing results that push the visual boundaries of the gaming industry.

7.7 Demo

The web materials accompanying this book contain an implementation of our technique and its variations in the form of an AMD RenderMonkey sample. HLSL code is also provided in a text file and a short video demonstration of the technique is included.

7.8 Acknowledgments

We would like to thank the following individuals at Electronic Arts for reviewing this paper: Sergei Savchenko, Johan Andersson and Dominik Bauset. We are also grateful for the support of EA's Wessam Bahnassi, Frédéric O'Reilly, David "Mojette" Giraud, Gabriel Lassonde, Stéphane Lévesque, Christina Coffin and John White. Further, we would like to thank Sandie Jensen from Concordia University for her genuine and meticulous style editing. We would also like to thank our section editor, Carsten Dachsbacher, for his thorough reviews and inspiring savoir-faire in search of technical excellence through simplicity. Finally, Marc Bouchard would like to thank Ling Wen Kong and Elliott Bouchard, and Colin Barré-Brisebois would like to thank Simon Barré-Brisebois, Gene-viève Barré-Brisebois and Robert Brisebois.

Bibliography

[Hable 09] J. Hable, G. Borshakov, and J. Heil. "Fast Skin Shading." In *ShaderX^7*, pp. 161–173. Hingham, MA: Charles River Media, 2009.

[Dachsbacher 03] Carsten Dachsbacher and Marc Stamminger. "Translucent Shadow Maps." In *Proceedings of the 14th Eurographics Workshop on Rendering*, pp.197-201. Aire-la-Ville, Switzerland: Eurographics Association, 2003.

[d'Eon 09] Eugene d'Eon and David Luebke. "Advanced Techniques for Realistic Real-Time Skin Rendering." In *GPU Gems 3*, edited by Hubert Nguyen, pp.293–347. Reading, MA: Addison-Wesley, 2008.

[Green 04] Simon Green. "Real-Time Approximations to Subsurface Scattering." In *GPU Gems: Programming Techniques, Tips, and Tricks for Real-Time Graphics*, edited by Randima Fernando, pp. 263-278. Reading, MA: Addison-Wesley, 2004.

[Hejl 09] Jim Hejl. "Fast Skin Shading." In *ShaderX^7: Advanced Rendering Techniques*, edited by Wolfgang Engel, pp. 161–173. Hingham, MA: Charles River Media, 2009.

[Jensen 01] Henrik Wann Jensen, Stephen R. Marschner, Marc Levoy, and Pat Hanrahan. "A Practical Model for Subsurface Light Transport." In *Proceedings of the 28th Annual Conference on Computer Graphics and Interactive Techniques*, pp. 511-518. New York: ACM, 2001.

[Ki 09] Hyunwoo Ki. "Real-Time Subsurface Scattering Using Shadow Maps." In *ShaderX^7: Advanced Rendering Techniques*, edited by Wolfgang Engel, pp 467–478. Hingham, MA: Charles River Media, 2009.

[Kurt 09] Murat Kurt and Dave Edwards. "A Survey of BRDF Models for Computer Graphics," *ACM SIGGRAPH Computer Graphics* 43:2 (2009), 4:1–4:7.

[Oat 08] Christopher Oat and Thorsten Christopher. "Computing Per-Pixel Object Thickness in a Single Render Pass," In *ShaderX^6: Advanced Rendering Techniques*, edited by Wolfgang Engel, pp. 57–62. Hingham, MA: Charles River Media, 2008.

[Sousa 08] Tiago Sousa. "Vegetation Procedural Animation and Shading in Crysis." In *GPU Gems 3*, edited by Hubert Nguyen, pp. 373–385. Reading, MA: Addison-Wesley, 2008.

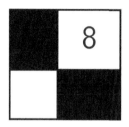

8

Diffuse Global Illumination with Temporally Coherent Light Propagation Volumes

Anton Kaplanyan, Wolfgang Engel, and Carsten Dachsbacher

8.1 Introduction

The elusive goal of real-time global illumination in games has been pursued for more than a decade. The most often applied solution to this problem is to use precomputed data in lightmaps (e.g., Unreal Engine 3) or precomputed radiance

Figure 8.1. Example of indirect lighting with Light Propagation Volumes in the upcoming blockbuster *Crysis 2*.

transfer (e.g., *Halo 3*). Both techniques increase the complexity and decrease the efficiency of a game production pipeline and require an expensive infrastructure (e.g., setting up a cloud for precomputation and incorporating the result into a build process).

In this chapter we describe the light propagation volumes, a scalable real-time technique that does not require a preprocess and storing additional data. The basic idea is to use a lattice storing the light and the geometry in a scene. The directional distribution of light is represented using low-order spherical harmonics. The surfaces of the scene are sampled using reflective shadow maps and this information is then used to initialize the lattice for both light propagation and blocking. A data-parallel light propagation scheme allows us to quickly, and plausibly, approximate low-frequency direct and indirect lighting including fuzzy occlusion for indirect light. Our technique is capable of approximating indirect illumination on a vast majority of existing GPUs and is battle-tested in the production process of an AAA game. We also describe recent improvements to the technique such as improved temporal and spatial coherence. These improvements enabled us to achieve a time budget of 1 millisecond per frame on average on both Microsoft Xbox 360 and Sony PlayStation 3 game consoles.[1]

8.2   Overview

The light propagation volume technique consists of four stages:

- At the first stage we render all directly lit surfaces of the scene into reflective shadow maps [Dachsbacher and Stamminger 05] (see Figure 8.2).

- Next, a sparse 3D grid of radiance distributions is initialized with the surface samples generated in the first pass (see Figure 8.3).

DEPTH   ALBEDO   NORMALS

Figure 8.2. Reflective Shadow Maps store not only depth, but also information about surfaces' normals and reflected flux.

---

[1] *Crysis 2*, *Halo 3*, and CryENGINE 3 are trademarked. PlayStation 3, Microsoft Xbox 360, Unreal Engine 3, and Microsoft DirectX are all registered trademarks.

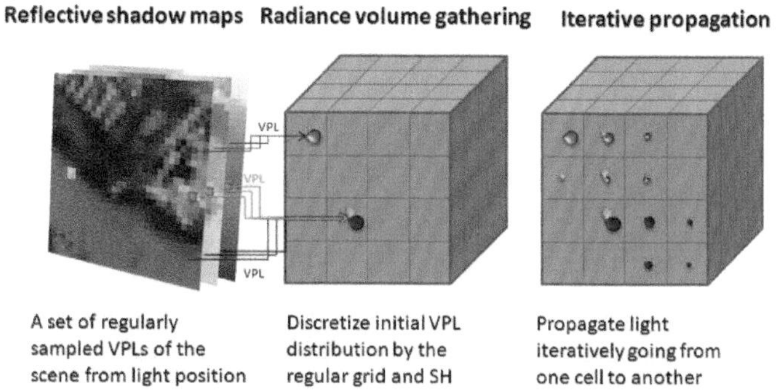

Reflective shadow maps   Radiance volume gathering   Iterative propagation

A set of regularly sampled VPLs of the scene from light position

Discretize initial VPL distribution by the regular grid and SH

Propagate light iteratively going from one cell to another

Figure 8.3. The basic steps of our method: surfaces causing one-bounce indirect illumination are sampled using RSMs, next this information is used to initialize the light propagation volumes where light is propagated, and finally this information is used to light the surfaces in the scene.

- Light is propagated in the grid using an iterative propagation scheme.

- Lastly, the scene is illuminated using the resulting grid, similar to using irradiance volumes [Tatarchuk 04].

Our light propagation volumes (LPV) technique works completely on the GPU and has very modest GPU requirements.

8.3 Algorithm Detail Description

In this section we recapitulate the core algorithm presented in [Kaplanyan and Dachsbacher 10] and emphasize several small, yet important, details. Besides the main steps of the technique we will present an important extension: cascading the reflective shadow maps. This extension allows our technique to be used in large scenes while maintaining real time performance. We also describe important general as well as platform-specific optimizations at the end of this section.

8.3.1 Reflective Shadow Maps

Reflective shadow maps (RSMs) are an extension to regular shadow maps and store not only a depth buffer, but also a normal buffer and flux buffer (Figure 8.2). It is a very fast method for sampling directly lit surfaces of a scene on the GPU, and all pixels of such an RSM can be seen as virtual light sources that generate the indirect illumination in a scene. This representation allows generating and storing samples of a scene's lit surfaces in a very efficient manner.

The size of an RSM should be chosen such that one surface sample (*surfel*) represents an area that is much smaller than one cell of the LPV to provide

Figure 8.4. A reflective shadow map captures the directly lit surfaces of the scene with a regular sampling from the light's origin.

sufficient detail in the lighting computation. We recommend an RSM size that is four times larger than the number of elements along the diagonal of an LPV (e.g., for a LPV of $32 \times 32 \times 32$, an RSM of at least 128×128 size is recommended).

As in the original approach, we assume indirect lighting from diffuse surfaces and store reflected flux in the RSM, which accounts for surface albedo as well as incident lighting (i.e., effects such as a colored projected light can be used as well).

Note that many techniques developed for shadow maps can be applied to RSMs. For example, an RSM can be cascaded like cascaded shadow maps to capture global illumination from a light source such as the sun, or it can be stored in cube maps similar to which cube shadow maps for point light sources. Figure 8.4 shows the surfels created from an RSM that is created for a directional light source.

Temporally stable rasterization. Temporal flickering can occur when an RSM frustum moves, and obviously becomes visible when the resolution of the RSM is rather low and thus scene surfaces are sampled at a coarser level. A simple solution to this problem is to move the frustum of the RSM with world-space positions snapped to the size of one texel in world space. This leads to consistently sampled points during rasterization and largely removes the sampling problems [Dimitrov 07]. If this is not possible, e.g. for perspective projections, then higher resolution RSMs are required for consistently sampling surfaces. Kaplanyan et al. [Kaplanyan 09] proposed downsampling RSMs to reduce the number of surfels for the injection stage. However, additional experiments showed that the downsampling if sometimes even slower than injecting the same number of surfaces directly into the LPV.

8.4 Injection Stage

The injection stage transforms the reflected flux of the surfels obtained from the RSMs into an initial light distribution represented using spherical harmonics (SH) stored into the LPV as spatial discretization. As we assume diffuse surfaces, the reflected flux of each surfel (neglecting if spatial extend) can be represented using a cosine lobe and thus using a low-order SH approximation. Note that we store the energy as directional intensity distribution in the LPV as described in [Kaplanyan and Dachsbacher 10].

The LPV is stored as a texture on the GPU and thus the SH approximations of the surfels can be easily accumulated into the LPV using additive blending. At this point the spatial discretization comes into play as the surfels' positions are snapped to the centers of LPV cells (see Figure 8.5). At the end of the injection stage, each cell of the LPV represents the initial radiant intensity approximated using spherical harmonics.

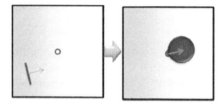

Figure 8.5. The reflected intensity distribution of a surfel obtained from an RSM is approximated using SH and snapped to the center of the closest LPV cell.

Projecting into spherical harmonics. To represent the intensity distribution of a surfel we use the first two bands of the spherical harmonics basis (i.e., four coefficients). This proved to be sufficient to represent the mostly low-frequency indirect lighting in diffuse scenes (Figure 8.6). As previously mentioned, the outgoing intensity distribution of each surfel is a (clamped) cosine lobe centered around its surface normal that is projected into the SH basis. Given the normal vector of the surfel, $\mathbf{n}$, we can obtain the SH coefficients $\mathbf{c} = (c_0, c_1, c_2, c_3)$ as [Sloan 08]:

$$c_0 = \frac{\sqrt{\pi}}{2},$$

$$c_1 = -\sqrt{\frac{\pi}{3}}y,$$

$$c_2 = \sqrt{\frac{\pi}{3}}z,$$

$$c_3 = -\sqrt{\frac{\pi}{3}}x.$$

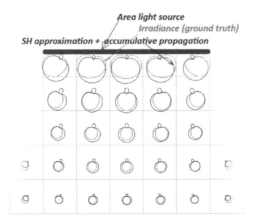

Figure 8.6. Illustration of the approximation error with 4 SH coefficients and a coarse lattice. Note that both the analytical result (green) and propagated result (red) are represented as a final convolved irradiance.

These coefficients are scaled according to the corresponding world-space size and reflected flux of the surfel, yielding four coefficients per color channel. In order to simplify the following description, we show only one set of SH coefficients.

Offsetting surfels. As the LPV is a coarse grid, we have to take care when injecting surfels, as their exact position inside a cell is no longer available after injection. If a surfel's normal points away from the cell's center, its contribution should not be added to this cell, but rather to the next cell, in order to avoid self-illumination (see Figure 8.7). For this, we virtually move each VPL by half the cell-size in the direction of its normal before determining the cell. Note that this shifting of the surfels still does not guarantee completely avoiding self-illumination and light bleeding, but largely removes artifacts from the injection stage.

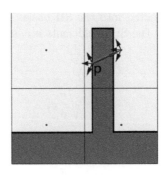

Figure 8.7. Example of a VPL injection causing self-illumination of the thin geometry.

8.4.1 Propagation

The propagation stage consists of several iterations, where every iteration represents one step of light propagation. The propagation stage has some similarity to the *SH discrete ordinate method* [Chandrasekhar 50, Evans 98]. These techniques are typically employed for light-propagation simulation in scattering media. Essentially we use the same process; however, we use a different cell-to-cell propagation scheme. The application of this method to light propagation through vacuum instead of scattering media suffers from the fact that propagation directions are blurred out. Fortunately, our results show that this is an acceptable artifact in many application scenarios.

Intensity propagation. The propagation consists of the following steps:

- The input for the first iteration step is the initial LPV obtained from the injection stage. Each cell stores the intensity as an SH-vector and we propagate the energy to the six neighbors along the axial directions.

- All subsequent propagation steps take the LPV from the previous iteration as input and propagate as in the first iteration.

The main difference from SHDOM methods is the propagation scheme. Instead of transferring energy from a source cell to its 26 neighbor cells in a regular grid, we propagate to its 6 neighbors only, thus reducing the memory footprint. To preserve as much directional information as possible, we compute the transfer to the faces of these neighbor cells and reproject the intensities to the cells' center (see Figure 8.8). This mimics, but is of course not identical to, the use of 30 unique propagation directions. Please see [Kaplanyan and Dachsbacher 10] for the details. There are two ways to implement this propagation process: scattering and gathering light. The gathering scheme is more efficient in this case due to its cache-friendliness.

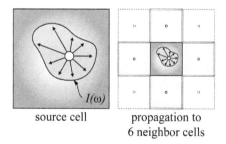

source cell   propagation to
6 neighbor cells

Figure 8.8. Propagation from one source cell (center) to its neighbor cells. Note that we compute the light propagation according to the intensity distribution $I(\omega)$ to all yellow-tagged faces of the destination cells (blueish).

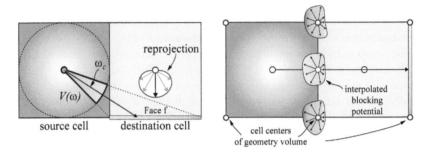

Figure 8.9. Left: Light propagation from the source cell (gray) to the bottom face of the destination cell (blueish). Right: during propagation we can account for occlusion by looking up the blocking potential from the geometry volume.

When propagating the light from a source cell to one face of the destination cell, we compute the incoming flux onto the face using the solid angle $\Delta\omega$ of the face and the central direction ω_c of the propagation cone (see Figure 8.9). The flux reaching the face is then computed as

$$\Phi_f = \frac{\Delta\omega}{4\pi} I(\omega_c),$$

where $I(\omega_c)$ is the intensity of the source cell towards the center of face obtained by evaluating the SH approximation. Here we assume that the intensity does not vary over the solid angle of the face.

Reprojection. The flux incident on a face is then reprojected back into the intensity distribution of the destination cell. The reprojection is accomplished by creating a new virtual surfel at the destination cell's center, pointing toward the face and emitting exactly as much flux as the face received from the propagation (Φ_f):

$$\Phi_l = \int_\Omega \Phi_f \langle n_l, \omega \rangle d\omega = \frac{\Phi_f}{\pi}.$$

Similar to the light injection stage, the corresponding clamped cosine lobe is scaled by Φ_l and accumulated into SH coefficients of the destination cell. In other words, we compute the incoming flux for each face of the destination cell and transform it back into an intensity distribution.

Blocking for indirect shadows. Indirect shadows, i.e., the blocking of indirect light due to scene geometry, can also be incorporated into the LPVs. In order to add indirect shadows, we construct a volumetric representation of the scene's surfaces (see Section 8.4.2). This so-called geometry volume (GV) is a grid of the same resolution as the LPV and stores the blocking potential (also represented as SH) for every grid cell. The GV is displaced by half the grid size with respect to the LPV. That is, the cell centers of the GV reside on the corners of the LPV cells. Whenever we propagate from a source to a destination cell, we obtain the bilinearly interpolated SH coefficients—at the center of the face through which we propagate—from the GV, and evaluate the blocking potential for the propagation direction to attenuate the intensity. Note that this occlusion should not be considered for the very first propagation step after injection, in order to prevent immediate self-shadowing.

Iterations. The sum of all intermediate results is the final light distribution in the scene. Thus we accumulate the results of every propagation in the LPV into a separate 3D grid. The number of required iterations depends on the resolution of the volume. We recommend using two times the longest dimension of the grid (when not using a cascaded approach). For example, if the volume has dimensions of $32 \times 32 \times 8$, then the light can travel the whole volume in 64 iterations in the worst case (which is a diagonal of the volume). However, when using a cascaded approach it is typically sufficient to use a significantly lower number of iterations.

Illustrative example of light propagation process in the Cornell Box–like scene. The light propagation is shown in Figure 8.10. The top-left image shows the coarse LPV initialized from the RSM in the injection stage. The noticeable band of reflected blue and red colors has a width of one cell of LPV. Note that after four iterations the indirect light is propagated and touches the small white cube. After eight iterations the indirect light has reached to the opposite wall.

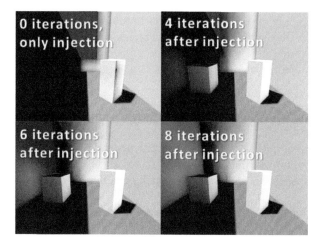

Figure 8.10. Example of the light propagation process in a simple scene.

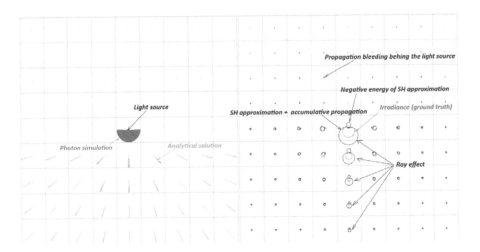

Figure 8.11. Light from a small area light source (smaller than the cell size). The analytical result shows the ground truth solution (left). The light propagation illustrates the ray effect and an unwanted propagation behind the light source (right).

Limitations. The iterative propagation has three main limitations. First, the coarse resolution of the grid does not capture fine details and might even cause light bleeding. Second, due to the SH representation of the intensity distribution and the propagation process itself, the light strongly diffuses and a strictly directed light propagation is not possible. Consequently, there is also no reasonable chance of handling glossy surfaces during propagation. Lastly, the propagation together with the reprojection introduces spatial and directional discretization; this is called the ray effect and is common to all lattice-based methods (see Figure 8.11). Note that some of these artifacts can be suppressed to an acceptable level using cascaded grids to provide finer grids closer to the camera and smart filtering when looking up the LPV.

8.4.2 Indirect Occlusion (Optional Step for Indirect Shadows)

The geometry volume storing the blocking potential of the scene geometry is only required when computing indirect shadows. To this end, we again sample the surfaces using RSMs (and deferred shading buffers, see below) and each texel represents a small part of a surface. Using this sampled scene information, we model the occlusion in the spirit of [Sillion 95], using the accumulated blocking potential of surfels in a grid cell as a probability for blocking light from a certain direction. In this way we can render soft shadows, but shadows of objects smaller than the GV's cell size can of course not be resolved.

Constructing the geometry volume. The blocking potential of a surfel is approximated using the first two bands of the SH basis again. The amount of blocking by one surfel depends on its size and the cosine of the angle between its normal and the light direction in question. The blocking probability of a single surfel with area A_s (computed based on the RSM's texel size in world space), and normal n_s in a cell of grid size s is

$$B(\omega) = \frac{A_s \langle n_s | \omega \rangle}{s^2}.$$

Note that we assume that scene objects are closed surfaces. This is important and allows us to use a clamped cosine lobe for the blocking potential again, as low-order SH projections of absolute cosine lobes tend to degrade to near isotropic functions. Similar to the VPL injection, we accumulate the SH projections of the blocking potential into the GV.

Reusing G-buffers from RSMs and cameras. Aiming at fully dynamic scenes without precomputation requires the creation of the GV—and thus the surface sampling—on the fly. First of all, we can reuse the sampling of the scene's surfaces that is stored in the depth and normal buffers of the camera view (when using a deferred renderer), and in the RSMs that have been created for the light sources. RSMs are typically created for numerous light sources and thus already represent a dense sampling of large portions of the scene. It is, at any time, possible to gather more information about the scene geometry by using depth-peeling for the RSMs or the camera view.

The injection (i.e., determining the blocking potential of a GV's cell) has to be done using separate GVs for every RSM or G-buffer in order to make sure that the same occluder (surfel) is not injected multiple times from different inputs. Afterwards, we combine all intermediate GVs into a single final GV. We experimented using the maximum operator for SH coefficients. Although this is not correct, it yields plausible result when using 2 SH-bands only and clamping the evaluation to zero, and thus yields more complete information about light-blocking surfaces.

8.4.3 Final Scene Illumination

The accumulated results of the propagation steps represent the light distribution in the scene. In the simplest form we query the intensity by a trilinearly interpolated lookup of the SH coefficients and compute the reflected radiance of a surface. We then evaluate the SH-intensity function for the negative normal of the surface, similar to irradiance volumes [Greger et al. 97], and next convert it into incident radiance. For this we assume that the cell's center (where the intensity is assumed to reside) is half the grid size s away from the surface.

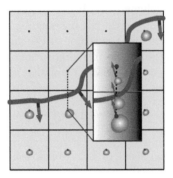

Figure 8.12. The interpolation of the intensity stored in the grid induced by the orange surface between two cells. Note the wrong result of linear interpolation behind the emitting object itself. Also note that the gradient is opposing in this case.

LPVs and light prepass rendering. In light prepass architecture [Engel 09] of the CryENGINE 3, the LPV lighting is directly rendered into the diffuse-light-accumulation buffer on top of multiple ambient passes. This allows us to use optimizations, such as stencil prepass and depth-bound tests, for this pass as well. Moreover, it is also possible to compose complex layered lighting.

Improving filtering by using directional derivatives. The trilinear interpolation of SH coefficients for looking up the LPV can cause serious artifacts such as self-illumination and light bleeding. We found that a damping factor based on the directional derivative of the intensity distribution greatly reduces these artifacts. For a surface location x with normal n, we determine the trilinearly interpolated SH coefficients c and the directional derivative in the normal direction ∇c (computed via final differencing) (see Figure 8.12):

$$\nabla c(x) = \frac{c(x) - c(x + n)}{\|n\|} = c(x) - c(x + n).$$

Whenever the derivative is large, and c and ∇c are deviating, we damp c before computing the lighting.

This additional filtering during the final rendering phase yields sharper edges between lit and shadowed areas.

8.4.4   A Multi-Resolution Approach Using Cascaded Light Propagation Volumes

So far we have considered a single LPV only; however, a regular 3D grid does not provide enough resolution everywhere in scenes with large extent, or otherwise requires prohibitively high memory storage and propagation cost. In this section

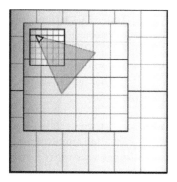

Figure 8.13. Cascaded approach. Cascades are nested and attached to the camera; note that cascades are slightly shifted toward the view direction.

we propose a multi-resolution approach to this problem keeping both memory consumption and computation cost low, even for large scenes (see Figure 8.13).

Cascaded LPVs. In spirit of the cascaded shadow map (CSM) approach [Engel 05, Dimitrov 07], we use multiple nested grids, or cascades, for light propagation that move with the camera. For every cascade, we not only store an LPV, but we also create a separate RSM for every light source, where the RSM resolution is chosen proportional to the grid cell sizes as described above. However, unlike CSMs, the indirect lighting can also be propagated from behind to surfaces in front of the camera (see Figure 8.14). In practice we use a 20/80 ratio for cascade shifting, i.e., the cascades are not centered around the camera but shifted in view directions such that 20% of their extent is located behind the camera. Usually it is sufficient to use three nested grids with a respective double size.

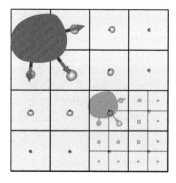

Figure 8.14. Indirect light propagated from objects of different sizes in the respective resolution.

The idea of LPVs naturally transfers to the multi-resolution approach, and every cascade requires RSM generation, injection, propagation, and LPV lookup almost as before. However, before the RSM generation starts, we determine for every object in the scene to which cascade it belongs, and thus in which RSM it has to be considered. This ensures that we do not account for the indirect light contribution of an object multiple times.

Light propagation with cascades. So far we detailed light propagation within a single grid, but handling multiple cascades simultaneously imposes new questions: How do we propagate across different cascades? How do we combine the contributions of different cascades for the final rendering? In this section we propose two options depending on whether indirect shadows are a required feature or not.

If no indirect shadows are required, we can handle the cascades independent from each other, and the multi-resolution approach is straightforward to implement. With indirect shadows, we have to correctly deal with light propagating across the edges of cascades and, of course, blocking.

Cascaded LPVs without indirect shadows. Assuming that light propagates without blocking, we can completely decouple the cascades and compute a LPV solution with the following steps:

- Every RSM for a each cascade should contain unique objects causing indirect light. Objects are normally rendered into the RSM for the cascade for which they have been selected; in RSMs for other cascades they are rendered with black albedo in order to prevent indirect light contribution, but correctly rendering direct shadows.

- The propagation is done for each cascade independently.

- The scene is illuminated by the accumulated contribution of all cascades.

In this case, we determine the respective cascade for every object by estimating its contribution to the indirect illumination, which in turn heavily depends on its surface area and the distance to the camera. To this end, we account for large and distant objects in the coarser cascades while injecting smaller, close objects into the finer grids. Note that this means that distant, small objects might not be considered during the computation (if they lie outside the finer cascades). However, the indirect illumination stemming from such objects typically has a significant contribution only within a certain (small) proximity of the object.

Cascades with indirect shadows. When accounting for light blocking we cannot decouple the propagation process of the cascades. In this case every object is injected into the finest grid at its respective location. This also means that those parts of coarser grids that are overlapped by finer grids are empty and not used during the propagation. Although we apply the propagation steps to each cascade separately, we have to make sure that light leaving one grid can further propagate in the next grid. This is simple when the grid cell sizes of two cascades differ by a power-of-two factor. Note that intensity has to be redistributed when propagating light from a single cell of a coarse grid to multiple cells of a fine grid, and accumulated when propagating light from multiple fine grid cells to a coarse grid cell (as intensity already accounts for the surface area).

Stable lighting through snapping. The LPV cascades are oriented along the world space axes and do not rotate, only translate, with the camera. It is important to snap the cascade positions in world-space to multiples of the cell sizes. This ensures that the distribution of surfels in the injection stage is stable and independent of the translation of the LPVs.

8.5 Optimizations

8.5.1 General Optimizations

The scene illumination stage with a final LPV is usually a very expensive pass (see the timing table in Section 8.6.1). It is important to note that the hardware capability to render into a volume texture tremendously improves performance at this stage. This simplifies the shader workload as the emulation of a trilinear filtering in the pixel shader is not necessary. Instead, the hardware unit is utilized and cache coherency is highly improved due to the optimized memory layout of a swizzled 3D texture.

Unfortunately, not every platform supports rendering into a 3D texture. However, it is possible to inject the VPLs directly into the volume texture on consoles. To do so, the 3D texture should be treated as a horizontally unwrapped 2D render target; note that this is not possible with the Microsoft DirectX 9.0 API.

Using an 8 bit/channel texture format for the LPV has proven to be sufficient for diffuse indirect lighting stored in two bands of SH. Note that this detail is very important because it speeds up the final rendering pass significantly due to decreased bandwidth and texture-cache misses.

8.5.2 Temporal Coherence

As the diffuse indirect lighting is inherently smooth, the observer is usually quite unaware of temporally changing smooth gradients. Exploiting this fact, we recommend caching each resulting LPV and reusing the results across several frames. The temporal reprojection can easily be done in a straightforward way with accumulation of the old results and a smooth substitution by the newly propagated results.

In practice, we perform the full pass of LPV computation (RSM generation, injection, and propagation) each fifth frame. With the target frame rate of 30 frames/second that means that the refresh rate for the indirect lighting is six times/second. This proved to be sufficient in the vast majority of cases. The workload can be distributed either stage-by-stage across several frames or can be executed all at once (RSM rendering, injection, and propagation) during one frame. In CryENGINE 3 we do not spread separate stages; however, we update different cascades in different frames. In addition, we use different update frequencies for different cascades of cascaded shadow maps. The LPV update workload is interleaved with updates of shadow map cascades, which ensures that we have a balanced rendering and consistent performance.

8.5.3 Xbox 360-Specific Optimizations

When doing the injection directly into a 3D texture on the Xbox 360, we recommend redundantly unwrapping this texture vertically as well (so a $32 \times 32 \times 32$ 3D texture becomes a 32×1024 2D texture after being aliased as a 2D render target, but it should additionally be duplicated vertically). This trick significantly reduces the h/w bank conflicts caused by multiple surfels being written to the same pixel.

Note that the redundant copies of the texture should be accumulated together afterwards and added into the final 3D texture. Also, the resolve GPU command from the EDRAM into a 3D texture has some API issues; a work-around solution for these issues is proposed in the Appendix of [Kaplanyan 09].

8.5.4 PlayStation 3-Specific Optimizations

The 3D texture is essentially implemented as an array of contiguous 2D textures. This means that the layout of unwrapped 2D render targets should be vertical on PlayStation 3 in order to match the memory layout of the 3D texture. Then the injection goes directly into a 3D texture and can be done by using the simple memory aliasing of this texture as a 2D render target. The RSX pipeline should obviously be flushed after the injection rendering in order to make sure that all the surfels are injected before the propagation is started.

Another suggestion for speeding up the final illumination pass is to alias the target buffer as a $2\times$ MSAA and do the shading in a half-resolution horizontally. This is possible only on PlayStation 3 because the layout of samples in the sampling scheme matches the layout of the render target with the same pitch. This trick can help to reduce the pixel work without noticeable quality degradation, as the diffuse indirect lighting typically exhibits low frequencies only.

8.6 Results

In this section we provide several example screenshots showing diffuse global illumination in Crysis 2 (see Figure 8.15). In Crysis 2 we use one to three cascades depending on the graphics settings, platform, and level specifics.

Figure 8.15. In *Crysis 2* we use from one to three cascades depending on graphics settings, platform, and level specifics.

8.6.1 Tools and Tweaking Parameters for Artists

Because artists want to have more control over the indirect lighting, it was decided to expose multiple controlling parameters for the technique:

- Global intensity of indirect lighting: This parameter helps to tweak the overall composition and can also be tweaked during the game play from the game logics.

- Per-object indirect color: This parameter affects only the color and the intensity of indirectly bounced lighting from a specific object. It is mostly used to amplify or attenuate the contribution of some particular objects into indirect lighting.

- Propagation attenuation: This parameter is used to tweak the attenuation of the indirect color.

- Per-object "indirect receiver" parameter for particles: This is mostly used to tag some particle effects as those illuminated by the indirect lighting (disabled by default).

These parameters are frequently used by artists to tweak some particular places and moments in the game. They proved to be particularly important for cut scenes and some in-game movies.

8.6.2 Timings

Detailed timings for a single cascade for the Crytek Sponza[2] scene are provided in Table 8.1. Note that the timings for multiple cascades can be estimated by multiplying the timings for a single cascade by the number of cascades when using the cascaded approach, as the work is spread across several RSMs.

For all screenshots in this chapter we used the same settings: the size of the LPV grid is $32 \times 32 \times 32$, the propagation uses 12 iterations and 1 1 cascade, and the rendering was at 1280×720 resolution (no MSAA). The cost of the final illumination pass obviously depends on the target buffer resolution. The RSM size is 256^2 for the timings with the NVIDIA GTX285 and 128^2 for both consoles. Of course the cost of the RSM rendering also depends on the scene complexity.

Stage	NVIDIA GTX 285	Xbox	PlayStation
RSM Rendering	0.16 (256^2)	0.5 (128^2)	0.8 (128^2)
VPL Injection	0.05	0.2	0.4
Propagation (12 iterations)	0.8	0.8	0.7
Final illumination (720p)	2.4 (RGBA16F format)	2.0	1.5
Total (per frame)	1.5	1.1	1.2

Table 8.1. Detailed timings for a single cascade for the Crytek Sponza scene. All measurements are in milliseconds for the individual stages.

8.7 Conclusion

In this chapter we described a highly parallel production-ready and battle-tested (diffuse) global illumination method for real-time applications without any pre-computation. To our knowledge, it is the first technique that employs a light propagation for diffuse global illumination. It features a very consistent and scalable performance, which is crucial for real-time applications such as games. We also described how to achieve indirect illumination in large-scale scenes using a multi-resolution light propagation.

We demonstrated our method in various scenes in combination with comprehensive real-time rendering techniques. In the future we would like to reduce the limitations of our method by investigating other grid structures and other adaptive schemes, where the compute shaders of DirectX 11 will probably of great help.

---

[2]The Crytek Sponza scene is the original Sponza Atrium scene improved for global illumination experiments. This scene is granted to the rendering community and can be downloaded from this link: http://crytek.com/cryengine/cryengine3/downloads.

8.8 Acknowledgments

Thanks to Sarah Tariq and Miguel Sainz for implementing this technique as a sample of the NVIDIA SDK[3]. And of course the whole Crytek R&D team as well as all others who helped and discussed the real-time graphics with us!

Bibliography

[Chandrasekhar 50] S. Chandrasekhar. *Radiative Transfer*. New York: Dover, 1950.

[Dachsbacher and Stamminger 05] C. Dachsbacher and M. Stamminger. "Reflective Shadow Maps." In *Proc. of the Symposium on Interactive 3D Graphics and Games*, pp. 203–213. Washington, DC: IEEE Computer Society, 2005.

[Dimitrov 07] R. Dimitrov. "Cascaded Shadow Maps." Technical report, NVIDIA Corporation, 2007.

[Engel 05] W. Engel. "Cascaded Shadow Maps." In *Shader X^5*, pp. 129–205. Hingham, MA: Charles River Media, 2005.

[Engel 09] W. Engel. "Light Prepass." In *Advances in Real-Time Rendering in 3D Graphics and Games Course—SIGGRAPH 2009*. New York: ACM Press, 2009.

[Evans 98] K. F. Evans. "The Spherical Harmonic Discrete Ordinate Method for Three-Dimensional Atmospheric Radiative Transfer." In *Journal of Atmospheric Sciences*, pp. 429–446, 1998.

[Greger et al. 97] G. Greger, P. Shirley, P. Hubbard, and D. Greenberg. "The Irradiance Volume." *IEEE Computer Graphics & Applications* 18 (1997), 32–43.

[Kaplanyan and Dachsbacher 10] Anton Kaplanyan and Carsten Dachsbacher. "Cascaded Light Propagation Volumes for Real-Time Indirect Illumination." In *Proceedings of the 2010 ACM SIGGRAPH Symposium on Interactive 3D Graphics and Games*, pp. 99–107, 2010.

[Kaplanyan 09] A. Kaplanyan. "Light Propagation Volumes in CryEngine 3." In *Advances in Real-Time Rendering in 3D Graphics and Games Course—SIGGRAPH 2009*. New York: ACM Press, 2009.

[Sillion 95] F. Sillion. "A Unified Hierarchical Algorithm for Global Illumination with Scattering Volumes and Object Clusters." *IEEE Trans. on Visualization and Computer Graphics* 1:3 (1995), 240–254.

[Sloan 08] P.-P. Sloan. "Stupid Spherical Harmonics (SH) Tricks." In *GDC'08*, 2008.

[Tatarchuk 04] N. Tatarchuk. "Irradiance Volumes for Games." Technical report, ATI Research, Inc., 2004.

---

[3]Publicly available for download at: http://developer.nvidia.com/object/sdk_home

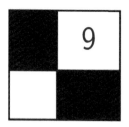

9

Ray-Traced Approximate Reflections Using a Grid of Oriented Splats
Holger Gruen

9.1 Overview

This chapter introduces a method to generate approximate ray-traced reflections of dynamic scene elements. It uses a dynamic 3D grid containing lists of oriented surface splats to generate these reflections on DX11-class GPUs. It is shown how a straightforward implementation of this technique allows for real-time frame rates for low to moderate grid sizes. The resulting reflections are plausible for rough reflectors. The chapter further describes a future implementation that utilizes a flat hierarchical grid to improve the quality of the reflections while keeping the memory requirements for the 3D grid at an acceptable level.

9.2 Introduction

Real-time reflections in dynamic scenes are still one of the most desired features for real-time 3D applications like computer games, and they pose a really challenging problem in the general case. Recent advances in programmable hardware allow real-time rendering into data structures that capture properties of dynamic scene elements (see e.g., [Yang et al. 10]). This chapter makes use of these capabilities to construct a data structure that allows for computing approximate reflections of dynamic scene elements.

Until now, real-time reflections have been realized by one or a combination of the following techniques:

1. Flat Reflectors: Mirror the camera to render a reflection texture.

2. Reflections through a set of environment maps: An approximation of the real reflections seen at a specific surface point in the scene is generated. Usually environment maps are used to realize reflections of distant objects.

3. Screen space reflections: An approximation is generated that ignores reflections from objects that are not visible onscreen.

4. Image-based reflections: Examples are the billboard reflections in the last Unreal Engine 3 demo presented at GDC 2011.

The DX11 rasterizer is used to generate a splat-based intermediate representation of the dynamic objects' surfaces in a scene. In the context of this chapter, the minimum set of attributes stored for each splat are the 3D position of the center of the splat, a surface normal, and some other surface properties used for lighting. This approach shares some of the benefits of image-based rendering, as there is no longer a need to access the full scene geometry. The rasterizer also eliminates some of the geometric complexity of the scene, as small triangles that do not straddle the center of a pixel will not generate any splats.

The use of the rasterizer makes it possible to render exactly the same geometry that is used by other rendering passes of the 3D application. As a result, no memory for an additional scene representation is needed.

GPU-based ray tracing of the full-scene geometry can also be used to generate high-quality reflections. However, ray tracing of fully dynamic scenes is not yet fast enough for a real-time solution. Also, ray-tracing algorithms can become memory limited if they need to parse the full geometric complexity of the scene. This can be especially bad for nonplanar reflectors, as reflected rays in general do not show good coherence.

9.3   The Basic Algorithm

The basic algorithm for generating approximate splat-based reflections works in three phases. These will be now described in detail. Please note that all phases must be carried out per frame for all dynamic scene elements.

9.3.1   Phase 1: Generating a Grid of Splats

In order to generate a good set of point splats, one renders a set of orthogonal views of the geometry in question. Typically three views, for example, a top view, a front view, and a side view are used. To render these views efficiently, we use hardware instancing to replicate the geometry for each of the views . The DX11 system value SV_InstanceID is used inside the vertex shader to select what view matrix and what orthogonal projection matrix are to be used.

DX11-class graphics hardware allows for scattering pixel shaders. In other words, a pixel shader can write data to an arbitrary location inside a buffer.

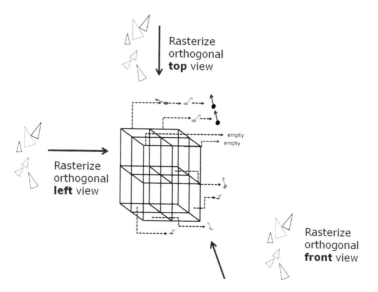

Figure 9.1. Rasterizing oriented splats for a set of orthogonal views into a 3D grid of single linked lists.

When rendering the splats, one needs to disable depth tests and backface culling, and one doesn't actually bind any valid render target but only two output buffers for scattering writes. These output buffers are used to represent a 3D grid with a list of splats in each grid cell (see [Yang et al. 10]). We typically use a $64 \times 64 \times 64$ grid around the dynamic scene elements to capture splats.

We set up a viewport that is big enough to generate a reasonable number of splats along each view direction, and then the scattering pixel shader is used to insert a splat entry for each pixel into the 3D grid. Please consult Figure 9.1 for a high-level abstraction of this process.

In fact, we construct a small bounding box around each pixel in the pixel shader and add the oriented splat to all grid cells that are touched by the bounding box. This avoids popping artifacts for dynamic objects. The size of the bounding box is typically chosen to be around 25% of the world-space size of a grid cell for our demo implementation.

The splat entry for each pixel can contain every piece of information that may be needed by later rendering operations. The minimum set of attributes is:

1. the 3D position of the splat,

2. the surface normal of the splat,

3. surface properties used for lighting the splat.

Listing 9.1 shows an implementation of the scattering pixel shader mentioned above. Please note that the shader uses a shadow map to apply a shadow term to the coloring of the splats.

```
#define CELLS_XYZ 64

struct LINKEDSPLAT
{
  float3 pos;
  float3 n;
  float3 col;
  uint   prev;
};

struct PS_RenderSceneInput
{
  float4 f4Position          : SV_POSITION;
  float4 f4Diffuse           : COLOR0;
  float2 f2TexCoord          : TEXTURE0;
  float3 f3WorldSpacePos     : TEXTURE1;
  float3 f3WorldSpaceNormal  : TEXTURE2;
};

RWStructuredBuffer<LINKEDSPLAT> LinkedSplatsBuffer;
RWByteAddressBuffer             StartOffsetBuffer;

uint offset( uint3 pos )
{
    return ( pos.x + pos.y * CELLS_XYZ +
             pos.z * CELLS_XYZ * CELLS_XYZ );
}

void PS_RenderSplats( PS_RenderSceneInput I )
{
  // compute initial splat color
  float4 f4Col = I.f4Diffuse* g_txCurrentObject.Sample(
                   g_SampleLinearWrap, I.f2TexCoord );

  // compute shadow term
  float4 f4SMC = mul(float4(I.f3WorldSpacePos.xyz, 1.0f ),
                     g_f4x4WorldViewProjLight );
  float2 rtc   = float2( 0.0f, 1.0f ) +  float2( 0.5f, -0.5f ) *
                 ( (1.0f).xx + ( f4SMC.xy / f4SMC.w ) );
  float fShadow = filter_shadow(float3(rtc, f4SMC.z/f4SMC.w) );

  LINKEDSPLAT ls;

  ls.pos = I.f3WorldSpacePos.xyz;
  ls.n   = normalize( I.f3WorldSpaceNormal.xyz );
  ls.col = 1.3f * saturate( fShadow + 0.3f ) * f4Col.xyz;

  // compute position normalized to grid coord system
  // g_LBFbox holds left, bottom, front corner of box of grid
  float3 f3GridP = max( I.f3WorldSpacePos - g_LBFbox.xyz,
                   (0.0f).xxx );

  // set up small bounding box around splat (EPS = small number)
  float3 f3TLBF = max( f3GridP - EPS * g_GridCellSize.xyz,
                  (0.0f).xxx );
  float3 f3TRTB = max( f3GridP + EPS * g_GridCellSize.xyz,
                  (0.0f).xxx );
```

```
            // figure out the range of cells touching the bb
            float3 f3Start = min( (float(CELLS_XYZ-1)).xxx,
                              max( f3TLBF * g_InvGridCellSize.xyz,
                              (0.0f).xxx ) );
            float3 f3Stop  = min( (float(CELLS_XYZ-1)).xxx,
                              max( f3TRTB * g_InvGridCellSize.xyz,
                              (0.0f).xxx ) );

            // compute integer range of grid cells to iterate over
            uint3   start = uint3( f3Start );
            uint3   stop  = uint3( f3Stop );

            // iterate over cells
            for( uint zi = start.z; zi <= stop.z; ++zi )
            {
              for( uint yi = start.y; yi <= stop.y; ++yi )
              {
                for( uint xi = start.x; xi <= stop.x; ++xi )
                {
                  uint oldOffset;

                  // alloc new offset
                  uint newOffset = LinkedSplatsBuffer.IncrementCounter();

                  // update grid offset buffer
                  StartOffsetBuffer.
                  InterlockedExchange( 4 * offset(uint3(xi,yi,zi) ),
                                       newOffset, oldOffset );

                  ls.prev = oldOffset;

                  // add splat to the grid cell
                  LinkedSplatsBuffer[ newOffset ] = ls;
                }
              }
            }
```

Listing 9.1. Scattering pixel shader that adds splat information to all grid cells touching a small box around the splat.

9.3.2 Phase 2: Lighting of the Splats

Depending on the lighting requirements of the application, it may be necessary to perform deferred lighting operations on the splats stored in the grid. All deferred light sources and shadow operations must be carried out on the splats to compute the final lit color of each splat.

If the lighting model is simple, then one can carry out these steps in Phase 1 as set forth in Listing 9.1. The simple proof-of-concept implementation that accompanies this chapter also does carries out a diffuse lighting operation and a shadow map lookup in Phase 1 to immediately arrive at a lit and shadowed color for each splat.

9.3.3   Phase 3: Ray Tracing the Grid of Splats

Now we use the grid of splats for speeding up ray casting to compute where reflected rays hit dynamic scene geometry.

It is of course possible to trace a ray along the reflected view direction even for forward rendering applications. Nevertheless it is more efficient to run this operation on a full-screen g-buffer that has been generated while rendering the main scene.

Using the camera position, the surface normal, and the position at each g-buffer-pixel, the direction to trace along for finding reflections is computed. The pixel shader then traces a ray through the grid starting at the surface position stored in the g-buffer.

For each grid cell entered by the ray, a weight is assigned to each splat in the cell. The lit color of each splat is multiplied by the weight and the weighted colors and weights of all splats are accumulated.

The weights chosen will be zero for splats that point away from the current g-buffer pixel and also take the distance of the center of the splat from the traced ray into account. As a consequence, splats that are too far away will receive a zero weight as well.

If the resulting sum of weights is above zero, the shader assumes that the ray has hit a surface splat and it returns the ratio of the accumulated weighted color and the accumulated weight as the color for the reflection.

Listing 9.2 shows the implementation of the weighting function used in the demo for this chapter. Please note that in order to make efficient use of ALU resources, four splats are handled simultaneously by this shader function.

```
float4
intersect_splats( float3 orig, float3 dir,
                  LINKEDSPLAT s0,
                  LINKEDSPLAT s1,
                  LINKEDSPLAT s2,
                  LINKEDSPLAT s3,
                  float4 f4Mask )
{
    float4 w, denom, k, dw;

    // compute initial weights
    w.x = saturate( dot( normalize( orig - s0.pos ), s0.n ) );
    w.y = saturate( dot( normalize( orig - s1.pos ), s1.n ) );
    w.z = saturate( dot( normalize( orig - s2.pos ), s2.n ) );
    w.w = saturate( dot( normalize( orig - s3.pos ), s3.n ) );

    // compute closest distance to splat
    // ( ( orig + k * dir ) - s.pos ) * s.n = 0
    // s.n * orig + k * dir * s.n  - s.pos * s.n = 0
    // k = ( s.pos * s.n - orig * s.n ) /  ( dir * s.n )
    denom.x = dot( dir, s0.n );
    denom.y = dot( dir, s1.n );
    denom.z = dot( dir, s2.n );
    denom.w = dot( dir, s3.n );
```

```
        k.x = dot( ( s0.pos - orig ), s0.n );
        k.y = dot( ( s1.pos - orig ), s1.n );
        k.z = dot( ( s2.pos - orig ), s2.n );
        k.w = dot( ( s3.pos - orig ), s3.n );

        k /= denom;

        k *= ( denom != (0.0f).xxxx ? (1.0f).xxxx : (0.0f).xxxx );

        w *= ( k > ( 0.0f ).xxxx ) ? ( 1.0f ).xxxx : ( 0.0f ).xxxx;

        // change w to reflect distance from splat center
        float3 temp0 = orig + k.x * dir - s0.pos;
        dw.x = 0.001f + dot( temp0, temp0 );
        float3 temp1 = orig + k.y * dir - s1.pos;
        dw.y = 0.001f + dot( temp1, temp1 );
        float3 temp2 = orig + k.z * dir - s2.pos;
        dw.z = 0.001f + dot( temp2, temp2 );
        float3 temp3 = orig + k.w * dir - s3.pos;
        dw.w = 0.001f + dot( temp3, temp3 );

        // combine weights
        w *= ( dw < (0.08f).xxxx ? 1.0f : 0.0f ) * f4Mask;

        // compute result
        return float4( w.x * s0.col + w.y * s1.col +
                       w.z * s2.col + w.w * s3.col,
                       dot( w, (1.0f).xxxx ) );
}
```

Listing 9.2. Computing a weighted combined color for four splats.

9.4   Results

The proof-of-concept implementation for this technique renders splats to a low-resolution grid of $64 \times 64 \times 64$ cells. In order to generate a good frame rate ($>$ 60 fps), we have chosen to generate reflections for only one out of four pixels of the scene image. Intermediate values are generated using bilateral upsampling [Tomasi and Manduchi 98].

The way the weights are chosen for each splat leads to the perception that the grid contains a sphere-based scene representation. In order to hide this fact—in the end an artifact that comes from the use of a low-resolution grid—we use a bilateral blurring operation to blur the reflections. The resulting blurry reflections look plausible if one assumes rough reflectors.

Figures 9.2–9.4 show screenshots from our demo—all are taken on an AMD HD6870 GPU at frame rates above 60 Hz.

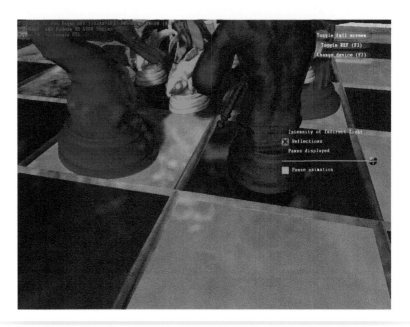

Figure 9.2. Screenshot 1 using a 64 × 64 × 64 grid of splats.

Figure 9.3. Screenshot 2 using a 64 × 64 × 64 grid of splats.

Figure 9.4. Screenshot 3 using a $64 \times 64 \times 64$ grid of splats without ground textures.

9.5 Future Work

We hope that in the future, we will overcome the quality limitations that stem from the use of a fairly low-resolution grid. To do so, we must meet two requirements:

1. Increase the resolution of the grid without making its memory footprint prohibitively high.

2. Keep the ray-traversal performance at a level similar to the one in the low-resolution grid.

The most obvious idea is to make use of a hierarchical grid that only uses memory to store a subgrid for nonempty cells of the coarser grid cells. The following steps describe details of how to implement such an approach:

1. When rendering the splats, one just adds them to an append buffer A. At the same time, the scattering pixel shader doing the append marks the grid cells of a coarse level-0 low-resolution grid as occupied. Also, one needs to allocate a buffer B that is big enough to hold an offset for each cell of the level-0 low-resolution grid.

2. Next, run a compute shader pass to store a valid offset to a subgrid (e.g., 32 × 32) into the cells of offset buffer B for all nonempty grid cells of the level-0 grid.

   Each cell of the subgrid initially contains an empty list of splats.

3. Another compute shader pass runs over the splats in the buffer (from Step 1) and inserts them into the nonempty subgrids accessible via B.

4. When casting rays, we traverse the coarse grid and only descend into subgrids if the coarse grid cell is nonempty.

Implementing all these steps will result in heavily reduced memory requirements and should enable a jump in image quality. Also, the two-level hierarchical grid should keep ray-traversal speed close to speeds achieved by the demo using just a grid. DX11-class hardware already allows for implementing this approach. The most optimal implementation is still a topic of active research, which will be presented in a later publication. At this point in time it is easy to realize the expected memory savings, yet it is hard to reach the performance of the simple nonhierarchical prototype.

Bibliography

[Tomasi and Manduchi 98] C. Tomasi and R. Manduchi. "Bilateral Filtering for Gray and Color Images." In *Proceedings of the Sixth International Conference on Computer Vision (ICCV '98)*. pp. 839–846. Washington, DC: IEEE Computer Society, 1998.

[Yang et al. 10] J. Yang, J. Hensley, H. Gruen, and N. Thibieroz. "Dynamic Construction of Concurrent Linked-Lists for Real-Time Rendering." Presented at *Eurographics Symposium on Rendering*, 2010.

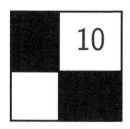

10

Screen-Space Bent Cones: A Practical Approach
Oliver Klehm, Tobias Ritschel, Elmar Eisemann, and Hans-Peter Seidel

10.1 Overview

Ambient occlusion (AO) is a popular technique for visually improving both real-time as well as offline rendering. It decouples occlusion and shading, providing a gain in efficiency. This results in an average occlusion that modulates the surface shading. However, this also reduces realism due to the lack of directional information. Bent normals were proposed as an amelioration that addresses this issue for offline rendering. Here, we describe how to compute bent normals as a cheap byproduct of screen-space ambient occlusion (SSAO). Bent cones extend bent normals to further improve realism. These extensions combine the speed and simplicity of AO with physically more plausible lighting.

10.2 Introduction

AO is a physically incorrect but perceptually plausible approximation of environmental lighting and global illumination (GI). It has been used in many games, in particular when implemented in screen space. AO achieves high performance by averaging occlusion that modulates the surface shading instead of respecting the directionality of the lighting. However, the lack of directionality can be visually unpleasant and leaves room for improvement.

To this end, Landis [Landis 02] introduced so-called bent normals. While AO stores the average occlusion, bent normals are modified normals bent according to an estimate of the direction that is most disoccluded, in other words, the average unblocked direction. Using these bent normals in shading—for example, with preconvolved environment maps—leads to improved lighting. Usually, bent

Figure 10.1. Lighting computed using bent cones: 2048×1024 pixels, 60.0 fps, including direct light and DOF on an Nvidia GF 560Ti.

normals can be easily integrated in rendering engines; the only required change is to apply a bending of the normal. Adjusting the length of the bent normal by multiplying it with the corresponding AO value leads to automatically integrating AO in the shading evaluation.

Computing AO in screen space (SSAO) is one popular implementation of the approach [Mittring 07, Shanmugam and Arikan 07, Bavoil et al. 08, Ritschel et al. 09, Loos and Sloan 10]. In this chapter, we will describe a technique to extend SSAO. Our idea is to keep the simplicity of SSAO by relying on a screen-space solution, but to add the advantages of bent normals. Additionally, a new extension to further improve accuracy is introduced: bent cones. Bent cones capture the distribution of unoccluded directions by storing its directional average and variance.

10.3   Ambient Occlusion

Ambient occlusion [Zhukov et al. 98] decouples shading and visibility by moving visibility outside of the integral of the rendering equation [Kajiya 86]:

$$L_o(\mathbf{x}, \omega_o) \approx AO(\mathbf{x}) \int_{\Omega^+} f_r(\mathbf{x}, \omega \to \omega_o) \, L_i(\mathbf{x}, \omega) \, (\mathbf{n} \cdot \omega) \, d\omega,$$

$$AO(\mathbf{x}) := \frac{1}{2\pi} \int_{\Omega^+} V(\mathbf{x}, \omega) \, d\omega,$$

where $L_o(\omega_o)$ is the outgoing radiance in direction ω_o, Ω^+ is the upper hemi-sphere, f_r is the bidirectional reflectance distribution function (BRDF), $\mathbf{n}$ is the surface normal, L_i is the incoming light, and V is the visibility function that is zero when a ray is blocked and one otherwise. We assume that the diffuse surfaces f_r are constant and then ω_o can be dropped. Applying AO, light from all directions is equally attenuated by the average blocking over all directions.

Landis [Landis 02] used Monte-Carlo integration based on ray tracing to compute the hemispherical integral of AO. The idea of *bent normals* also dates back to the work of Landis, where it was proposed as a generalization of AO. Bent normals are the mean free direction scaled by the mean occlusion and are used for shading instead of the normals. Different from AO, their definition includes the direction ω inside the integral:

$$N(\mathbf{x}) := \frac{1}{\pi} \int_{\Omega^+} V(\mathbf{x}, \omega)\, \omega \; \mathrm{d}\omega.$$

For lighting computations, bent normals simply replace the surface normal and the visibility term:

$$L_o(\mathbf{x}) \approx \frac{1}{\pi} \int_{\Omega^+} L_i(\mathbf{x}, \omega)\, (N(\mathbf{x}) \cdot \omega)\; \mathrm{d}\omega.$$

In the case of bent normals, the visibility has to be multiplied with the direction using Monte-Carlo computation of bent normals $N(\mathbf{x})$, which is computationally simple and efficient compared to AO alone.

AO—in particular in screen space—has become a key ingredient in the shading found in a range of contemporary games [Mittring 07, Shanmugam and Arikan 07,

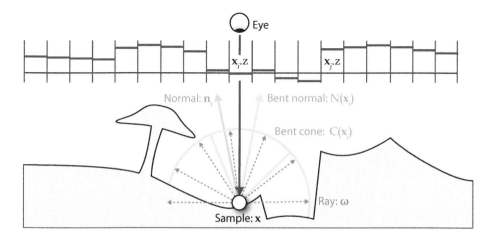

Figure 10.2. Overview: AO, bent normals, and bent cones in flatland.

Bavoil et al. 08, Ritschel et al. 09, Loos and Sloan 10]. SSAO is based on deferred shading [Mittring 09]. We propose to use bent cones, which are easy to integrate and program, and result in smooth illumination at high speed.

Usually, SSAO (Figure 10.2) is computed for a pixel i by counting occlusion of random point samples S. We ignore the 2D structure of the image for a moment, and enumerate all pixels using a 1D index i. The samples are chosen within a sphere, respectively, hemisphere (if the normal at i is known) centered at the point in world space that corresponds to pixel i (its back projection). The sphere corresponds to a pixel neighborhood, which can either be of constant size in screen space or be scaled according to the distance to the camera, thereby having constant world-space radius. Each sample is tested against the depth buffer to check for an occlusion by objects that are closer to the camera. If the samples S are distributed in the upper hemisphere, each sample S_i itself is tested for occlusion. Whereas, if the samples S are directly chosen in a pixel neighborhood of i, it is checked to see if the back-projected point of S_i occludes the back-projected point of i. For now, we stick to the latter.

For a pixel i, we compare its camera space location $\mathbf{x}_i$ with other pixels' camera space position $\mathbf{x}_j$ in a pixel neighborhood $P_i \subset \mathbb{N}$:

$$AO_{\text{ss}}(i) := \frac{1}{|P_i|} \sum_{j \in P_i} d(\Delta_{ij}), \tag{10.1}$$

where $\Delta_{ij} := \mathbf{x}_j - \mathbf{x}_i$. Intuitively, this function is 0 for blocking pixels, and 1 otherwise, depending on their relative position, most particularly, their relative depth. One possible implementation of $d(\Delta)$ is $d_{\text{x}}(\Delta)$, defined as

$$d_{\text{x}}(\Delta) := \begin{cases} 0 & \text{if } \Delta.z > 0, \\ 1 & \text{otherwise.} \end{cases}$$

Improvements are possible by accounting for outliers that should not cast shadows [Shanmugam and Arikan 07, Ritschel et al. 09, Loos and Sloan 10] if $\Delta.z$ is greater than z_{max}, and by including the normal at the ith pixel [Ritschel et al. 09]:

$$d_{\text{xn}}(\Delta, \mathbf{n}) := \begin{cases} 0 & \text{if } z_{\text{max}} > \Delta.z > 0 \text{ and } (\Delta \cdot \mathbf{n}) > 0, \\ 1 & \text{otherwise.} \end{cases}$$

It is further possible to replace the binary function d by some falloff function [Filion and McNaughton 08] depending on the distance and angle of the occluder, which results in smoother AO.

The underlying assumption of SSAO is that summing occlusion of "nearby" occluders approximates true visibility. However, visibility is a nonlinear effect: two occluders behind each other in one direction do not cast a shadow twice. Hence, other approaches find the correct occlusion for a set of directions in screen space via ray marching in the depth buffer. Alternatively, one can also compute a horizon angle [Bavoil et al. 08]. As an in-between solution, others [Szirmay-Kalos et al. 10, Loos and Sloan 10] considered the free volume over a height field of depth values inside a sphere around a pixel as a better approximation.

10.4 Our Technique

In this section, we will describe our approach for interactive AO and GI based on screen-space bent normals. We will first introduce their computation (Section 10.4.1), and then generalize them to bent cones (Section 10.4.2).

10.4.1 Bent Normals

Our technique is mostly orthogonal to the used type of SSAO. We will describe here the basic implementation along the lines of the original Crytek SSAO [Mittring 07]. Instead of just computing AO at the ith pixel (Equation (10.1)), we additionally compute a new normal N_{ss}. The basic principle behind our approach is that when computing AO in screen space, the direction Δ_{ij} is known and can be used to accumulate an unblocked direction that defines the bent normal. Thus, we simply sum up the normalized unoccluded directions defined by our samples, and divide the resulting vector by the number of nonblocked directions:

$$N_{\mathrm{ss}}(i) := \left(\sum_{j \in P_i} d(\Delta_{ij}) \right)^{-1} \sum_{j \in P_i} \frac{\Delta_{ij}}{|\Delta_{ij}|} d(\Delta_{ij}) \approx N(\mathbf{x}_i). \qquad (10.2)$$

The resulting bent normal is the mean of the unoccluded directions at $\mathbf{x}_i$.

10.4.2 Bent Cones

Bent cones are bent normals augmented by an angle (Figure 10.2). As the mean of the unoccluded directions gives the bent normal, the variance defines the angle. However, directions require the use of directional statistics instead of linear statistics in Euclidean spaces. To this end, we use an approach similar to the computation of variance in von Mises-Fisher (vMF) distributions. There, variance is approximated from the length of the non-normalized bent normal as computed in Equation (10.2). While vMF distributions are defined for spheres, we estimate a distribution on a hemisphere. This leads to a simple estimation of angle, corresponding to the variance of the unoccluded directions as

$$C(i) := (1 - \max(0, 2\,|N_{\mathrm{ss}}(i)| - 1))\,\frac{\pi}{2}.$$

Bent normal and bent cone define a certain spherical cap of visibility. Figure 10.3 shows possible unblocked directions and the resulting bent normal and cone. We use this cap in combination with shading methods that compute the incoming

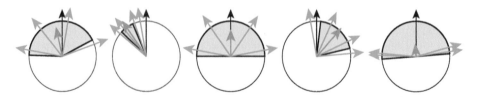

Figure 10.3. Resulting bent normal and cone of different visibility configurations. Blue arrows show unblocked directions within the hemisphere centered around the normal (black). Bent normals form the average direction (orange). The length of the bent normal describes the variance of the unblocked directions and is used to calculate the angle of the bent cone with the bent normal as center (darkened sector of circle).

light inside a spherical cap, such as preconvolved environment maps [Heidrich and Seidel 99] or irradiance volumes [Greger et al. 98]. Note that the clamping ensures that the length of the bent normal of an unoccluded point is mapped to a cone that covers the entire hemisphere.

We only use the bent cone to limit the directions from which we gather light. The cone does not describe a concrete visibility approximation. We still use AO to estimate the overall visibility. One can think of the cone as describing the illumination color whereas the AO controls brightness. This also allows that a cone does not need to match the actual visibility configuration very accurately. Using a cone with an angle of 90 degrees means a fallback to illumination with bent normals only. In Section 10.4.3, we describe how to use the cones to evaluate the incoming illumination.

10.4.3 Shading

For shading using bent cones, preconvolved environment maps are used [Heidrich and Seidel 99], which are indexed using bent cones. The same concept applies to irradiance volumes [Greger et al. 98]. Such precomputations are done at application start-up or once per frame, and avoid needing to do computations when shading each pixel. The convolutions involved are known to give very smooth results without noticeable noise, which fit well with the perceptual requirements of games.

Preconvolution of environmental illumination computes a directional function $L_p(\mathbf{n})$. For every possible normal $\mathbf{n}$, it convolves the BRDF (a constant for the diffuse surfaces we consider, therefore there is no dependence on ω_o), the geometric term, and the environmental illumination $L_i'(\omega)$:

$$L_p(\mathbf{n}) := \frac{1}{\pi} \int_{\Omega+} L_i'(\omega') (\omega' \cdot \mathbf{n}) \, d\omega'.$$

To query this convolved environment map, the bent normal is used in place of $\mathbf{n}$: the computation reduces to a lookup in the preconvolved environment map and

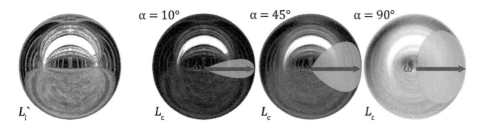

Figure 10.4. Preconvolution of environmental lighting (left) into a series of triple products of light, BRDF, and visibility of cones with varying angle α (left to right, 10, 45, and 90 degrees).

a multiplication with SSAO, which accounts for visibility:

$$L_o(\mathbf{x}) = AO(\mathbf{x})\, L_p(N(\mathbf{x})).$$

However, the preconvolution has to assume that no shadows occur as the point $\mathbf{x}$ and its visibility configuration are not known at preconvolution time. With bent cones, we propose to include a proxy visibility inside the preconvolution leading to a trivariate function

$$L_c(\mathbf{n}, \alpha) := \frac{1}{\pi} \int_{\Omega^+} L_i'(\omega')\, \bar{V}(\omega', \mathbf{n}, \alpha)\, (\omega' \cdot \mathbf{n})\, \mathrm{d}\omega'$$

that stores the outgoing radiance for a bent cone in direction $\mathbf{n}$ with angle α (Figure 10.4). The function $\bar{V}$ returns one if ω' and $\mathbf{n}$ form an angle smaller than α and zero otherwise. Note that by doing so, with increasing α the preconvolved values get larger. To include bent cones, we look up the appropriate convolved environment map. The term becomes

$$L_o(\mathbf{x}) = AO(\mathbf{x})\, L_c(N(\mathbf{x}), C(\mathbf{x}))\, (1 - \cos(C(\mathbf{x})))^{-1}.$$

The last part of the equation is a "normalization" of the preconvolved incoming light. The reason for this is that we do not use the cone as the actual visibility approximation of the visibility configuration at $\mathbf{x}$, which is usually much more complicated than a simple cone. Instead, we use it as a proxy to select directions from which we gather light. AO is then used to account for the average visibility. By doing so, we shift the lighting to the correct result compared to a convolution over the entire hemisphere. Only if AO and the cone angle match ($AO(\mathbf{x}) = 1 - \cos(C(\mathbf{x}))$), we get the same result as using the cone as visibility approximation. Due to the decoupling, bent cones are even able to handle visibility configurations, which cannot be well represented with a cone. Note that by our definition of the cone angle, the spherical cap is usually larger than or of equal size as AO ($AO(\mathbf{x}) \leq 1 - \cos(C(\mathbf{x}))$).

In practice, we move the normalization term to the preconvolution step to account for a given angle α. We thereby limit the sampling to the cone, such that $\bar{V}(\omega', \mathbf{n}, \alpha)$ returns one, and the normalization is included implicitly. Therefore, we can skip the normalization $((1 - \cos(C(\mathbf{x})))^{-1})$ during lighting. During preconvolution, one can do the sampling exactly by looping over all pixels, resulting in a complexity of $O(n^2)$, where n is the number of pixels. For every output pixel, a loop computes a cone-weighted sum of all other pixels. Samples are ignored if $\bar{V}(\omega', \mathbf{n}, \alpha)$ returns zero. Alternatively, one can use a Monte-Carlo approach with a fixed set of samples, which turns complexity into $O(nm)$, where m is the number of Monte-Carlo samples and $m \ll n$. This can help to reduce precomputation time, especially for high-resolution environment maps. Further, it is very easy to distribute the Monte-Carlo samples in a way that $\bar{V}(\omega', \mathbf{n}, \alpha)$ returns one and no samples need to be ignored. However, m has to be chosen carefully, depending on the frequency of the environment map and its resolution.

10.4.4   Geometric Term

We use a heuristic to combine the geometric term (cosine of incoming light and normal) with our bent cones. The geometric term must be a part of the preconvolution because the incoming light per direction is only known at this moment.

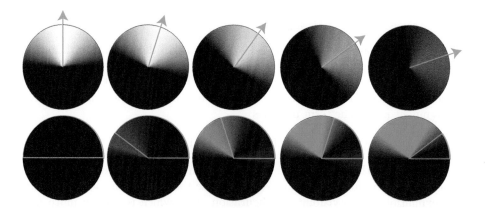

Figure 10.5. A 2D showcase of the effect of the approximation of the geometric term. The heuristic is shown in the top row, error is shown in the bottom row (compared to a normal with direction upward (left)). Red color encodes overestimation and green encodes underestimation compared to the correct geometric term. The bent normal is increasingly rotated in the images to the right. If normal and bent normal point to the same direction, the heuristic weights all directions correctly (left). The more normal and bent normal diverge (images to the right), the greater the error becomes. However, at the same time, the angle of the bent cone becomes smaller and so the error within the cone remains low. Note that the bent cone can have a different size than shown.

Correctly integrating the geometric term would be five dimensional: 2D for the mean direction (bent normal), 1D for the cone angle, and 2D for the surface normal. However, we can approximate the correct geometric term by

$$(\omega \cdot \mathbf{n}) \approx (\omega \cdot N(\mathbf{x}))\,(N(\mathbf{x}) \cdot \mathbf{n}).$$

Figure 10.5 illustrates the heuristic for different angles between $\mathbf{n}$ and $N(\mathbf{x})$. If $(N(\mathbf{x}) \cdot \mathbf{n}) \approx 1$, we can use the cosine between bent normal and incoming light and, thus, our heuristic approximates the geometric term very well. In the other case, if $(N(\mathbf{x}) \cdot \mathbf{n}) < 1$, using the bent normal only would result in visible artifacts. Fortunately, if normal and bent normal diverge, we have a concentration of the incoming light and also the angle of the bent cone is small, thus, $(\omega \cdot \mathbf{n}) \approx (N(\mathbf{x}) \cdot \mathbf{n})$. We also tried to interpolate between both versions $((\omega \cdot N(\mathbf{x}))$ and $(N(\mathbf{x}) \cdot \mathbf{n}))$ depending on $(N(\mathbf{x}) \cdot \mathbf{n})$, which is known at runtime, but this underestimates the geometric term and causes artifacts. Instead, the multiplication uses the original normal and should be preferred to only using $(\omega \cdot N(\mathbf{x}))$. The heuristic avoids a 5D preconvolution and gives correct results for unoccluded points (where $\mathbf{n} = N(\mathbf{x})$).

10.5 Implementation

Variants. Our approach can be used in conjunction with different SSAO techniques. Differences remain small, mostly depending on the sampling radius (Figure 10.6).

Crytek2D SSAO [Mittring 07] uses a 2D sampling pattern to distribute samples in screen space. For higher quality, we perform jittering and reject samples outside the unit disc.

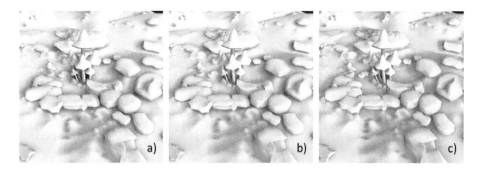

Figure 10.6. Our approach is largely orthogonal to the particular SSAO implementation used. Bent normals implemented with: (a) fixed screen-space radius (Crytek2D), (b) fixed world-space radius (Crytek3D), (c) horizon-based ray marching (HBAO). Note, that the results are very similar.

Crytek3D [Mittring 09] uses a 3D sampling pattern to distribute samples in space that are projected to screen space. We generate samples in a hemisphere, which is then transformed using an orthonormal basis according to **n**. Optionally, we add ray marching (multiple AND-combined samples per random 3D direction), which drastically improves AO and bent normal quality, even for a low number of marching steps (two to three) and a reduced number of ray directions. Here, the samples are distributed on the unit hemisphere to get random directions, and randomized starting points per direction turn aliasing into more eye-pleasing noise.

HBAO [Bavoil et al. 08] uses random 3D directions that are marched to find the highest intersection. We generate samples on the unit disc, apply randomized offsets, and then transform them according to **n**.

We rely on OpenGL 3 and store all sample patterns in uniform variables. If a large pattern or many samples are required, we store the data in a texture. Listing 10.1 gives pseudocode showing how AO and bent normals are computed in a pixel / fragment shader.

Filtering. Interleaved sampling [Keller and Heidrich 01] in combination with filtering of illumination guided by positions and normals [Laine et al. 07] is used to compute AO and bent normals using only a small number of samples per pixel. At a resolution of 2048×1024, downsampled 2×2 for antialiasing, three to six samples are enough for AO when applying an 8×8 joint-bilateral filtering. However, bent cones usually require at least six samples to avoid visible artifacts. Obviously, the quality of the filtering depends on the coherence of the neighboring pixels.

Instead of interpolating the bent normal directly, we compute the difference between normal and bent normal and filter this difference. The change is then added back to the original high-frequency normals per-pixel. Thus, the details in the normal field itself are preserved as shown in Figure 10.7 and the bent information is propagated.

Figure 10.7. Fine geometric details, for example, those due to bump maps, are lost when directly filtering bent normals (left). When filtering the change-of-normals instead, details are preserved (right).

```
void main() {
  // get point properties at pixel i
  vec3 positionX = backproject(depthTexture(pixelCoordinateI),
                               inverseViewProjectionMatrix );
  vec3 normalX = normalTexture(pixelCoordinateI);
  // get ONB to transform samples
  mat3 orthoNormalBasis = computeONB(normalX);
  // select samples for pixel out of pattern
  int patternOffset = getPatternOffset(pixelCoordinateI);

  float ao = 0.0;
  int validAODirectionCount = 0;
  vec3 bentNormal = vec3(0.0);
  float unoccludedDirections = 0.0;

  for(int index=0; index<sampleCount; ++index) {
    vec3 sampleDirection = orthoNormalBasis *
                  getSampleDirection(index, patternOffset);
    bool isOutlier = false;
    // use float instead of bool and
    // apply a fall-off function to get smooth AO
    float visibility = 1.0;
    // this function tests for occlusion in SS
    // depending on the actual technique
    // and sample distribution,
    // the implementation of this function varies
    checkSSVisibilityWithRayMarchingSmooth(
      sampleDirection, maxOccluderDistance,
      depthTexture, inverseViewProjectionMatrix ,
      positionX, normalX,
      rayMarchingSteps, rayMarchingStartOffset,
      visibility, isOutlier);

    // we have insufficient information in SS
    // here, we simply ignore samples,
    // which cannot be handled properly
    if(!isOutlier) {
      validAODirectionCount ++;
      ao += visibility;
    }

    // for bent normals, we assume,
    // that outlier occluders are NOT real occluders!
    // sum up unoccluded directions
    // direction may be partially visible
    // => only counts accordingly
    bentNormal += normalize(sampleDirection) * visibility;
    unoccludedDirections += visibility;
  }

  ao /= float(validAODirectionCount );
  bentNormal /= unoccludedDirections;
}
```

Listing 10.1. Fragment shader pseudo-code for screen-space bent cones.

Preconvolved lighting. For preconvolved environment maps, we store L_p as a floating-point cube texture. Preconvolution including visibility L_c is trivariate and can be stored most efficiently using the recent cube map array extension of OpenGL [Bolz et al. 09]. This extensions stores an array of cube maps, which can be accessed with a direction and an index. We discretize α to eight levels and apply linear filtering between the levels. The preconvolved environment maps require a high dynamic range, which is why we chose to use RGB 16 bit floating-point textures. Due to the convolution, low resolution cube maps provide sufficient quality, resulting in $\sim$7 MB of storage for a typical 64×64 cube-map array with eight layers. More efficiently, in the context of glossy reflections Kautz and McCool [Kautz and McCool 00] propose to store the third dimension in cube-map MIP levels. This could even allow for a fully dynamic convolution of the environment map at reduced quality, but also reduced storage costs.

Practical considerations. Bent normal and cones integrate very well in an existing deferred shading rendering pipeline. The bent normal easily replaces the normal without requiring special handling. Further, the bent normal can be scaled with AO. Using the scaled bent normal for shading, AO is included automatically, also avoiding further storage requirements. For bent cones, no extra storage is required in addition to that for the bent normal and AO. A special preconvolution step is required for a number of possible cone angles.

10.6   Results

In this section, we present our results that increase accuracy while adding only a small performance penalty when compared to previous SSAO techniques.

A typical performance breakdown at resolution 2048×1024 of Figure 10.1 on an Nvidia Geforce 560Ti is as follows: 6.0 ms for AO and bent normals (16×16 pattern, four samples per pixel, two ray-marching steps per sample), 5.2 ms for geometry-aware blurring, 1.0 ms for the cone computation and environment map lookup, 1.5 ms for the deferred shading buffer, and 1.6 ms for direct light with 2×2-sample PCF shadows (shadow map resolution 4096×4096). The overhead for bent cones compared to only AO with the same number of samples is 6 % for the computation and 25 % for the blur, in total less than 9 %. We still see some room for engineering improvements, depending on the actual quality and performance constraints in real applications. For example, using data packing and 8 bits for bent normals may especially improve the blur speed.

Lighting using our bent normals is closer to a reference solution than AO alone (see Figure 10.8 (a)–(c)). It can be seen how AO decouples lighting and visibility, which leads to gray shadows that are perceived as a change of reflectance, rather than an effect of lighting. The reference solutions were created using path-tracing using several hundred samples. Our screen-space bent normals are similar to real bent normals (see Figure 10.8 (d)–(f)), which leads to only a small difference

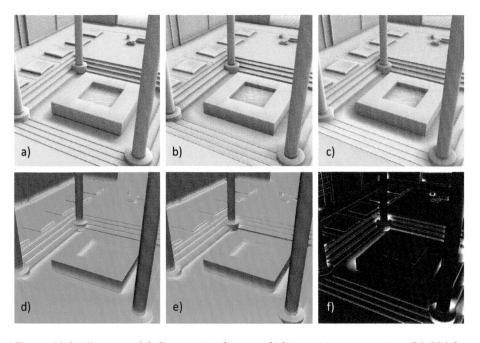

Figure 10.8. Top row: (a) Comparison between lighting using ray tracing, (b) SSAO, and (c) SS bent normals. Bottom row: (d) ray-traced bent normals, (e) SS bent normals, and (f) the 8 × angle difference. Note that SS bent normals is similar to ray tracing in quality, while performance is similar to SSAO. Further, the shadow's shapes are more similar to the reference.

when comparing lighting using accurate bent normals and our bent normals. Additionally, it shows that testing visibility in screen space is sufficient in most cases.

Bent cones further improve the directionality of lighting, which is limited with bent normals as their input remains the incoming light from all directions of a hemisphere (see Figure 10.9). Ritschel et al. [Ritschel et al. 09] apply a brute-force sampling for unblocked directions, which is inefficient in two ways. First, the additional texture lookup in the SSAO shader causes an overhead of about 10% in our tests. Second, more samples are required per pixel to avoid noise. Even with a randomization pattern and a postprocessing blur, at least 16 to 24 samples are required to avoid block noise in the final image. For high-resolution and high-frequency illumination this number is much higher. In contrast, bent cones return smooth results with a very small number of per-pixel samples (see Figure 10.10). In our experiments we were able to use eight samples at a minimum with similar minor artifacts. The cone does not need to be very accurate and AO is smooth anyway, which is why the sample count can be low. We also compared

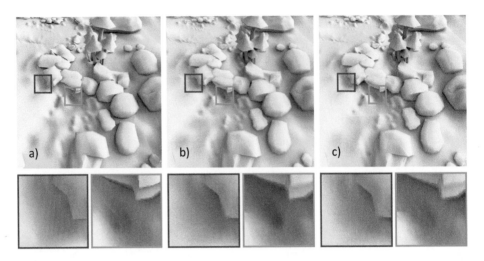

Figure 10.9. Left to right: (a) Lighting using ray tracing, (b) SS bent normals, and (c) SS bent cones. Applying cones, shadows are more colored and appear similar to the Monte-Carlo reference, because only visible light is gathered (see insets).

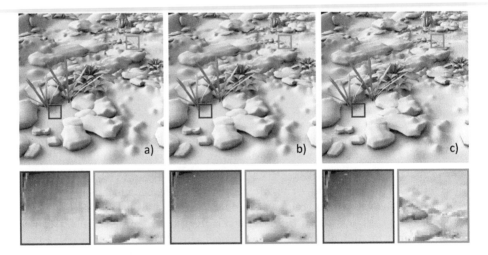

Figure 10.10. Left to right: (a) Environment map importance sampling, (b) SSDO [Ritschel et al. 09], and (c) SS bent cones. Importance sampling required 32 samples per pixel (18.8 ms), SSDO 16 samples (14.1 ms), and bent cones only eight samples (6.0 ms for bent normal, 0.7 ms for single bent cone environment map sample) to achieve the results. We set the sample count such that all techniques produce similar results with acceptable minor noise (red inset). For all techniques, we applied an 8×8 randomization pattern and a geometry-aware blur. Bent cones allow for blurring the change, which preserves normal details (green inset). In all cases, we used three ray-marching steps per sample for the SS visibility tests and computed lighting at a resolution of 1024×1024 to create the images.

bent cones to importance sampling, which in our tests required at least 24 to 32 samples for an equal quality. However, in contrast to sampling-based techniques, bent cones are not able to handle high-frequency illumination.

We removed high-frequency illumination changes in our test cases to allow for a fair comparison. Since bent cones simply blur the high frequencies, the brute-force sampling technique [Ritschel et al. 09] requires many more samples (up to hundreds), and the importance sampling requires at least 64 samples.

10.7 Discussion and Conclusion

Screen-space bent normals improve accuracy of shading without imposing much additional computation cost. The bent cones further improve on the directionality of lighting. Bent cones can limit the spherical cap depending on the variance of the unoccluded directions. The success clearly depends on whether the actual visibility configuration fits a cone. The cone is chosen such that it mostly includes unblocked directions, possibly overestimating the overall visibility. The overestimation is not a problem as we still rely on AO to account for the actual overall visibility. As a worst case, bent cones compare to lighting with bent normals. While screen-space directional occlusion [Ritschel et al. 09] achieves similar results, it requires the evaluation of shading for every sample. This is closer to screen-space Monte-Carlo rendering involving many samples, but does not agree with the original goal of AO to decouple shading and visibility as much as possible. In contrast, our approach keeps shading and visibility separated, leading to a significant speedup.

Bent normals and cones are most suitable for lighting techniques that compute lighting within a spherical cap, such as environmental lighting with light coming from many directions. They are less useful for direct illumination of very directed light such as from the common directional, spot, or point-light sources. Consequently, bent normals and cones are not able to handle high-frequency illumination changes.

We showed that our extension is mostly orthogonal to the particular SSAO implementation used [Mittring 07, Bavoil et al. 08], and thus can be easily integrated in existing implementations. It is intended to be used as part of a deferred shading pipeline, most interestingly for real-time applications. By performing the visibility test in screen space, only an incomplete scene representation is available, sharing the screen-space limitations with previous SSAO techniques. However, the screen-space visibility test could be replaced with a more accurate test, such as testing against a voxel representation of the scene.

In future work, we plan to investigate dynamic convolution of cube maps, other representations of the occlusion function, new interpolation methods, and a combination with irradiance volumes [Greger et al. 98] for local prefiltered directional occlusion.

10.8   Acknowledgments

This work was partly funded by the Intel Visual Computing Institute at Saarland University and the ANR iSpace & Time of the French government.

Bibliography

[Bavoil et al. 08] Louis Bavoil, Miguel Sainz, and Rouslan Dimitrov. "Image-Space Horizon-Based Ambient Occlusion." In *ACM SIGGRAPH 2008 Talks*. New York: ACM, 2008.

[Bolz et al. 09] Jeff Bolz, Yunjun Zhang, Bill Licea-Kane, Graham Sellers, Daniel Koch, and Mark Young. "ARB_texture_cube_map_array." OpenGL Extension, Available at http://www.opengl.org/registry/specs/ARB/texture_cube_map_array.txt, 2009.

[Filion and McNaughton 08] Dominic Filion and Rob McNaughton. "Starcraft: Effects & Techniques." In *Advances in Real-Time Rendering in 3D Graphics and Games Course*, edited by Natalya Tatarchuk, Chapter 5, pp. 133–164. ACM, 2008.

[Greger et al. 98] G. Greger, P. Shirley, P. M. Hubbard, and D. P. Greenberg. "The Irradiance Volume." *IEEE Computer Graphics and Applications* 18:2 (1998), 32–43.

[Heidrich and Seidel 99] Wolfgang Heidrich and Hans-Peter Seidel. "Realistic, Hardware-Accelerated Shading and Lighting." In *Proceedings of SIGGRAPH '99, Computer Graphics Proceedings, Annual Conference Series*, edited by Alyn Rockwood, pp. 171–178. Reading, MA, 1999.

[Kajiya 86] J. T. Kajiya. "The Rendering Equation." *Proc. SIGGRAPH '86, Computer Graphics* 20:4 (1986), 143–150.

[Kautz and McCool 00] Jan Kautz and Michael D. McCool. "Approximation of Glossy Reflection with Prefiltered Environment Maps." In *Graphics Interface*, pp. 119–126. Toronto, Canada: Canadian Human-Computer Communications Society, 2000.

[Keller and Heidrich 01] Alexander Keller and Wolfgang Heidrich. "Interleaved Sampling." In *Proceedings of the 12th Eurographics Workshop on Rendering Techniques*, pp. 269–276. London: Springer-Verlag, 2001.

[Laine et al. 07] Samuli Laine, Hannu Saransaari, Janne Kontkanen, Jaakko Lehtinen, and Timo Aila. "Incremental Instant Radiosity for Real-Time Indirect Illumination." In *Proceedings of Eurographics Symposium on Rendering 2007*, pp. 277–286. Aire-la-Ville, Switzerland: Eurographics Association, 2007.

[Landis 02] Hayden Landis. "Production-Ready Global Illumination." In *RenderMan in Production, SIGGRAPH Course*, pp. 87–102. New York: ACM, 2002.

[Loos and Sloan 10] Bradford James Loos and Peter-Pike Sloan. "Volumetric Obscurance." In *Proceedings of the 2010 ACM SIGGRAPH Symposium on Interactive 3D Graphics and Games, I3D '10*, pp. 151–156. New York: ACM, 2010.

[Mittring 07] Martin Mittring. "Finding next gen: CryEngine 2." In *Advanced Real-Time Rendering in 3D Graphics and Games, SIGGRAPH Course*, edited by Natalya Tatarchuk, pp. 97–121. NY: ACM, 2007.

[Mittring 09] Martin Mittring. "A Bit More Deferred – CryEngine 3." In *Triangle Game Conference*, 2009.

[Ritschel et al. 09] Tobias Ritschel, Thorsten Grosch, and Hans-Peter Seidel. "Approximating Dynamic Global Illumination in Image Space." In *Proceedings of the 2009 Symposium on Interactive 3D Graphics and Games, I3D '09*, pp. 75–82. New York: ACM, 2009.

[Shanmugam and Arikan 07] Perumaal Shanmugam and Okan Arikan. "Hardware Accelerated Ambient Occlusion Techniques on GPUs." In *Proceedings of the 2007 Symposium on Interactive 3D Graphics and Games, I3D '07*, pp. 73–80. New York: ACM, 2007.

[Szirmay-Kalos et al. 10] L. Szirmay-Kalos, T. Umenhoffer, B. Tóth, L. Szécsi, and M. Sbert. "Volumetric Ambient Occlusion for Real-Time Rendering and Games." *IEEE Computer Graphics and Applications* 30 (2010), 70–79.

[Zhukov et al. 98] S. Zhukov, A. Iones, G. Kronin, and G. Studio. "An Ambient Light Illumination Model." In *Rendering Techniques '98, Proceedings of the Eurographics Workshop in Vienna, Austria, June 29–July 1, 1998*, pp. 45–56. New York: Springer, 1998.

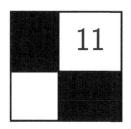

11

Physically Based Area Lights
Michal Drobot

11.1 Overview

This chapter presents the physically based area lighting system used in *Killzone: Shadow Fall*, developed by Guerrilla Games for Playstation 4 (see Figure 11.1).

We present a novel, real-time, analytical model for area lights, capable of supporting multiple light shapes. Each shape can be represented by simple 3D or 2D functions on a plane. Discussed applications include the following light shapes: sphere, disk, and rectangle.

The model supports diffuse and specular lighting. BRDF (bidirectional reflectance distribution function) implementation in *Killzone: Shadow Fall* rendering engine explicitly splits the material reflectance model from the lighting model itself. This allows a separation between different surface simulation algorithms and light types, which supply the former with required light quantities. To achieve this, we use the importance sampling principle to approximate nonfinite or computationally expensive integrals in the material reflectance part of the BRDF. This chapter focuses only on the derivation of the proposed framework and actual light modeling part.

All lights in the rendering engine are physically based area lights, described by radiometric quantities such as light intensity in lumens, dimensions in meters, world orientation, and light shape type. We introduce a specialized description of surface roughness that is shared or adapted to match various surface reflectance models. The light model uses light description and surface roughness, at the point being shaded, to deliver light quantity arriving at the point—split between the light model and the surface reflectance model.

In addition we discuss integration of the proposed model into deferred renderer and how it was used as a principle for environmental probe generation and dynamic analytical texture-based area lights.

Figure 11.1. Usage of area lights in *Killzone: Shadow Fall.*

11.2   Introduction

The current game industry standard for lighting models is Blinn-Phong BRDF
or models directly based on it. In recent years we have seen multiple advances
extending the model to support more varied materials, surface properties, and
physically based properties [McAuley et al. 13] or ways to tackle aliasing problems [Baker and Hill 12]. The result of this technological push is widespread
access to an efficient, predictable, well-known lighting model, capable of capturing most material properties that we might observe in common scenarios. Most
research focused on refining material interactions, including well-known geometric and fresnel terms proposed in the Cook-Torrance lighting model [Cook and
Torrance 81]. However, a very basic constraint of the model still exists, as it can
only simulate point-based lights. In almost every scenario, the source of light
has a physical size, which in real life is reflected by the correct shape of specular reflection and diffuse lighting response. Using Blinn-Phong point lighting for
dynamic lights proves inadequate in many situations, creating a visual disjoint
between visible lights in the scene and lighting result (see Figures 11.2 and 11.3).

Several methods exist to tackle this issue. Some of them include pre-computing
"light cards" or billboard reflections and raytracing them at runtime to simulate
accurate specular reflections [Mittring and Dudash 11]. Unfortunately, this system is an addition on top of standard analytical, dynamic lighting that is point
based. Moreover, it doesn't provide a solution for area-based diffuse lighting.

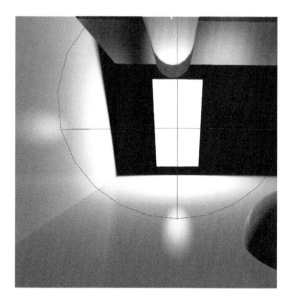

Figure 11.2. Visual disparity between the light shape and Blinn-Phong specular reflection.

Figure 11.3. Specular reflection matches the light shape using the proposed model.

Another way of solving the problem involves switching to global illumination–based solutions. Several systems were already implemented in commercial engines, mostly voxel based [Mittring 12]; however, they can't fully substitute for analytical lights, due to stability, resolution, or quality difference.

During our research on a new iteration of the *Killzone* engine for next generation platform, we wanted to leverage current knowledge about lighting models and extend it to cover non-point-based lights. A unified way to deal with art production was also our priority. With our transition to physically based material modeling, we also wanted to have physically based lights, using real-world radiometric quantities, thus achieving a predictable shading model.

We decided to utilize existing BRDFs to model surface reaction to light and remodel the way lighting information is actually provided to those models. Standard BRDFs assume light incoming from only one direction with intensity given as a per-light set quantity. When dealing with an area-based light source, we would have to solve an integral of the lighting model over all points of the light shape. This can be achieved numerically, but unfortunately that proves unfeasible performance-wise in real-time applications. However, parts of that integral can be calculated analytically using radiometric integrals, while the rest can be efficiently approximated.

11.3 Area Lighting Model

11.3.1 Radiometric Integrals and BRDF Definition

In this section we introduce basic radiometric quantities such as light intensity, irradiance, and radiance [Pharr and Humphreys 04]. Then, we define radiometric integrals essential to solving area lighting models.

Let *intensity* be defined as the light flux density per solid angle:

$$I = \frac{d\phi}{d\omega},$$

where $d\phi$ is the light flux differential and $d\omega$ is the solid angle differential. Intensity is meaningful only for a point light source.

Irradiance defines the total amount of light flux per area:

$$E = \frac{d\phi}{dA},$$

where dA is the differential area receiving light flux.

Radiance describes the light flux density per unit area, per unit solid angle:

$$L = \frac{d\phi}{d\omega dA^{\perp}},$$

where $dA^{\perp}$ is the projected area of dA on a hypothetical surface perpendicular to the solid angle.

We also define radiance emitted $L_o(p, \omega)$ and incoming $L_i(p, \omega)$ to a point on a surface as a function of the point and direction.

Irradiance at point p with normal vector n would be defined as

$$E(p, n) = \int_{\mathcal{H}^2(n)} L_i(p, \omega) \cos\theta d\omega,$$

where $\cos\theta d\omega$ is the projected solid angle $d\omega^{\perp}$, with θ the angle between ω and the surface normal n. This term comes from the definition of radiance. In other words, this equation integrates incoming light from all directions on a hemisphere, around a point of integration with a given normal, with respect to the projected solid angle.

A *bidirectional reflectance distribution function* (BRDF) defines a ratio of the light reflecting from a surface point, in the viewer's direction, and the amount of light incoming to a surface from a specific direction. Therefore, a basic definition of BRDF is

$$f_r(p, \omega_o, \omega_i) = \frac{dL_o(p, \omega_o)}{dE(p, \omega_i)}.$$

In the case of real-time graphics, we are interested in finding the integral of $L_o(p, \omega_o)$ over the whole hemisphere $\mathcal{H}$ set around point p with surface normal vector n. Therefore, we are looking for

$$L_o(p, \omega_o) = \int_{\mathcal{H}^2} f_r(p, \omega_o, \omega_i) L d\omega_i.$$

Using the definition of radiance L,

$$L_o(p, \omega_o) = \int_{\mathcal{H}^2} f_r(p, \omega_o, \omega_i) L_i(p, \omega_i) \cos \theta_i d\omega_i. \tag{11.1}$$

During rendering we evaluate a finite number of lights. Therefore, we are interested in expressing integrals over area. In the case of irradiance over area A, we can define

$$E(p, n) = \int_A L_i(p, \omega_i) \cos \theta_i d\omega_i.$$

In the simplified case of n contributing lights, we can express the integral from Equation (11.1) as a sum of integrals over all area lights that are visible from point p:

$$L_o(p, \omega_o) = \sum_{1..n} \int_{A(n)} f_r(p, \omega_o, \omega_i) L_i(p, \omega_i) \cos \theta_i d\omega_{i(n)}. \tag{11.2}$$

Equation (11.2), our main lighting equation, will be the basis of all derivations.

For simplicity we can assume that the light source has uniform light flux distribution so $L(p, w)$ is constant and denoted L; therefore,

$$L_o(p, \omega_o) = \sum_{1..n} L_n \int_{A(n)} f_r(p, \omega_o, \omega_i) \cos \theta_i d\omega_{i(n)}.$$

The differential solid angle is also in relation with the differential area.

In the case of a light source defined on a quadrilateral, the differential solid angle can be expressed as a function of differential area of light:

$$d\omega = \frac{dA \cos\theta_o}{r^2}, \tag{11.3}$$

where r is the distance from point p on the surface to point p' on dA and θ_o is the angle between surface normal dA at point p' and $\overrightarrow{p'p}$ (see Figure 11.4).

It is worth noting that the solid angle is well defined for multiple primitives that can be used as a light source shape, such as a disk and a rectangle.

To finalize, radiance at a point per single light is defined as

$$L_o(p, \omega_o) = \sum_{1..n} L_n \int_{A(n)} f_r(p, \omega_o, \omega_i) \cos\theta_i \frac{dA \cos\theta_o}{r^2}. \tag{11.4}$$

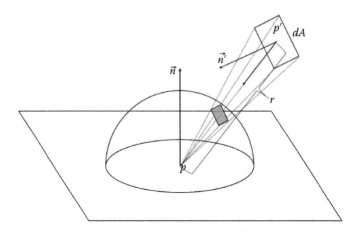

Figure 11.4. Solid angle of quadrilateral as visible from point p.

11.3.2   Material and Lighting Models

After deriving the principal integral (Equation (11.4)) for light rendering, we assume that the light area is well defined and therefore possible to integrate. For simplification we restrict our reasoning to simple shapes—a sphere, a disk, and a rectangle—which are relatively easy to integrate and compute.

Our light is defined by the following parameters:

- position,

- orientation,

- outgoing light radiance in lumens,

- shape type (sphere, disk, rectangle),

- dimensions.

With those parameters we can instantly calculate L in lumens. We need to find a way to solve or approximate the integral from Equation (11.4). To simplify the problem, let us look at the generalized physically based BRDF combining diffuse and specular reflectance models:

$$f_r\left(p,\omega_o,\omega_i\right) = k_d + k_s, \qquad (11.5)$$

where k_d is the diffuse light model and k_s is the specular model.

We also need to set additional requirements to make this BRDF physically based:

$$f_r(p, \omega_o, \omega_i) \geq 0,$$
$$f_r(p, \omega_o, \omega_i) = f_r(p, \omega_i, \omega_o), \tag{11.6}$$
$$\bigvee_{\omega_o} \int_{\mathcal{H}^2} f_r(p, \omega_o, \omega_i) \cos\theta_i d\omega_i \leq 1.$$

For our k_d we can use the standard Lambertian diffuse model [Lambert 60]. When expressed as a part of $f_r(p, \omega_o, \omega_i)$, it takes a very simple form:

$$k_d = C_d, \tag{11.7}$$

where C_d defines the surface diffusion color.

We choose the generalized Cook-Torrance BRDF [Cook and Torrance 81] for a base of our microfacet specular model:

$$k_s(p, \omega_o, \omega_i) = \frac{D(\vec{h})F(\omega_o, \vec{h})G(\omega_i, \omega_o, \vec{h})}{4(cos\theta_i)(cos\theta_o)}, \tag{11.8}$$

where $D(\vec{h})$ is the distribution of micro-facets around surface normal n'', $F(\omega_o, \vec{h})$ is the Fresnel reflectance function, and $G(\omega_i, \omega_o, \vec{h})$ is the geometric function. As previously defined, θ_i is the angle between $\vec{n}$ and ω_i, and θ_o is the angle between $\vec{n}$ and ω_o. Generally, $\vec{h}$ is called the *half vector*, defined as

$$\vec{h} = \frac{\omega_o + \omega_i}{\|\omega_o + \omega_i\|}. \tag{11.9}$$

We are interested in finding radiance in the direction of the viewer, per light, described as follows:

$$L_o(p, \omega_o) = \int_{A(n)} f_r(p, \omega_o, \omega_i) L_i(p, \omega_i) \cos\theta_i d\omega_{i(n)}.$$

For now, we can assume, as in Equation (11.2), that $L_i(p, \omega_i)$ is constant over light:

$$L_o(p, \omega_o) = L_n \int_{A(n)} f_r(p, \omega_o, \omega_i) \cos\theta_i d\omega_{i(n)}. \tag{11.10}$$

Now substitute parts of Equation (11.10) with Equations (11.5), (11.7), and (11.8):

$$L_o(p, \omega_o) = L_n \int_{A(n)} \left(C_d + \frac{D(\vec{h})F(\omega_o, \vec{h})G(\omega_i, \omega_o, \vec{h})}{4(cos\theta_i)(cos\theta_o)} \right) cos\theta_i d\omega_{i(n)}.$$

In the end we can define two integrals:

$$Diffuse\,(p, \omega_o) = L_n \int\limits_{A(n)} C_d \cos\theta_i d\omega_{i(n)}, \tag{11.11}$$

$$Specular\,(p, \omega_o) = L_n \int\limits_{A(n)} \frac{D(\vec{h})F(\omega_o, \vec{h})G(\omega_i, \omega_o, \vec{h})}{4(\cos\theta_o)} d\omega_{i(n)}. \tag{11.12}$$

To get the final form of specular integral, we need to choose functions DFG. There are multiple sources available that discuss the best choice for a specific use scenario [Burley 12].

Unfortunately, independent of the chosen function, the integrals from Equations (11.11) and (11.12) are not easily solvable for shapes other than a sphere. Therefore, we will focus on finding a suitable approximation for light shapes that can be expressed as a 2D function on a quadrilateral.

11.3.3 Approximating Diffuse Integral

Monte Carlo methods and importance sampling. One of the known ways to solve an integral is numerical integration by discretized parts. There are multiple ways and techniques to accelerate this process. A particularly interesting one for us is the Monte Carlo technique, which in general can be described in the following steps:

1. Define a domain of possible inputs.

2. Generate inputs randomly from a probability distribution over the domain.

3. Calculate the function being integrated for given inputs.

4. Aggregate the results.

With a given probability distribution, the expected variance is also known as well as the estimator for minimal acceptable error. This process can be significantly sped up using importance sampling techniques [Pharr and Humphreys 04].

The principle of *importance sampling* is to prioritize samples that would have maximum impact on the final outcome. We can find such samples using spatial heuristics. Another solution is to run an initial pass of Monte Carlo integration with a low number of samples to estimate the result variance and therefore decide which regions of integration would use more important samples.

Importance sampling is an actively researched subject with multiple different solutions. The takeaway for our reasoning is that, in any integration, there are samples more important than others, therefore minimizing the error estimator for a given amount of samples.

Application to diffuse integral. We would like to apply the Monte Carlo method to our diffuse integral. In order to simplify that process, we assume that the light shape has uniform surface normal n. Another assumption is that dA does not change for integrated points, meaning the whole shape is always visible. Therefore, we can conceptually move $dA cos\theta_o$ out of our integral and compute it once for the entire domain:

$$dA cos\theta_o \int_A \frac{cos\theta_i}{r^2}. \tag{11.13}$$

The integrated function is dependent only on the distance and cosine between the surface normal and the directions subtended by the light shape. Those are continuous and well-defined functions.

Immediately we can see that the global minimum and maximum of the integrated function are inside the sampling domain defined by the light shape. Therefore, there is a single point, on the light shape, that is able to represent the integral, thus minimizing the error estimator.

If we could find this point, we could essentially solve the integral by approximation using importance sampling with one point of highest importance. We would just need to evaluate the function once for that specific point. However, we are only interested in points that are easy to find at GPU program runtime. The ideal candidate would be given by a function of light parameters, the position of point p, and the normal n. We need to find a function that returns a point minimizing the error estimator. We also need to minimize the function complexity, to maintain runtime performance. To simplify the problem's domain, we prefer to work in the 2D space of a light quadrilateral.

Our function of interest is bounded by the light shape and defined as

$$\frac{cos\theta_i}{r^2}. \tag{11.14}$$

We know that the function integral over area is bounded by local minima and maxima in limits of given area. The function from Equation (11.14) has one global maximum and one global minimum at the shape bounds. Therefore, we know that a single point best representing the integral can be found on a segment between the maximum and minimum. In order to find it, we would have to calculate the global minimum and maximum, which we deemed to be too computationally expensive.

Instead, we decided to find an approximate important point in the proximity of the global maximum, accepting the risk of overestimation. In order to do so, we need to set boundary conditions for our search. The function from Equation (11.14) is a component-wise multiplication of two functions. The maximum of their products can be found along a segment connecting their local maximums.

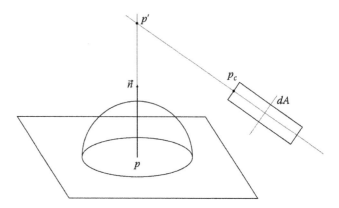

Figure 11.5. Geometric construction of point p_c.

We can easily find $cos\theta_o$ maximum on A geometrically by casting a ray from point p in the direction of the normal n of the surface, creating point p', intersecting with the light plane and finding the closest location on the shape to p', called p_c (see Figure 11.5). It is worth noting that in the case when the light plane is pointing away from the surface normal (i.e., $n \cdot n' > 0$), vector $\overline{pp'}$ should be skewed in the direction of the light plane in order to obtain intersection (see Figure 11.5).

A maximum of $\frac{1}{r^2}$ can be found by projecting point p on the light plane, creating point p_p, finding the closest point on positive hemisphere to p_p, called p'', and finally finding a closest point on the light shape to p_r (see Figures 11.6 and 11.7).

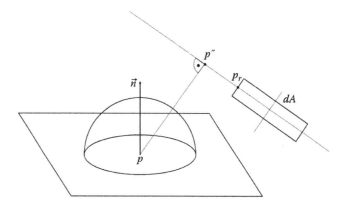

Figure 11.6. Geometric construction of point p_r when the light plane is pointing toward the surface.

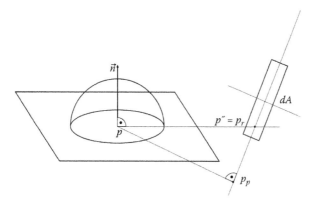

Figure 11.7. Geometric construction of point p_r when the light plane is pointing away from the surface.

As previously discussed, we were searching for the most important sample of the integral on a segment between points p_r and p_c representing component-wise local maximums (see Figure 11.8).

With those conditions set, we used a computational software package to numerically find a point on line $\overline{p_c p_r}$ that approximates the most important point as much as possible. We worked on a data set of several hundred area lights randomly generated as disk or rectangle light shapes. For every light shape we found a point on the plane that best resembles the full integral. Then, we computed the end points of our line between p_c and p_r (as if it would be calculated at runtime). Then, we numerically checked the points along the line, computing the lighting equation and comparing against a reference, using the least squares method to find point p_d, which would most accurately represent the integral.

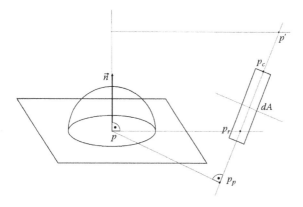

Figure 11.8. Geometric construction of line $\overline{p_c p_r}$.

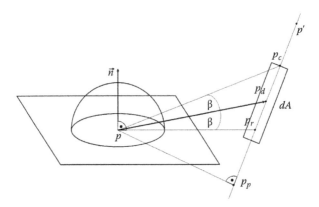

Figure 11.9. Geometric construction of point p_d.

After evaluating many test cases and several functions of various complexity, we noticed that intersecting a simple halfway vector between $\overrightarrow{pp_c}$ and $\overrightarrow{pp_r}$ with the light plane to create p_d (see Figure 11.9) works reasonably well in the majority of our cases, having a statistical error less than 0.05 against best-point approximating the integral.

After visual assessment we decided it works well enough in our use case (see Figure 11.10) and is visually indifferent from the raytaced solution (see Figure 11.11). It also proves simple enough for real-time per-pixel calculation on modern GPUs.

As another level of simplification, we used the halfway vector between $\overrightarrow{pp'}$ and $\overrightarrow{pp''}$. It allowed the important optimization of skipping the closest point to the shape calculation. Unfortunately, it yields a statistical error of more than 0.15. However, the disparity is mostly visible in an edge case scenario, where the light shape is pointing away from surface normal. There are no visual artifacts noticeable, and our artists decided it is good enough for our needs.

Area diffuse approximation algorithm. Our final approximation for diffuse integral can therefore be expressed by the following pseudo code:

- For point p with normal n:

    - Intersect a ray from p in direction n'' with light plane, creating new point p'.

    - Project point p on the light plane, creating point p''.

    - Create halfway vector $\overrightarrow{d_h}$ between $\overrightarrow{pp'}$ and $\overrightarrow{pp''}$:

$$\overrightarrow{d_h} = \frac{\overrightarrow{pp'} + \overrightarrow{pp''}}{\|\overrightarrow{pp'} + \overrightarrow{pp''}\|}.$$

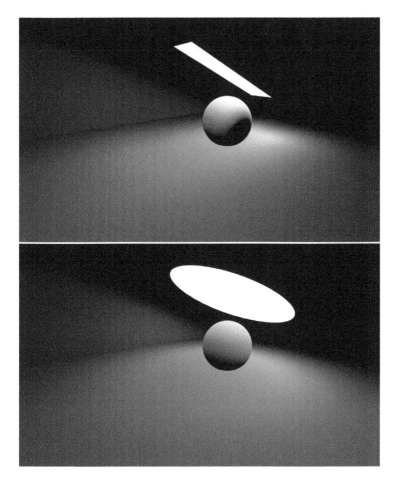

Figure 11.10. Correct wrapped diffuse lighting from rectangular (top) and disk (bottom) area light.

○ Intersect a ray from p in direction $\vec{h}$ with the light plane creating point p_d. This is the most important point in terms of importance sampling.

○ Treat vector $\overrightarrow{pp_d}$ as a light vector for the diffuse equation, effectively approximating the diffuse integral from Equation (11.11):

$$Diffuse\,(p,\omega_o) = L_n \int\limits_{A(n)} C_d \cos\theta d\omega_{i(n)} \sim L_n C_d \cos\theta_{\overrightarrow{pp_d}} d\omega_{\overrightarrow{pp_d}}. \quad (11.15)$$

In Equation (11.15) we assume that L_n is constant for the whole area of the light. The angle between the new light vector $\overrightarrow{pp_d}$ and surface normal n is $\theta_{\overrightarrow{pp_d}}$.

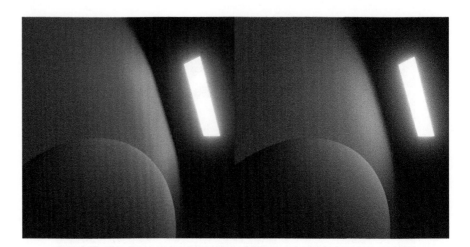

Figure 11.11. Comparison between Monte Carlo raytraced reference and proposed analytical solution: proposed model (left) and Monte Carlo sampled reference (right).

We can also express the differential solid angle as a function of distance and differential area using Equation (11.3). Therefore, our final approximated diffuse integral is

$$Diffuse\,(p, \omega_o) \sim L_n C_d \cos \theta_{\overrightarrow{pp_d}} \frac{dA cos\theta_o}{r^2}, \qquad (11.16)$$

where θ_o is the angle between the surface normal n and the light plane orientation normal n_l and dA is given by the light shape.

11.3.4 Approximating Specular Integral

Introduction. We followed the idea of leveraging importance sampling to estimate the specular integral. First we analyzed the behavior of typical specular lighting models relying on probability distribution functions (PDFs). This led us to the definition of a specular cone of importance sampling, used to find the most important point for the specular integral and the actual integration area.

Specular in importance sampling. If we were to render specular reflection using Monte Carlo methods, we would cast a ray in every direction around the point being shaded and evaluate specular BRDF for given functions DFG from Equation (11.12). Also, every PDF used to model D depends on some kind of surface-roughness parameter, denoted g. This parameter describes how focused lighting remains after reflecting off the surface.

In the case of specular reflection, we can define a vector created by reflecting in the viewer's direction ω_o against the surface normal n. Such a vector is called the reflection vector $\vec{r}$.

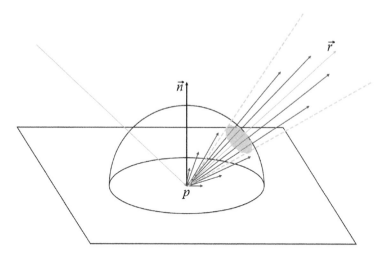

Figure 11.12. Visualization of reflection ray spread due to surface roughness.

Due to the nature of specular reflection, most samples that have meaningful weights would focus around $\vec{r}$. Their weights toward a final solution would be directly correlated to the angular distance of the ray being integrated to $\vec{r}$. They would also relate directly to material parameter g. Therefore, we can define a specular cone of importance sampling, centered around $\vec{r}$, encompassing all important ray samples (see Figure 11.12).

By the term *important*, we mean every ray that has absolute weight greater than a threshold σ (assuming that a ray shot in the direction of $\vec{r}$ would have a weight of 1.0). We can easily see that, with a constant σ, the cone apex angle α depends only on the surface glossiness factor g (see Figure 11.13). Therefore, we are interested in finding a function that calculates the specular cone angle from the surface glossiness, with a given specular model and constant σ.

As an example, we can apply this reasoning to find such a function for the Phong specular model:

$$k_{Phong} = (r \cdot n)^g . \tag{11.17}$$

We prepare data containing the specular cone angles α, at which $k_{Phong} > \sigma$. Then, for a given dataset, we find an approximation function. From possible candidates we pick a function with the lowest computational cost. In our case the function of choice is

$$\alpha\left(g\right) = 2\sqrt{\frac{2}{g+2}} . \tag{11.18}$$

It coincides with the Beckmann distribution definition of roughness m [Beckmann and Spizzichino 63], where m is given as the root mean square of the specular cone slope.

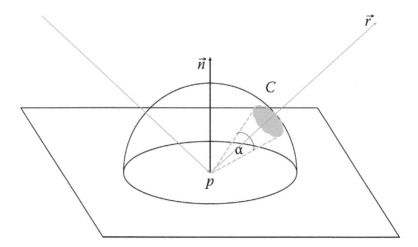

Figure 11.13. Visualization of cone of specular importance sampling.

We successfully applied this method to various specular models such as Phong, Blinn-Phong, Beckmann and GGX [Walter et al. 07]. However, it is worth noting that a cone shape is a relaxed bound on the actual distribution 3D shape, the complexity of which varies over different BRDF. Therefore, the cone shape is only approximate. In the case of Phong, the cone is actually a perfect match. However, in the case of Blinn-Phong, due to the use of the half vector, a pyramid with an ellipse base or even more complex shape would provide tighter, more accurate bounds.

Now we have an approximation model for the most important samples of our specular function. In the case of a single area light source, we would be interested in calculating the integral of our specular function over the portion of area of the light subtending the cone—defining integration limits. We can approximate the final solution by applying reasoning and methodology similar to Section 11.3.3. Again, a varied database was prepared, an integral numerically calculated, and the most important points estimated. In the end we found out that the geometric center of the integration limits area is a good point to estimate the unbounded specular integral. Let's call it p_{sc}. Therefore, to obtain the final result, we must calculate $Specular\,(p,\omega_o)$ for a single point light at p_{sc} and normalize the result by the integration limits area (see Figure 11.14).

To simplify our problem, we move to the light space (see Figure 11.15) by projecting our specular cone onto the light plane. In that case we are looking at a 2D problem, of finding the area of intersection between an ellipsoid (projected specular cone) and a given light shape (in our case a disk or rectangle, as spheres prove to be easily solvable working exclusively with solid angles).

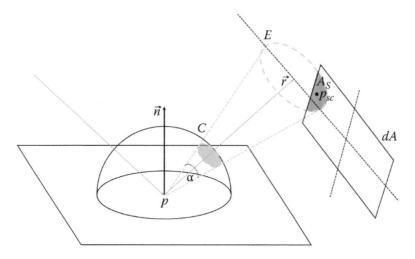

Figure 11.14. Construction of point p_{sc} and computing the intersection area A_S.

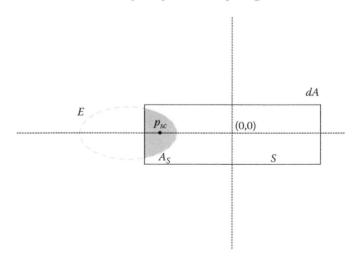

Figure 11.15. Situation from Figure 11.14 visible in 2D on the light plane.

Area specular approximation algorithm. Here is pseudo code of the algorithm to approximate area specular integral (see Figures 11.14 and 11.15 for reference):

- For every shaded point p, find reflection vector r.

- Calculate the specular importance cone apex angle $\alpha_{BRDF}(g)$ from point p and glossiness g, where $\alpha_{BRDF}(g)$ is defined per the BRDF used to model specular lighting.

- Create cone C with apex at point p and opening angle α, oriented around vector r.

- Project cone C onto the light plane of area light L, creating ellipsoid E.

- Find area A_S of the intersection between ellipsoid E and function S describing specular light shape.

- Find geometric center p_{sc} of A_S—the importance point of the specular integral.

- Calculate $Specular\,(p, \omega_o)$ as if p_{sc} was a point light, therefore vector $\overrightarrow{pp_{sc}}$.

- Normalize the result by the actual area of A_S as an effective solid angle differential.

Applying this to Equation (11.12) results in

$$Specular\,(p, \omega_o) \sim L_n \frac{D(\vec{h})F(\omega_o, \vec{h})G(\omega_i, \overrightarrow{pp_{sc}}\vec{h})}{4(cos\theta_o)} d\omega_{\overrightarrow{pp_{sc}}}, \qquad (11.19)$$

$$\vec{h} = \|\omega_o, \overrightarrow{pp_{sc}}\|.$$

After substituting the solid angle differential from Equation (11.19) by A_S normalization, we get

$$Specular\,(p, \omega_o) \sim L_n \frac{D(\vec{h})F(\omega_o, \vec{h})G(\omega_i, \overrightarrow{pp_{sc}}\vec{h})}{4(cos\theta_o)A_S}. \qquad (11.20)$$

When solving for specific light, we use the appropriate method per light type to calculate A_S. The following section focuses on approximations for various light-shape intersections with the specular importance cone.

Intersection area calculation. Finding an accurate area of intersection, between various 2D shapes, at runtime is not a trivial task. In our case we are looking at ellipse-disk or ellipse-rectangle intersections. Disks and rectangles are axis aligned in light space and centered at $(0,0)$, as they represent the actual light shape. Ellipses can be rotated. See Figures 11.14 and 11.15 for reference. To minimize shader complexity, we decided to approximate an ellipsoid by a simple disk. Calculating the area of intersection of two disks, or an axis-aligned box and a disk, is a reasonably easy problem to solve. In the case of a disk-disk intersection, we use the known smooth step approximation proposed by [Oat 06]:

$$A_{D0D1} = A_{min} smoothstep\left(0, 1, 1 - \|c0 - c1\| - \frac{|r0 - r1|}{r0 + r1 - |r0 - r1|}\right), \qquad (11.21)$$

where $c0$, $r0$, $c1$, and $r1$ are the center and radius of disks $D0$ and $D1$, respectively (see Figure 11.16).

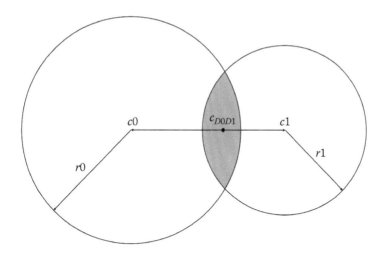

Figure 11.16. Finding area and center of intersection of disks.

The geometric center of intersection (if intersection exists) is given by

$$c_{D0D1} = c0 + (c1 - c0)\left(\frac{r0 - r1}{2\|c0 - c1\|} + 0.5\right). \qquad (11.22)$$

Both Equations (11.21) and (11.22) simplify under the assumption that $c0$ is at $(0,0)$.

In the case of a rectangle-disk intersection, we treat the disk as a square adjusted to have the same area as the original disk. Therefore, we can resort to simple axis-aligned rectangle-rectangle intersection mathematics. A_{R0R1} and c_{R0R1} are given by

$$tl = \max\left(c0 - \frac{d0}{2}, c1 - \frac{d1}{2}\right),$$
$$br = \min\left(c0 + \frac{d0}{2}, c1 + \frac{d1}{2}\right), \qquad (11.23)$$

$$A_{R0R1} = \max\left(tl.x - br.x, 0\right)\max(tl.y - br.y, 0),$$

$$c_{R0R1} = \frac{tl + br}{2},$$

where $c0$, $d0$, $c1$, and $d1$ are the center points and dimensions of rectangles $R0$ and $R1$, respectively, and tl and br are top left and bottom right intersection corners, respectively (assuming Euclidian space with inverse y; see Figure 11.17).

It is worth noting that accurate results can only be achieved for models based on radially symmetrical PDFs. If we strip away the projection part, by substituting the projected ellipse with a disk during our intersection tests and further

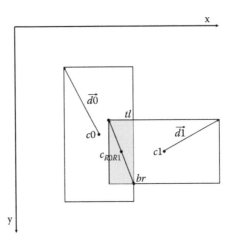

Figure 11.17. Finding the area and center of the intersection of rectangles.

integral calculation, we not only approximate the final result, but we also limit the model to radially symmetric PDFs. In the case of most microfacet BRDFs based on half vectors (Equation (11.9)), the initial shape of the specular cone would be similar to an elliptical base, which would result in an ellipse shape on the light plane—thus an integral over an ellipse.

This is a rather crude approximation; however, it proved good enough in visual assessment of final results, when tested with Phong, Blinn-Phong, and GGX, using radially symmetrical light shapes (see Figures 11.18 and 11.19).

11.3.5 Nonuniform Light Sources

Up to this point we were only considering light sources with constant $L_i(p, \omega_i)$. We will now change this assumption and for simplicity assume that light intensity I is constant over the light and that $L_i(p, \omega_i)$ returns a normalized, wavelength dependent value. Looking at integrals from Equations (11.11) and (11.12) and following intuitions from Sections 11.3.3 and 11.3.4, we can see that in order to acquire the correct result, we could pre-integrate Equations (11.11) and (11.12) with varying $L_i(p, \omega_i)$ over the light source and then normalize by the source area. Assuming we can approximate diffuse and specular integrals at runtime, due to Equations (11.16) and (11.20), we would just need to multiply those results by the pre-integrated, normalized full integral from Equations (11.11) and (11.12) at our most important points for diffuse and specular integrals, respectively.

In the case of a diffuse (Equations (11.11) and (11.16)), we need to integrate

$$Diffuse_{Lookup}(p_d, r) = \int_A L_i(p_d + rn_l, \omega_i)\, d\omega_i,$$

Figure 11.18. Disk area light fit to Phong distribution.

where p_d is a point on the light plane with normal n_l and r is the distance away from the light.

To simplify, we assume that occlusion does not influence the result. Then the integral can be pre-computed in a 3D lookup table indexed by $p_d.xy$ coordinates in the light space and by distance r between points p and p_d. The distance can be normalized against the maximum distance at which computing the integral still makes a visual difference. Such a distance maximum can be calculated by solving the light shape's solid angle (Equation (11.3)) for r, irrespective of $cos\theta_o$, where σ sets the boundary importance of the solid angle weight:

$$r_{max} > \sqrt{\frac{dA}{\sigma}}.$$

For distances larger than r_{max}, the solid angle would be too small and, as a result, the integral would not further change visually.

Every Z layer of the lookup table would contain the diffuse integral for point p_d, set on coordinates $p_d.xy$ in the light space, $\max(r/r_{max}, 1)$ away from the light plane. Finally, the full diffuse integral approximation is

$$Diffuse\,(p, \omega_o) \sim IC_d \cos\theta_{\overrightarrow{pp_d}} \frac{dA cos\theta_o}{r^2} Diffuse_{Lookup}\,(p_d, r)\,. \qquad (11.24)$$

Figure 11.19. Disk area light fit to GGX distribution.

In the case of specular (Equation (11.12)), we need to integrate

$$Specular_{Lookup}(\overrightarrow{p}\,p_{sc}, g) = \int_A L_i(p, \omega_i) \frac{D(\vec{h}, g)F(\omega_o, \vec{h})G(\omega_i, \omega_o, \vec{h})}{4(cos\theta_o)} d\omega_i, \quad (11.25)$$

where p is the point being shaded and p_{sc} is the most important point of the specular integral with g defined as surface roughness. Unfortunately, such a representation would require a 4D lookup table. We would like to free ourselves from knowledge of point p. According to reasoning from Section 11.3.4, we know that the integral will effectively depend on the projected cone of importance sampling radius. We also know how to create functions to calculate the specular importance cone apex angle from the surface roughness for given BRDFs (Equations (11.17) and (11.18)). The projected importance cone radius depends on distance r to the light and the cone opening angle α (see Figure 11.20). Therefore, we can calculate the integral from Equation (11.25) for point p_{sc} and the new roughness g', where

$$g' = f_{BRDF}(g, r). \quad (11.26)$$

To make this assumption viable, we have to restrict only to radially symmetrical PDFs:

$$Specular_{Lookup}(p_{sc}, g') = \int_A L_i(p, \omega_i) \frac{D(\vec{h}, g')F(\omega_o, \vec{h})G(\omega_i, \omega_o, \vec{h})}{4(cos\theta_o)} d\omega_i, \quad (11.27)$$

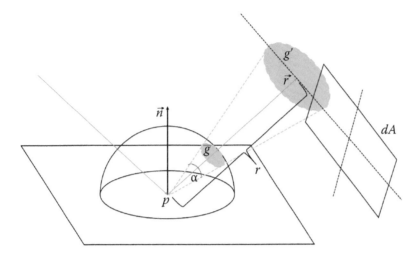

Figure 11.20. Relationship between cone angle, projected cone, and roughness.

where $\vec{h}$ is orthogonal to view direction ω_o. This effectively forces us to use Phong as our D function.

With these assumptions we can calculate Equation (11.27) as a 3D lookup table indexed by $p_{sc}.xy$ coordinates in the light space and g' calculated using Equation (11.26) derived for the used BRDF.

Finally, the full specular integral approximation is

$$Specular\,(p, \omega_o, g) \sim L_n \frac{D(\vec{h},)F(\omega_o, \vec{h})G(\omega_i, \overrightarrow{pp_{sc}}, \vec{h})}{4(cos\theta_o)A_S} Specular_{Lookup}(p_{sc}, g').$$

$$(11.28)$$

It is worth noting that, based on choice, functions DFG might depend on g or other surface parameters. Every additional parameter, apart from already included g, would add one more dimension to our lookup table or would have to be factored out. This is entirely based on the final choices for the specular model.

11.3.6   Solving Area Light BRDF

We presented a framework for efficient derivation of area-based lighting models based on currently known and well-researched BRDFs. The final lighting model should follow all procedures from Section 11.3, with the choice of particular DFG functions and appropriate derivation of additional parameters based directly on them. Then, diffuse and specular lighting per point can be approximated for various light types (Equations (11.16) and (11.20)), including colored, non-uniform lights (Equations (11.24) and (11.28)). See Figures 11.21, 11.22, and 11.23.

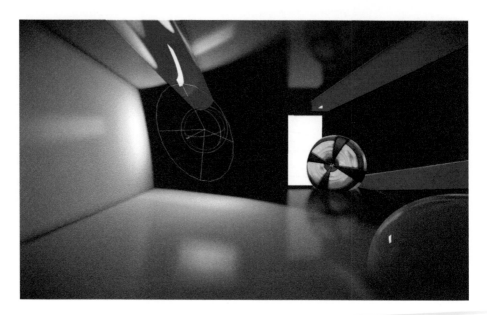

Figure 11.21. Rectangular area light.

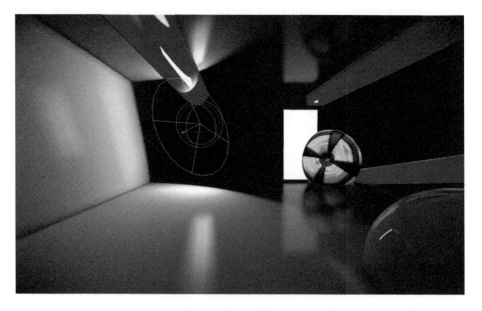

Figure 11.22. Rotated rectangular area light.

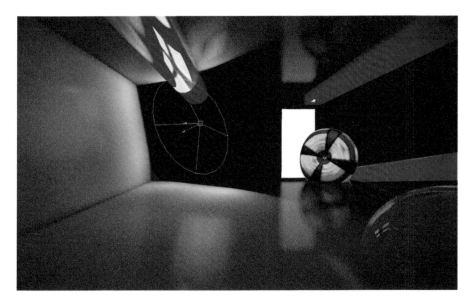

Figure 11.23. Textured rectangular area light.

11.4 Implementation

11.4.1 Introduction

Multiple ideas from this chapter were combined and used as the basis of the lighting model in *Killzone: Shadow Fall*. The light rendering engine relies heavily on real-time screen-space reflections and localized environmental reflection probes. Both solutions could efficiently support only radially symmetrical distribution-based specular (Phong). One of the dynamic texture-based lights requirements was to blend perfectly with existing image-based systems. Essentially we wanted a capability to swap dynamic area light, with image-based light card, with cube-map reflection at a distance without visual artifacts. We also wanted to support analytical shape lights allowing the highest visual quality and advanced material reflectance models.

11.4.2 Motivation

We used Cook-Torrance BRDF as the basis for our reflectance model. Normalized Blinn-Phong was used as the distribution function. Fresnel and geometric terms were calculated according to Smith-Schlick approximations [Schlick 94], matched and normalized to Blinn-Phong. We also prepared a radially symmetrical version of this BRDF. It was refitted to use Phong as the base, normalized and matched as closely as possible to reference solution.

Figure 11.24. Pre-integrated integral of environmental cube-map.

All lights use the same diffuse integral approximation reasoning shown in Section 11.3.3. Every light, depending on the light shape function, implements Equation (11.16) or Equation (11.24) in the case of a textured light source, to approximate the diffuse integral. That includes sunlight, omnidirectional lights, and spot lights with sphere, disk, or rectangular light shapes.

Standard analytical dynamic lights, depending on the light shape function, implement Equation (11.20) to approximate the specular integral. In the case of textured area lights, we support only rectangular lights with Phong-based BRDF.

Phong-based Cook-Torrance was also used for image-based lighting convolutions and texture-based area lights. Similar to already-known methods for cube map generation [Lazarov 11], we build our kernel based on our Phong-based BRDF and generate multiple mip-map levels of cube-maps for different specular cone widths (see Figure 11.24). Similar reasoning, described mathematically in Section 11.3.5, was applied to generate image-based light cards used with textured rectangular area.

Different light shape implementation. The *Killzone* renderer supports the following light shapes: sphere, rectangle, and disk. All lights follow the framework set by the disk light implementation. They require only minor changes to the code responsible for the closest point to the shape or normalized solid angle. Therefore, we were able to efficiently share code between different light shapes.

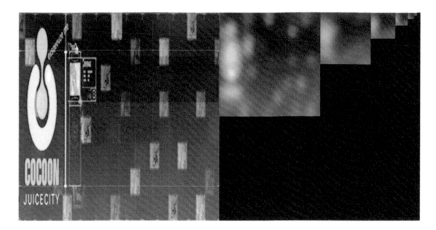

Figure 11.25. Pre-integrated specular integral of light card used with texture area lights.

It is also worth noting that sphere shape diffuse integral implementation can be vastly simplified by analytically integrating the integral as it has a closed form dependent only on the light position and radius. The sphere specular integral can also be optimized by working exclusively with the solid angle differential. There is no need to project computation into the light space, as the sphere shape is easily defined in 3D. Also, the projected solid angle is equal to the solid angle, as a sphere always subtends the same solid angle, independent of viewing direction and orientation.

Nonuniform light source implementation. We support texture-based lights using a rectangle shape as the base. We apply reasoning from Section 11.3.5 to directly compute and store pre-computed data in mip-maps of a 2D texture. Initial light intensity is provided by the texture generated by the in-game impostor rendering system or hand-painted by artists. Computed values are normalized and stored in two compressed RGB8 format textures (see Figures 11.25 and 11.26). At runtime, the rectangle light evaluates diffuse and specular integral, and multiplies the result by pre-computed partial integral from textures indexed in a similar fashion as described in Section 11.3.5.

11.5   Results Discussion

Using area lights exclusively during the production of *Killzone: Shadow Fall* proved to be an important pillar of the physically based rendering pipeline. Due to the proposed model, we were able to unify lighting incoming from different sources—analytical or image based—keeping a similar response and quality. Our

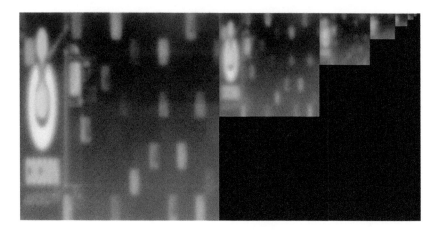

Figure 11.26. Pre-integrated diffuse integral of light card used with texture area lights.

art production pipeline was able to produce assets in a hermetic review environment, prepared as HDR pre-integrated BRDF cube-maps, and expect similar,
high-quality results in game (see Figures 11.27 and 11.28).

Also due to the implicit split of material and lighting handling, teams could
efficiently work on level assets, without interference between lighting and environmental departments. Previously, that kind of clash was unavoidable, as environmental artists had a tendency to tweak assets to simulate physically larger
lights (i.e., by changing roughness). This habit resulted many times in duplicated
assets per different in-game scenarios.

Figure 11.27. Typical usage of analytical area lights.

Figure 11.28. Typical usage of textured area lights.

The area lighting model proved to be efficient on the next generation console Playstation 4 GPU. The model itself is heavy on ALU operations (see Table 11.1), which in our case helped to amortize waiting time for multiple texture fetches from bandwidth intensive G-buffer and shadow maps. Therefore, we did not experience a noticeable slowdown in comparison with more standard point-based light models such as Blinn-Phong.

Unfortunately, several shortcuts we took during the model derivation resulted in artifacts, under certain circumstances, when using Blinn-Phong–based BRDF rectangular area lights. Due to those cases, we decided to use the rectangle shape exclusively with Phong-based BRDF, which is a better fit for the used approximations in the case of nonradially symmetrical light shapes.

Blinn-Phong Lights	Scalar ALU	% Against Base
Point	222	0%
Sphere	252	+13%
Disk	361	+62%
Rectangle	382	+72%
Texture Rectangle	405	+82%

Table 11.1. Comparision of Different light shaders assembly. Counts includes full deferred shadowed light code.

Figure 11.29. Square light shape using Phong distribution.

11.6 Further Research

In the near future we would like to focus on enhancing the normalization part of
the specular integral, which currently, due to disk approximation (Section 11.3.4),
is lacking in visual quality when compared to the reference solution. We would
be especially interested in pursuing a good approximation for Blinn-Phong and
therefore other microfacet distributions with a similar base such as the recently
popular GGX.

In order to do so, we would need to find an efficient way of finding intersections
between rotated ellipses and disks or rectangles.

We also feel that the rectangular lights specular approximation, when using
nonradially symmetrical PDFs, needs more research. As of now, the current algorithm for the most important point might result in severe artifacts at a rotation
angle of light that is orthogonal to the anisotropy direction of the PDF. A proper
search algorithm would require taking anisotropy direction into account. It is
worth noting that even in its current form, artifacts might be visually bearable
for rectangular shapes close to square (see Figures 11.29 and 11.30).

One proposed heuristic would be to treat the projected specular cone as an
elongated rectangle, oriented and extending in the direction of anisotropy. Such
shape change could be dynamic, calculated for specific BRDFs. Then, the most
important point for specular sampling would be the geometric center of the intersection between the specular rectangle and the light shape. The intersection
area could also be used as A_s for normalization (see Equation (11.20)).

Figure 11.30. Square light shape using GGX distribution exhibiting minor visual artifacts.

We prototyped this approach, for rectangular lights, by analytically finding a polygon representing the light shape and the projected specular cone intersection. To find the intersection at runtime, we used a GPU-optimized version of the Liang-Barsky clipping algorithm [Liang and Barsky 84]. A light shape rectangle was treated as the clipping window, then a polygon representing the projected specular cone was clipped against it. The end result was an array of vertices representing a planar, non-self-intersecting polygon. In order to find the polygon's area, we used the Gauss formula for arbitrary polygon area.

Unfortunately, a busy production schedule has prevented further research in that promising direction. Figure 11.31 shows the proposed idea geometrically with reference shader-based solution results (Figure 11.32).

Another proposed area of research includes nonradially symmetrical PDFs support for texture-based area lights. We experimented with multisampling approaches and approximating the PDF at runtime; however, it proved to be too expensive for our real-time budgets.

11.7 Conclusion

We provided a tested framework for developing various physically based, area-based lighting models using currently researched BRDFs as the starting point. Implementation proved to be robust and efficient enough for the rendering engine of *Killzone: Shadow Fall*, a launch title for Playstation 4.

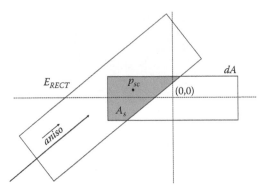

Figure 11.31. Geometric construction of point p_{sc} respecting distribution anisotropy direction. A_S due to Liang-Barsky clipping algorithm.

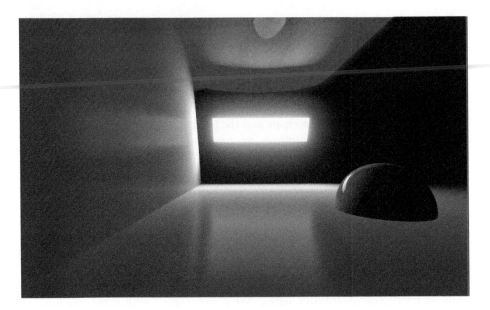

Figure 11.32. Runtime shader results using method from Figure 11.31.

We hope that the proposed ideas will provide other researchers and developers with tools to tackle problems of area lights and further extend the concept. In future, we hope that area-based lighting will become the de facto standard in modern video games, providing unified, predictable lighting solutions supplementing physically based material reflectance models.

Bibliography

[Baker and Hill 12] D. Baker and S. Hill "Rock-Solid Shading." SIGGRAPH 2012, Advances in Real-Time Rendering in 3D Graphics and Games Course, Los Angeles, CA, August 8, 2012.

[Beckmann and Spizzichino 63] Petr Beckmann and André Spizzichino. *The Scattering of Electromagnetic Waves from Rough Surfaces.* Oxford, UK: Pergamon Press, 1963. (Republished by Artech House in 1987.)

[Burley 12] B. Burley. "Physically-Based Shading at Disney." SIGGRAPH 2012, Practical Physically Based Shading in Film and Game Prduction Course, Los Angeles, CA, August 8, 2012.

[Cook and Torrance 81] R. Cook and K. Torrance. "A Reflectance Model for Computer Graphics." *Computer Graphics (Siggraph 1981 Proceedings)* 15:3 (1981), 301–316.

[Lambert 60] Johann Heinrich Lambert. *Photometria, sive De mensura et gradibus luminus, colorum et umbrae.* Augsburg, 1760.

[Lazarov 11] D. Lazarov. "Physically-Based Lighting in *Call of Duty: Black Ops.*" SIGGRAPH 2011, Advances in Real-Time Rendering in 3D Graphics and Games Course, Vancouver, Canada, August, 2011.

[Liang and Barsky 84] Y.D. Liang and B. Barsky. "A New Concept and Method for Line Clipping," *ACM Transactions on Graphics* 3:1 (1984), 1–22.

[Mittring and Dudash 11] M. Mittring and B. Dudash. "The Technology Behind the DirectX 11 Unreal Engine 'Samaritian' Demo." Presentation, Game Developers Conference 2011, San Francisco, CA, March, 2011.

[Mittring 12] M. Mittring. "The Technology Behind the 'Unreal Engine 4 Elemental Demo'." SIGGRAPH 2012, Advances in Real-Time Rendering in 3D Graphics and Games Course, Los Angeles, CA, August, 2012.

[Oat 06] C. Oat. "Aperture Ambient Lighting." *ACM Siggraph 2006 Courses*, pp. 143–152. New York: ACM, 2006.

[Pharr and Humphreys 04] M. Pharr and G. Humphreys. *Physically Based Rendering: From Theory to Implementation.* San Francisco, CA: Morgan Kaufman, 2004.

[Schlick 94] C. Schlick. "An Inexpensive BRDF Model for Physically-Based Rendering." *Proc. Eurographics '94, Computer Graphics Forum* 13:3 (1994), 233–246.

[McAuley et al. 13] S. McAuley et al. "Physically Based Shading in Theory and Practice." In *ACM SIGGRAPH 2013 Courses*, Article no. 22. New York: ACM, 2013.

[Walter et al. 07] B. Walter, S.R. Marschner, H. Li, and K.E. Torrance. "Microfacet Models for Refraction through Rough Surfaces." In *Proceedings of the 18th Eurographics Conference on Rendering Techniques*, pp. 195–206. Aire-la-Ville, Switzerland: Eurographics Association, 2007.

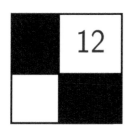

High Performance Outdoor Light Scattering Using Epipolar Sampling

Egor Yusov

12.1 Introduction

Light scattering effects in the atmosphere are crucial for creating realistic images of outdoor scenes. These effects generate the blue color in a clear sky as well as the spectrum of colors painting the horizon at sunset or sunrise. Light shafts, or god rays, are also produced by the same physical phenomenon when some sunlight is blocked by terrain features, such as mountains. Due to the complexity and numerous computations required to accurately evaluate the airlight integral, only rudimentary sky models are usually used in real-time rendering, which have a number of limitations. For example, simple models cannot handle daytime changes, restrict the camera to ground level, etc. Using screen-space imitation is a common technique to render god rays.

This chapter presents a new high performance, physically based method for computing outdoor light scattering effects while taking shadowing into account. The method combines two key concepts: epipolar sampling, which significantly reduces the number of samples for which expensive ray marching is performed, and 1D minimum/maximum binary trees, which accelerate ray marching procedure. The method is fully dynamic, and requires only a little pre-computation. It renders scattering effects for all times of day and for all camera locations, from ground views to outer space. The method is integrated with cascaded shadow maps, which are commonly used to handle large outdoor environments.

12.2   Previous Work

There were a lot of methods for rendering scattering in the Earth's atmosphere, starting with the work by Klassen [Klassen 87]. Early real-time approaches used very simple models due to hardware limitations of the time. Assuming flat Earth, constant density atmosphere and constant light intensity, Hoffman and Preetham derived a fully analytical solution for the airlight integral [Hoffman and Preetham 02]. The resulting model produces reasonable results, but only for ground views. Still, the sky looks unnatural, especially near the horizon. A more accurate model was proposed by Riley et al. [Riley et al. 04]. They also assumed Earth was flat, but the density of the atmosphere in their model decreased exponentially. To obtain a closed form solution for airlight integral, they ignored scattering on aerosols. Some attempts were made to approximate complex effects in the atmosphere with analytic functions [Preetham et al. 99]. Mitchell simulated light shafts using screen-space radial blur [Mitchell 08].

More physically accurate approaches perform numerical integration of the scattering integral with either slicing [Dobashi et al. 02] or ray marching [O'Neil 04, Schüler 12]. To accelerate numerical integration, different techniques were proposed related basically to the way optical depth is computed inside the integral. Nishita et al. [Nishita et al. 93], Dobashi et al. [Dobashi et al. 02] and O'Neil [O'Neil 04] used different pre-computed lookup tables. In his later work, O'Neil replaced the lookup table with a combination of ad hoc analytic functions [O'Neil 05]. Schüler presented sufficiently accurate analytical expression based on the approximation to the Chapman function [Schüler 12].

Some researchers tried to pre-compute the scattering integral as much as possible. While generally it depends on four variables, Schafhitzel et al. dropped one parameter and stored the integral using 3D texture [Schafhitzel et al. 07]. Bruneton and Neyret elaborated on this idea and used complete 4D parameterization [Bruneton and Neyret 08]. Their algorithm also approximates multiple scattering, and accounts for Earth surface reflection. It uses an array of 3D textures to store the resulting data; manual interpolation for the fourth coordinate is also required. To render light shafts, they used shadow volumes to compute the total length of the illuminated portion of the ray. Then they computed inscattering, assuming that the illuminated part of the ray is continuous and starts directly from the camera.

Engelhardt and Dachsbacher developed an elegant and efficient algorithm for rendering scattering effects in a homogenous participating medium [Engelhardt and Dachsbacher 10]. They noticed in-scattered light intensity varies smoothly along the epipolar lines emanating from the position of the light source on the screen. To account for this, they proposed a technique that distributes ray marching samples sparsely along these lines and interpolates between samples where adequate. It preserves high-frequency details by placing additional samples at depth discontinuities.

Chen et al. also took advantage of epipolar geometry [Chen et al. 11]. They noticed that they could accelerate the ray marching process by using a 1D min/-max binary tree constructed for each epipolar slice. Their algorithm is rather sophisticated. It relies upon a singular value decomposition of the scattering term, and requires special care of the area near the epipole.

In this chapter we apply our previous approach [Yusov 13] to rendering scattering effects in the Earth's atmosphere. We reduce the number of samples for which the airlight integral is numerically integrated with the epipolar sampling and exploit 1D min/max binary trees to accelerate ray marching. We also discuss practical details, like integration with cascaded shadow maps [Engel 07].

12.3 Algorithm Overview

The following is a high-level overview of our algorithm. The remaining sections provide details on each step. The algorithm can be summarized as follows:

1. Generate epipolar sampling.

    (a) Compute entry and exit points of each epipolar line on the screen.

    (b) Distribute samples.

2. Select ray marching samples.

    (a) Compute coarse in-scattering for each sample.

    (b) Sparsely locate initial ray marching samples along epipolar lines.

    (c) Place additional samples where coarse in-scattering varies notably.

3. Construct 1D min/max binary tree for each epipolar slice.

4. Perform ray marching.

5. Interpolate in-scattering radiance for the rest of the samples from ray marching samples.

6. Transform scattering from epipolar coordinates to screen space and combine with the attenuated back buffer.

12.4 Light Transport Theory

Since our method ultimately boils down to efficiently solving the airlight integral, it requires an introduction. We will start with the key concepts of the light transport theory.

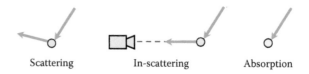

Figure 12.1. Types of interaction of light with particles.

12.4.1 Physical Model of the Air

Sunlight interacts with the particles distributed in the air as it propagates through the atmosphere. Two types of interaction are important: scattering (Figure 12.1, left), which changes the light direction, and absorption (Figure 12.1, right), which transforms the energy into other forms. Scattering in the view direction is called *in-scattering* (Figure 12.1, center). The amount of light energy per unit length scattered at point x is expressed by the total scattering coefficient $\beta^s(x)$. The angular distribution of the scattered light is described by the phase function $p(\theta)$ where θ is the angle between incident and outgoing directions.[1] The total losses of energy per unit length caused by absorption and both absorption and scattering are given by the absorption and extinction coefficients $\beta^a(x)$ and $\beta^e(x) = \beta^s(x) + \beta^a(x)$, respectively.

Air is usually modeled as a mix of two types of particles: air molecules and aerosols. Scattering by air molecules is accurately described by the Rayleigh theory. It is considerably wavelength-dependent, and almost isotropic with the following phase function: $p_R(\theta) = \frac{3}{16\pi}(1 + \cos^2(\theta))$. Precise derivation of scattering coefficients is irrelevant for this paper and can be found for instance in [Nishita et al. 93, Preetham et al. 99]. As in previous works [Riley et al. 04, Bruneton and Neyret 08], we use the following values for Rayleigh scattering coefficient at sea level: $\beta_R^s.rgb = (5.8, 13.5, 33.1)10^{-6} m^{-1}$.

Scattering by aerosols is described by the Mie theory. Cornette-Shanks function is commonly used as an approximation to the phase function of Mie particles [Nishita et al. 93, Riley et al. 04]:

$$p_M(\theta) = \frac{1}{4\pi} \frac{3(1 - g^2)}{2(2 + g^2)} \frac{(1 + \cos^2(\theta))}{(1 + g^2 - 2g\cos(\theta))^{3/2}}.$$

As in [Bruneton and Neyret 08], we use $g = 0.76$ and $\beta_M^s.rgb = (2, 2, 2)10^{-5} m^{-1}$. For aerosols we also assume slight absorption with $\beta_M^a = 0.1\beta_M^s$.

In the model of the atmosphere it is assumed that the particle density decreases exponentially with the altitude h: $\rho = \rho_0 e^{-h/H}$, where ρ_0 is the density at sea level and H is the particle scale height (which is the height of the atmosphere if the density was uniform). We use the following scale heights for Rayleigh and

---

[1] We assume that the phase function is normalized to unity such that $\int_\Omega p(\theta)d\omega = 1$ where integration is performed over the whole set of directions Ω.

Mie particles: $H_R = 7994m$, $H_M = 1200m$ [Nishita et al. 93]. Both scattering and absorption are proportional to the particle density, thus scattering/absorption coefficient at altitude h is given by scaling the appropriate coefficient at sea level with the factor $e^{-h/H}$.

12.4.2 Scattering Integral and Aerial Perspective

In our derivation of the airlight integral, we will follow a single scattering model that assumes that sunlight can only be scattered once before it reaches the camera. This is a reasonable approximation for day time. During twilight, multiple scattering becomes more important and should be considered in the production of realistic images [Haber et al. 05]. Still, a single scattering model produces reasonably convincing results. As we understand it, the only real-time method that approximates multiple scattering was proposed by Bruneton and Neyret [Bruneton and Neyret 08]. It requires a 4D lookup table with nonlinear parameterization. Performing multiple lookups into the table at runtime is quite expensive.

Consider some point P on the view ray starting at camera location C and terminating at point O (Figure 12.2). If the ray does not hit Earth or the camera is located outside the atmosphere, then either O or C is assumed to be the corresponding intersection of the ray with the top of the atmosphere. The amount of light that reaches P after attenuation by air molecules and aerosols can be expressed as $L_{Sun} \cdot e^{-T(A \to P)}$, where L_{Sun} is the sunlight radiance before entering the atmosphere, and A is the point on the top of the atmosphere through which the light reached P. The $T(A \to B)$ term is called optical depth along the path from point A to point B. It is essentially the integral of the total extinction

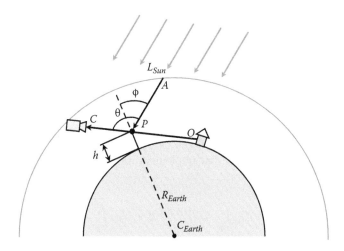

Figure 12.2. Scattering in the atmosphere.

coefficient over the path, which is given by the following equation:

$$T(A \to B) = \int_A^B (\beta_R^e e^{-h(t)/H_R} + \beta_M^e e^{-h(t)/H_M}) dt. \tag{12.1}$$

Scattering by molecules and aerosols happens independently and is proportional to the corresponding scattering coefficient $(\beta_{R/M}^s)$ at sea level and to the particle density scale factor $(e^{-h/H_{R/M}})$ at P. The fraction of scattered light going in the view direction is given by the phase function $p_{R/M}(\theta)$ for each type. Light in-scattered at P is attenuated on the way to the camera by a factor of $e^{-T(P \to C)}$. Finally, to account for shadowing, we also need to introduce a visibility term $V(P)$, which equals 1 if P is visible from light and 0 otherwise. Total in-scattering along the view ray is thus given by the following integral:

$$L_{In} = \int_C^O L_{Sun} \cdot e^{-T(A(s) \to P(s))} \cdot e^{-T(P(s) \to C)} \cdot V(P(s))$$
$$\cdot \left(\beta_R^s e^{-h(s)/H_R} p_R(\theta) + \beta_M^s e^{-h(s)/H_M} p_M(\theta) \right) ds. \tag{12.2}$$

Initial object radiance L_O is attenuated in the atmosphere before it reaches the camera by a factor of $e^{-T(O \to C)}$. The final radiance measured at the camera is a sum of the attenuated object radiance and in-scattered light, which stands for a phenomenon called *aerial perspective*:

$$L = L_O \cdot e^{-T(O \to C)} + L_{In}. \tag{12.3}$$

12.5   Computing Scattering Integral

Integral (12.2) cannot be solved analytically. Nor it is feasible to compute it directly with numerical integration, because at each step we will have to solve two optical depth integrals (12.1). Numerical integration can be significantly optimized using a number of tricks. To begin, we can eliminate computation of the optical depth integrals $T(A \to P)$ and $T(P \to C)$. O'Neil noticed that Equation (12.1) depends on two parameters: the altitude h and the angle φ between the vertical direction and the light direction [O'Neil 04]. Optical depth $T(A \to P)$ can thus be pre-computed and stored in a lookup table. We follow the same idea, but use slightly different implementation. First we rewrite the optical depth integral (12.1) as follows:

$$T(A \to B) = \beta_R^e \int_A^B e^{-h(t)/H_R} dt + \beta_M^e \int_A^B e^{-h(t)/H_M} dt. \tag{12.4}$$

Now one can see that while β_R^e and β_M^e are 3-component vectors, both integrals in Equation (12.4) are scalar. We can use a two-channel lookup table storing total

Rayleigh and Mie particle densities up to the top of the atmosphere. With the help of this lookup table, optical depth to the top of the atmosphere $T(A \rightarrow P)$ can be computed as follows:

$$T_{A \rightarrow P} = \beta_R^e.\text{xyz} * D[h, \cos(\varphi)].\text{x} + \beta_M^e.\text{xyz} * D[h, \cos(\varphi)].\text{y}.$$

If the ray hits the Earth, the corresponding table entry should contain a large number to account for occlusion. To eliminate interpolation artifacts, in our practical implementation we avoid discontinuities in the table by allowing the altitude to become negative. This provides fast but continuous growth of the total particle density.

We also tried using the analytical expression based on an approximation to the Chapman function as proposed by Schüler [Schüler 12]. However, we found that it is quite complex and the lookup table works significantly faster.

Optical depth $T(P \rightarrow C)$ is computed by maintaining net particle densities from the camera to the current point during the numerical integration process. Finally, we can observe that angle θ does not vary across the ray, and both phase functions $p_R(\theta)$ and $p_M(\theta)$ can be evaluated outside the integral. To implement this, we integrate Rayleigh and Mie in-scattering separately and apply corresponding phase functions at the end. Pseudo-shader for the numerical integration procedure is given in Listing 12.1.

```
// Compute integration step
dP.xyz = (O.xyz-C.xyz) / N_Steps;
ds = ||dP||;

// Initialize integration variables
D_{P→C}.xy = 0; // Net density from camera to integration point
L_{Rlgh}.rgb = 0; // Rayleigh in-scattering
L_{Mie}.rgb = 0; // Mie in-scattering

for(float s = 0.5f; s < N_Steps; s += 1.f)
{
    // Compute position of the current point
    P.xyz = C.xyz + dP.xyz * s;
    // Compute altitude and normal to the Earth surface
    h = ||P - C_{Earth}|| - R_{Earth};
    N_{Earth}.xyz = (P.xyz - C_{Earth}.xyz)/||P.xyz - C_{Earth}.xyz||;
    // Compute Rayleigh and Mie particle density scale at P
    ρ_{RM}.xy = e^{-h/H_{RM}.xy};
    // Compute cos(φ) and look-up for the net particle
    // density from P to the top of the atmosphere
    cosφ = (N_{Earth},-l); // l is the light direction
    D_{A→P}.xy = D[h,cosφ];

    // Accumulate net particle density from the camera
    D_{P→C}.xy += ρ_{RM}.xy * ds;

    // Compute total particle density from the top of the
    // atmosphere through the integration point to camera
    D_{A→P→C}.xy = D_{A→P}.xy + D_{P→C}.xy;
```

```
// Compute optical depth for Rayleigh and Mie particles
T_R.xyz = D_{A→P→C}.x * β_R^e.xyz;
T_M.xyz = D_{A→P→C}.y * β_M^e.xyz;

// Compute extinction for the current integration point
E_{R+M}.rgb = e^{-(T_R.xyz + T_M.xyz)};

// Compute differential amounts of in-scattering
dL_{Rlgh}.rgb = ρ_{RM}.x * β_R^s.rgb * E_{R+M}.rgb * ds;
dL_{Mie}.rgb = ρ_{RM}.y * β_M^s.rgb * E_{R+M}.rgb * ds;

// Compute visibility V

// Update Rayleigh and Mie integrals
L_{Rlgh}.rgb += dL_{Rlgh}.rgb * V;
L_{Mie}.rgb += dL_{Mie}.rgb * V;
}

// Apply Rayleigh and Mie phase functions
cosθ = (-v⃗, l⃗); // v⃗ is the view direction
ApplyPhaseFunctions(L_{Rlgh}.xyz, L_{Mie}.xyz, cosθ);

// Compute in-scattering and extinction from the camera
L_{In}.rgb = (L_{Rlgh}.rgb + L_{Mie}.rgb) * L_{Sun};
Ext.rgb = e^{-(D_{P→C}.x * β_R^e.xyz + D_{P→C}.y * β_M^e.xyz)};
```

Listing 12.1. Numerical integration of the in-scattering integral.

12.6   Epipolar Sampling

Although the integration procedure presented in Section 12.5 is much faster than the straightforward numerical integration of Equation (12.2), it is still too expensive to perform it for every screen pixel at real-time frame rates. The number of computations can be dramatically reduced with epipolar sampling, which smartly distributes expensive ray marching samples along the epipolar lines on the screen. We perform sample generation using the method described in Engelhardt and Dachsbacher's paper [Engelhardt and Dachsbacher 10] with some improvements. Epipolar lines are obtained by connecting the light source projected position with a user-defined number of points equidistantly placed along the border of the screen (Figure 12.3). Note that border coordinates should correspond to the centers of the outermost pixels, which are biased by 0.5 pixel size inward. In projection space, this defines the following rectangle: $[-1 + 1/W, 1 - 1/W] \times [-1 + 1/H, 1 - 1/H]$, where W and H are width and height of the viewport.

If the sun is on the screen, the entry point for each line is its position (Figure 12.3, left). If the sun is outside the screen, the entry point for each line is placed at the intersection of the line with the screen boundary (Figure 12.3, right). Lines that are completely behind the screen (shown in gray in Figure 12.3, right) are invalid and discarded from further processing. Then, a predefined num-

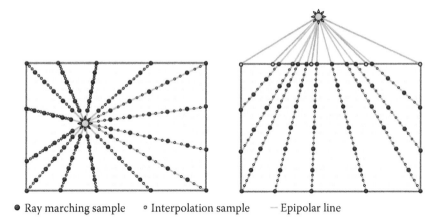

● Ray marching sample   ○ Interpolation sample   — Epipolar line

Figure 12.3. Distributing ray marching and interpolation samples along epipolar lines.

ber of samples are evenly distributed between the entry and exit points of each line. Every Nth sample is then flagged as an initial ray marching sample (in our experiments we use $N = 16$). Entry and exit points are always ray marching samples. To eliminate oversampling for short lines, which occurs when the light source is close to the screen boundary, we elongate such lines, striving to provide 1:1 correspondence between samples on the line and screen pixels.

Sample refinement in the original algorithm [Engelhardt and Dachsbacher 10] was performed by searching for depth discontinuities. We found out this is not an optimal strategy since what we really need are discontinuities in light intensity. In our method, we first compute coarse unshadowed ($V = 1$) in-scattering for each epipolar sample. For this, we perform trapezoidal integration, which can be obtained by a couple of modifications to the algorithm in Listing 12.1. We store particle density in previous point and update total density from the camera as follows:

```
D_{P→C}.xy += (ρ_{RM}.xy + Prev_ρ_{RM}.xy)/2 * ds;
Prev_ρ_{RM}.xy = ρ_{RM}.xy;
```

Rayleigh and Mie in-scattering are updated in the same way:

```
L_{Rlgh}.rgb += (dL_{Rlgh}.rgb + Prev_dL_{Rlgh}.rgb) / 2;
L_{Mie}.rgb += (dL_{Mie}.rgb + Prev_dL_{Mie}.rgb) / 2;
Prev_dL_{Rlgh}.rgb = dL_{Rlgh}.rgb;
Prev_dL_{Mie}.rgb = dL_{Mie}.rgb;
```

Finally, loop variable s now runs from 1 to N_{Steps} inclusively and $Prev\_\rho_{RM}$, $Prev\_dL_{Rlgh}$, and $Prev\_dL_{Mie}$ variables are initialized by appropriate values for camera position C before entering the loop. Trapezoidal integration requires fewer steps to achieve the same precision. We found out that $N_{Steps} = 7$ are enough to provide good refinement results. After coarse in-scattering is calculated for each sample, we search for discontinuities and place additional ray marching samples directly before and after each one. This algorithm is implemented with the compute shader as described in Section 12.8.

12.7 1D Min/Max Binary Tree Optimization

12.7.1 General Idea

At this point we have selected a number of ray marching samples on each epipolar line and need to compute the in-scattering integral for each one taking shadowing into account. For each sample, we cast a ray, then transform its start and end positions into the light projection space and perform ray marching in shadow map space (Figure 12.4).

Stepping through each shadow map texel would be too expensive, especially for a high-resolution shadow map. Using a fixed number of samples can cause undersampling and result in banding artifacts. We took advantage of epipolar geometry to improve performance without sacrificing visual quality. Consider camera rays casted through ray marching samples on some epipolar line (Figure 12.5). The rays clearly lie in the same plane, which we will call epipolar slice. The most important property of the slice is that the light direction also belongs to it.

The intersection of an epipolar slice with the light projection plane is a line. All camera rays in the slice project to this line and differ only in the end point.

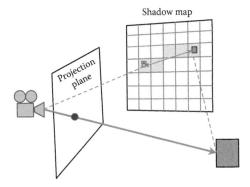

Figure 12.4. Projecting the view ray onto the shadow map.

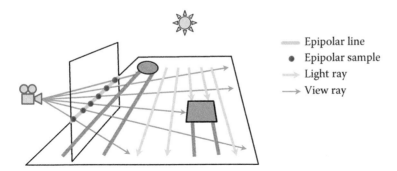

Figure 12.5. Epipolar geometry: camera rays casted through the samples on an epipolar line and light rays lie in the same plane.

Taking shadow map samples along this line results in a one-dimensional height map, which is the same for all camera rays in the slice. To perform a visibility test $V(P)$ in Equation (12.2) and Listing 12.1, we essentially need to check if the current position on the view ray is under this height map or above it (Figure 12.6). It is clear that if there is a long consecutive lit or shadowed section on the ray, we can process it right away without stepping through all the underlying shadow map samples. To detect such sections, a one-dimensional minimum/maximum binary tree can be used as suggested by Chen et al. [Chen et al. 11]. Note that in contrast to their method, we do not perform rectification of the shadow map, which makes our algorithm significantly simpler. If the maximum value of depths of the ray section end points is less than the minimum depth value stored in the tree node, then the section is fully in light (such as AB in Figure 12.6). On the other hand, if the minimum of depths is greater than the node's maximum value, then the section is in shadow (CD in Figure 12.6).

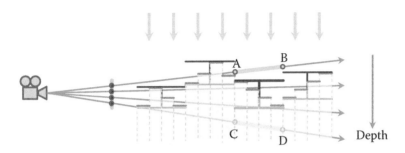

Figure 12.6. Detecting long lit and shadowed ray sections with 1D min/max binary tree.

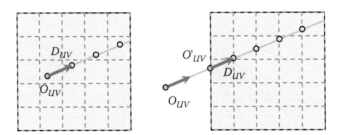

Figure 12.7. Epipolar slice origin and direction in shadow map UV space as well as locations of sampling points for creating min/max trees.

12.7.2 Constructing Min/Max Trees

To construct a binary tree for the slice, we need to define the intersection of the slice with the shadow map. Since all camera rays in the slice project onto this line, this can be done by taking any two points on the ray and transforming them into the shadow map UV space. In our implementation, we use camera location as the first point. Its projected position O_{UV} gives us the zeroth sample in the 1D height map. To compute the direction $\vec{D}_{UV}$, we take the termination point of the ray casted through the slice exit point, transform it into the UV space and compute direction from O_{UV} to the resulting point. Then we normalize $\vec{D}_{UV}$ so that the maximum of its projections on u and v axes equals 1. If O_{UV} falls outside the shadow map boundary $[0,1] \times [0,1]$ (which is a very common case in multi-cascade set-up), we continue the line along the $\vec{D}_{UV}$ and move the origin to the first intersection with the boundary (Figure 12.7, right).

Now when we know the location O_{UV} of the zeroth sample in the 1D height map and direction $\vec{D}_{UV}$, we can determine the location of ith sample as $O_{UV} + i \cdot \vec{D}_{UV}$. The first level of the tree can be constructed by computing the min/max of every $2i$th and $(2i + 1)$th samples. All the coarser levels can be built by propagating these min/max values upwards. As Figure 12.7 shows, the locations of the original samples on the shadow map do not fall in texel centers. To obtain correct results, we compute the conservative min/max bound by considering the nearest four samples, which would be used for PCF filtering (see Section 12.8). Note that the number of samples in the 1D height map built as described above is always not greater than the maximum shadow map dimension.

12.7.3 Ray Marching with 1D Min/Max Trees

In our optimized ray marching algorithm we adopted the method proposed by Tevs et al. [Tevs et al. 08] and reused by Chen et al. [Chen et al. 11]. Min/max tree traversal is implemented without recursion in this method. Transitions to coarser levels are performed one at a time so that the transition from level l to the next coarser level $l + 1$ can be performed when the sample index is divisible by 2^{l+1}. Transitions to the finer levels are done when a section is neither fully lit nor shadowed. We incorporate min/max tree traversal into the base procedure (presented in Listing 12.1). The optimized algorithm keeps track of the current min/max level l, increasing or decreasing it as necessary. When Rayleigh and Mie in-scattering integrals are updated, current section length ds is scaled by a factor of 2^l. Section 12.8 shows the shader code for the optimized algorithm.

Strictly speaking, computing the scattering contribution from a single ray section having a length of $2^l \cdot ds$ samples does not yield the same result as stepping through all the samples because the integral is nonlinear. For a point light source, we solved this problem by pre-computing the in-scattering integral and storing it in a 2D lookup table [Yusov 13]. An air-light integral for outdoor light scattering requires a 4D lookup table as shown in [Bruneton and Neyret 08] to be pre-computed. Performing lookups into this table at each step would be prohibitively expensive as the table has nonlinear parameterization. The manual interpolation for the fourth coordinate is necessary (in their work, the authors estimate the total lit length and then only perform two lookups in the table assuming lit section starts at the camera). Fortunately, integrand function varies slowly, thus even stair-step integration yields quite accurate results. We also attempted to use trapezoidal integration, but did not observe any notable quality improvement while performance plummeted. Note that in contrast to computation of the coarse in-scattering integral, which is done using only seven steps, many more steps are performed during the actual ray marching.

12.8 Implementation

We used DirectX 11 to implement our algorithm. The full source code can be found in the book's supplemental materials. It is also available on Intel Developer Zone (http://software.intel.com/en-us/blogs/2013/09/19/otdoor-light -scattering-sample-update) and GitHub (https://github.com/GameTechDev/ OutdoorLightScattering). Some important implementation details follow.

12.8.1 Algorithm Workflow

The algorithm goes through the following steps:

1. Render the camera-space z coordinate to a screen-size texture `tex2DCam SpaceZ` ($W_{Scr} \times H_{Scr}$, $R32F$) by inverting the depths from the depth buffer `tex2DDepthBuffer` ($W_{Scr} \times H_{Scr}$, $D32F$).

2. Compute the screen-space coordinates of the end points of each epipolar line (Section 12.6) and render them to a $N_{Slices} \times 1$ auxiliary texture `tex2DSliceEndPoints` ($RGBA32F$).

3. Render coordinate texture `tex2DCoordinates` ($N_{Samples} \times N_{Slices}$, $RG32F$), epipolar camera-space z texture `tex2DEpipolarCamSpaceZ` ($N_{Samples} \times N_{Slices}$, $R32F$) and set up stencil buffer `tex2DEpipolarStencil` ($N_{Samples} \times N_{Slices}$, $D24US8$).

   (a) The screen-space coordinates of each epipolar sample on the line are computed by interpolating the line end points loaded from the `tex2DSliceEndPoints` texture (Section 12.6).

   (b) To compute the camera-space z coordinate for the sample, `tex2DCamSpaceZ` texture is linearly filtered at the sample location.

   (c) Stencil buffer `tex2DEpipolarStencil` is set up to mark only these samples that are located on the screen. This is implemented by setting up increment stencil function and discarding those samples that fall outside the screen.

4. For each valid epipolar sample, compute the coarse in-scattering integral as described in Section 12.6 and store it in the `tex2DInitialInsctr` texture ($N_{Samples} \times N_{Slices}$, $RGBA16F$).

   (a) Stencil `tex2DEpipolarStencil` is used to cull all invalid samples.

   (b) Trapezoidal integration with $N_{Steps} = 7$ provides a good trade-off between accuracy and performance.

   (c) Here we also render extinction texture `tex2DEpipolarExtinction` ($N_{Samples} \times N_{Slices}$, $RGBA8U$), which will be used to attenuate background.

5. Next, coarse in-scattering stored in the `tex2DInitialInsctr` texture is used to refine sampling and compute interpolation source texture `tex2DInterpolationSource` ($N_{Samples} \times N_{Slices}$, $RG16U$). Details follow in Section 12.8.2.

6. After that, determine the slice origin and direction for each epipolar slice in each shadow cascade as described in Section 12.7.2, and store them in another auxiliary texture `tex2DSliceUVDirAndOrigin` ($N_{Slices} \times N_{Cascades}$, $RGBA32F$).

7. Min/max binary trees are then constructed as described in Section 12.7.2 and stored in the `tex2DMinMaxDepth` ($SM_{Dim} \times (N_{Slices} \cdot N_{Cascades})$, $RG16U$) texture. Details follow in Section 12.8.3.

   (a) `tex2DSliceUVDirAndOrigin` texture is used to fetch zeroth sample and direction, compute locations of the required samples, and build the first level.

   (b) All coarse levels are then rendered.

8. Next, use interpolation source texture `tex2DInterpolationSource` to update the stencil `tex2DEpipolarStencil` and mark these samples, for which we will execute ray marching. For all these samples, the interpolation source indices are the same, which is how they can be detected. Note that all culled samples are not processed.

9. Perform ray marching for all the marked samples. The resulting in-scattering is rendered to `tex2DInitialInsctr` texture (which previously contained coarse in-scattering and is now reused). Details can be found in Section 12.8.4.

10. Next, the initial in-scattering `tex2DInitialInsctr` is interpolated on all eipolar samples using interpolation source texture `tex2DInterpolationSource` and is rendered to `tex2DEpipolarInscattering`.

11. Finally, in-scattering from `tex2DEpipolarInscattering` is transformed from epipolar space back to rectangular and added to the attenuated back buffer (Section 12.8.5).

Important details of the stages are presented in the following subsections.

12.8.2 Sample Refinement

The sample refinement stage generates the interpolation source texture `tex2DInterpolationSource`, which stores the indices of the two samples on the same line, from which the sample will be interpolated. This stage is implemented with a compute shader and consists of two steps. On the first step, a shared-memory array is populated with 1-bit flags indicating if there is significant difference in coarse in-scattering (loaded from `tex2DInitialInsctr`) between each two adjacent samples in this segment. Flags are computed as follows:

```
float3 f3MaxI = max(max(f3I0, f3I1), 1e-2);
bool NoBreak = all( (abs(f3I0 - f3I1)/f3MaxI) < Threshold );
```

The flags are packed as 32 bit uints using `InterlockedOr()`. On the second step, the interpolation source samples are identified using `firstbitlow()` and `firstbithigh()` intrinsic functions. They return the bit position of the first nonzero bit starting from the lowest-order bit and the highest-order bit, respectively.

12.8.3 1D Min/Max Binary Tree Construction

We store min/max binary trees as a $SM_{Dim} \times (N_{Slices} \cdot N_{Cascades})$ `RG_16UNORM` texture `tex2DMinMaxDepth`, which contains all trees for all slices in all shadow cascades. As discussed in Section 12.7.2, each 1D height map cannot contain more than SM_{Dim} samples. It is not necessary to store the height map itself, so all coarser levels can be packed into $SM_{Dim} - 1$ samples (in case the shadow map dimension is a power of two). We pack data so that level 1 starts at column $x = 0$, level 2 starts at column $x = SM_{Dim}/2$ and so on. The data for the ith cascade begins at row $y = N_{Slices} \cdot i$.

The first tree level is obtained by reading the slice origin O_{UV} and direction $\vec{D}_{UV}$ from the `tex2DSliceUVDirAndOrigin` texture, computing the locations of the two required samples on the shadow map ($O_{UV}+2i \cdot \vec{D}_{UV}$ and $O_{UV}+(2i+1) \cdot \vec{D}_{UV}$) and the min/max depth. To obtain conservative bounds, we use the `Gather()` instruction to fetch four depths, which would be used if PCF filtering was performed, for each location. We use the 16-bit unorm texture to save memory and bandwidth. Since conversion from 32-bit float to 16-bit uint can lose precision, we have to be careful with proper rounding, as shown in the following snippet:

```
const float R16U_PRECISION = 1.f / (float)(1<<16);
fMinDepth = floor(fMinDepth/R16U_PRECISION)*R16U_PRECISION;
fMaxDepth =  ceil(fMaxDepth/R16U_PRECISION)*R16U_PRECISION;
```

Coarser levels are computed by reading min/max bounds from the two finer level nodes and taking minimum/maximum of these values. To implement this, we use two textures, setting them alternately as a source and destination. Since it is unlikely that very coarse tree levels could be reached, we limit the coarsest level step by 1/16 of the shadow map resolution. Rendering to low-resolution textures is inefficient on modern GPUs and numerical integration is less accurate when performing very long steps.

12.8.4 Ray Marching Shader

Ray marching shader implements the algorithm described in Section 12.7.3. `tex2D InitialInsctr` texture is set as the render target, while stencil `tex2DEpipolar Stencil` is used to execute the shader only for the marked ray marching samples. The shader full code is too long to be presented here, and Listing 12.2 contains only the most important lines, mentioning the remaining parts in comments.

We tried three strategies to process cascades. The first strategy renders each cascade in a single draw call and accumulates in-scattering in `tex2DInitialInsctr` texture using alpha blending. The second strategy uses instancing to perform this in a single draw call. The third strategy (shown in the listing) goes through all cascades in the shader. The last method works slightly better because common computations, like intersection with top of the atmosphere, are not duplicated, but the GPU is still fully utilized.

```
// Compute ray termination point, full ray length and view
// direction; truncate the ray against the top of the atmosphere
float3 f3RlghIn = 0;
float3 f3MieIn = 0;
float2 f2NetDensFromCam = 0;

for(uint Cascade=g_StartCscd; Cascade<g_NumCascades; ++Cascade)
{
  // Truncate view ray against min/max z range for the current
  // cascade, project onto the shadow map

  // Load slice origin and direction, compute integration
  // step f3UVAndDepthStep in shadow map space and in world
  // space, set up current position f3CurrUVAndDepth

  // Compute initial sample location in 1D height/map
  uint uiSamplePos =
    length(f2StartUV.xy - f2SliceOriginUV.xy)/fUVStepLen + 0.5;
  uint uiLevel = 0;
  int iDataOffset = -g_iSMDim; // Level 0 is not stored
  float fMarchedDist = 0;
  uint uiMinMaxTexYInd =
    uiSliceInd + (Cascade - g_StartCscd) * g_NumSlices;
  float fStep = 1.f;
  while( fMarchedDist < fRayLength )
  {
    IsInLight = 0;

    // If the sample is located at the appropriate position,
    // advance to the next coarser level
    if( (uiSamplePos & ((2<<uiLevel)-1)) == 0 )
    {
      iDataOffset += g_iSMDim >> uiLevel;
      uiLevel++;
      fStep *= 2.f;
    }

    while(uiLevel > 0)
    {
      // Compute depths at the ends of the current ray section
      float2 f2StartEndDepth;
      f2StartEndDepth.x = f3CurrUVAndDepth.z;
      f2StartEndDepth.y = f3CurrUVAndDepth.z +
                          f3UVAndDepthStep.z * (fStep-1);

      // Load min/max depths for the node
      float2 f2MinMaxDepth = g_tex2DMinMaxDepth.Load(
          uint3( (uiSamplePos>>uiLevel) + iDataOffset,
                 uiMinMaxTexYInd,
                 0) );

      IsInShadow = all( f2StartEndDepth >= f2MinMaxDepth.yy );
      IsInLight  = all( f2StartEndDepth <  f2MinMaxDepth.xx );

      if( IsInLight || IsInShadow )
          break; // If the ray section is fully lit or shadowed,
                 // we can break the loop
      // If the ray section is neither fully lit, nor
      // shadowed, we have to go to the finer level
      uiLevel--;
      iDataOffset -= g_iSMDim>>uiLevel;
      fStep /= 2.f;
    };
```

```
[branch]
if( uiLevel == 0 )
{
    // If we are at the finest level, sample the shadow
    // map with PCF at location f3CurrUVAndDepth.xy
    IsInLight = ...
}

// Execute body of the loop from Listing 12.1, using
// fStep as the scaler for the step length ds,
// update f3RlghIn, f3MieIn, f2NetDensFromCam
...

f3CurrUVAndDepth += f3UVAndDepthStep * fStep;
uiSamplePos += 1 << uiLevel;
fMarchedDist += fRayStepLengthWS * fStep;
}//while( fMarchedDist < fRayLength )

}//for(uint Cascade...)

// Add contribution from the ray section behind the shadow map

// Apply Rayleigh and Mie phase functions
```

Listing 12.2. Shader code for the optimized ray marching algorithm.

To improve performance, we skip one or two of the smallest cascades (global variable g_StartCscd stores index of the first cascade to process). Since light scattering effects are only visible at a large scale, this has negligible visual impact. We also limit maximum distance that is covered by shadow cascades to 300 km. Therefore we need to account for the scattering from the part of the ray behind the largest cascade, which is accomplished by trapezoidal integration in the end of the shader.

To distribute cascades, we use mixed logarithmic/linear partitioning. Note that shadow cascades must cover all the view frustum, because visibility is queried not only on surfaces, but in the whole visible volume. Optimized cascade distribution techniques, like those based on determining minimum/maximum extents of the visible geometry, should be used with care. Note also that the first cascade used for ray marching must cover camera.

12.8.5 Unwarping

The final stage of the algorithm transforms the interpolated radiance stored in the ptex2DEpipolarInscattering texture from epipolar to rectangular space. We perform this by finding the two closest epipolar lines and projecting the sample onto them. Then we use Gather() instruction to fetch camera-space z coordinates from tex2DEpipolarCamSpaceZ texture for the two closest samples on each line and compute bilateral weights by comparing them with z coordinate of the target screen pixel (loaded from tex2DCamSpaceZ). Using these bilateral weights, we tweak filtering locations to obtain weighted sums of in-scattering values on each epipolar line using Sample() instruction.

At the final step, we combine the in-scattering value with the attenuated back buffer according to Equation (12.3). Calculating extinction factor $T(O \to C)$ also requires some attention. One way to do this is to use a lookup table for the optical depth to the top of the atmosphere. Unfortunately, this method produces very noticeable artifacts near the horizon due to the limited precision of 32-bit float values and interpolation issues. Numerically integrating optical thickness (Equation (12.1)) is also not an option. We use another method. When computing coarse in-scattering required to refine sampling, we also compute extinction anyway. So we store it in `tex2DEpipolarExtinction` texture and then transform it back to rectangular coordinates in the same manner as in-scattering. The resulting extinction is then used to attenuate background.

Since in-scattering is computed in high dynamic range, we perform simple tone mapping to convert the final color to low dynamic range using the following expression: `1.0 - exp(-fExposure * f3Color)`.

12.9   Results and Discussion

Figure 12.8 shows different images produced by our algorithm for various times of day and camera locations. Our technique is suitable for a wide range of graphics hardware, as it has a number of different parameters, such as $N_{Samples}$ and N_{Slices}, which enable trading quality for performance. We conducted our experiments on two different platforms. The first platform was a desktop workstation equipped with the Intel Core i7 CPU and NVidia GeForce GTX 680 high-end discrete GPU (195W TDP). The second platform was an ultrabook powered by Intel Core i5 processor and Intel HD graphics 5000 integrated GPU (15W TDP

Figure 12.8. Visual results generated by our algorithm.

Profile	SM Res $\times N_{Cscd}$	First cascade	N_{Slices}	$N_{Samples}$	Time, ms	Mem, MB
Brute force	$2048^2 \times 6$	1			304	
High qual	$2048^2 \times 6$	1	2048	1024	9.14	160
Balanced	$1024^2 \times 5$	1	1024	1024	3.45	56
High perf	$1024^2 \times 4$	2	1024	512	2.73	28

Table 12.1. Profile settings for NVidia GeForce GTX 680 (2560 × 1600 resolution).

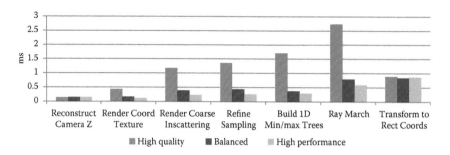

Figure 12.9. Performance of different stages of the algorithm on NVidia GeForce GTX 680 (2560 × 1600 resolution).

shared between CPU and GPU). On each platform, we rendered the scattering effects using brute force ray marching (which is run for every screen pixel and does not exploit 1D min/max trees) and three different quality profiles: high quality, balanced, and high performance. Results for the first test platform (images rendered at resolution of 2560 × 1600) can be found in Table 12.1 and Figure 12.9. Table 12.2 and Figure 12.10 show results for the second platform (images rendered at resolution of 1280 × 720). Initial epipolar line sampling step was set to 16 in all the experiments.

On both platforms, the results in the high quality profile are visually identical to the image generated by the brute force ray marching. At the same time, the performance improvement over brute force algorithm is more than 33× and 8.8× on NVidia and Intel platforms correspondingly. The balanced quality profile generates an image that is only slightly different from high quality and brute force ray marching, but it gives an additional performance advantage of 2.6× and 2.3× on our test platforms. On NVidia GTX 680, less than 3.5 ms are required to render the artifacts-free image at 2560 × 1600 resolution. The high performance profile reduces the computation times further, but image quality suffers. It must be noted that even in high performance profile, the rendered image still looks very convincing, as Figure 12.11 shows. The image does not exhibit aliasing artifacts, like stair-step patterns. Some temporal artifacts could be visible, but these are caused by low shadow map resolution, which generally affects shadow quality.

Profile	SM Res $\times N_{Cscd}$	First cascade	N_{Slices}	$N_{Samples}$	Time, ms	Mem, MB
Brute force	$1024^2 \times 6$	1			209.6	
High qual	$1024^2 \times 6$	1	1024	1024	23.6	60
Balanced	$1024^2 \times 5$	1	512	512	10.35	18
High perf	$512^2 \times 4$	2	512	256	6.19	7

Table 12.2. Quality settings for Intel HD Graphics 5000 (1280×720 resolution).

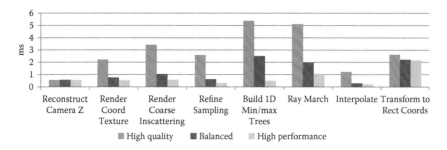

Figure 12.10. Performance of different stages of the algorithm on Intel HD Graphics 5000 (1280×720 resolution).

Memory requirements shown in the tables reflect only the amount of memory required to store algorithm-specific resources. They do not take into account shadow map size, back buffer size or camera-space z coordinate texture. The memory requirements may seem to be high, but if we take into account the fact that 16-bit float color buffer and 32-bit depth buffer at 2560×1600 resolution occupy 49 MB, memory consumption starts to look reasonable. Besides, 56 MB required for balanced profile is less than 3% of 2GB video memory available on GTX 680.

Timings for the individual steps of the algorithm are given in Figures 12.9 and 12.10. Some minor steps are not shown on the charts. The algorithmic complexity of the first and last steps does not depend on the quality settings and so is almost constant. Slight variations are caused by different sizes of textures being accessed from the shaders. Transformation from epipolar to rectangular coordinates takes ~ 0.9 ms on NVidia hardware. The ray marching step dominates in the high quality profile, while in the balanced profile it takes about the same time as final un-warping. In the high performance profile, the time of the last step dominates, so decreasing quality settings even further will not give noticeable speed-up (but will save some memory).

On Intel HD graphics 5000 hardware, the picture differs because this GPU has lower relative memory bandwidth. As a result, constructing 1D min/max binary trees, a purely bandwidth-limited step, takes more time than ray marching for

Figure 12.11. In-scattering only rendered on Intel HD graphics 5000 in high performance profile.

high-resolution shadow maps. Even when taking this time into account, the optimized algorithm is always faster.

Table 12.3 shows performance speed-ups obtained by using 1D min/max binary trees for different quality profiles for both test platforms. The RM column displays the performance improvement to the ray marching algorithm alone; the RM+MMT column shows the speed-up of the two steps: ray marching and constructing 1D min/max tees. The third column shows the performance improvement of the whole algorithm.

As Table 12.3 shows, using 1D min/max trees significantly reduces the execution times of the ray marching step. The performance gain is higher for high-resolution shadow maps (high quality profiles) as longer ray sections in shadow map space can be efficiently processed. This results in a speed-up of up to $8.6\times$ on NVidia and up to $5.3\times$ on the Intel platform. Taking the tree construction

Profile	NVidia GTX 680			Intel HD graphics 5000		
	RM	RM+MMT	Total	RM	RM+MMT	Total
High qual	8.6	5.3	3.8	5.3	2.6	1.7
Balanced	3.6	2.5	1.5	4.0	1.8	1.3
High perf	2.7	1.8	1.3	1.6	1.1	1.1

Table 12.3. Performance gains obtained by using 1D min/max trees.

time into account, up to 5.3× and up to 2.6× speedup is observed. Even in the high performance profile when a low-resolution shadow map is used, the ray marching still benefits from using 1D min/max binary trees.

In our algorithm, we exploited a simple strategy to place $N_{Slices}/4$ exit points on each boundary of the screen, primarily for the sake of simplicity. Therefore, the maximum distance between the two closest epipolar lines is always less than $\Delta_{Slice} = 4 \cdot \max(H_{Scr}, W_{Scr})/N_{Slices}$ pixels. Maximum distance between two samples on one epipolar line does not exceed

$$\Delta_{Sample} = \frac{\sqrt{H_{Scr}^2 + W_{Scr}^2}}{N_{Samples} - 1}.$$

Thus maximum screen-space distance from any pixel to the closest epipolar sample is bounded by the

$$0.5\sqrt{\Delta_{Slice}^2 + \Delta_{Sample}^2}.$$

For our first test platform this formula gives us 2.9, 5.2 and 5.8 pixels of maximum error for the high quality, balanced and high performance profiles, respectively. For our second platform, it gives 2.6, 5.2 and 5.7 pixels of maximum error. Since this analysis accounts for the worst case scenario, in practice the error is always much smaller than this estimation. Therefore, bilateral filtering can be performed accurately for the majority of pixels, producing convincing visual results even in the high performance profile. Note that a more sophisticated slice distribution method could be used to guarantee a predefined maximum screen-space error [Baran et al. 10].

Our algorithm can be extended to support MSAA. Most steps are performed in epipolar space and will thus be the same. The only step that requires modification is the transformation from epipolar to rectangular space. It could be broken into two sub-passes: pixel pass and sample pass. The pixel pass will be identical to the one described in Section 12.8.5 and will render to non-MSAA buffer. The per-sample pass will execute over the MSAA buffer. It will use an antialiasing mask (which is usually available when MSAA-enabled post-processing is performed) to distinguish between pixels that do not require antialiasing and those that require it. For pixels from the first group, the algorithm would read in-scattering from the non-MSAA back buffer and store it in all samples. For these pixels, which require antialiasing, the shader performs the same unwarping steps, but for each particular sample. To improve performance, the last two sub-passes can be split using stencil masking.

It is also relatively easy to extend our algorithm to approximate multiple scattering by pre-computing the secondary and higher-order scatterings and storing them in a lookup table (refer to [Bruneton and Neyret 08]). After completing ray marching, two lookups into the table will be required to approximate the effects of higher-order scattering along the ray. The average light occlusion along the ray could also be easily estimated and accounted for. While having only subtle impact during the day time, multiple scattering will improve appearance of twilight sky notably.

12.10   Conclusion and Future Work

We presented a high-performance technique for rendering light scattering effects in the Earth's atmosphere. This technique exploits epipolar sampling to efficiently reduce the number of times expensive ray marching is executed. The 1D min/max binary trees accelerate in-scattering integral calculation, and integration with cascaded shadow maps allows rendering large outdoor environments. Thanks to the number of different parameters that trade quality for performance, the technique scales from high-end discrete GPUs to low-power integrated graphics solutions. We plan on adding support for rendering dynamic clouds in the future.

Bibliography

[Baran et al. 10] Ilya Baran, Jiawen Chen, Jonathan Ragan-Kelley, Frédo Durand, and Jaakko Lehtinen. "A Hierarchical Volumetric Shadow Algorithm for Single Scattering." *ACM Transactions on Graphics* 29:6 (2010), 178:1–178:9.

[Bruneton and Neyret 08] Éric Bruneton and Fabrice Neyret. "Precomputed Atmospheric Scattering." *Special Issue: Proceedings of the 19th Eurographics Symposium on Rendering 2008, Computer Graphics Forum* 27:4 (2008), 1079–1086.

[Chen et al. 11] J. Chen, I. Baran, F. Durand, and W. Jarosz. "Real-Time Volumetric Shadows Using 1D Min-max Mip-maps." In *Proceedings of the Symposium on Interactive 3D Graphics and Games*, pp. 39–46. New York: ACM, 2011.

[Dobashi et al. 02] Y. Dobashi, T. Yamamoto, and T. Nishita. "Interactive Rendering of Atmospheric Scattering Effects Using Graphics Hardware." In *Graphics Hardware 2002*, pp. 99–107. Aire-la-Ville, Switzerland: Eurographics Association, 2002.

[Engel 07] Wolfgang Engel. "Cascaded Shadow Maps." In *ShaderX5: Advanced Rendering Techniques*, edited by Wolfgang Engel, pp. 197–206. Hingham, MA: Charles River Media, 2007.

[Engelhardt and Dachsbacher 10] T. Engelhardt and C. Dachsbacher. "Epipolar Sampling for Shadows and Crepuscular Rays in Participating Media with Single Scattering." In *ACM SIGGRAPH Symposium on Interactive 3D Graphics and Games*, pp. 119–125. New York: ACM, 2010.

[Haber et al. 05] Jörg Haber, Marcus Magnor, and Hans-Peter Seidel. "Physically-Based Simulation of Twilight Phenomena." *ACM Transactions on Graphics* 24:4 (2005), 1353–1373.

[Hoffman and Preetham 02] N. Hoffman and A. J. Preetham. "Rendering Outdoor Light Scattering in Real Time." Presentation, Game Developers Conference 2002, San Jose, CA, March, 2002.

[Klassen 87] R. Victor Klassen. "Modeling the Effect of the Atmosphere on Light." *ACM Transactions on Graphics* 6:3 (1987), 215–237.

[Mitchell 08] Kenny Mitchell. "Volumetric Light Scattering as a Post-Process." In *GPU Gems 3*, edited by Hubert Nguyen, pp. 275–285. Upper Saddle River, NJ: Addison-Wesley, 2008.

[Nishita et al. 93] Tomoyuki Nishita, Takao Sirai, Katsumi Tadamura, and Eihachiro Nakamae. "Display of the Earth Taking into Account Atmospheric Scattering." In *Proceedings of the 20st Annual Conference on Computer Graphics and Interactive Techniques, SIGGRAPH 1993*, pp. 175–182. New York: ACM, 1993.

[O'Neil 04] Sean O'Neil. "Real-Time Atmospheric Scattering." *GameDev.net*, http://www.gamedev.net/page/resources/_/technical/graphics-programming-and-theory/real-time-atmospheric-scattering-r2093, 2004.

[O'Neil 05] Sean O'Neil. "Accurate Atmospheric Scattering." In *GPU Gems 2*, edited by Matt Pharr. Upper Saddle River, NJ: Addison-Wesley, 2005.

[Preetham et al. 99] A. J. Preetham, P. Shirley, and B. Smits. "A Practical Analytic Model for Daylight." In *Proceedings of ACM SIGGRAPH*, pp. 91–100. New York: ACM, 1999.

[Riley et al. 04] Kirk Riley, David S. Ebert, Martin Kraus, Jerry Tessendorf, and Charles D. Hansen. "Efficient Rendering of Atmospheric Phenomena." In *Rendering Techniques*, edited by Alexander Keller and Henrik Wann Jensen, pp. 374–386. Aire-la-Ville, Switzerland: Eurographics Association, 2004.

[Schafhitzel et al. 07] Tobias Schafhitzel, Martin Falk, and Thomas Ertl. "Real-Time Rendering of Planets with Atmospheres." *Journal of WSCG* 15:1–3 (2007), 91–98.

[Schüler 12] Christian Schüler. "An Approximation to the Chapman Grazing-Incidence Function for Atmospheric Scattering." In *GPU Pro 3*, edited by Wolfgang Engel, pp. 105–118. Natick, MA: A K Peters, 2012.

[Tevs et al. 08] A. Tevs, I. Ihrke, and H.-P. Seidel. "Maximum Mip-maps for Fast, Accurate, and Scalable Dynamic Height Field Rendering." In *Proceedings of the 2008 Symposium on Interactive 3D Graphics and Games*, pp. 183–190. New York: ACM, 2008.

[Yusov 13] Egor Yusov. "Practical Implementation of Light Scattering Effects Using Epipolar Sampling and 1D Min/Max Binary Trees." Presentation, Game Developers Conference 2013, San Francisco, CA, March, 2013. Available online (http://gdcvault.com/play/1018227/Practical-Implementation-of-Light-Scattering).

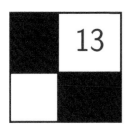

Hi-Z Screen-Space
Cone-Traced Reflections
Yasin Uludag

13.1 Overview

This chapter will introduce a novel approach for calculating reflections on dynamic 3D scenes, one that works on arbitrary shaped surfaces. Algorithms and techniques that were researched during the early development of *Mirror's Edge* are presented and shared.

The methods we will look into outperform any other methods both in terms of performance and image quality, as can be seen in Section 13.8, "Performance," and Section 13.9, "Results."

We will take a look into the latest work done in the area of real-time reflections, analyze their pros and cons and where they fail to deliver. Then we'll look into a new approach for calculating reflections in real time at game interactive frame rates.

First we will present the algorithm itself, which uses a screen-space aligned quad tree we call *Hierarchical-Z* (Hi-Z) buffer to accelerate the ray tracing. The hierarchy is stored in the MIP channels of the Hi-Z texture. This acceleration structure is used for empty space skipping to efficiently arrive at the intersection point. We will further discuss all the pre-computation passes needed for glossy reflections and how they can be constructed. We will also look into a technique called screen-space cone tracing for approximating rough surfaces, which produce blurred reflections. Moreover, performance and optimization for the algorithm are discussed. Then extensions to the algorithm are shown for improving and stabilizing the result. One such extension is temporal filtering, which allows us to accumulate the reflection results of several previous frames to stabilize the output result of the current frame by re-projecting the previous images even when the camera moves. The ability to approximate multiple ray bounces for reflections within reflections comes for free when doing temporal filtering because the previous frames already contain the reflections. Research and development techniques currently being developed will be mentioned, such as packet tracing for grouping several rays together into a packet and then refining/subdividing and shooting smaller ray packets once a coarse intersection is found. Another direction for future research that will be mentioned is screen-space tile-based tracing where if an entire tile contains mostly rough surfaces we know we can shoot fewer rays because the result will most likely be blurred, thereby gaining major performance, which gives us more room for other types of calculations for producing better images.

Finally timers will be shown for PCs. For the PC we will use both NVIDIA- and AMD-based graphics cards. Before we conclude the chapter, we will also mention some future ideas and thoughts that are being currently researched and developed.

This novel and production-proven approach (used in *Mirror's Edge*), proposed in this chapter guarantees maximum quality, stability, and good performance for computing local reflections, especially when it is used in conjunction with the already available methods in the game industry such as local cube-maps [Bjorke 07, Behc 10]. Specific attention is given to calculating physically accurate glossy/rough reflections matching how the stretching and spreading of the reflections behave in real life from different angles, a phenomenon caused by micro fractures.

13.2   Introduction

Let's start with the actual definition of a reflection:

> *Reflection* is the change in direction of a wave, such as a light or sound wave, away from a boundary the wave encounters. Reflected waves remain in their original medium rather than entering the medium they encounter. According to the *law of reflection*, the angle of reflection of a reflected wave is equal to its angle of incidence (Figure 13.1).

Reflections are an essential part of lighting; everything the human eye perceives is a reflection, whether it's a specular (mirror), glossy (rough), or diffusive

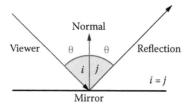

Figure 13.1. Law of reflection states that incident angle i equals reflection angle j.

Figure 13.2. Impact of reflections toward the goal of achieving photorealism. Notice the reflection occlusion near the contact points of the floor and the door blocking the incident light.

reflection (matte). It's an important part of achieving realism in materials and lighting. Reflection occlusion also helps out with grounding the object being reflected into the scene at the contact points, as we can see in Figures 13.2 and 13.3. It's an important part of our visual understanding of reality and it shouldn't be taken lightly, as it can make a big difference in achieving realism.

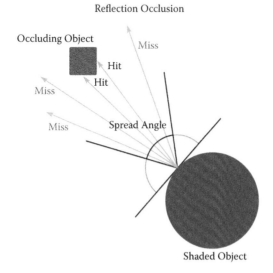

Figure 13.3. Illustration showing reflection occlusion where the hit rays block the light just like the door blocks the white light in Figure 13.2.

There has been little development lately for producing accurate reflections, especially glossy reflections, in the real-time graphics industry at high performance game frame-rate levels, meaning an algorithm has to run at a fraction of our per frame millisecond budget.

Solving reflections in computer games has been a big challenge due to the high performance requirements of the computations. We have a limited budget of milliseconds to spare for each frame, 16.6 milliseconds for 60 FPS and 33.33 milliseconds for 30 FPS, to recalculate everything and present an image to the user. This includes everything from game simulation, physics, graphics, AI to Network, etc. If we don't keep the performance level at such small fractions of a second, the user will not experience feedback in real time when giving input to the game. Now imagine that a fraction of those milliseconds needs to go to reflections only. Coming up with an algorithm that runs as fast as a few milliseconds and still keeps the quality level at maximum is hard using rasterization-based techniques that GPU hardware runs on.

Though game developers have been able to produce fake reflections for a very long time on simple cases, there is no solution that fixes every issue up to an acceptable level of realism with the performance levels required. For planar surfaces, meaning walls and floors, it's easy to flip the camera and re-render the entire scene and project the resulting image onto the planar surface to achieve what we today call planar reflections. This works for planar surfaces such as floors and walls but it's a completely different story for arbitrarily shaped surfaces that can reflect toward any direction per pixel. Re-rendering the entire scene and re-calculating all the lightings per plane is also an expensive operation and can quickly become a bottleneck.

The only solution that gives perfect results existing today is what we call ray tracing. But, tracing reflected rays and mathematically intersecting geometric primitives (a bunch of small triangles that make up the 3D world) is computationally and also memory heavy both in terms of bandwidth and size, because the rays could really go anywhere and we would need to keep the entire 3D scene in memory in a traversable and fast-to-access data structure. Even today, with the most optimized algorithms and data structures, ray tracing is still not fast enough in terms of performance to be deployed on games.

13.3　Previous Work

Generating 100% accurate and efficient reflections is difficult if not impossible with rasterization-based hardware used in GPUs today. Though we have moved on toward more general computing architectures allowing us more freedom, it's still not efficient enough to use a real ray tracer. For this reason game developers have for a long time relied on planar reflections where you re-render the scene from a mirrored camera for each plane, such as floors or walls, and project the image

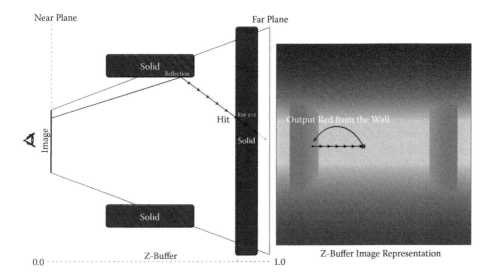

Figure 13.4. Ray marching by taking small steps in screen space using the Z-buffer (depth buffer, an image representing scene depth in floating point numbers) until the ray depth is below the surface. Once it is below the surface, we can stop the ray marching and use the new coordinates to acquire the reflection color and apply it on the pixel we started the marching from.

to create a planar reflection. Another technique that has been relied upon for a very long time is cube-maps, six images capturing 360 degrees of the surrounding environment from a single point with a 90-degree field of view for each side, hence these reflections are only valid from that specific point only.

A new idea called screen-space local reflections was first showed by [Graham 10] at Beyond3D forums and then later introduced into Crysis 2 DX11 patch by Crytek [Tiago et al. 12]. They both proposed a simple ray marching algorithm in screen space. Screen space means that we do everything in 2D framebuffer objects, images, as a post-processing effect.

It's a fairly simple idea; you just compute a screen-space reflection vector using the scene normal buffer and ray-march through the pixels at a certain step size until the ray depth falls below the scene depth stored in what we call a depth buffer. Once the ray depth is below the scene depth, we detect a hit and use the new screen-space coordinate to read the scene color, which is used as reflection for the pixel we started the ray-marching from. This technique is illustrated in Figure 13.4.

However since this computation is performed in screen space, there are limitations that need to be taken care of. A built-in problem with this kind of technique is that not all of the information is available to us. Imagine a mirror reflecting the ray in the opposite direction of the view direction; this information is not available in screen space. This means that occlusion and missing information is a huge challenge for this technique and if we do not deal with this problem we will have artifacts and produce incorrect reflection colors. Smoothly fading rays that fall outside the screen borders, fall behind objects that occlude information and rays that point toward the camera are recommended.

On the other hand this type of linear ray marching can be really efficient if you do a low number of steps/samples for very short range reflections. As soon as you have really long rays this method starts to perform really slowly because of all the texture fetches it requires at each loop to acquire the scene depth from the Z-buffer. Due to this latency hiding starts to diminish and our cores basically stall, doing nothing.

It's also error prone such that it can miss very small details due to taking a fixed constant step size at each sample. If the small detail next to the ray is smaller than the step size, we might jump over it and have an incorrect reflection. The number of steps taken and how large those steps are make a huge difference in terms of quality for this kind of linear ray marching. This technique also produces staircase artifacts, for which you have to employ some form of a refinement once an intersection point is found. This refinement would be between the previous ray-march position and the ray-march intersection point to converge into a much more refined intersection. A low number of binary search steps or a single secant search is usually enough to deal with the staircase artifacts for pure specular rays. (See Figure 13.5.) Crytek employs ray length jittering at each iteration step to hide the staircase artifacts.

A simple linear ray-marching algorithm that traverses the depth buffer can be written with fewer than 15 lines of code, as we can see in Listing 13.1.

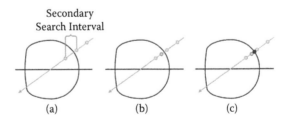

Figure 13.5. Binary search illustration between the intersection position and the last position of the ray. Basically it takes the middle point of the two and checks if it's still intersecting; if true it does it again until it can resurface, which is a refined position. We can also visualize the constant step sizes linear ray marching takes and end up in the wrong coordinate, which results in staircase artifacts, so we need some form of a refinement. Binary search and secant search are popular ones. [Original image courtesy of [Risser 07].]

```
#define LINEAR_MARCH_COUNT 32
for(int i = 0; i < LINEAR_MARCH_COUNT; ++i)
{
    // Read scene depth with current ray.
    float d = depthBuffer.SampleLevel( pointSampler, ray.xy, 0 );

    // Check if ray is greater than the scene, it means we
    // intersected something so end.
    if( ray.z > d )
        break;

    // Else advance the ray by a small step and continue the
    // loop. Step is a vector in screen space.
    ray += step;
}
```

Listing 13.1. A simple linear ray marching to illustrate the concept of walking a depth buffer until an intersection is found. We can quickly see that this technique is fetch bound. The ALU units are not doing a lot of work as there are too few ALU instructions to hide the latency of the global memory fetches the shader has to wait to complete.

So let's take a close look at some major problems for this kind of a technique.

1. It takes small-sized steps, it conducts many fetches, and latency starts to bottleneck quickly.

2. It can miss small details in the case that the step it takes is larger than the small detail next to the ray.

3. It produces staircase artifacts and needs a refinement such as a secant or binary search.

4. It is only fast for short travels; ray-marching an entire scene will stall the cores and result in slow performance.

Our goal is to introduce an algorithm that can solve all four points.

All of those points can be solved by introducing an acceleration structure, which can then be used to accelerate our rays, basically traversing as much distance as the ray can possibly take without risking missing any details at all. This acceleration structure will allow the ray to take arbitrary length steps, and especially large ones as well whenever it can. It's also going to conduct fewer fetches and thereby perform faster. The acceleration structure is going to produce great results without needing an extra refinement pass, although it doesn't hurt to do a final secant search between the previous pixel and the current pixel because an acceleration structure is usually a discrete set of data. Since we gain major speedups by using an acceleration structure, we will also be able to travel longer and ray-march an entire scene with much better performance.

The algorithm called Hi-Z Screen-Space Cone Tracing proposed in this chapter can reflect an entire scene with quick convergence and performs orders of magnitude faster than the linear constant step-based ray-marching algorithm.

13.4   Algorithm

The proposed algorithm can be divided into five distinct steps:

1. Hi-Z pass,

2. pre-integration pass,

3. ray-tracing pass,

4. pre-convolution pass,

5. cone-tracing pass.

We will go through each step by step now.

13.4.1   Hi-Z Pass

The *Hierarchical-Z buffer*, also known as the Hi-Z buffer, is constructed by taking the minimum or maximum of the four neighboring values in the original Z-buffer and storing it in a smaller buffer at half the size. In our case for this chapter, we will go with the minimum version.

The Z-buffer holds the depth values of the 3D scene in a buffer such as a texture/image. The figure below represents the minimum value version of how a Hi-Z construction works:

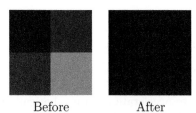

Before   After

The result is a coarse representation of the original buffer. We do this consecutively on the resulting buffers until we arrive at a buffer with the size of 1, where we no longer can go smaller. We store the computed values in the mip-channels of a texture. This is represented in Figure 13.6.

The result is what we call a Hi-Z buffer, because it represents the Z values (also known as scene depth values) in a hierarchical fashion.

This buffer is the heart of the algorithm. It's essentially a screen/image aligned quad tree that allows us to accelerate the ray-tracing algorithm by noticing and

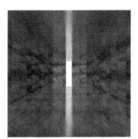

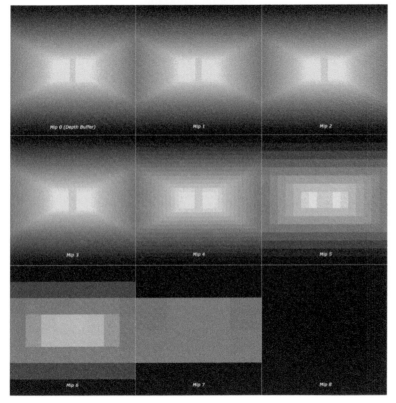

Figure 13.6. The original scene (top) and the corresponding Hi-Z (Hierarchical-Z) buffer (bottom) where the 2×2 minimum depths have been used successively to construct it. It serves as an acceleration structure for our rays in screen space. Mip 0 is our depth buffer that represents the scene depth per pixel. At each level we take the minimum of 2×2 pixels and produce this hierarchical representation of the depth values.

skipping empty space in the scene to efficiently and quickly arrive at our desired intersection point/coordinate by navigating in the different hierarchy levels. Empty space in our case is the tiles we see in the image, the quads.

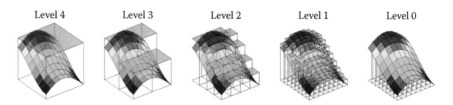

Figure 13.7. The Hi-Z (Hierarchical-Z) buffer, which has been unprojected from screen space into world space for visualization purposes. [Image courtesy of [Tevs et al. 08].]

Unlike the previously developed methods, which take constant small steps through the image, the marching method we investigate runs much faster by taking large steps and converges really quickly by navigating in the hierarchy levels.

Figure 13.7 shows a simple Hierarchical-Z representation unprojected from screen space back into world space for visualization purposes. It's essentially a height field where dark values are close to the camera and bright values are farther away from the camera.

Whether you construct this pass on a post-projected depth buffer or a view-space Z-buffer will affect how the rest of the passes are handled, and they will need to be changed accordingly.

13.4.2   Pre-integration Pass

The pre-integration pass calculates the scene visibility input for our cone-tracing pass in a hierarchical fashion. This pass borrows some ideas from [Crassin 11], [Crassin 12], and [Lilley et al. 12] that are applied to voxel structures and not 2.5D depth. The input for this pass is our Hi-Z buffer. At the root level all of our depth pixels are at a 100% visibility; however, as we go up in this hierarchy, the total visibility for the coarse representation of the cell has less or equal visibility to the four finer pixels:

$$\text{Visibility}_n \leq \text{Visibility}_{n-1}.$$

(See also Figure 13.8.) Think about the coarse depth cell as a volume containing the finer geometry. Our goal is to calculate how much visibility we have at the coarse level.

The cone-tracing pass will then sample this pre-integrated visibility buffer at various levels until our ray marching accumulates a visibility of 100%, which means that all the rays within this cone have hit something. This approximates the cone footprint. We are basically integrating all the glossy reflection rays. We start with a visibility of 1.0 for our ray; while we do the cone tracing, we will keep subtracting the amount we have accumulated until we reach 0.0. (See

Figure 13.8. The area of interest between the minimum and maximum depth plane of the four pixels for which we calculate the visibility; basically, take the percentage of empty volume.

Figure 13.9.) We cannot rely on only the visibility buffer, though. We must know how much our cone actually intersects the geometry as well, and for that we will utilize our Hi-Z buffer. Our final weight will be the accumulated visibility multiplied by how much our cone sphere is above, in between, or below the Hi-Z buffer.

The format for this pre-integration buffer is an 8 bit per channel texture that gives 256 values to represent our visibility. This gives 0.390625% of increments for our visibility values $(1.0/256.0)$, which is good enough precision for transparency.

Again, this pass is highly dependent on whether we have a post-projected depth Hi-Z or a view-space Hi-Z buffer.

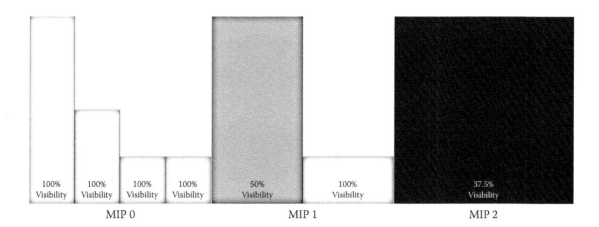

Figure 13.9. A 2D representation of the hierarchical pre-integrated visibility buffer. The percent is calculated between the minimum and maximum depths. The height is the depth and the color is the amount of visibility.

13.4.3 Ray-Tracing Pass

The following function is the reflection formula where $\vec{V}$ is the view direction and $\vec{N}$ is the surface normal direction (surface orientation) and the return value is the reflection vector:

$$Reflect(\vec{V}, \vec{N}) = 2(\vec{V} \cdot \vec{N})\vec{N} - \vec{V}.$$

The dot is the dot product, also known as the scalar product, between the two vectors. We will later use this function to calculate our reflection direction for the algorithm.

Before we continue with the ray-tracing algorithm, we have to understand what the depth buffer of a 3D scene actually contains. The depth buffer is referred to as being nonlinear, meaning that the distribution of the depth values of a 3D scene does not increase linearly with distance to the camera. We have a lot of precision close to the camera and less precision far away, which helps with determining which object is closest to the camera when drawing, because closer objects are more important than farther ones.

By definition division is a nonlinear operation and there is a division happening during perspective correction, which is where we get the nonlinearity from. A nonlinear value can't be linearly interpolated. However, while it is true that the Z-values in the depth buffer are not linearly increasing relative to the Z-distance from the camera, it is on the other hand indeed linear in screen space due to the perspective. Perspective-correct rasterization hardware requires linear interpolation across an entire triangle surface when drawing it from only three vertices. In particular the hardware interpolates 1/Z for each point that makes up the surface of the triangle using the original three vertices.

Linear interpolation of Z directly does not produce correct depth values across the triangle surface, though 1/Z does [Low 02]. Figure 13.10 explains why non-perspective interpolation is wrong.

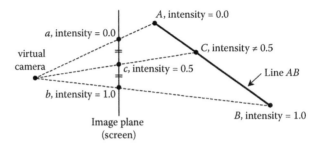

Figure 13.10. Illustration of interpolating an attribute directly in screen space giving incorrect results. One must do perspective correct interpolation as described in [Low 02]. The depth buffer value, 1/Z, is perspective correct so this allows us to interpolate it in screen space without any further computation.

We can observe the fact that the depth buffer values are linear in screen space, due to perspective, by taking the partial derivatives, gradients, of them using `ddx` and `ddy` instructions in Microsoft HLSL and outputting them as color values. For any planar surface the result is going to be a constant color, which tells us a linear rate of change the farther the planes are from the camera in screen space.

Anything that behaves linearly is also going to allow us to interpolate it, just like the hardware, which is a very powerful fact. It's also the reason we did the Hi-Z construction on the nonlinear depth buffer. Our ray tracing will happen in screen space, and we would like to exploit the fact that the depth buffer values can be interpolated correctly in screen space because they're perspective-corrected. It's like the perspective cancels out this nonlinearity of the values.

In the case that one desires to use a view-space Hi-Z buffer and not a post-projected buffer, one has to manually interpolate the Z-value just as perspective interpolation does, $1/Z$. Either case is possible and affects the rest of the passes as mentioned earlier. We will assume that we use a post-perspective Hi-Z from now on. Now that we know the depth buffer values can be interpolated in screen space, we can go back to the Hi-Z ray-tracing algorithm itself and use our Hi-Z buffer.

We can parameterize our ray-tracing algorithm to exploit the fact that depth buffer values can be interpolated. Let $\mathbf{O}$ be our starting screen coordinate, the origin, let the vector $\vec{D}$ be our reflection direction, and finally let t be our driving parameter between 0 and 1 that interpolates between the starting coordinate $\mathbf{O}$ and ending coordinate $\mathbf{O} + \vec{D}$:

$$Ray(t) = \mathbf{O} + \vec{D} * t,$$

where the vector $\vec{D}$ and point $\mathbf{O}$ are defined as

$$\vec{D} = \vec{V}_{ss}/\vec{V}_{ss_z},$$

$$\mathbf{O} = \mathbf{P_{ss}} + \vec{D} * -\mathbf{P_{ss_z}}.$$

$\vec{D}$ extends all the way to the far plane now. The division by $\vec{V}_z$ sets the Z-coordinate to 1.0, but it still points to the same direction because division by a scalar doesn't change a vector's direction. $\mathbf{O}$ is then set to the point that corresponds to a depth of 0.0, which is the near plane. We can visualize this as a line forming from the near plane to the far plane in the reflection direction crossing the point we are shading in Figure 13.11.

We can now input any value t to take us between the starting point and ending point for our ray-marching algorithm in screen space. The t value is going to be a function of our Hierarchical-Z buffer.

But we need to compute the vector $\vec{V}$ and $\mathbf{P}$ first to acquire $\mathbf{O}$ and $\vec{D}$. $\mathbf{P}$ is already available to us through the screen/texture coordinate and depth. To get $\vec{V}$ we need another screen-space point $\mathbf{P}'$, which corresponds to a point somewhere

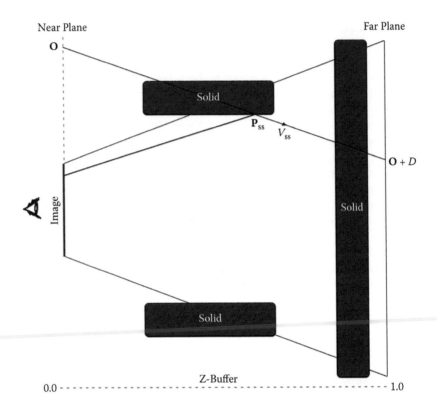

Figure 13.11. An illustration showing $\mathbf{O}$, $\vec{D}$, $\mathbf{P}$, and $\vec{V}$ variables from the equations. $\mathbf{O} + \vec{D} * t$ will take us anywhere between starting point $\mathbf{O}$ and ending point $\mathbf{O} + \vec{D}$ where t is between 0 and 1. Note that $\vec{V}$ is just a vector, direction, and has no position. It was put on the line for visualization purposes.

along the reflection direction. Taking the difference of these two will yield us a screen-space reflection vector:

$$\vec{V}_{ss} = \mathbf{P}'_{ss} - \mathbf{P}_{ss},$$

where the available $\mathbf{P}$ is defined as

$$\mathbf{P}_{ss} = \{\mathbf{texcoord_{xy}}\ \mathbf{depth}\}.$$

The other $\mathbf{P}'$ along the reflection direction can be computed by taking the view-space point, view-space direction, and view-space surface normal, computing a view-space reflection point, projecting it into clip space $[-1, 1]$ range, and finally converting from clip space into screen space $[0, 1]$ range, as we can see below:

$$\mathbf{P_{cs}} = (\mathbf{P_{vs}} + Reflect(\vec{V}_{vs}, \vec{N}_{vs})) * \mathbf{M_{proj}},$$

$$\mathbf{P'_{ss}} = \frac{\mathbf{P_{cs}}}{\mathbf{P_{cs_w}}} * [0.5 \quad -0.5] + [0.5 \quad 0.5].$$

Once we have a screen-space reflection vector, we can run the Hi-Z traversal to ray-march along the acceleration structure using $\mathbf{O}$, $\vec{D}$, and t.

We'll first look at the pseudo code in Listing 13.2. The algorithm uses the Hi-Z buffer we constructed earlier to accelerate the ray marching. To visualize the algorithm in Listing 13.2 step by step, follow Figure 13.12.

Once the ray-tracing algorithm has run, we have our new coordinate in screen space that is our ray intersection point. Some ideas are borrowed from displacement mapping techniques found in the literature [Hien and Lim 09, Hrkalovic and Lundgren 12, Oh et al. 06, Drobot 09, Szirmay-Kalos and Umenhoffer 06]. One major difference is that we start on the root level while displacement techniques start on the leaf level for marching a ray. Ray-marching with a view-space Z-buffer is a bit more involved because we have to manually interpolate the Z-coordinate as it is not possible to interpolate it in screen space.

```
level = 0 // starting level to traverse from

while level not below N // ray-trace until we descend below the
                        // root level defined by N, demo used 2

    minimumPlane  = getCellMinimumDepthPlane( . . . )
    // reads from the Hi-Z texture using our ray
    boundaryPlane = getCellBoundaryDepthPlane( . . . )
    // gets the distance to next Hi-Z cell boundary in ray
    // direction

    closestPlane  = min( minimumPlane , boundaryPlane )
    // gets closest of both planes

    ray = intersectPlane( . . . )
    // intersects the closest plane , returns O + D * t only.

    if intersectedMinimumDepthPlane
    // if we intersected the minimum plane we should go down a
    // level and continue
        descend a level

    if intersectedBoundaryDepthPlane
    // if we intersected the boundary plane we should go up a
    // level and continue
        ascend a level

color = getReflection( ray ) // we are now done with the Hi-Z ray
                             // marching so get color from the intersection
```

Listing 13.2. Pseudo code for implementing the Hi-Z ray tracing.

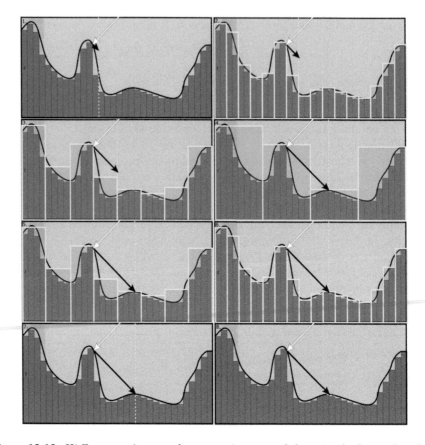

Figure 13.12. Hi-Z ray-tracing step by step going up and down in the hierarchy of the buffer to take longer jumps at each step. [Source image courtesy of [Drobot 09].]

13.4.4 Pre-convolution Pass

The pre-convolution pass is an essential pass for the algorithm for computing blurred glossy reflections emitted from microscopic rough surfaces. Just like in the Hi-Z pass, which outputs a hierarchy of images, this pass also does so, but with a different goal in mind.

We convolve the original scene color buffer to produce several different blurred versions out of it as we can see in Figure 13.13. The final result is another hierarchical representation, images at different resolutions with different levels of convolution, which is stored in the mip-map channels.

These blurred color buffers will help out with accelerating rough reflections to achieve results similar to what we can see in Figure 13.14.

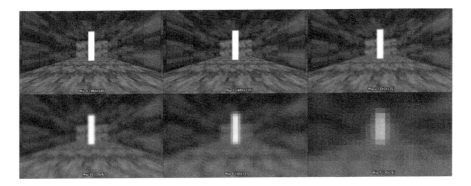

Figure 13.13. Convolved color texture of a simple scene with different level of convolution at each level. This will be later used to create our rough reflections.

Usually to simulate this kind of blurred reflections in ray-tracing-based renderers, we would shoot a lot of diverged rays defined by the cone aperture, say 32 more, and average the resulting colors together to produce a blurred reflection. (See Figures 13.15 and 13.16.)

However, this quickly becomes a very expensive operation and the performance decreases linearly with the number of rays we shoot, and even then the technique produces noisy and unacceptable results that need further processing to smooth out. One such technique is called image-space gathering [Robison and Shirley 09], which works really well even on pure mirror reflections to make them appear like rough reflections as a post-process.

Figure 13.14. Different levels of roughness on the spheres produce diverged reflection rays, which results in the viewer perceiving blurred reflections. [Image courtesy of [David 13].]

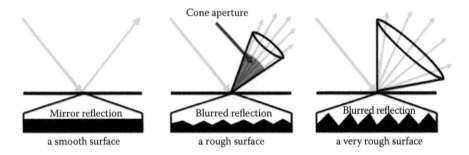

Figure 13.15. The rougher the surface is at a microscopic level, the more blurry and weaker the reflection appears. Fewer rays hit the iris of the perceivers' eye, which gives the weaker appearance. [Original image courtesy of [ScratchaPixel 12].]

Another drawback of shooting randomly jittered rays within the cone aperture is the fact that parallel computing hardware such as the GPU tends to run threads and memory transaction in groups/batches. If we introduce jittered rays we slow down the hardware because now all the memory transactions are in memory addresses far away from each other, slowing the computation by tremendous amounts because of cache-misses and global memory fetches, and bandwidth becomes a bottleneck.

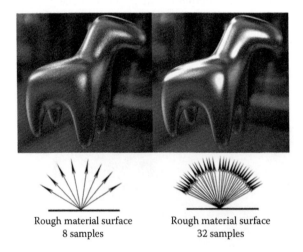

Figure 13.16. Noisy reflections produced by firing multiple diverged rays and averaging the results together for glossy reflections. Even 32 rays per pixel are not enough to create a perfectly smooth reflection and the performance decreases linearly with each additional ray. [Original images courtesy of [Autodesk 09] and [Luxion 12].]

Section 13.4.5 will propose a method that is merely an approximation but runs really fast without the need for firing multiple rays or jittering. By just navigating in the hierarchy of the blurred color images we discussed in this pass, depending on the reflection distance and roughness of the surface we are reflecting from, we can produce accurate glossy reflections.

13.4.5 Cone-Tracing Pass

The cone-tracing pass runs right after the Hi-Z ray-tracing pass finishes, and it produces the glossy reflections of the algorithm. This pass uses all our hierarchical buffers.

The output from the ray-tracing pass is our screen-space intersection coordinate as we saw earlier. With that we have all the knowledge to construct a screen-space aligned cone, which essentially becomes an isosceles triangle.

The idea is simple; Figure 13.17 shows a cone in screen space that corresponds to how much the floor diverges the reflection rays at maximum. Our goal is to accumulate all the color within that cone, basically integrate for every single ray that diverges. This integration can be approximated by sampling at the circle centers, where the size of the circle decides at which hierarchy level we read the color from our textures, as we saw in Section 13.4.3. Figure 13.18 illustrates this.

We determine whether the cone intersect our Hi-Z at all. If it does, we determine how much it intersects and multiply this weight with the pre-integrated visibility for that level and point. This final weight is accumulated until we reach 100%, and we weigh the color samples as well during the traversal. How you determine whether the cone intersects the Hi-Z for empty space is highly dependent on whether you use a post-projected Hi-Z or view-space Hi-Z.

First, we need to find the cone angle for a specific roughness level. Our reflection vector is basically the Phong reflection model because we just compute a reflection vector by reflecting the view direction on the normal. To approximate

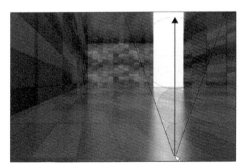

Figure 13.17. A cone in screen space is essentially an isosceles triangle with the in-radius circles that will be able to sample/read the hierarchical buffers.

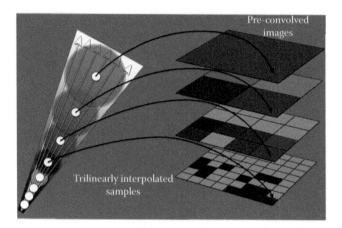

Figure 13.18. The cone integrates the rays, arrows, we see in the image by sampling, reading, at different levels in our convolved, blurred, color image depending on the distance and surface roughness. It blends both between the neighboring pixels and between the hierarchy levels, which is what we call *trilinear interpolation* for smooth transitions and blended results.

the cone angle for the Phong model, we use

$$\theta = \cos\left(\xi^{\frac{1}{\alpha+1}}\right), \tag{13.1}$$

where α is the specular power and ξ is hard-coded to 0.244. This is the basic formula used for importance sampling of a specular lobe; it is the inverse cumulative distribution function of the Phong distribution. Importance-sampling applications generate a bunch of uniform random variables [0–1] for ξ and use Equation (13.1) to generate random ray directions within the specular lobe in spherical coordinates [Lawrence 02]. The hard-coded value 0.244 seems to be a good number for covering a decent range of cone-angle extents. Figure 13.19 shows how well this equation maps to the cone angle extents of the Phong specular lobe in polar coordinates.

To get a perfectly mirrored ray with the Phong model, the specular power value would need to be infinity. Since that will not happen and graphics applications usually have a cap on their specular power value, we need a threshold value to support mirror reflections for the cone tracer. We can clearly see that there is not much change between a power of 1024 and 2048. So, any specular power in the range of 1024–2048 should be interpolated down to an angle of 0.

If we want another type of reflection model with more complicated distribution, we would need to pre-compute a 2D lookup table and index it with roughness as the u coordinate and $\vec{V}\cdot\vec{N}$ as the v coordinate, which would then return a local reflection direction. This local reflection direction would need to be transformed into a global reflection vector for the Hi-Z tracing pass.

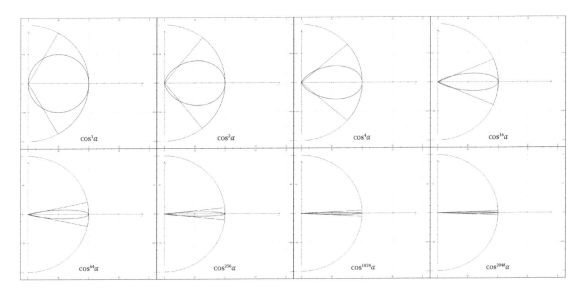

Figure 13.19. Polar coordinate plot of the specular lobe with various specular power values. The red ellipse is the specular lobe and the black isosceles triangle shows the cone angle extents using the formula presented earlier; α is the angle and $\cos \alpha$ is powered to various specular power values.

So, for any distribution model, we average at pre-computation time all the reflection vectors within the specular lobe—importance sampling using uniform random variables [0–1]—with a specific roughness value that gives the vector where the reflection vector is strongest, and then we store this vector in a 2D texture table. The reason we average all the reflection vectors within the lobe is the fact that complicated BRDF models often don't produce a lobe with respect to the pure specular reflection vector. They might be more vertically stretched or behave differently at grazing angles, and we are interested in finding the reflection vector that is the strongest within this specular lobe, which we can clearly see in Figure 13.20.

The RGB channel of this table would contain the local reflection vector and the alpha channel would contain either an isotropic cone-angle extent with a single value or anisotropic cone-angle extents with two values for achieving vertically stretched reflections, which we revisit later.

For this chapter, we just assume that we use a Phong model. We need to construct an isosceles triangle for the cone-tracing pass using the newly obtained angle θ. Let $\mathbf{P_1}$ be the start coordinate of our ray in screen space and $\mathbf{P_2}$ be the end coordinate of our ray, again in screen space. Then the length l is defined as

$$l = \|\triangle_{\mathbf{P}}\| = \|\mathbf{P_2} - \mathbf{P_1}\|.$$

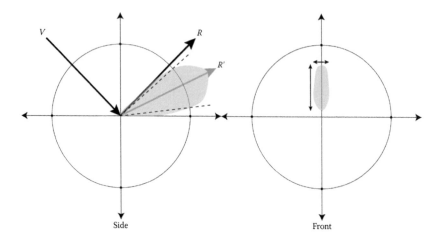

Side   Front

Figure 13.20. Spherical coordinate preview of a specular lobe for a complicated distribution. We can clearly see that the lobe does not necessarily need to be centered around the pure reflection vector. If we average all the vectors within the lobe, we get a new reflection vector $\vec{R}'$ that represents our reflection direction more precisely.

Once we have the length for our intersection, we can assume that it's the adjacent side of our isosceles triangle. With some simple trigonometry we can calculate the opposite side as well. Trigonometry says that the tangent of θ is the opposite side over the adjacent side:

$$\tan(\theta) = \frac{opp}{adj}.$$

Using some simple algebra we discover that the opposite side that we are looking for is the tangent of θ multiplied by the adjacent side:

$$opp = \tan(\theta)adj.$$

However, this is only true for right triangles. If we look at an isosceles triangle, we discover that it's actually two right triangles fused over the adjacent side where one is flipped. This means the opposite is actually twice the opposite of the right triangle:

$$opp = 2\tan(\theta)adj \tag{13.2}$$

Once we have both the adjacent side and the opposite side, we have all the data we need to calculate the sampling points for the cone-tracing pass. (See Figure 13.21.)

To calculate the in-radius (circle radius touching all three sides) of an isosceles triangle, this equation can be used:

$$r = \frac{a(\sqrt{a^2 + 4h^2} - a)}{4h},$$

where a is the base of the isosceles triangle, h is the height of the isosceles triangle, and r is the resulting in-radius. Recall that the height of the isosceles triangle is

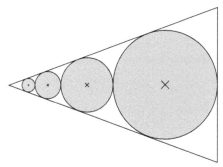

Sample ponts from ray start →ray finish

Figure 13.21. The isosceles triangle with the sampling points for the cone-tracing pass in screen space. To find the sample points of our cone in screen space, we have to use some geometry and calculate the in-radius of this isosceles triangle. Note that this is an approximation and we are not fully integrating the entire cone.

the length of our intersection we calculated before and the base of our isosceles triangle is the opposite side. Using this formula we find the radius of the in-radius circle. Once we have the in-radius of the isosceles triangle, we can take the adjacent side and subtract the in-radius from it to find the sampling point we are interested in. We can now read the color from the correct coordinate in screen space.

To calculate the rest of the sampling points, all we have to do is subtract the in-radius another time to reach the leftmost side of the circle and then recalculate the opposite side with this new adjacent side using Equation (13.2), and then rerun the in-radius formula to get the next smaller circle. We do this successively for as many samples as we want to take.

We accumulate the correct color by using a trilinear filtering scheme (smoothly filtering between the neighboring pixels and between the hierarchy levels). We also weigh the color with the transparency buffer and by how much our cone-sphere intersects the coarse depth cells. This is done in front-to-back order, so it is basically a linear search algorithm. The larger the cone is, the faster it runs. The weight is accumulated to know how much visibility is integrated. One might want to take smaller offsets between the circles to achieve smoother results; however, that gets more expensive. If the cone tracer doesn't accumulate a visibility of 100%, we can blend in the rest of the visibility using, say, cube-maps with the same roughness.

Again depending on the format of the Hi-Z buffer, if we use a view-space Z version, then how we determine whether the cone-sphere intersects the Hi-Z buffer—as well as how we calculate the sampling points on the cone—is different One can use the cone angle with the view-space Z distance to find the sphere size and then project this using perspective division into screen space, keeping aspect ratio in mind.

13.5   Implementation

We have now looked at all the algorithms; let's go through them in the same order again, looking at sample code for implementation details.

13.5.1   Hi-Z Pass

The code snippet in Listing 13.3 shows how to implement a Hi-Z construction pass in DirectX using Microsoft HLSL (High Level Shading Language). This shader is executed successively, and the results are stored in the mip-channels of the Hi-Z buffer. We read from level $N-1$ and write to N until we reach a size of 1×1 as mentioned in Section 13.4.1.

   To render into the same texture that we read from in DirectX 11 terms, we will have to make sure that our `ID3D11ShaderResourceView` objects point to a single mip-channel and not the entire range of mip-channels. The same rule applies to our `ID3D11RenderTargetViews` objects.

13.5.2   Pre-integration Pass

The code snippet in Listing 13.4 shows how to implement a pre-integration pass in DirectX using Microsoft HLSL. It basically calculates the percentage of empty

```
float4 main( PS_INPUT input ) : SV_Target
{
    // Texture/image coordinates to sample/load/read the depth
    // values with.
    float2 texcoords = input.tex;

    // Sample the depth values with different offsets each time.
    // We use point sampling to ignore the hardware bilinear
    // filter. The constant prevLevel is a global that the
    // application feeds with an integer to specify which level
    // to sample the depth values from at each successive
    // execution. It corresponds to the previous level.
    float4 minDepth;

    minDepth.x = depthBuffer.SampleLevel( pointSampler,
        texcoords, prevLevel, int2(  0,  0) );
    minDepth.y = depthBuffer.SampleLevel( pointSampler,
        texcoords, prevLevel, int2(  0, -1) );
    minDepth.z = depthBuffer.SampleLevel( pointSampler,
        texcoords, prevLevel, int2( -1,  0) );
    minDepth.w = depthBuffer.SampleLevel( pointSampler,
        texcoords, prevLevel, int2( -1, -1) );

    // Take the minimum of the four depth values and return it.
    float d = min( min(minDepth.x, minDepth.y), min(minDepth.z,
        minDepth.w) );

    return d;
}
```

Listing 13.3. How to implement the Hierarchical-Z buffer taking the minimum of 2×2 depth values from the depth buffer.

space within the minimum and maximum of a depth cell and modulates with the previous transparency.

```
float4 main( PS_INPUT input ) : SV_Target
{
    // Texture/image coordinates to sample/load/read the depth
    // values with.
    float2 texcoords = input.tex;

    float4 fineZ;
    fineZ.x   = linearize( hiZBuffer.SampleLevel( pointSampler,
        texcoords, mipPrevious, int2( 0,  0) ).x );
    fineZ.y   = linearize( hiZBuffer.SampleLevel( pointSampler,
        texcoords, mipPrevious, int2( 0, -1) ).x );
    fineZ.z   = linearize( hiZBuffer.SampleLevel( pointSampler,
        texcoords, mipPrevious, int2( -1, 0) ).x );
    fineZ.w   = linearize( hiZBuffer.SampleLevel( pointSampler,
        texcoords, mipPrevious, int2( -1, -1) ).x );

    // hiZBuffer stores min in R and max in G.
    float minZ = linearize( hiZBuffer.SampleLevel( pointSampler,
        texcoords, mipCurrent ).x );
    float maxZ = linearize( hiZBuffer.SampleLevel( pointSampler,
        texcoords, mipCurrent ).y );

    // Pre-divide.
    float coarseVolume = 1.0f / (maxZ - minZ);

    // Get the previous four fine transparency values.
    float4 visibility;
    visibility.x = visibilityBuffer.SampleLevel( pointSampler,
        texcoords, mipPrevious, int2( 0,  0 ) ).x;
    visibility.y = visibilityBuffer.SampleLevel( pointSampler,
        texcoords, mipPrevious, int2( 0, -1 ) ).x;
    visibility.z = visibilityBuffer.SampleLevel( pointSampler,
        texcoords, mipPrevious, int2( -1, 0 ) ).x;
    visibility.w = visibilityBuffer.SampleLevel( pointSampler,
        texcoords, mipPrevious, int2( -1, -1 ) ).x;

    // Calculate the percentage of visibility relative to the
    // calculated coarse depth. Modulate with transparency of
    // previous mip.
    float4 integration = fineZ.xyzw * abs(coarseVolume)
        * visibility.xyzw;

    // Data-parallel add using SIMD with a weight of 0.25 because
    // we derive the transparency from four pixels.
    float coarseIntegration = dot( 0.25f, integration.xyzw );

    return coarseIntegration;
}
```

Listing 13.4. The demo uses both a minimum Hi-Z buffer and a maximum Hi-Z buffer. With them, we calculate how much empty space there is in between the hierarchy depth cells. We linearize the post-projected depth into view-space Z for the computation. We could also output a linear Z-buffer during the Hi-Z pass, but this would require some changes in the ray-tracing pass and cone-tracing pass because view-space Z cannot be interpolated in screen space by default.

13.5.3   Ray-Tracing Pass

The implementation in Listing 13.5 is the Hi-Z ray-tracing code in Microsoft HLSL. The code snippet is heavily commented and should be easy to follow once the algorithm presented in Section 13.4.3 is clear.

```
float3 hiZTrace( float3 p, float3 v )
{
    const float rootLevel = mipCount - 1.0f; // Convert to 0
                                              // based indexing

    float level        = HIZ_START_LEVEL; // HIZ_START_LEVEL was
                                           // set to 2 in the demo
    float iterations   = 0.0f;

    // Get the cell cross direction and a small offset to enter
    // the next cell when doing cell crossing.
    float2 crossStep, crossOffset;
    crossStep.x    = ( v.x >= 0 ) ? 1.f : -1.f;
    crossStep.y    = ( v.y >= 0 ) ? 1.f : -1.f;
    crossOffset.xy = crossStep.xy * HIZ_CROSS_EPSILON.xy;
    crossStep.xy   = saturate( crossStep.xy );

    // Set current ray to the original screen coordinate and
    // depth.
    float3 ray = p.xyz;

    // Scale the vector such that z is 1.0f
    // (maximum depth).
    float3 d = v.xyz /= v.z;

    // Set starting point to the point where z equals 0.0f (minimum
        depth).
    float3 o = intersectDepthPlane(p.xy, d.xy, -p.z);

    // Cross to next cell so that we don't get a self-
    // intersection immediately.
    float2 rayCell     = getCell(ray.xy, hiZSize.xy);
    ray                = intersectCellBoundary(o.xy, d.xy, rayCell.xy,
        hiZSize.xy, crossStep.xy, crossOffset.xy);

    // The algorithm loop HIZ_STOP_LEVEL was set to 2 in the
    // demo; going too high can create artifacts.
    [loop]
    while( level >= HIZ_STOP_LEVEL && iterations < MAX_ITERATIONS )
    {
        // Get the minimum depth plane in which the current ray
        // resides.
        float minZ = getMinimumDepthPlane( ray.xy, level, rootLevel );

        // Get the cell number of our current ray.
        const float2 cellCount  = getCellCount(level, rootLevel);
        const float2 oldCellIdx = getCell(ray.xy, cellCount);

        // Intersect only if ray depth is below the minimum depth
        // plane.
        float3 tmpRay           = intersectDepthPlane( o.xy, d.xy, max(
            ray.z, minZ) );
```

```
        // Get the new cell number as well.
        const float2 newCellIdx = getCell(tmpRay.xy, cellCount);

        // If the new cell number is different from the old cell
        // number, we know we crossed a cell.
        [branch]
        if( crossedCellBoundary(oldCellIdx, newCellIdx) )
        {
            // So intersect the boundary of that cell instead,
            // and go up a level for taking a larger step next
            // loop.
            tmpRay = intersectCellBoundary(o, d, oldCellIdx,
                cellCount.xy, crossStep.xy, crossOffset.xy);
            level  = min(HIZ_MAX_LEVEL, level + 2.0f);
        }

        ray.xyz = tmpRay.xyz;

        // Go down a level in the Hi-Z.
        --level;

        ++iterations;
    } // end while

    return ray;
}
```

Listing 13.5. Some of the functions are not shown because of code length. This is only a minimum tracing for the sake of simplicity. The full implementation of those functions can be seen with the demo code in the book's web materials. The demo uses minimum-maximum tracing, which is a bit more complicated than this. View-space Z tracing is a bit more complicated and not shown.

13.5.4 Pre-convolution Pass

The pre-convolution pass is just a simple separable blur with normalized weights so that they add up to 1.0 when summed—otherwise we would be creating more energy than what we had to begin with in the image. (See Figure 13.22.)

The filter is executed successively on the color image and at each step we reduce the image to half the size and store it in the mip-channels of the texture. Assuming that we are at half resolution, this would correspond to 960×540; when convolving level 2 (240×135), we read from level 1 (480×270) and apply the separable blur passes.

The 1D Gaussian function for calculating our horizontal and vertical blur weights is

$$G(x) = \frac{1}{\sqrt{2\pi\sigma^2}} e^{-\frac{x^2}{2\sigma^2}}.$$

So, for example, a 7×7 filter would have an inclusive range from -3 to 3 for x.

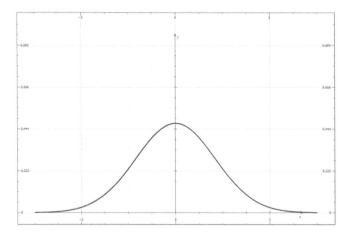

Figure 13.22. The normalized Gaussian curve used in the demo for weighting colors.

The normalized Gaussian weights then would be 0.001, 0.028, 0.233, 0.474, 0.233, 0.028, and 0.001, which when summed equal 1.0 exactly.

We don't want to produce more energy when doing the local blurring in the image, we want to keep the total energy in the image the same so the weights must equal 1.0 when summed—otherwise we are going to end up with more energy than what we started with so our image would have become brighter.

Listing 13.6 is a simple simple horizontal and vertical Gaussian blur implementation in the shading language Microsoft HLSL.

The final convolved images are produced by running the horizontal blur passes first and then the vertical blur passes successively for each level, which then are stored in the mip-channel of our color texture.

The choice of 7 × 7 seems to give good matching results for the needs of the demo. Using a wider kernel with a wider range of weights will cause wrong results because our transparency buffer and the colors associated with it will not match on a pixel basis anymore. Notice that our Gaussian weights take the colors mostly from the two neighboring pixels.

13.5.5 Cone-Tracing Pass

The cone-tracing pass is one of the smaller and easier-to-understand passes. In short it calculates the in-radiuses for the triangle made up from the cone and samples at different levels in our hierarchical color convolution buffer and pre-integrated visibility buffer (see Listing 13.7). Refer back to Section 13.4.5 for the algorithm explanation. The result can be seen in Figure 13.23.

```
// Horizontal blur shader entry point in
// psHorizontalGaussianBlur.hlsl
float4 main( PS_INPUT input ) : SV_Target
{
    // Texture/image coordinates to sample/load the color values
    // with.
    float2 texcoords = input.tex;
    float4 color;

    // Sample the color values and weight by the pre-calculated
    // normalized Gaussian weights horizontally.
    color += colorBuffer.SampleLevel( pointSampler, texcoords,
        prevLevel, int2( -3,  0 ) ) * 0.001f;
    color += colorBuffer.SampleLevel( pointSampler, texcoords,
        prevLevel, int2( -2,  0 ) ) * 0.028f;
    color += colorBuffer.SampleLevel( pointSampler, texcoords,
        prevLevel, int2( -1,  0 ) ) * 0.233f;
    color += colorBuffer.SampleLevel( pointSampler, texcoords,
        prevLevel, int2(  0,  0 ) ) * 0.474f;
    color += colorBuffer.SampleLevel( pointSampler, texcoords,
        prevLevel, int2(  1,  0 ) ) * 0.233f;
    color += colorBuffer.SampleLevel( pointSampler, texcoords,
        prevLevel, int2(  2,  0 ) ) * 0.028f;
    color += colorBuffer.SampleLevel( pointSampler, texcoords,
        prevLevel, int2(  3,  0 ) ) * 0.001f;

    return color;
}

// Vertical blur shader entry point in
// psVerticalGaussianBlur.hlsl
float4 main( PS_INPUT input ) : SV_Target
{
    // Texture/image coordinates to sample/load the color values
    // with.
    float2 texcoords = input.tex;
    float4 color;

    // Sample the color values and weight by the pre-calculated
    // normalized Gaussian weights vertically.
    color += colorBuffer.SampleLevel( pointSampler, texcoords,
        prevLevel, int2( 0,  3 ) ) * 0.001f;
    color += colorBuffer.SampleLevel( pointSampler, texcoords,
        prevLevel, int2( 0,  2 ) ) * 0.028f;
    color += colorBuffer.SampleLevel( pointSampler, texcoords,
        prevLevel, int2( 0,  1 ) ) * * 0.233f;
    color += colorBuffer.SampleLevel( pointSampler, texcoords,
        prevLevel, int2( 0,  0 ) ) * 0.474f;
    color += colorBuffer.SampleLevel( pointSampler, texcoords,
        prevLevel, int2( 0, -1 ) ) * 0.233f;
    color += colorBuffer.SampleLevel( pointSampler, texcoords,
        prevLevel, int2( 0, -2 ) ) * 0.028f;
    color += colorBuffer.SampleLevel( pointSampler, texcoords,
        prevLevel, int2( 0, -3 ) ) * * 0.001f;

    return color;
}
```

Listing 13.6. Simple horizontal and vertical separable blur shaders, with a 7×7 kernel.

```
// Read roughness from a render target and convert to a BRDF
// specular power.
float specularPower     = roughnessToSpecularPower( roughness );

// Depending on what BRDF used, convert to cone angle. Cone
// angle is maximum extent of the specular lobe aperture.
float coneTheta         = specularPowerToConeAngle(
    specularPower );

// Cone-trace using an isosceles triangle to approximate a cone
// in screen space
for(int i = 0; i < 7; ++i)
{
    // Intersection length is the adjacent side, get the opposite
    // side using trigonometry
    float oppositeLength    = isoscelesTriangleOpposite(
        adjacentLength, coneTheta );

    // Calculate in-radius of the isosceles triangle now
    float incircleSize      = isoscelesTriangleInradius(
        adjacentLength, oppositeLength );

    // Get the sample position in screen space
    float2 samplePos        = screenPos.xy + adjacentUnit *
        (adjacentLength - incircleSize);

    // Convert the in-radius into screen size (960x540) and then
    // check what power N we have to raise 2 to reach it.
    // That power N becomes our mip level to sample from.
    float mipChannel        = log2( incircleSize *
        max(screenSize.x, screenSize.y) );

    // Read color and accumulate it using trilinear filtering
    // (blending in xy and mip direction) and weight it.
    // Uses pre-convolved image and pre-integrated transparency
    // buffer and Hi-Z buffer. It checks if cone sphere is below,
    // in between, or above the Hi-Z minimum and maxamimum and
    // weights it together with transparency.
    // Visibility is accumulated in the alpha channel.
    totalColor += coneSampleWeightedColor( samplePos, mipChannel );

    if( totalColor.a > 1.0f )
        break;

    // Calculate next smaller triangle that approximates the cone
    // in screen space.
    adjacentLength          = isoscelesTriangleNextAdjacent(
        adjacentLength, incircleSize );
}
```

Listing 13.7. Again the full implementation of some of the functions is not shown because of code length. The demo code available online has the full implementation; the demo also comes with alternative toggle-able code for accumulating the colors such as basic averaging, distance-based weighting, and hierarchical pre-integrated visibility buffer weighting.

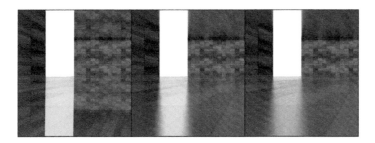

Figure 13.23. Cone-tracing algorithm capable of producing glossy reflections in screen space. Notice how the algorithm ensures that the further the reflection is from caster, the more spread it becomes like in the real world.

There is a conflict between the Hi-Z tracer and the cone tracer. Hi-Z tries to find a perfect specular as fast as possible while the cone tracer needs to take linear steps to integrate the total visibility in front-to-back order for correct occlusion.

This is not shown in this chapter because of complexity but the Hi-Z buffer is actually used together with the cone angle to find an early intersection at a coarse level to early exit out of the Hi-Z loop; then, we jump straight to the cone-tracing pass to continue with the linear stepping for glossy reflections. The Hi-Z functions as an empty-space determiner; once we have a coarse intersection with the cone, we can jump straight into the cone tracer to integrate the visibility and colors from that point onwards.

The more roughness we have on our surfaces, the cheaper this technique gets because we sample bigger circles and do larger jumps. Conversely, the less rough the surface is, the further the Hi-Z can travel for a perfect specular reflection so it all balances out evenly. Again, implementation is dependent on whether you use post-projected Hi-Z or view-space Hi-Z.

13.6 Extensions

13.6.1 Smoothly Fading Artifacts

We already talked about the inherent problems with screen-space local reflection in Section 13.2. Without further ado, rays traveling the opposite direction of the viewing ray and rays that fall close to the screen borders or outside the screen should be faded away due to lack of information available to us in the screen space. We can also fade rays based on ray travel distance.

A quick and simple implementation is shown in Listing 13.8. The demo ships with a more robust implementation.

One could fade away based on local occlusion as well, where a ray starts traveling behind an object and fails to find a proper intersection. One would

```
// Smoothly fade rays pointing towards the camera; screen space
// can't do mirrors (this is in view space).
float fadeOnMirror     = dot(viewReflect, viewDir);

// Smoothly fade rays that end up close to the screen edges.
float boundary       = distance(intersection.xy,
                       float2(0.5f, 0.5f) ) * 2.0f;
float fadeOnBorder = 1.0f - saturate( (boundary  - FADE_START) /
    (FADE_END - FADE_START) );

// Smoothly fade rays after a certain distance (not in
// world space for simplicity but shoudl be).
float travelled   = distance(intersection.xy, startPos.xy);
float fadeOnTravel     = 1.0f - saturate( (travelled - FADE_START)
    / (FADE_END - FADE_START) );

// Fade the color now.
float3 finalColor = color * ( fadeOnBorder   * fadeOnTravel *
    fadeOnMirror );                .
```

Listing 13.8. Artifact removal snippet for fading the rays that have a high chance of
failing and computing incorrect reflection results. FADE_START and FADE_END drive how
quickly the fading should happen, where they are between 0 and 1. Though the code
snippet shows the same parameters used for both the fading techniques, one should use
different parameters and tweak them accordingly.

store when the ray entered such a state and then, depending on the distance
traveled, fade the ray during that state to remove such unwanted artifacts.

13.6.2 Extrapolation of Surfaces

Since the ray-marching step might not find a true intersection, we could potentially extrapolate the missing information. Assuming the screen is covered with
mostly rough surfaces with glossy reflections, we could run a bilateral dilation
filter, which basically means take the surface normal and depth into account
when extrapolating the missing color (i.e., flood-filling the holes). For any surface other than rough surfaces, the dilation filter might fail horribly because of
potential high-frequency reflection colors.

One might be able to use a tile-based filter that finds good anchor points per
tile and then run a clone brush filter to extrapolate the missing information for
non-rough surfaces. The tile-based approach should work well for running the
dilation only on the needed pixels.

13.6.3 Improving Ray-Marching Precision

If we use a nonlinear, post-projected depth buffer, most of the depth values fall
very quickly into the range between 0.9 and 1.0, as we know. To improve the
precision of the ray marching, we can reverse the floating-point depth buffer.

This is done by swapping the near and the far planes in the projection matrix, changing the depth testing to greater than and equal instead of lesser than and equal. Then, we could clear the depth buffer to black instead of white at each frame because 0.0 is where the far plane is now. This will turn 1.0 to the near plane in the depth buffer and 0.0 to the far plane. There are two nonlinearities here: one from the post-perspective depth and one from the floating point. Since we reversed one, they basically cancel each other out, giving us better distribution of the depth values.

Keep in mind that reversing the depth buffer affects our Hi-Z construction algorithm as well.

One should always use a 32-bit floating-point depth buffer; on AMD hardware the memory footprint of 24-bit and 32-bit depth buffers is the same, with which the fourth generation consoles are equipped also.

Another technique that can be used to improve depth precision is to actually create the Hi-Z buffer over a view-space Z depth buffer. We would need to output this in the geometry pass into a separate render target because recovering it from a post-perspective depth is not going to help the precision. This gives us uniformly distributed depth values. The only issue with a view-space Z depth buffer is that since it's not post-perspective, we can't interpolate it in screen space. To interpolate it we would have to employ the same technique as the hardware interpolator uses. We take $1/Z$ and interpolate it in screen space and then divide this interpolated value again by $1/Z'$ to recover the final interpolated view-space Z. However, outputting a dedicated linear view-space Z buffer might be too costly. We should test a reversed 32-bit floating-point depth buffer first. The cone-tracing calculations are also a bit different with a view-space Z buffer. We would need to project the sphere back into screen space to find the size it covers at a particular distance. There are compromises with each technique.

13.6.4 Approximate Multiple Ray Bounces

Multiple bounces are an important factor when it comes to realistic reflections. Our brain would instantly notice that something is wrong if a reflection of a mirror didn't have reflections itself but just a flat color. We can see the effect of multiple reflections in Figure 13.24.

The algorithm presented in this chapter has the nice property of being able to have multiple reflections relatively easily. The idea is to reflect an already reflected image. In this case the already reflected image would be the previous frame. If we compute the reflection of an already reflected image, we'll accumulate multiple bounces over time. (See Figure 13.25.) But since we always delay the source image by a frame, we'll have to do a re-projection of the pixels. To achieve this re-projection, we'll basically transform the current frame's pixel into the position it belonged to in the previous frame by taking the camera movement into account [Nehab et al. 07].

 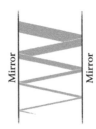

Figure 13.24. Infinite reflections when two mirrors are parallel against each other. Notice how the strength of the reflections decreases with the number of bounces we have due to absorption where the light is transferred to heat and some is reflected back again. The result is darker reflections at further ray depths. Notice the green tint as well that the ray accumulates over time from the glass as it bounces, due to iron oxide impurities in an ordinary soda-lime glass [Wikipedia 14]. The green tint is usually most noticeable on the edges of a glass. [Image courtesy of [Merry Monk 11].]

Once we know the position of where it belonged in the previous frame, we'll also need to detect if that pixel is valid or not. Some pixels might have moved outside the screen borders and some might have been blocked/occluded, etc. If the camera has moved drastically between the previous frame and the current frame, we might have to reject some of the pixels. The easiest way of doing this would be to store the previous frame's depth buffer; once we have done a re-projection of the current pixel into the previous frame, we just compare them by an epsilon and detect a fail or success. If they are not within an epsilon value we know the pixel is invalid. To get even more accurate results, one could also use the normal (surface orientation) of the previous frame and the normal of the re-projected pixel. The demo uses only the depth for rejection invalid pixels.

Mathematically speaking, we need to use the current inverted camera projection matrix and the previous camera projection matrix to take us from the current frame's pixel into the previous frame:

$$\mathbf{M}' = \mathbf{VP}_{\mathbf{curr}}^{-1}\mathbf{VP}_{\mathbf{prev}},$$

where $\mathbf{M}'$ is the concatenated re-projection matrix, $\mathbf{VP}_{\mathbf{curr}}^{-1}$ is the inverse view projection matrix from the current frame, and $\mathbf{VP}_{\mathbf{prev}}$ is the view projection matrix from the previous frame. When multiplied with a pixel $\mathbf{P}_n$ in clip space, this will take us to the corresponding pixel $\mathbf{P}_{n-1}$ in the previous frame in homoge-

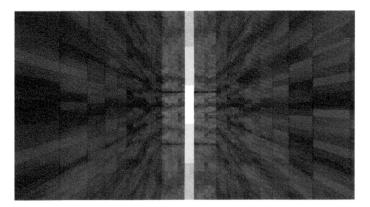

Figure 13.25. The effect of re-projecting an already reflected image and using it as a source for the current frame. This produces multiple reflections and just like in the real world the reflections lose intensity the further in reflection depth it gets.

nous space. We just need to divide the result with the w component to finally get the clip-space coordinate. Then we can just map it into screen space and start reading from the previous frame color buffer and thereby have an infinite number of reflection bounces. Figure 13.26 and Listing 13.9 show the concept of un-projecting and re-projecting a pixel into the previous camera's pixel position.

Another benefit of using the previous frame is the fact that we are taking the final lighting and all transparent object information into account as well as the possibility of including post-processing effects that have been applied to the image. If we would have used the current unfinished frame, we would lack all of those nice additions—though not all post-process effects are interesting.

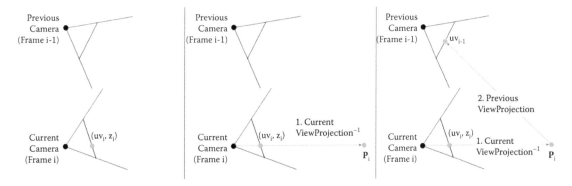

Figure 13.26. Illustration of how a pixel in screen space is transformed into its old coordinate by re-projection, which can be used to read from the previous color buffer.

```
float2 texcoords = input.tex.xy;

// Unpack clip position from texcoords and depth.
float depth          = depthBuffer.SampleLevel(pointSampler,
    texcoords, 0.0f);
float4 currClip      = unpackClipPos(texcoords, depth);

// Unpack into previous homogenous coordinates:
// inverse(view projection) * previous(view projection).
float4 prevHomogenous = mul(currClip,
    invViewProjPrevViewProjMatrix);

// Unpack homogenous coordinate into clip-space coordinate.
float4 prevClip      = float4( prevHomogenous.xyz /
    prevHomogenous.w, 1.0f);

// Unpack into screen coordinate [-1, 1] into [0, 1] range and
// flip the y coordinate.
float3 prevScreen    = float3(prevClip.xy * float2(0.5f, -0.5f)
    + float2(0.5f, 0.5f), prevClip.z);

// Return the corresponding color from the previous frame.
return prevColorBuffer.SampleLevel(linearSampler, prevScreen.xy,
    0.0f);
```

Listing 13.9. Re-projecting a pixel into its previous location in the previous frame's color image. Implementation details for rejecting pixels are omitted. Demo comes with the full code.

If you have a motion blur velocity vector pass, more specifically 2D instantaneous velocity buffer, you can use that instead of re-projecting with the code above. Using 2D instantaneous velocity is more stable but that is beyond the topic of this chapter.

13.6.5   Temporal Filtering

Temporal filtering is another enhancer that helps the algorithm to produce even more accurate and stable results by trying to recover and reuse pixels over several frames, hence the name *temporal*, over time. The idea is to have a history buffer that stores the old reflection computation, and then we run a re-projection pass over it just like we saw in Section 13.6.4, and reject any invalid pixels. This history buffer is the same buffer we write our final reflection computation to, so it acts like an accumulation buffer where we keep accumulating valid reflection colors. In case the ray-marching phase fails to find a proper intersection, due to the ray falling behind an object or outside of the screen, we can just rely on the previous re-projected result that is already stored in the history buffer and have a chance of recovering that missing pixel.

Temporal filtering helps stabilize the result because a failed pixel in frame N due to occlusion or missing information might be recovered from frame $N - 1$, which was accumulated over several frames by re-projection of pixels. Having the possibility of recovering pixels that were valid in the previous frames but invalid in the current frame is essential and is going to give much better results and stabilize the algorithm. It's also possible to get huge speedups by not running the ray-marching code if the recovery is accurate enough so that we don't need to recalculate the reflection at all.

This little enhancer walks hand in hand with Section 13.6.2, "Multiple Ray Bounces," since both rely on re-projection.

13.6.6   Travel Behind Surfaces

It is possible to travel behind objects using a Minimum and a Maximum Hi-Z buffer. In case the ray crosses a cell and ends up behind both the minimum and the maximum depth of the new cell, we can just cross that cell as well and continue with the Hi-Z traversal. This assumes that the surface has not infinitely long depth. A global small epsilon value can also be used, or a per object thickness epsilon value into a render target. Traveling behind objects is really a hard problem to solve if we do not have information on object thickness.

13.6.7   Ray Marching Toward the Camera

We've looked at the algorithm using a Minimum Hi-Z hierarchy for rays to travel away from the camera. It's also possible for mirror-like reflected rays to travel toward the camera and thereby have a chance of hitting something, though this chance is very small and would mostly benefit curved surfaces. A small change is required for the algorithm, which makes use of an additional hierarchy, the Maximum Hi-Z, for any ray that would want to travel toward the camera.

A texture format such as R32G32F would be appropriate for this change, the R channel would store the minimum and the G channel would store the maximum.

There is a very small amount of pixels that have a chance of actually hitting something, so this change might not be worth it as this would add an overhead to the entire algorithm.

13.6.8   Vertically Stretched Anisotropic Reflections

In the real world the more grazing angles we see on glossy surfaces, the more anisotropic reflections we perceive. Essentially the reflection vectors within the reflection lobe are spread more vertically than horizontally, which is the main reason why we get the vertical stretching effect.

To achieve this phenomenon with screen-space reflections, we have to use the `SampleGrad` function of our color texture during the cone-tracing accumulation pass of the reflection colors, give this sampler hardware some custom calculated vertical and horizontal partial derivatives, and let the hardware kick the anisotropic filterer to stretch the reflections for us. This is highly dependent on the BRDF used and how roughness values map to the reflection lobe.

We could also manually take multiple samples to achieve the same result. Basically, instead of sampling quads, we sample elongated rectangles at grazing angles.

We saw earlier in Section 13.4.5 that for complicated BRDF models we would need to pre-compute a 2D table of local reflection vectors and cone angles. A texture suited for this is R16G16B16A16. The RGB channels would store the local vector and the alpha channel would store either one isotropic cone-angle extent or two anisotropic vertical and horizontal cone-angle extents. These two anisotropic values for the cone would decide how many extra samples we would take vertically to approximate an elongated rectangle to stretch the reflections.

13.7   Optimizations

13.7.1   Combining Linear and Hi-Z Traversal

One drawback of the Hierarchical-Z traversal is that it is going to traverse down to lower hierarchy levels when the ray travels close to a surface. Evaluating the entire Hierarchical-Z traversal algorithm for such small steps is more expensive than doing a simple linear search with the same step size. Unfortunately the ray starts immediately close to a surface, the surface we are reflecting the original ray from. Doing a few steps of linear search in the beginning seems to be a great optimization to get the ray away from the surface and then let the Hierarchical-Z traversal algorithm do its job of taking the big steps.

In case the linear search finds intersections, we can just early-out in the shader code with a dynamic branch and skip the entire Hi-Z traversal phase. It's also worth it to end the Hi-Z traversal at a much earlier level such as 1 or 2 and then continue with another linear search in the end. The ending level could be calculated depending on the distance to the camera, since the farther away the pixel is, the less detail it needs because of perspective, so stopping much earlier is going to give a boost in performance.

13.7.2   Improving Fetch Latency

Partially unrolling dynamic loops to handle dependent texture fetches tends to improve performance with fetch/latency-bound algorithms. So, instead of handling one work per thread, we would actually pre-fetch the work for the next N loops. We can do this because we have a deterministic path on our ray. However, there is a point where pre-fetching starts to hurt performance because the register usage rises and using more registers means less buckets of threads can run in parallel. A good starting point is $N = 4$. That value was used on a regular linear tracing algorithm and a speedup of $2\times$–$3\times$ was measured on both NVIDIA and AMD hardware. The numbers appearing later in this chapter do not include these improvements because it wasn't tested on a Hi-Z tracer.

13.7.3   Interleaved Spatial Coherence and Signal Reconstruction

Because most of our rays are spatially coherent, we can shoot rays every other pixel—so-called interleaved sampling—and then apply some sort of signal reconstruction filter from sampling theory. This works very well with rough reflections since the result tends to have low frequency, which is ideal for signal reconstruction. This was tested on linear tracing-based algorithms, and a performance increase of about $3\times$–$4\times$ was achieved. The interleaving pattern was twice horizontally, twice vertically. These improvements were also not tested on a Hi-Z tracer, so the numbers presented later do not include these either.

13.7.4   Cross-Bilateral Upsampling or Temporal Super-Sampling

Since we run the ray tracing at half-resolution, we do need a smart upsampling scheme to make up for the low number of pixels. A cross-bilateral image upsampling algorithm is a perfect fit for this kind of a task [Kopf et al. 07], but a temporal super-sampling algorithm is even better: after four frames we will have full-resolution traced results using the temporal re-projection that was explained earlier.

For the cross-bilateral upsampler, The full-resolution depth buffer would be an input together with the half-resolution reflection color buffer. The algorithm would upsample the reflection color buffer to full resolution while preserving silhouettes and hard edges. It's way faster and cheaper to calculate the reflections at half-resolution than full-resolution. However, to recompose the image back to the original screen, at full-resolution, we need to scale it up while preserving the hard edges, and that's exactly what the Cross-Bilateral Upsampling algorithm is good for.

While upsampling one could also use another approach and append the pixels at depth discontinuities to an append/consume buffer and re-trace only those pixels at high resolution later for higher quality. This was not tested.

13.8   Performance

The demo runs at half-resolution, meaning 960×540, and it's running super-fast:

- 0.35–0.39 ms on NVidia GTX TITAN,

- 0.70–0.80 ms on NVidia GTX 670,

- 0.80–0.90 ms on AMD 7950.

The timers are the Hi-Z Ray-Marching and Cone-Tracing combined.

The demo is memory latency bound, and the memory unit is 80–90% active, which gives little to no room for our ALU units to work because they just sit there waiting for a fetch to complete.

According to GPU PerfStudio 2, we are having 50% cache misses because of nonlocal texture buffer accesses when traversing using the Hi-Z acceleration structure and we also suffer from noncoherent dynamic branching since a GPU executes branches in lock-step mode. If an entire bucket of threads (group of 32 threads for Nvidia called Warp, 64 for AMD called Wavefront) does not take the same branch, then we pay the penalty of stalling some threads until they converge again into the same path. This gets worse as the threads keep taking different branches for some pixels.

One optimization that was not tried, but mentioned by [Tevs et al. 08], is using a 3D texture to store the Hi-Z instead of a 2D texture. According to [Tevs et al. 08], using a 3D texture for a displacement mapping technique, where each slice represents the hierarchy levels of our Hi-Z, gives better cache hits and a performance boost of 20% due to less L2 traffic and more texture cache hits.

Since we are memory latency bound due to cache misses and incoherent texture accesses, while jumping up and down in the hierarchy, this might be a good optimization to try, though it would use much more memory.

13.9 Results

The presented algorithm works really well and produces great reflections, both specular and glossy, and it runs at easily affordable speeds for games. The most noticeable detail is the spread of reflections as they get farther away from the source, which is the selling point of the entire algorithm. (See Figures 13.27 and 13.28.)

13.10 Conclusion

In this chapter we looked at Hi-Z Screen-Space Cone Tracing to compute both specular and glossy reflections at game interactive frame rates and performance

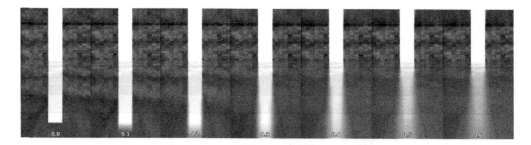

Figure 13.27. Cone-tracing algorithm with different level of glossiness on the tile material, giving the appearance of diverged reflection rays. The reflection becomes more spread the farther away it is, and it is stretching just like the phenomena we see in the real world.

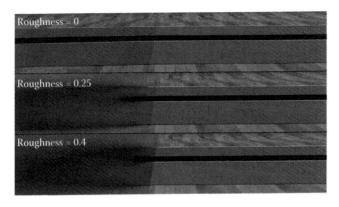

Figure 13.28. Another example of Hi-Z Screen-Space Cone Tracing producing spread reflections the farther it travels due to micro fracture simulation using material roughness.

levels. While the algorithm works well for local reflections, there are some edge cases where it may fail because of insufficient information on the screen. This algorithm can only reflect what the original input image has, as we have seen. You will not be able to look at yourself in the mirror since that information is not available to us in screen space. Hi-Z Screen-Space Cone Tracing is more of a supplementary effect for dynamic reflections in dynamic 3D scenes with the cheap glossy appearance on them, and it's recommended that you combine it with other types of reflection techniques such as local box projected [Behc 10] or sphere projected [Bjorke 07] cube-maps to take over when Hi-Z Screen-Space Cone Tracing fails as a backup plan. Hi-Z Screen-Space Cone Tracing should not be used on its own as a single solution because of the inherent problems the screen-space algorithm has, unless you have a very specific controlled scene with a specific camera angle where you can avoid the problems to begin with, such as flat walls and no mirrors, etc. The glossy reflections help hide artifacts that are otherwise visible as mirror reflections.

13.11 Future Work

The system could be extended in many ways. One idea is to take a screenshot of a 3D scene and store the color and depth information in conjunction with the camera basis. With this we could at run time re-project this local screenshot without any dynamic objects obscuring interesting information from us. The screenshots would act like local reflection probes, and we would pick the closest interesting one and do our Hi-Z traversal.

The Hi-Z Screen-Space Cone-Tracing technique could also be applied on cube-maps, where we construct a cube-mapped Hi-Z acceleration structure and ray-march within this cube volume. This would allow us to reflect anything outside the screen as well with pixel perfect ray-tracing-like results. This technique, Hi-Z Cube-Map Ray Tracing, is ongoing research and it will be published at a later time.

Another expansion could be packet tracing. This is ongoing research also and will be published at a later time. The basic idea is to group several rays together and basically shoot a packet of rays, like a frustum. As we intersect the coarse Hi-Z, we can refine/subdivide the packet and shoot several more rays. This way we can quickly intersect coarse Hi-Z levels and then do fewer operations as we travel, though this makes the implementation more complex and harder to maintain and relies heavily on compute shaders. Grouping coherent rays should give an excellent boost in performance.

One could also do tiled tracing, where each tile identifies the roughness value of the scene. In case the entire tile is very rough, we can probably get away with shooting fewer rays and extrapolating most of the pixel colors. This multi-resolution handling should also give an excellent boost in speed, though again this also relies heavily on compute shaders.

All of those topics are ongoing research and will be, as said before, published at a later time if it makes it out of the research and development phase.

13.12   Acknowledgments

I would like to give my special thanks to my co-workers who supported me at EA DICE—Mikael Uddholm, Rendering Engineer of *Mirror's Edge*, and Charles de Rousiers, Rendering Engineer of *Frostbite*—and to my leads for proofreading this chapter, also at EA DICE—Jonas Åberg, Technical Director of *Mirror's Edge*, and Daniel Johansson, Lead Software Engineer of *Mirror's Edge*.

I would also like to give my special thanks to the editors of *GPU Pro 5*—Michal Valient of Guerilla Games and Wolfgang Engel of Confetti FX—and to project editor Charlotte Byrnes of CRC Press.

Bibliography

[Autodesk 09] Autodesk. "General Utility Shaders." *mental ray Architectural and Design Visualization Shader Library*, http://download.autodesk.com/us/maya/2011help/mr/shaders/architectural/arch_util.html, 2009.

[Behc 10] Behc. "Box Projected Cubemap Environment Mapping." http://www.gamedev.net/topic/568829-box-projected-cubemap-environment-mapping/, 2010.

[Bjorke 07] Kevin Bjorke. "Image-Based Lighting." In *GPU Gems*, edited by Randima Fernando, Chapter 19. Upper Saddle River, NJ: Addison-Wesley, 2007.

[Crassin 11] Cyril Crassin. "GigaVoxels: A Voxel-Based Rendering Pipeline For Efficient Exploration of Large and Detailed Scenes." PhD thesis, Université de Grenoble, Saint-Martin-d'Hères, France, 2011.

[Crassin 12] Cyril Crassin. "Voxel Cone Tracing and Sparse Voxel Octree for Real-Time Global Illumination." http://on-demand.gputechconf.com/gtc/2012/presentations/SB134-Voxel-Cone-Tracing-Octree-Real-Time-Illumination.pdf, 2012.

[David 13] David. "The Layering Library (MILA) UI: BETA SHADERS." *Elemental Ray*, http://elementalray.wordpress.com/2013/01/22/the-layering-library-mila-ui-beta-shaders/, January 22, 2013.

[Drobot 09] Michal Drobot. "Quadtree Displacement Mapping with Height Blending." In *GPU Pro*, edited by Wolfgang Engel, pp. 117–148. Natick, MA: A K Peters, Ltd., 2009.

[Graham 10] Graham. "Screen Space Reflections." *B3D Forum*, forum.beyond3d.com/showthread.php?t=56095, January 10, 2010.

[Hien and Lim 09] Tu The Hien and Low Kok Lim. "Real-Time Rendering of Dynamic Dispalcement Maps." http://www.nus.edu.sg/nurop/2009/SoC/TuTheHien_NUROP.pdf, 2009.

[Hrkalovic and Lundgren 12] Ermin Hrkalovic and Mikael Lundgren. "Review of Displacement Mapping Techniques and Optimization." Blekinge Institute of Technology, http://www.bth.se/fou/cuppsats.nsf/all/9c1560496a915078c1257a58005115a0?OpenDocument, 2012.

[Kopf et al. 07] Johannes Kopf, Michael F. Cohen, Dani Lischinski, and Matt Uyttendaele. "Joint Bilateral Upsampling." *ACM Transactions on Graphics (Proceedings of SIGGRAPH 2007)* 26:3 (2007), Article no. 96.

[Lawrence 02] Jason Lawrence. "Importance Sampling of the Phong Reflectance Model." www.cs.virginia.edu/~jdl/importance.doc, 2002.

[Lilley et al. 12] Ian Lilley, Sean Lilley, and Nop Jiarathanakul. "Real-Time Voxel Cone Tracing." http://cis565-fall-2012.github.io/lectures/11-01-GigaVoxels-And-Sparse-Textures.pdf, 2012.

[Low 02] Kok-Lim Low. "Perspective-Correct Interpolation." http://www.gamedev.net/topic/416957-z-bufferperspective-correct-interpolation/, March 12, 2002.

[Luxion 12] Luxion Inc. "Roughness Parameter (Glossy)." *KeyShot 3 User's Manual*, http://www.keyshot.com/keyshot3/manual/material_types/glossy_samples_parameter.html, 2012.

[Merry Monk 11] The Merry Monk. "Infinite Mirror image." http://www.themerrymonk.com/wp-content/uploads/2011/05/infinite_mirror.jpg, 2011.

[Nehab et al. 07] Diego Nehab, Perdo V. Sander, Jason Lawrence, Natalya Tatarchuk, and John R. Isidoro, "Accelerating Real-Time Shading with Reverse Reprojection Caching." In *Proceedings of the 22nd ACM SIG-GRAPH/EUROGRAPHICS Symposium on Graphics Hardware*, pp. 25–35. Aire-la-Ville, Switzerland: Eurographics Association, 2007.

[Oh et al. 06] Kyoungsu Oh, Hyunwoo Ki, and Cheol-Hi Lee. "Pyramidal Displacement Mapping: A GPU based Artifacts-Free Ray Tracing through an Image Pyramid." In *Proceedings of the ACM Symposium on Virtual Reality Software and Technology*, pp. 75–82. New York: ACM, 2006.

[Risser 07] Eric Risser. "True Impostors." In *GPU Gems 3*, edited by Hubert Nguyen, Chapter 21. Upper Saddle River, NJ: Addison-Wesley, 2007.

[Robison and Shirley 09] Austin Robison and Peter Shirley. "Image Space Gathering." In *Proceedings of the Conference on High Performance Graphics 2009*, pp. 91–98. New York: ACM, 2009.

[ScratchaPixel 12] ScratchaPixel. "Material Appearance." http://www.scratchapixel.com/lessons/3d-basic-lessons/lesson-14-interaction-light-matter/material-appearance/, 2012.

[Szirmay-Kalos and Umenhoffer 06] Laszlo Szirmay-Kalos and Tamas Umenhoffer. "Displacement Mapping on the GPU—State of the Art." http://sirkan.iit.bme.hu/~szirmay/egdis_link.htm, 2006.

[Tevs et al. 08] Art Tevs, I. Ihrke, and H.-P. Seidel. "Maximum Mipmaps for Fast, Accurate, and Scalable Dynamic Height Field Rendering." In *Proceedings of the 2008 Symposium on Interactive 3D Graphics and Games*, pp. 183–190. New York: ACM, 2008.

[Tiago et al. 12] Tiago Souse, Nickolay Kasyan, and Nicolas Schulz. "CryENGINE 3: Three Years of Work in Review." In *GPU Pro 3*, edited by Wolfgang Engel, pp. 133–168. Boca Raton, FL: A K Peters/CRC Press, 2012.

[Wikipedia 14] Wikipedia. "Glass Coloring and Color Marking." https://en.wikipedia.org/wiki/Glass_coloring_and_color_marking, 2014.

14

TressFX: Advanced Real-Time Hair Rendering

Timothy Martin, Wolfgang Engel, Nicolas Thibieroz, Jason Yang, and Jason Lacroix

14.1 Introduction

Hair is one of the key materials in the realm of realistic real-time character rendering that has proven to be a difficult endeavour. The conventional approach would be to author hair using "fins and shells" or a standard mesh, then use a combination of textures, noise maps, and anisotropic lighting to produce the effect of a full head of hair [Scheuermann 04]. In this chapter, we cover a real-time hair rendering technique that renders hair as individual strands and how that technique was modified and optimized to integrate into a game and run at peak performance. (See Figure 14.1.) Hair-specific topics that will be covered include geometry expansion, antialiasing, lighting, shadows, and the usage of per-pixel

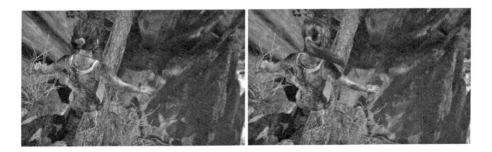

Figure 14.1. Here is a comparison of hair rendered in *Tomb Raider* using a mesh with a cloth simulation applied to the ponytail in the left image versus the TressFX advanced real-time hair rendered as individual strands in the image on the right.

linked lists for order independent transparency. Lastly, we cover further ideas that may be worthwhile to expand the use of the hair technique or advance it further.

To look into the technology demo that this chapter follows and that was used as a base for integration into *Tomb Raider*, download the latest TressFX demo at http://developer.amd.com/tools-and-sdks/graphics-development/amd-radeon -sdk/.

14.1.1 Overview

In order to cover each part of the hair rendering in the easiest way to follow, it is best to trace through the data flow path from raw hair vertices to the final rendered image. So, here we give a high-level overview of the chapter, outlining what to expect in each section.

Section 14.2 covers the *geometry expansion* step. We cover how hair geometry is expanded from line primitives into quads that properly cover the pixels on screen to represent hair.

The next step involves lighting and shadowing, covered in separate sections. In Section 14.3, we cover details on the hair lighting model. In the separate section on shadows, called "Shadowing and Approximated Hair Self-Shadowing," we cover the hair self-shadowing approximation calculations and implementation as well as how we handle hair casting and receiving environment shadows.

Section 14.5 covers *antialiasing*. In this section, we cover how antialiasing is specifically applied to hair and the image-based approach that was used in *Tomb Raider*.

The next section, titled "Transparency," covers how transparency is handled with per-pixel linked lists. The section covers the two relevant shader passes: *A-Buffer Fill* and *Sort and Draw*. We also describe where each of the steps, covered in the previous sections, occurs relative to or within the transparency shader passes.

Section 14.7 covers integration specifics. In this section, we cover how to handle writing hair depth, because the final rendering of hair may need to be treated as an opaque (or partially opaque) object when dealing with other transparent objects or depth-based effects such as depth of field.

Lastly, we have the "Conclusion" section to sum up the content of the chapter and cover possible paths of further work or improvement.

14.2 Geometry Expansion

We represented hair geometry data as individual strands made up of line segments. The line segments are represented as successive vertices. In order to render hair in a typical triangle rasterizing graphics pipeline, each of the line segments undergoes an expansion to a quad made up of two triangles [Yu et al. 12].

To generate these two triangles, each line segment results in six vertices. The full
extent of the geometry expansion occurs in the vertex shader. Here are the two
steps involved in the hair geometry expansion:

- World-space hair fiber radius expansion: The rasterized hair fibers end up
  being a sequence of view plane aligned billboards for each hair fiber segment.
  The individual hair fiber segments are expanded by the hair fiber radius in
  world space when these billboards are generated.

- Screen-space pixel expansion: After projecting the expanded hair fiber vertices, an additional expansion occurs to ensure that a single hair fiber covers
  at least one pixel width by adding $\sqrt{2}/2 \approx 0.71$ to the projected hair fiber
  radius.

See Listing 14.1 to see how both of these described steps are performed in the
vertex shader that performs the hair geometry expansion.

```
static const uint  HairVertexSelection[] = {0, 1, 0, 1, 1, 0};
static const float OffsetDir[] =
    {-1.f, -1.f, 1.f, -1.f, 1.f, 1.f};
static const uint OffsetDirIndex[] = {0, 0, 1, 0, 1, 1};

HairPSInput HairVS( uint vertexId : SV_VertexID )
{
  HairPSInput Output = (HairPSInput)0;
  float thicknessFactor[] = ... // normalized thickness scaler
// two tangents and vertices of the hair fiber segment
  float3 t[2], v[2];
// calculate right vector for billboarding the hair fiber quad
  float3 right[] = { cross(t[0], normalize(v[0] - g_vEye)),
          cross(t[1], normalize(v[1] - g_vEye))};
  float2 proj_right[] =
    { normalize( mul(float4(right[0], 0), g_mViewProj).xy ),
      normalize( mul(float4(right[1], 0), g_mViewProj).xy ) }

  // Setting up the indexing for calculating one of the
  // 6 verts of the 2 triangles making a quad

  // indexing vert 0 to 5
  uint localVertId = vertexId % GENERATED_VERTEX_COUNT;

  // choosing vertex in the fiber segment
  uint idx        = HairVertexSelection[localVertId];

  // choosing which direction to offset from the fiber segment
  uint offDirIndex = OffsetDirIndex[localVertId];

  float4 hairEdgePositions[2]; // 0 is negative, 1 is positive

  // World-space expansion
  hairEdgePositions[0] = float4(v[idx] +
    -1.f * right[idx] * thicknessFactor[idx] * fiberRadius, 1.f);
  hairEdgePositions[1] = float4(v[idx] +
    1.f * right[idx] * thicknessFactor[idx] * fiberRadius, 1.f);
  hairEdgePositions[0] = mul(hairEdgePositions[0], g_mViewProj);
  hairEdgePositions[1] = mul(hairEdgePositions[1], g_mViewProj);
```

```
// Output after screen-space expansion
Output.Position = hairEdgePositions[offDirIndex] +
 hairEdgePositions[offDirIndex].w * OffsetDir[localVertId] *
 float4(proj_right[idx] * 0.71f / g_WinSize, 0.0f, 0.0f);
Output.Tangent  = t[idx];
Output.WorldPos = v[idx];

// Used for image-space-based antialiasing,
//   for having the nearest edge positions of
//   the hair fiber in the pixel shader
Output.p0 = hairEdgePositions[0].xy/hairEdgePositions[0].w;
Output.p1 = hairEdgePositions[1].xy/hairEdgePositions[1].w;
return Output;
}
```

Listing 14.1. The vertex shader that performs the hair geometry expansion.

14.3 Lighting

After the geometry expansion occurs in the vertex shader, lighting calculations follow as one of the first steps in the pixel shader during the hair geometry pass.

The lighting calculations for the hair stem from a fur rendering model introduced by [Kajiya and Kay 89], as well as from work done by in [Marschner et al. 03]. The lighting equation in [Kajiya and Kay 89] provides a basis for the lighting with a tangent-based diffuse and specular component. Hair lighting in [Marschner et al. 03] is based on an analytical approach and adds the concept of a dual specular highlight. The result of combining these two works can be seen in a presentation by Scheuermann, where a practical real-time lighting equation is defined for hair [Scheuermann 04].

14.3.1 Diffuse

The diffuse component is based on applying lambert diffuse lighting to a cylinder. Kajiya's paper [Kajiya and Kay 89] provides a derivation of the diffuse component, which is found by integrating along the circumference of a half cylinder and accumulating the reflected diffuse component along that circumference. The derivation ends with a simple equation for the diffuse component:

$$K_d \sin(t, l),$$

where K_d is the diffuse reflectance, t is the hair fiber tangent, and l is the light vector. Given this derivation, the diffuse component will be strongest when the light direction is perpendicular to the tangent of the hair.

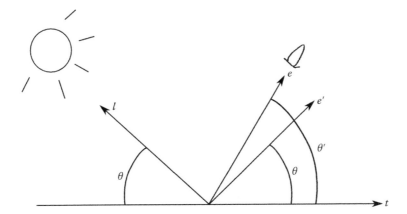

Figure 14.2. This figure serves as a visual supplement to the calculations necessary for the hair specular component. See Section 14.3.2.

14.3.2 Specular

The specular component from the hair lighting model described by [Kajiya and Kay 89] is based on the Phong specular model [Phong 73], where light is reflected off a hair strand based on the tangent direction of the hair. The tangent of the hair fiber represents the tangent of the surface that the light will reflect off of. See Figure 14.2 and the following derivation for the hair specular component:

$$K_s \cos (e, e')^p$$

$$K_s \cos (\theta - \theta')^p$$

$$K_s (\cos (\theta) \cos (\theta') + \sin (\theta) \sin (\theta'))^p$$

$$K_s ((t \cdot l)(t \cdot e) + \sin (t, l) \sin (t, e))^p,$$

where K_s is the specular reflectance. The eye vector is represented with e, while l is the light vector and e' is the corresponding reflection vector. the angle between the hair tangent t and the light vector l is θ, and θ' is the angle between the eye vector e and the hair fiber tangent t.

14.3.3 Practical Real-Time Hair Lighting

Given the defined diffuse and specular hair shading components and Marschner's more analytical approach, Scheuermann presents a phenomenologically derived hair lighting model [Scheuermann 04]. Figure 14.3 shows the dual specular highlights in a real-world image that the Scheuermann model attempts to reproduce.

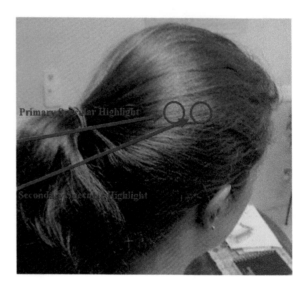

Figure 14.3. An image, found in and courtesy of [Scheuermann 04], which shows the dual specular highlights in hair that the resulting practical real-time hair lighting model attempts to produce.

Marschner's paper [Marschner et al. 03] describes a primary and secondary high-light. The primary highlight is shifted toward the hair tip, and is primarily influenced by the light color. The secondary highlight is shifted toward the hair root, and is influenced by the light color and hair color. To combine the two spec-ular highlights, the reflection vector for the primary highlight is shifted in toward the direction of the hair tangent, pointing from root to tip, and the secondary highlight may be shifted in the opposite way, away from the direction of the hair fiber tangent (see Figure 14.4).

14.4   Shadows and Approximated Hair Self-Shadowing

In addition to lighting calculations, the hair receives environment shadows and self-shadowing. In this section, we explain what we used to handle hair receiving and casting shadows as well as hair self-shadowing in *Tomb Raider*.

We chose to approximate the self-shadowing calculation because of the com-parative cost of generating and applying a deep shadow map in order to apply accurate self-shadowing effects [Lacroix 13, Engel and Hodes 13]. For the approx-imation, a regular shadow map may be used, which will hold the depth of the hair fibers closest to the light source. This shadow map of the hair serves as a representation of the topmost layer of the hair. Using this shadow map, an ap-proximated *number of fibers* occluding the hair fragment can be calculated and

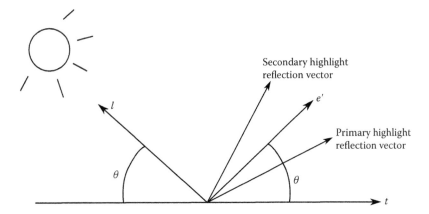

Figure 14.4. This figure shows a simple representation of the reflection vector shift that occurs to generate the dual highlights. The secondary highlight reflection vector is shifted toward the root of the hair fiber (which is against the direction of the hair fiber tangent), and the primary highlight reflection vector is shifted toward the hair fiber tip.

used to apply a volumetric self-shadowing term. The resulting effect is similar to deep shadow maps but at a much lower cost. Here is the approximated deep shadow maps calculation:

$$number\ of\ fibers = \frac{(depth\ range)}{(fiber\ spacing) * (fiber\ radius)},$$

$$hair\ shadow\ term = (1 - hair\ shadow\ alpha)^{number\ of\ fibers}.$$

In these calculations *depth range* is the distance between the hair fragment being shaded and the corresponding shadow map depth. *Fiber spacing* and *fiber radius* are artistic tweakables that help define how dense the hair is when calculating the hair self-shadowing term. *Fiber radius* is considered in the geometry expansion step (see Section 14.2), so it is best to adjust the *fiber spacing* when tuning hair self-shadowing. A larger *fiber spacing* means a lower *number of fibers* count, which leads to a lighter self-shadowing term. The *hair shadow alpha* defines how much light energy goes through each of the approximated *number of fibers*. Each fiber allows $(1 - hair\ shadow\ alpha)$ light through, so $(1 - hair\ shadow\ alpha)^{number\ of\ fibers}$ calculates the amount of light that goes through the approximated *number of fibers* and reaches the hair fragment being shadowed.

In order to take care of hair casting shadows on the environment as well as hair self-shadowing, hair was rendered into the engine's shadow maps just like any other shadow casting object. This allowed hair to cast shadows on the environment as any typical shadow mapping occurs. These shadow maps were also useful for applying hair self-shadowing. Due to the nature of the self-shadowing approximation calculation, there was no need to separate hair from the engine's shadow maps when dealing with the environment casting shadows on the hair because typically environment objects will be a large distance away from the hair. The relatively large distance will generate a large number of fibers, which will drive the shadow term to zero, as would be expected for a solid object casting a shadow on the hair.

14.5   Antialiasing

After lighting and shadow calculations are completed, antialiasing calculations occur for each hair pixel fragment. In this section, we explain the reasoning for having specialized hair antialiasing. Then we will cover how the hair antialiasing is performed. Lastly, we'll cover an alternative image-space approach we developed [Engel and Hodes 13, Lacroix 13], which we found to perform faster than the geometrically based approach proposed by [Yu et al. 12].

Rendering individual hair strands can result in heavy aliasing issues. (See Figure 14.5.) An individual hair strand will look like a jagged line once projected into screen space. Also, with a large amount of hair strands, aliasing will not only cause jagged hair strands, but there can also be noise among the final result of shading a clump of hair strands. With hair, we can take advantage of special geometry information and apply a specialized hair antialiasing to improve the overall render quality.

An additional important benefit of the specialized hair antialiasing is to simulate the thinness of individual hair strands. Previous real-time hair rendering simulations would run into issues where individual hair strands would appear too thick. Applying the specialized hair antialiasing helps soften the edges of

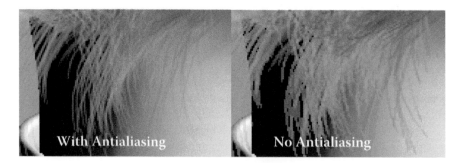

Figure 14.5. Here is a comparison of hair rendered with and without the specialized hair antialiasing. The largest noticeable difference is the jagged staircasing present in the image without antialiasing versus the softer hair edge pixels in the image with antialiasing.

individual hair strands, which is especially important when the hair strands are sub-pixel in width.

In order to apply antialiasing to the hair pixels, the strategy is to calculate the percentage of the screen pixel that is covered by the hair fiber. This percentage value is called *coverage* and this *coverage* value directly modifies the hair alpha. By using the *coverage* value to modulate the hair alpha, hair pixels become more transparent near the edges of hair strands in order to produce the antialiasing effect. One approach to antialiasing uses a ray-cone intersection of the pixel and hair fiber [Yu et al. 12]. With the ray-cone intersection approach, the area of the ray-cone cross section at the intersection with the hair fiber is determined, then the percentage of this area that is covered by the hair fiber becomes the *coverage* value for the corresponding pixel.

An alternative approach we took to apply the specialized hair antialiasing is handled in image space instead. A related generic antialiasing approach that inspired our image-space approach for hair is *geometric post-process antialiasing* (GPAA) [Persson 12], for applying antialiasing to polygon edges in a screen-space pass. Pixels that lie on polygon edges are evaluated for their distance to the actual image space projected edge locations. The distances to each polygon edge are used to generate blend weights for blending between the bordering polygons.

Our image-based hair antialiasing approach uses the location of the hair fiber edges to evaluate each hair fragment's distance with respect to these edges. The farther the pixel is outside the hair fiber, the more we decrease the *coverage* value. The farther the pixel is inside of the hair fiber, the more we increase the *coverage* value. A pixel directly on the hair fiber edge has a 0.5 *coverage* value. A hair fragment 0.5+ pixel distance outside the hair fiber edge has a *coverage* of 0. A hair fragment 0.5+ pixel distance inside the hair fiber edge has a *coverage* value of 1. See Listing 14.2 to see how the image-based hair antialiasing calculation is performed in the pixel shader.

In Figure 14.6, we see a hair fiber segment's outline after being projected onto the screen. The blue lines in the figure show the "hair fiber edge"-to-"pixel center" that is calculated for each hair fragment for the image-space-based antialiasing. The pixels are marked **A**, **B**, and **C** depending on their resulting *coverage* values. The pixels marked **A** have *coverage* values near 0 because the pixel centers are nearly a half-pixel outside the hair fiber. Pixels marked **B** are the pixels that are near the hair fiber edge, which result in *coverage* values near 0.5. **C** pixels are nearly a half-pixel distance within the hair fiber, so these pixels will have *coverage* values near 1.

14.6 Transparency

Transparency for hair rendering is important for a high-quality implementation. Working together with hair antialiasing, transparency helps to simulate the pres-

```
float ImageBasedHairAA(float2 p0, float2 p1, float2 pixelLoc)
{
    // p0, p1, pixelLoc are in d3d clip space (-1 to 1)x(-1 to 1).
    // p0 and p1 are the two nearest hair fiber edge positions
    //    to the hair fragment being shaded.

    // Scale positions so 1.f = half pixel width
    p0 *= g_WinSize.xy;
    p1 *= g_WinSize.xy;
    pixelLoc *= g_WinSize.xy;

    float p0dist = length(p0 - pixelLoc);
    float p1dist = length(p1 - pixelLoc);
    float hairWidth = length(p0 - p1);

    // will be 1.f if pixel outside hair, 0.f if pixel inside hair
    float outside = any( float2(step(hairWidth, p0dist),
                        step(hairWidth,p1dist)) );

    // if outside, set sign to -1, else set sign to 1
    float sign = outside > 0.f ? -1.f : 1.f;

    // signed distance
    //(positive if inside hair, negative if outside hair)
    float relDist = sign * saturate( min(p0dist, p1dist) );

    // returns coverage based on the relative distance
    // 0, if completely outside hair edge
    // 1, if completely inside hair edge
    return (relDist + 1.f) * 0.5f;
}
```

Listing 14.2. This is the function used to perform the image-based hair antialiasing calculation. See Listing 14.1 to see where **p0** and **p1** are calculated.

ence of thin individual hair strands. Also, where each hair fragment has its own lighting and shadowing applied separately, transparency is important for a high-quality volumetric result.

Due to the large amount of geometry and high possibility of a large number of transparent layers within a single pixel, dealing with correctly blending the many transparent layers of hair becomes a challenge. The hair transparency is handled through the use of Order Independent Transparency with per-pixel linked lists [Thibieroz 11]. For every pixel on screen that has one or more layers of hair, a linked list is generated containing each overlapping hair fragment.

The transparency for hair is handled by two separate passes. The first pass, the *A-Buffer Fill*, generates the unsorted linked lists for each pixel on screen that contains hair fragments. The second pass, *Sort and Draw*, traverses the per-pixel linked lists, sorting and blending for the final hair pixel result [Yu et al. 12]. In the rest of this section, we'll go through some of the specifics of the hair transparency passes and how that works with per-pixel linked lists.

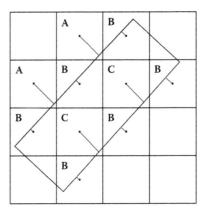

Figure 14.6. The specialized hair antialiasing calculation is performed by finding the distances between the pixels and the closest hair fiber edge. The blue segments here represent the distances that are found then used to modify the hair *coverage* value. The pixels marked **A** are nearly a half-pixel distance outside the hair fiber, so their *coverage* values will be near 0. Pixels marked **B** are pixels near the hair fiber edge, which means these pixels will have *coverage* values near 0.5. The pixels marked **C** are nearly a half-pixel distance within the hair fiber resulting in *coverage* values close to 1.

14.6.1 Hair Fragment Linked List Node

The linked list node consists of color, depth, and a next node pointer. Each component of the linked list node is stored as a 32-bit unsigned integer. The color is the final shaded hair fragment (from a single hair fiber) and includes alpha for hair transparency blending and hair antialiasing (see Section 14.5 for more information on hair antialiasing). When stored into the linked list node, color is packed into eight bits per channel (red, green, and blue) and eight bits for alpha. The hair fragment's depth relative to the camera is stored, which will be used for sorting the layers of hair fragments in the linked lists. The next node pointer points to another fragment in the linked list or no fragment if the node is at the end of the list [Yu et al. 12, Lacroix 13, Engel and Hodes 13].

14.6.2 A-Buffer Fill

During the *A-Buffer Fill* pass, the hair goes through a geometry pass and all strands are rendered (see the section on Geometry Expansion for more specifics on the geometry pass), then each individual hair fragment gets processed in the pixel shader. Each hair fragment undergoes lighting and shading. The *coverage* calculation for the specialized hair antialiasing occurs here and is applied to the hair fragment's alpha. Lastly, the fragment is stored in the linked list of the corresponding screen space pixel.

Having the main scene depth buffer readily usable here allows for the use of early depth stencil, so the depth comparison for hair fragments occurs before pixel shader execution, effectively reducing the number of pixels that need to be shaded and stored in the linked lists. In preparation for the *Sort and Draw* pass, a stencil for the hair pixels is written. The *Sort and Draw* pass is a fullscreen pass, so in order to make use of the early depth stencil again, a stencil comparison must be used.

14.6.3 Sort and Draw

During the *Sort and Draw* pass, the per-pixel linked list (PPLL) generated by the *A-buffer Fill* pass is traversed, sorted for the topmost hair pixels, then the final blended hair pixel result is generated. This is a fullscreen pass, where each pixel location is used to look up the corresponding per-pixel linked list. The topmost fragments are found and stored locally. While searching for the topmost hair fragments, the remaining hair fragments are blended out of order. The locally stored topmost layers are then blended in order.

Finding the eight topmost fragments is sufficient because of the contribution of a fragment at layer eight and beyond start to get minimal, so the out of order blending produces little to no variation in the final shaded result. The maximum influence m of a hair fragment on the final shaded result can be calculated based on the layer number n and the maximum alpha a possible for a hair fragment:

$$m = a * (1 - a)^{n-1}.$$

Given this formula, the maximum influence of a hair fragment at the eighth layer is ≈ 0.01715, meaning the influence at layer eight is barely over one percent. Layers beyond layer eight will influence the final shaded result less and less. Because of this, using the top eight layers is sufficient enough to minimize variation in the final shaded result.

The sorting is performed using the depth stored in the linked list node. To search for the to most hair fragments, the linked list is simple iterated over, while keeping a local copy of the current topmost hair fragments readily available for a simple comparison.

14.7 Integration Specifics

One thing not addressed in this chapter so far is writing depth for the hair in order for hair to work correctly with depth-based effects, such as depth of field. We cover three different ways to handle the depth write: writing a constant depth for all hair pixels, precise depth per hair pixel, and a selective depth write with precise depth per hair pixel. We chose to go with the last approach in *Tomb Raider* because it was the solution that maximized quality and was tolerant enough to deal with the large variance of camera conditions, close-ups with depth of field, and hair rendering with other transparent materials and effects [Lacroix 13, Engel and Hodes 13].

14.7.1 Constant Depth for Hair Pixels

In the same pass as the *Sort and Draw*, when the fullscreen quad is drawn, the quad may be drawn with a depth at the average depth or "hair object" position. Because the stencil is used during the *Sort and Draw* pass, the depth writes can be turned on and set to always pass and always write if the stencil comparison is successful. This is the most relaxed approach with the smallest overhead. One drawback is that depth is written for all hair pixels, even when hair is sparse, and edge hair pixels have near zero alpha, which will appear almost completely transparent. This drawback means the possibility for some noticeable visual artifacts with depth-based effects. One such example is in depth of field, where pixels that have nearly transparent hair fragments in them will not be blurred into the background far-focus, and there will be a "transparent halo" artifact around the hair. Another drawback is because of the lack of more precise depth information for all hair pixels.

14.7.2 Depth Per Hair Pixel

In order to get depth data for all hair pixels, a separate render target may be used during the *Sort and Draw* pass to capture the depth of the hair fragment in each per-pixel linked list that is closest to the viewer. A second pass is needed after this to copy the depth information collected into the depth buffer. The reason for separating this into two passes, rather than writing the more precise depth in the *Sort and Draw* pass, is because depth writes through the pixel shader are not possible when the depth result is influenced by flow control in shader code. This approach will result in more precise depth information per-pixel, but will still suffer from the "transparent halo" problem previously described in Section 14.7.1.

14.7.3 Selective Depth Write

To deal with the "transparent halo" problem, this last depth writing solution takes a conditional approach to writing depth, by evaluating final shaded hair fragments during the *Sort and Draw* pass for opaque or near-opaque final hair pixels. The criteria for evaluating pixels includes examining the number of hair fragment layers and the final alpha value being used for blending. Pixels with a large number of hair fragment layers or a large final alpha value can be marked as opaque and have their precise depth captured and written in a second pass, like the previously described depth writing solution.

Pass	Number of Draw Calls	Time (ms)
Shadow map render	16	0.7414
Shading and AA	4	2.0303
Sort and Draw	1	0.8660
Total	21	3.6377

Table 14.1. Performance numbers for the scene in Figure 14.7 for TressFX in *Tomb Raider* on an AMD Radeon HD 7970.

14.8 Conclusion

We were able to take a technology demo for hair and integrate that into a game. This chapter explains how each part of the advanced real-time hair works, and covers optimizations that we developed to improve the original hair technology demo and make it more viable for use in a game. In the rest of the conclusion, we cover details on performance and ideas for future work and improvements.

14.8.1 Performance

The performance of the hair technology is another interesting topic, because it is highly reliant on scene conditions. Given the large amount of hair geometry data and varying (but can be large) amount of hair pixels to process, the overall performance of the advanced real-time hair can vary depending on the amount of hair fragments on screen. If there are enough hair fragments on screen, then the technique becomes pixel shader limited, but if hair is far away from the screen, then the technique is vertex shader limited. Given this, pixel shader-based optimizations (such as simpler lighting calculations or the image-based hair antialiasing presented in this chapter) become effective when scene conditions cause the technique to be pixel shader limited.

Refer to Tables 14.1 and 14.2 for performance numbers for TressFX in *Tomb Raider* in two separate scenes. For these two scenes, the performance numbers vary because of the different scene conditions. The main factor to consider here is the number of hair fragments being processed. The scene used for the performance numbers in Table 14.2 (see Figure 14.8) has many more hair fragments on screen than the scene used for Table 14.1 (see Figure 14.7).

Pass	Number of Draw Calls	Time (ms)
Shadow map render	4	0.1992
Shading and AA	4	3.7104
Sort and Draw	1	3.0181
Total	9	6.9277

Table 14.2. Performance numbers for the scene in Figure 14.8 for TressFX in *Tomb Raider* on an AMD Radeon HD 7970.

Figure 14.7. The first scene used for gathering performance numbers.

Figure 14.8. The second scene used for gathering performance numbers.

14.8.2 Future Work and Improvements

An important point to explore is also where the technique can use improvements. Here are some possible improvement ideas:

- Reduce the need for random access patterns of memory in the *Sort and Draw* pass by storing or rendering a limited number of transparent hair pixel layers.

- Integrate the advanced real-time hair rendering into a deferred lighting engine. This will require storing data needed for hair lighting into the per-pixel linked lists instead of the shaded hair fragment color. AMD has an example implementation of this available in the latest TressFX sample available on the AMD website at http://developer.amd.com/tools-and-sdks/graphics-development/amd-radeon-sdk/.

- Improve the way vertex and other geometry data is utilized for geometry expansion, by reducing the amount of data to process in the hair geometry pass. It should be possible to take advantage of vertex buffers and index buffers rather than manually indexing into structured buffers in the vertex shader to perform the geometry expansion.

Bibliography

[Engel and Hodes 13] Wolfgang Engel and Stephan Hodes. "Hair Rendering in Tomb Raider: AMD's TressFX." Presentation, FMX 2013, Stuttgart, Germany, April 24, 2013.

[Kajiya and Kay 89] James T. Kajiya and T. L. Kay. "Rendering Fur with Three Dimensional Textures." In *Proceedings of the 16th Annual Conference on Computer Graphics and Interactive Techniques*, pp. 271–280. New York: ACM, 1989.

[Lacroix 13] Jason Lacroix. "A Survivor Reborn: Tomb Raider on DX11." Presentation, Game Developers Conference 2013, San Francisco, CA, April 23, 2013.

[Marschner et al. 03] Stephen R. Marschner, Henrik Wann Jensen, Mike Cammarano, Steve Worley, and Pat Hanrahan. "Light Scattering from Human Hair Fibers." *ACM Transactions on Graphics* 22:3 (2003), 780–791.

[Persson 12] Emil Persson. "Geometric Antialiasing Methods." In *GPU Pro 3*, edited by Wolfgang Engel, pp. 71–87. Natick, MA: A K Peters, Ltd., 2012.

[Phong 73] Bui Tuong Phong. "Illumination for Computer-Generated Images." Ph.D. thesis, The University of Utah, Salt Lake City, UT, 1973.

[Scheuermann 04] Thorsten Scheuermann. "Practical Real-Time Hair Rendering and Shading." In *ACM SIGGRAPH 2004 Sketches*, p. 147. New York: ACM, 2004.

[Thibieroz 11] Nicolas Thibieroz. "Order-Independent Transparency Using Per-Pixel Linked Lists." In *GPU Pro 2*, edited by Wolfgang Engel, pp. 409–431. Natick, MA: A K Peters, Ltd., 2011.

[Yu et al. 12] Xuan Yu, Jason C. Yang, Justin Hensley, Takahiro Harada, and Jingyi Yu. "A Framework for Rendering Complex Scattering Effects on Hair." In *Proceedings of the ACM SIGGRAPH Symposium on Interactive 3D Graphics and Games, I3D '12*, pp. 111–118. New York: ACM, 2012.

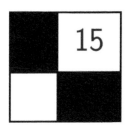

15

Wire Antialiasing

Emil Persson

15.1 Introduction

There are many sources of aliasing in rendered images. The two most common culprits are geometric edges and shading. Historically these sources of aliasing have been resolved by Multi-Sample Antialiasing (MSAA) and mip-mapping with trilinear filtering respectively. With mip-mapping and trilinear filtering, which were supported on consumer-level hardware even way back in the 1990s, textures on surfaces were essentially free from aliasing. In the early 2000s, as consumer-level hardware gained MSAA support, the remaining problem of edge aliasing, often referred to as "jaggies," was more or less a solved problem. Games of this era could then be relatively aliasing free since the geometric detail was limited enough that MSAA effectively eliminated all geometric aliasing, and shading was typically simple and low frequency and did not introduce any additional aliasing on top of the surface texture. The main exception was alpha-tested objects, such as fences and foliage, which sorely stood out in an otherwise relatively aliasing-free environment.

As games have adopted increasingly more sophisticated lighting models and with geometric density constantly on the rise, aliasing has unfortunately made a strong comeback in modern games. Mip-mapping alone no longer fully solves the shader aliasing problem. Complex lighting introduces aliasing where the mip-mapped textures alone exhibit none. In particular the specular component tends to cause lots of aliasing. This field is poorly researched and only a few approaches exist to properly deal with the problem. The most notable work here is LEAN mapping [Olano and Baker 10]. On the geometry side we are getting increasingly denser geometry, and as geometry gets down to the sub-pixel level, MSAA is no longer sufficient.

Much research remains to be done to solve these problems once and for all. This chapter does not present a final solution to all these problems; however, it presents a technique for solving one specific, but common, subset of geometric aliasing in games, namely that of phone wires and similar long and thin objects.

While the technique has been dubbed Wire Antialiasing, it applies to any object that can be decomposed to a set of cylindrical shapes. This includes wires, pipes, poles, railings, light posts, antenna towers, many types of fences, and even grass if represented as actual geometry rather than as alpha textures. Tree trunks and branches may also be cylindrical enough to work. These are all common elements in games and frequent sources of aliasing.

15.2 Algorithm

15.2.1 Overview

The problem with very thin geometry, such as wires, is that it tends to degenerate into a set of flickering and disconnected pixels when it gets sub-pixel sized. Why is that? In technical terms, what happens is that the visibility function gets undersampled. In plain English, the wire simply misses the pixels. A pixel only gets shaded if the geometry covers the pixel center. If the wire is thinner than a pixel, chances are that at some points it will simply slide in between two pixel centers and end up not shading any of them. In this case there will be a gap. The thinner the wire gets, the worse the problem gets. However, if the geometry is wider than a pixel, we are guaranteed to have a continuous line with no gaps. The problem thus occurs when geometry goes sub-pixel sized. The idea of this technique, then, is to simply keep the wire one pixel wide or larger. To emulate a sub-pixel coverage, we simply fade away the wire by outputting the coverage to alpha and applying blending.

What about MSAA? Unfortunately, MSAA does not solve the problem. It alleviates it somewhat, but the improvement is rather marginal. With 4× multisampling, the visibility function is now sampled at twice the rate horizontally and vertically. In other words, the wire can now be about half a pixel wide (depending on sample locations) without risking missing all samples somewhere. This is not much of an improvement, and all we have accomplished is to push the problem into the distance. We can now have the wire twice as far away before the problem occurs, or have a half as thin wire, but that is all. Actually, when we enable MSAA, we normally want to eliminate "jaggies." If we have a half-pixel wide wire, MSAA may keep it continuous in this case; however, it will be jagged, because it only hits a single sample per pixel. There is not enough resolution to estimate the coverage, but it simply boils down to more or less a binary on/off per pixel.

While MSAA does not by itself solve the thin geometry problem, it is still valuable for this technique. While we are guaranteeing gap-free wires, we are not producing smooth antialiased results as such. In fact, the wires will be jagged by default. So we use MSAA for what it excels at, namely removing those jaggies. So despite increased visibility function sampling rate with MSAA enabled, we still limit wires to a one pixel width and keep the additional resolution for MSAA to estimate coverage and eliminate the jaggies, just like MSAA normally does. Our technique is thus independent of the MSAA mode. It can also run without MSAA, but the wires will then look as jagged as (but not worse than) the rest of the scene.

15.2.2 Method

The wire is represented in the vertex buffer much like one might normally design a wire, with the exception that we need to be able to vary the wire's radius at runtime, so we do not store final vertex positions but instead store the center of the wire. The final vertex position will then be computed by displacing the vertex along the normal. For this we provide a wire radius, in world-space units. This would typically be a constant for wires and would be best passed in the constant buffer, but for some types of objects (such as antenna towers, light posts, and grass straws), it could make sense to store a radius value per vertex instead.

The first step is to estimate how small a radius we are allowed without violating our minimum one pixel width requirement given the current vertex position in the view frustum. This scales linearly with the w-value of the transformed vertex, depending on the field of view (FOV) angle and render-target resolution. With a projection matrix computed the usual way with a vertical FOV, a constant scale factor can be computed as in Equation (15.1):

$$PixelScale = \frac{\tan(FOV/2)}{height}.\tag{15.1}$$

This value can be computed once and passed as a constant. The radius of a pixel-wide wire is then given by multiplying by the vertex's w-value. The w-value can be found by doing a dot product between the vertex position and the last row of the view-projection matrix (or column, depending on the matrix convention used). Once we know the radius of a pixel-wide wire, we can simply clamp our radius to this value to ensure our wire is always at least one pixel wide. The shader code for this is in Listing 15.1.

While adjusting the radius guarantees that we get gap-free wires, the result is inevitably also that the wires will appear wider and wider as they go farther into the distance if we do not also take the original unexpanded wire's pixel coverage into account. Compare Figure 15.1 and Figure 15.2 for an illustration of this effect. What we need to do is to compensate by computing the coverage of the real unexpanded wire and fading the contribution accordingly. This is what will give the wire its natural and alias-free appearance. This can be accomplished by outputting the coverage value to alpha and enabling alpha blending. As shown on the last line in Listing 15.1, the coverage fade factor is simply the original real radius of the wire divided by the expanded radius. In other words, if the radius was expanded to twice the size to cover one pixel, then the wire is half a pixel wide and the coverage consequently 0.5. As the wire gets farther into the

```
// Compute view-space w
float w = dot(ViewProj[3], float4(In.Position, 1.0f));

// Compute what radius a pixel-wide wire would have
float pixel_radius = w * PixelScale;

// Clamp radius to pixel size.
float new_radius = max(Radius, pixel_radius);

float3 position = In.Position + radius * In.Normal;

// Fade out with the reduction in radius versus original.
float fade = Radius / new_radius;
```

Listing 15.1. Computing radius and fade factor.

Figure 15.1. Original wire. Note how the wire is aliased and full of holes despite $4\times$ MSAA being enabled.

distance, it will now appear fainter and fainter, maintaining the appearance of a thin wire, as illustrated in Figure 15.3. Comparing Figure 15.3 to Figure 15.1, it can be seen that the wires look identical, except for the fact that Figure 15.3 does not suffer from aliasing artifacts.

15.2.3 Lighting

The technique as described so far works fairly well; we have eliminated the geometric aliasing, but unfortunately thin wires also tend to suffer from shading aliasing as the lighting function gets sampled very sparsely and pseudo-randomly. When the wire reaches pixel size, any texture sampling would likely go down to the lowest mip-map and get uniformly colored by default; however, the normal

Figure 15.2. Expanded wire. Note that the wire is now free from gaps and aliasing, but appears unnaturally thick in the distance.

Figure 15.3. Final wire. Wire now appears natural and alias free.

can go from pointing straight up to straight down over the course of a single pixel, potentially resulting in severe aliasing from the lighting. The simplest approach to deal with this problem is to choose a soft lighting model that results in a minimum amount of aliasing, such as Half Lambert [Valve 08]. For many wires this could be good enough as it blends fairly well into an environment otherwise lit by more physically correct models. However, even with this simple model (and even more so for more complex ones), it is crucial to enable centroid sampling on the interpolators. The error introduced from sampling outside of the wire is simply far too great.

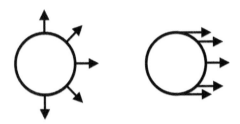

Figure 15.4. Left: Original normals. Right: Normals by the time the wire goes sub-pixel, assuming the viewer is to the right of the wire.

If sticking to Half Lambert is not enough, there are a few different approaches for dealing with this. We have tried a couple of methods that both work relatively well and can also be combined. Both involve fading over from our regular lighting model into something uniformly colored over some distance before reaching pixel size. The first method is simply computing our lighting as usual, then computing the Half Lambert as well, and then fading between these two. In our test scene a good fade range was from about 4 pixels wide and fully faded over to Half Lambert as it reached a single pixel. This is not based on any science but purely from testing various ranges and subjectively selecting what looked best for us. Depending on your lighting model and parameters, this could be tweaked differently. The advantage of this method is that it is straightforward and simple and tends to work fairly well.

The other method we tried involves flattening the normals over the distance. The thinner the wire gets, the more we are bending the normals toward the center normal from the viewer's point of view. As the wire goes down to a single pixel width, the normal will be entirely flat, and consequently result in a uniform lighting result. (See Figure 15.4.)

Since all this does is modify the input normal, this method is compatible with any lighting model, although results may vary.

15.2.4   Use with Deferred Shading

Deferred shading typically has a single global lighting model. This could make it tricky to fade between a soft light model, such as Half Lambert, and the engine's regular lighting model. The most straightforward approach is to simply render wires in a forward pass after the deferred lighting pass. The blended part of the wire (i.e., where it is smaller than a pixel wide) will have to be rendered as a translucent object anyway because of the blending. Typically wires take up a very small amount of screen space, so rendering the entire wire, including fully opaque parts, would normally have a minimal impact on performance. In the case where it is desirable to render opaque parts into the G-buffer, the normal bending approach above integrates very well as all it does is modify the input normal. The bent normal can then be written to the G-buffer and shaded as part of the regular deferred lighting pass.

15.2.5 Use with FXAA

This technique works very well together with MSAA, where MSAA takes care of all the jaggies, just like it is designed to do. But not all games use MSAA anymore; a whole bunch of filtering-based approaches to antialiasing have been used recently [Jimenez et al. 11a] and several have gone into shipping games. Arguably the most popular ones are FXAA [Lottes 09] and MLAA [Reshetov 09, Jimenez et al. 11b]. We have tested this technique in conjunction with FXAA and found that FXAA became nearly ineffective on the pixel-wide wires left by this technique. Consequently, as a workaround, the wire needs to be expanded somewhat for FXAA to take effect. Fortunately, as little as about 1.3 pixels width is enough for FXAA to pick up the edges. Somewhat wider wires do result in a somewhat lower quality overall, but not too bad. Other similar techniques, such as MLAA, may be better suited for dealing with pixel-thin wires, but the author has not verified that this is the case.

15.3 Conclusion and Future Work

A technique has been presented that effectively deals with aliasing on a specific (but frequently occurring) subset of aliasing-prone geometry. This is a welcome tool to reduce aliasing in games, but it does not solve the entire problem space of aliasing in real-time rendering. Much research is still needed. An obvious next step would be to explore ways to extend this technique to other shapes than cylinders. We believe extending it to rectangular shapes such as bricks and planks should be relatively straightforward and could work fundamentally the same, with the exception that we need to take view orientation into account for estimating size in terms of pixels. From there it may be possible to solve the staircase. Stairs are a frequent source of aliasing artifacts in games, as the top and side view of the steps tend to get lit differently, resulting in ugly Moiré patterns when the steps get down to pixel size.

Solving all these special cases may be enough for games, but ideally it would be desirable to solve the general case, where a model with any amount of fine detail and thin sub-pixel sized triangles could be rendered in an alias-free manner, without resorting to super-sampling, and preferably without a preprocessing step.

Bibliography

[Jimenez et al. 11a] Jorge Jimenez et al. "Filtering Approaches for Real-Time Antialiasing." SIGGRAPH 2011 Course, Vancouver, Canada, August, 2011. (Available at http://iryoku.com/aacourse/.)

[Jimenez et al. 11b] Jorge Jimenez, Belen Masia, Jose I. Echevarria, Fernando Navarro, and Diego Gutierrez. "Practical Morphological Antialiasing." In *GPU Pro 2*, edited by Wolfgang Engel, pp. 95–120. Natick, MA: A K Peters, Ltd., 2011. (See also http://www.iryoku.com/mlaa/.)

[Lottes 09] Timothy Lottes. "FXAA." White Paper, Nvidia, http://developer. download.nvidia.com/assets/gamedev/files/sdk/11/FXAA_WhitePaper.pdf, 2009.

[Olano and Baker 10] Marc Olano and Dan Baker. "LEAN Mapping." http:// www.csee.umbc.edu/~olano/papers/lean/, 2010.

[Reshetov 09] Alexander Reshetov. "Morphological Antialiasing." Preprint, http://visual-computing.intel-research.net/publications/papers/2009/mlaa/ mlaa.pdf, 2009.

[Valve 08] Valve Developer Community. "Half Lambert." https://developer. valvesoftware.com/wiki/Half_Lambert, 2008.

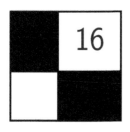

16

Real-Time Lighting via Light Linked List

Abdul Bezrati

16.1 Introduction

Deferred lighting has been a popular technique to handle dynamic lighting in video games, but due to the fact that it relies on the depth buffer, it doesn't work well with translucent geometry and particle effects, which typically don't write depth values. This can be seen in Figure 16.1, where the center smoke effect and the translucent water bottles are not affected by the colorful lights in the scene.

Common approaches in deferred engines have been to either leave translucent objects unlit or apply a forward lighting pass specifically for those elements. The forward lighting pass adds complexity and an extra maintenance burden to the engine.

At Insomniac Games, we devised a unified solution that makes it possible to light both opaque and translucent scene elements (Figure 16.2) using a single path. We have named our solution Light Linked List (LLL), and it requires unordered access views and atomic shader functions introduced with DirectX 10.1–level hardware.

The Light Linked List algorithm shares the performance benefits of deferred engines in that lighting is calculated only on the pixels affected by each light source. Furthermore, any object not encoded in the depth buffer has full access to the lights that will affect it. The Light Linked List generation and access is fully GPU accelerated and requires minimal CPU handholding.

16.2 Algorithm

The Light Linked List algorithm relies on a GPU-accessible list of light affecting each pixel on screen. A GPU Linked List has been used in the past to implement

Figure 16.1. Smoke effect and translucent water bottles don't receive any scene lighting in a traditional deferred lighting engine.

Figure 16.2. Smoke effects and translucent water bottles receive full-scene lighting via the LLL.

Order Independent Transparency as well as Indirect Illumination [Gruen and Thibieroz 10].

For each new frame in the game, we populate the linked list of lights and we later access it to evaluate lighting at each pixel.

16.2.1 GPU List Structure

For efficient lighting using the Light Linked List, we need to store each light's minimum and maximum depths so we can quickly reject any pixel that is outside of the light's boundaries. We also store the index of the light into a global array, where we keep each light's attributes such as colors, radii, intensities, etc.

Finally, we store a link to the next light at the current screen pixel: The Light Linked List algorithm follows a LIFO convention, where the last linked element stored is evaluated first.

```
struct LightFragmentLink
{
  float m_MinDepth;    // Light minimum depth at the current pixel
  float m_MaxDepth;    // Light maximum depth at the current pixel

  uint m_LightIndex;   // Light index into the full information array
  uint m_Next;         // Next LightFragmentLink index
};
```

16.2.2 GPU Structure Compressed

Because memory can be scarce on some systems and in an effort to reduce bandwidth usage, we chose to compress the `LightFragmentLink` structure and shave off half of the original memory requirements.

Both minimum and maximum light depths were converted to half precision and packed into a single unsigned integer `uint`. HLSL provides the useful intrinsic `f32tof16` to convert from full precision to half precision float. The light index was compressed from 32 to 8 bits, which puts an upper limit of 256 maximum visible lights at any frame. In practice, we found out that our scenes rarely ever exceed 75 lights per shot, but if the need for more than 256 lights ever comes up, we can either allocate more bits for the index or place it back in its own unsigned integer.

The link to the next fragment bits were reduced from 32 down to 24 bits in order to fit with the 8-bit light index. A 24-bit unsigned integer allows for more than 16 million actively linked fragments at once. The compressed `LightFragmentLink` structure stands at 8 bytes, whereas previously it required 16 bytes of memory.

```
struct LightFragmentLink
{
    uint m_DepthInfo; // High bits min depth, low bits max depth
    uint m_IndexNext; // Light index and link to the next fragment
};
```

16.2.3   Required Resources

To generate the Light Linked List, we use a total of four buffers, though the algorithm can easily be modified to require only three.

The first buffer is a pool of all the `LightFragmentLinks` that can be allocated and linked during a single frame. This resource is a read and write structured buffer:

$$\text{RWStructuredBuffer} < \text{LightFragmentLink} > \text{g\_LightFragmentLinkedBuffer}$$

The `LightFragmentLink` minimum and maximum depth values will be generated in separate draw calls, and thus we need a buffer to temporarily store one value while waiting for the matching depth to render. The second required buffer is a read and write byte address buffer:

$$\text{RWByteAddressBuffer} \qquad\qquad \text{g\_LightBoundsBuffer}$$

The third buffer is also a read and write byte address buffer that will be used to track the index of the last `LightFragmentLink` placed at any given pixel on screen:

$$\text{RWByteAddressBuffer} \qquad\qquad \text{g\_LightStartOffsetBuffer}$$

The final buffer is an optional depth buffer that will be used to perform software depth testing within a pixel shader. We chose to store the depth as linear in a FP32 format instead of the typical hyper values.

16.2.4   Light Shells

To render the dynamic lights into the LLL buffers, we represent the lights as geometry: Point lights are represented by spheres (Figure 16.3), spotlights are represented by cones, and area lights are represented by boxes.

To perfectly represent a sphere or a cone in 3D space with polygons, we need an extremely well-tessellated mesh, which places a heavy burden on both memory resources and GPU rendering time. To work around the tessellation problem, we resort to creating coarsely tessellated geometry that is oversized enough to fully contain the original high-resolution mesh.

16.3   Populating the Light Linked List

The pixel shader that generates the light linked list can be described in three steps. The first step is to perform a software depth test to reduce the number of `LightFragmentLinks` allocated in a single frame. The depth test is followed by collecting the light's minimum and maximum depth, before moving forward with the allocation of a `LightFragmentLink` element.

Figure 16.3. The light shell displayed in gray is used to describe a point light in the scene.

16.3.1 Software Depth Test

The Light Linked List algorithm allocates and links `LightFragmentLink` elements when the back faces of the light geometry get rasterized and sent to the pixel shader. In the common scenario where the scene geometry intersects the light sources, the hardware depth test can let the front faces pass through but occlude the back faces and thus interfere with the allocation of a `LightFragmentLink` (Figure 16.4).

To guarantee that back faces get processed by the pixel shader, we disable the hardware depth test and only perform the software test against the front faces; this will be explained in detail in the next section.

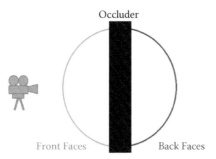

Figure 16.4. Front faces in green pass the hardware depth test, whereas back faces fail.

16.3.2 Depth Bounds

The LightFragmentLink structure stores both minimum and maximum light depth; however, those two values are rasterized by the hardware and sent to the pixel shaders at different times: The minimum depth will be carried through by the light geometry's front faces, whereas the maximum depth will be provided by the geometry's back faces.

We first draw the light geometry with back-ace culling turned on to allow rasterization of only the front faces. A pixel is determined to belong to a front- or back-facing polygon by the use of the HLSL semantic SV_IsFrontFace.

We perform a software depth test by comparing the light depth against the scene's depth. If the test fails, we turn the light depth into a negative value. If the test passes, we leave the target value unaltered.

The light's incoming depth is stored in an unsigned integer's lower 16 bits, the global light index in the upper 16 bits, and this value is then written to the g_LightBoundsBuffer resource.

```
// Detect front faces
if(front_face == true)
{
    // Sign will be negative if the light shell is occluded
    float depth_test = sign( g_txDepth[vpos_i].x - light_depth);

    // Encode the light index in the upper 16 bits and the linear
    // depth in the lower 16
    uint bounds_info = (light_index << 16) | f32tof16( light_depth*
        depth_test );

    // Store the front face info
    g_LightBoundsBuffer.Store( dst_offset, bounds_info );

    // Only allocate a LightFragmentLink on back faces
    return;
}
```

Once we have processed the front faces, we immediately rerender the light geometry but with front-face culling enabled.

We fetch the information previously stored into g_LightBoundsBuffer, and we decode both the light ID and the linear depth. At this point, we face two scenarios.

In the first scenario, the ID decoded from the g_LightBoundsBuffer sample and the incoming light information match. In this case, we know the front faces were properly processed and we proceed to check the sign of the stored depth: if it's negative we early out of the shader since both faces are occluded by the regular scene geometry.

The second scenario occurs when the decoded ID doesn't match the light information provided by the back faces. This scenario can happen when the frustum near clip intersects the light geometry. In this case, the minimum depth to be stored in the `LightFragmentLink` is set to zero.

```
// Load the content that was written by the front faces
uint bounds_info = g_LightBoundsBuffer.Load( dst_offset );

// Decode the stored light index
uint stored_index = (bounds_info >> 16);

// Decode the stored light depth
float front_depth = f16tof32( bounds_info >> 0 );

// Check if both front and back faces were processed
if(stored_index == light_index)
{
  // Check the case where front faces rendered but were occluded
  // by the scene geometry
  if(front_depth < 0)
  {
      return;
  }
}
// Mismatch, the front face was culled by the near clip
else
{
front_depth = 0;
}
```

16.3.3 Allocation of LightFragmentLink

Now that we know both minimum and maximum light depths are available to us, we can move forward with the allocation of a `LightFragmentLink`. To allocate a `LightFragmentLink`, we simply increment the internal counter of our `StructuredBuffer` containing all the fragments. To make the algorithm more robust and to avoid driver-related bugs, we must validate our allocation and make sure that we don't overflow:

```
// Allocate
uint  new_lll_idx = g_LightFragmentLinkedBuffer.IncrementCounter();

// Don't overflow
if(new_lll_idx >= g_VP_LLLMaxCount)
{
    return;
}
```

Once we have allocated a `LightFragmentLink`, we need to update our second `RWByteAddressBuffer` to keep track of the last inserted LLL element. Again, we make use of the HLSL atomic function `InterlockedExchange`:

```
uint        prev_lll_idx;

// Get the index of the last linked element stored and replace
// it in the process
g_LightStartOffsetBuffer.InterlockedExchange( dst_offset, new_
    lll_idx, prev_lll_idx );
```

At this point, we have all four of the required values to populate and store a valid **LightFragmentLink**:

```
// Encode the light depth values
uint light_depth_max = f32tof16( light_depth );// Back face depth
uint light_depth_min = f32tof16( front_depth );// Front face depth

// Final output
LightFragmentLink element;

// Pack the light depth
element.m_DepthInfo = (light_depth_min << 16) | light_depth_max;

// Index/Link
element.m_IndexNext = (light_index << 24) | (prev_lll_idx &
    0xFFFFFF);

// Store the element
g_LightFragmentLinkedBuffer[ new_lll_idx ] = element;
```

16.4   Accessing the Light Linked List

Accessing the Light Linked List is the same whether your engine uses a deferred or a forward renderer.

The first step is to convert the incoming pixel position from viewport space to an LLL index, and we do so by first converting the vPos to the LLL resolution, as shown below.

```
uint lll_x     = uint( (vpos_f.x / g_VP_Width ) * g_VP_LLLWidth );
uint lll_y     = uint( (vpos_f.y / g_VP_Height) * g_VP_LLLHeight );
uint src_index = lll_y * g_VP_LLLWidth + lll_x;
```

With the LLL index calculated, we fetch our first link from the unordered access view resource **g_LightStartOffsetView** and we start our lighting loop; the loop stops whenever we find an invalid value.

```
uint src_index = ScreenUVsToLLLIndex( screen_uvs );
uint first_offset = g_LightStartOffsetView[ src_index ];

  // Decode the first element index
  uint element_index = (first_offset & 0xFFFFFF);
```

```
// Iterate over the Light Linked List
while( element_index != 0xFFFFFF )
{
    // Fetch
    LightFragmentLink element   = g_LightFragmentLinkedView[element
    _index];

    // Update the next element index
    element_index          = (element.m_IndexNext & 0xFFFFFF);
    ...
}
```

Once we have acquired a valid `LightFragmentLink`, we decode the stored light depths and we perform a simple bounds test against the incoming pixel: if the pixel lies outside the light's bounds, we skip the rest of the lighting loop.

```
// Decode the light bounds
float light_depth_max    = f16tof32( element.m_DepthInfo >> 0 );
float light_depth_min    = f16tof32( element.m_DepthInfo >> 16 );

// Do depth bounds check
if( (l_depth > light_depth_max) || (l_depth < light_depth_min) )
{
    continue;
}
```

If our pixel lies within the light's bounds, we decode the global light index stored in the `LightFragmentLink` and we use it to read the full light information from a separate global resource.

```
// Decode the light index
uint light_idx = (element.m_IndexNext >> 24);

// Access the light environment
GPULightEnv light_env = g_LinkedLightsEnvs[ light_idx ];
```

16.5   Reduced Resolution

One way to reduce the memory footprint of the algorithm is to shrink the resolution at which the Light Linked List is stored. Running at a full resolution of 1080p and assuming an even light distribution of 32 lights per pixel, the total memory required for the linked list would be

$$1920 \times 1080 \times 32 \times \texttt{LightFragmentLink} = 506.25 \text{ MB}.$$

In practice, generating the Light Linked List at one quarter of the native game resolution, or even one eighth, is largely sufficient and reduces the required memory footprint by a significant amount:

$$(1920 \div 8) \times (1080 \div 8) \times 32 \times \texttt{LightFragmentLink} = 7.91 \text{ MB}.$$

16.5.1   Depth Down-Sampling

For engines that perform either a depth prepass or have a G-buffer, layer we need to down-sample the depth buffer to match the resolution of the LLL.

Scaling down the depth buffer must be done via point sampling and the use of the function max to avoid missing light information due to aggressive Z-culling. To speed up the down-sampling of the depth buffer, we make extensive use of the GatherRed function, which allows us to read four depth samples at once. Below is an example of how to down-sample a full-resolution depth buffer down to one eighth across the width and height:

```
float4 d4_max;

{
 float4 d4_00 = g_txDepth.GatherRed(g_samPoint, screen_uvs, int2(-3, -3));
 float4 d4_01 = g_txDepth.GatherRed(g_samPoint, screen_uvs, int2(-1, -3));
 float4 d4_10 = g_txDepth.GatherRed(g_samPoint, screen_uvs, int2(-3, -1));
 float4 d4_11 = g_txDepth.GatherRed(g_samPoint, screen_uvs, int2(-1, -1));
        d4_max = max(d4_00, max( d4_01, max( d4_10, d4_11)));
}

{
  float4 d4_00 = g_txDepth.GatherRed(g_samPoint, screen_uvs, int2(-3, 3));
  float4 d4_01 = g_txDepth.GatherRed(g_samPoint, screen_uvs, int2(-1, 3));
  float4 d4_10 = g_txDepth.GatherRed(g_samPoint, screen_uvs, int2(-3, 1));
  float4 d4_11 = g_txDepth.GatherRed(g_samPoint, screen_uvs, int2(-1, 1));
        d4_max = max(d4_max, max(d4_00, max( d4_01, max( d4_10, d4_11))));
}

{
  float4 d4_00 = g_txDepth.GatherRed(g_samPoint, screen_uvs, int2(3, -3));
  float4 d4_01 = g_txDepth.GatherRed(g_samPoint, screen_uvs, int2(1, -3));
  float4 d4_10 = g_txDepth.GatherRed(g_samPoint, screen_uvs, int2(3, -1));
  float4 d4_11 = g_txDepth.GatherRed(g_samPoint, screen_uvs, int2(1, -1));
        d4_max = max(d4_max, max(d4_00, max( d4_01, max( d4_10, d4_11))));
}

{
  float4 d4_00 = g_txDepth.GatherRed(g_samPoint, screen_uvs, int2( 3, 3));
  float4 d4_01 = g_txDepth.GatherRed(g_samPoint, screen_uvs, int2( 1, 3));
  float4 d4_10 = g_txDepth.GatherRed(g_samPoint, screen_uvs, int2( 3, 1));
  float4 d4_11 = g_txDepth.GatherRed(g_samPoint, screen_uvs, int2( 1, 1));
        d4_max = max(d4_max, max(d4_00, max( d4_01, max( d4_10, d4_11))));
}

// Calculate the final max depth
float depth_max = max(d4_max.x, max( d4_max.y, max(d4_max.z, d4_max.w)));
```

16.6 Conclusion

The Light Linked List algorithm helped us to drastically simplify our lighting pipeline while allowing us to light translucent geometry and particle effects, which were highly desirable. With Light Linked List, we were able to match or improve the performance of our deferred renderer, while reducing memory use. Additionally, the flexibility of Light Linked List allowed us to easily apply custom lighting for materials like skin, hair, cloth, and car paint.

In the future, we intend to further experiment with a more cache-coherent layout for the `LightFragmentLink` buffer, as this seems likely to yield further performance improvements.

Bibliography

[Gruen and Thibieroz 10] Holger Gruen and Nicolas Thibieroz. "Order Independent Transparency and Indirect Illumination Using Dx11 Linked Lists." Presentation at the Advanced D3D Day Tutorial, Game Developers Conference, San Francisco, CA, March 9–13, 2010.

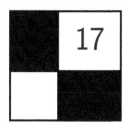

Deferred Normalized Irradiance Probes

John Huelin, Benjamin Rouveyrol, and Bartłomiej Wroński

17.1 Introduction

In this chapter we present deferred normalized irradiance probes, a technique developed at Ubisoft Montreal for *Assassin's Creed 4: Black Flag*. It was developed as a cross-console generation scalable technique and is running on all of our six target hardware platforms: Microsoft Xbox 360, Microsoft Xbox One, Sony Playstation 3, Sony Playstation 4, Nintendo WiiU, and PCs. We propose a partially dynamic global illumination algorithm that provides high-quality indirect lighting for an open world game. It decouples stored irradiance from weather and lighting conditions and contains information for a whole 24-hour cycle. Data is stored in a GPU-friendly, highly compressible format and uses only VRAM memory. We present the reasoning behind a higher achieved quality than what was possible with other partially baked solutions like precomputed radiance transfer (under typical open-world game constraints).

We also describe our tools pipeline, including a fully GPU-based irradiance baking solution. It is able to generate bounced lighting information for a full-day cycle and big game world in less than 8 minutes on a single PC machine. We present multiple optimizations to the baking algorithm and tools that helped achieve such performance and high productivity.

We provide details for both CPU and GPU runtime that stream and generate data for a given world position, time of day, and lighting conditions.

Finally, we show how we applied the calculated irradiance information in a fullscreen pass as part of our global ambient lighting and analyze the performance of whole runtime part of the algorithm. We discuss achieved results and describe how this technique affected art pipelines.

In the last section of our chapter, we propose potential improvements to developed solutions: analysis of pros and cons of different irradiance data storage basis and possible next-generation runtime extensions to improve the quality even more.

17.1.1 Overview

Achieving realistic, runtime lighting is one of biggest unsolved problems in real-time rendering applications, especially in games. Simple direct lighting achieved by analytical lights is quite easy to compute in real time. On the other hand, indirect lighting and effects of light bouncing around the scene and its shadowing are very difficult to compute in real time. Full-scene lighting containing both direct and indirect lighting effects is called *global illumination* (GI), and full runtime high-quality GI is the Holy Grail of rendering.

A full and proper solution to the light transport equation is impossible in the general case—as it is an infinite integral and numerical solutions would require an infinite number of samples. There are lots of techniques that approximate results, but proper GI solutions are far from being close to real time (they achieve timing of seconds, minutes, or even hours).

In games and real-time rendering, typically used solutions fall into three categories:

1. static and baked solutions,

2. dynamic crude approximations,

3. partially dynamic, partially static solutions.

The first category includes techniques like light mapping, radiosity normal mapping [McTaggart 04], or irradiance environment mapping [Ramamoorthi and Hanrahan 01]. They can deliver very good final image quality, often indistinguishable from ground truth for diffuse/Lambertian lighting. Unfortunately, due to their static nature, they are not usable in games featuring very dynamic lighting conditions (like changing time of day and weather).

The second category of fully dynamic GI approximation is gaining popularity with next-generation consoles and powerful PCs; however, it still isn't able to fully replace static GI. Current dynamic GI algorithms still don't deliver a comparable quality level as static solutions (light propagation volumes [Kaplanyan 09]), rely on screen-space information (deep screen-space G-buffer global illumination [Mara et al. 14]), or have prohibitive runtime cost (voxel cone tracing [Crassin 11]).

There are some solutions that try to decouple some elements of the light transport equation—for example, shadowing like various screen-space ambient occlusion techniques—but they capture only a single part of the phenomenon.

The final category containing partially dynamic and partially static solutions is the most interesting one thanks to a variety of different approaches and solutions working under different constraints. Usually in computer games we can assume that some of scene information is static (like placements of some objects and scene geometry) and won't change, so it is possible to precompute elements of a light transport integral and apply them in the runtime. In our case, some constraints were very limiting—very big open world size, previous generations of consoles as two major target platforms, dynamic weather, and dynamic time of day. On the other hand, due to the game setting, we didn't need to think about too many dynamic lights affecting GI and could focus only on sky and sun/moon lighting.

An example of partially dynamic solutions is precomputed radiance transfer [Sloan et al. 02]. It assumes that shaded scene is static, and lighting conditions can be dynamic but are fully external (from faraway light sources). Under such constraints, it is possible to precompute radiance transfer, store it using some low-frequency basis, and then in runtime compute a product integral with similar representation of lighting in the scene. Using orthonormal storage functions like spherical harmonics, the product integral is trivial and very efficient, as it simplifies to a single dot product of basis functions coefficients. The biggest problem of typical partially resident texture (PRT) solutions is a long baking time and large memory storage requirements (if stored per vertex or in PRT texture maps). Interesting and practical variations and implementations of this technique for an open-world game with dynamic weather, sky, and lighting conditions was presented as *deferred radiance transfer volumes* by Mickael Gilabert and Nikolay Stefanov at GDC 2012 [Gilabert and Stefanov 12].

Its advantages are numerous—relatively small required storage, real-time performance on previous generations of consoles, good quality for open-door rendering scenarios, and full dynamism. For *Assassin's Creed 4*, we tried integrating this technique in our engine. Unfortunately, we found that while it delivered good quality for uninhabited and rural areas, it wasn't good enough in case of dense, colonial towns with complex shadowing. Achieved results were too low of frequency, both in terms of temporal information (indirect lighting direction and irradiance didn't change enough when changing time of day and the main light direction) as well as spatial density (a probe every 4 meters was definitely not enough). We realized that simple second-order spherical harmonics are not able to capture radiance transfer in such complex shadowing of the scene (the result was always a strong directional function in the upper hemisphere, so lighting didn't change too much with changing time of day). We decided to keep parts of the solution but to look for a better storage scheme fitting our project requirements.

17.1.2 Theory and Introduced Terms

In general, rendering an equation for a single point and angle can be expressed as

$$L_o(x, \omega_o) = L_e(x, \omega) + \int_\Omega f(x, \omega_o, \omega) L_i(x, \omega)(\underline{\omega \cdot n}) d\omega,$$

where L_o is outgoing radiance, x is position in space, ω_o is outgoing radiance direction, ω is incoming radiance direction, L_e is radiance emitted by the surface, f is the bidirectional reflectance distribution function, L_i is incident radiance, n is the surface normal, and Ω is the hemisphere centered around the surface normal; $(\omega \cdot n)$ is the dot product of the incoming radiance direction and surface normal clamped to positive-only values (and equals 0 for the lower hemisphere).

This equation applies to a single point in space and is recursive (the outgoing radiance of one point becomes part of the incoming radiance to another point in space). Therefore, it's impossible to simply solve it for any generic case or just precompute some of its terms. However, if we are interested in light transport only for diffuse (Lambertian) lighting for nonemissive surfaces, we can simplify this equation a lot:

$$L_o(x, \omega_o) = \frac{c_{diff}}{\pi} \int_\Omega L_i(x, \omega)\underline{(\omega \cdot n)}d\omega,$$

where c_{diff} is the albedo color of the shaded surface.

The integral in this equation is called *irradiance*. We introduce the term *normalized irradiance* as the final irradiance of a shaded point caused by a single directional light source of white color and unified brightness. Our key reasoning behind using this term in our algorithm is that because such simplified lighting transport equation is linear, we can compute light transport for the whole scene for such normalized lighting from a single light direction and then de-normalize it for specific lighting conditions by multiplying it by a given color.

17.2   Deferred Normalized Irradiance Probes Algorithm

17.2.1   Requirements

We needed an algorithm that could handle the dynamic and changing time-of-day cycle and multiple weather presets very well.

Due to *Assassin's Creed 4* being shipped on the previous generation of consoles—Microsoft Xbox 360 and Sony Playstation 3—we had quite strict memory and performance budgets: a maximum 1 MB of used memory for relatively large effect ranges (at least several blocks away in colonial towns), preferably using only VRAM (not to take memory away from gameplay systems on Playstation 3) and under 1 millisecond of runtime cost on those consoles over seven years old.

Our game required coherent and simple handling of both static and dynamic objects—the lighting system and renderer should be transparent to this information and light the whole scene in a single pass.

Finally, as we decided to add a global illumination algorithm during actual game production when some levels were almost ready, its impact on the art pipelines had to be minimal. Baking times needed to be short enough to allow the artist to do many lighting iterations per hour, and, in the case of changing scene geometry, lighting shouldn't be completely broken. Therefore, we decided to do the baking on the artists' computers and wanted to allow them to re-bake quickly (within seconds) some parts of levels instead of having to set up lighting server farms and rely on nightly builds.

17.2.2 Assumptions and Limitations

We observed that we can simplify diffuse global illumination in *Assassin's Creed 4* with the following conditions being met and assumptions being made:

1. Game levels are fully static in terms of object placement and diffuse materials.

2. There is no diffuse GI caused by dynamic objects.

3. There is only a single dominant light: sun/moonlight affects GI.

4. Weather affects only light color and intensity, not light direction.

5. Worlds are very big, but only parts of them are fully accessible to the player and need global illumination.

6. We had a good-quality and optimal system for handling direct sky lighting and its occlusion already [St-Amour 13].

Based on this information, we were able to decouple normalized irradiance from dominant light transferred from the weather-modified parameters—weather-specific lighting color and intensity. As sky lighting was a separate term, this was even easier as our algorithm could focus only on diffuse indirect sunlight. It is a low-frequency term, so it allowed us to reduce the temporal and spatial resolution and meet memory requirements.

17.2.3 Algorithm Overview

Our algorithm is based on baking normalized irradiance into a grid of light probes covering world areas that are accessible for players. To support dynamic time of day, we decided to keyframe eight different times of day (spaced three hours apart). Our keyframes are captured at midnight, 3AM, 6AM, 9AM, noon, 3PM, 6PM, and 9PM. In the runtime, we interpolate diffuse normalized irradiance information from textures storing keyframed data, de-normalize the irradiance in the runtime using sun radiance, and then apply it in a deferred manner.

As we are storing only a single layer of information, it must be interpolated correctly with changing height. We do it in the runtime using available height information texture and blend the stored GI with a *neutral* global light probe with irradiance specified by lighting artists.

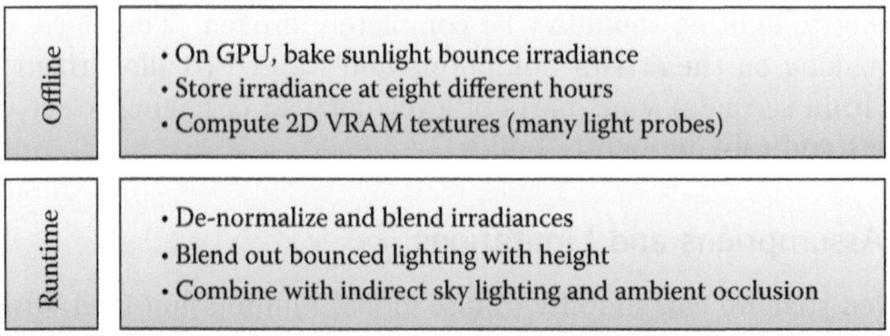

Figure 17.1. Simplified diagram of our algorithm split into two parts.

The whole algorithm is split into two parts: the static, tool-side part and the final runtime part.

The tool-side part consists of the following steps:

1. Spawn a uniform 2.5D grid of light probes, placing them on the lowest point accessible to the player (near the ground).

2. Split the probes into regularly sized *sectors* of 16×16 probes.

3. For each sector, render a cube map with G-buffer information for each probe and a single, high-resolution shadow map for every keyframed hour for the whole sector using calculated light direction.

4. Using pixel shaders, compute normalized irradiance for every light probe and keyframed hour, and store it in a texture.

Having such baked textures storing this information, we are able to use them in the runtime in the following steps:

1. Stream in textures in the sectors around the camera.

2. Determine a probe-snapped 2D viewport of the sectors around the camera.

3. Blend normalized irradiance information from two keyframed hours. De-normalize it while drawing irradiance data from the offscreen buffer.

4. On the CPU or SPU, prepare height information from available gameplay data.

5. In the deferred ambient pass, combine all computed information with sky lighting and SSAO into the final per-pixel ambient lighting.

A simplified diagram showing these steps and split between the editor and runtime parts is shown in Figure 17.1. Both parts will be covered in detail in following sections.

Figure 17.2. A light probe and the four vectors constructed using the irradiance basis.

17.2.4 Data Structure

Our light probes are using the *Far Cry 3* storage basis. The basis is constructed using three vectors pointing up in space (as in the *Half Life 2* irradiance storage basis) and an additional vector that points directly down (shown in Figure 17.2). Every vector stores directly normalized irradiance (irradiance response to unified-intensity white light) information in 8-bit sRGB. Unfortunately, such basis is not normalized, not orthonormal, and prone to ringing, ground color bleeding, and errors. We were aware of such mathematical limitations and improperness, but in our case it didn't produce any artifacts that artists would consider unacceptable. We will discuss this basis usage and propose better alternatives in Section 17.5.2.

Every light probe contains information for eight keyframed hours. Therefore, every probe takes exactly 96 bytes:

$$3 \text{ bytes normalized irradiance} \times 4 \text{ basis vectors} \times 8 \text{ hours.}$$

We store light probes in a uniform 2.5D grid. The grid density is 1 probe every 2 meters, and such assumptions helped us to keep the runtime code very simple. We organized light probes into sectors of 16×16 light probes (32×32 meters). Therefore, such a sector takes 24 kB of memory. We store sectors

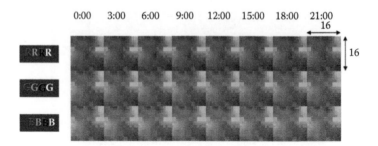

Figure 17.3. Packed normalized irradiance texture for a single sector.

as noncompressed 2D RGBA textures—texture color channels correspond to the different basis vectors (see Figure 17.3). Having our memory budget of 1 MB, we were able to load GI data of up to around 200 meters, but it wasn't necessary and was larger than our engine's regular streaming grid size.

17.3   Tool Side of the Algorithm

Our goal was to generate all this data directly on the artist's computer, provide interactive iterations on the lighting, and not rely on a render farm approach that would generate the GI data overnight.

A typical *Assassin's Creed* world is a square sized approximately 1 km on each 2D axis. Because we had to handle current-generation and next-generation consoles, our target resolution was 1 probe every 2 meters. This meant spawning more than 110,000 probes on just a single layer. Trimming this data as much as possible was a necessity to keep the baking times reasonable.

17.3.1   Probe-Spawning Process

We wanted the transition process in our pipelines between the old system and our new solution to be as fast and transparent for game editor users as possible. Placing probes by hand would mean too much manual work in a project with such a big scope, and we decided that we need some other, automatic solution— even if manual placement would give us better results. We decided to find a probe-placement solution that would require as little artist input as possible.

Using a simple uniform 2.5D grid gave us a few advantages: it not only usually is easy to implement, but it also guarantees a perfect repartition and easy interpolation of the probes. It can be a really good thing to get a good overall quality quickly, but, on the other hand, it means that many probes generated are not adapting to the actual mesh layout and the frequency of GI information. We observed that sometimes we ended up having probes at places we didn't

Figure 17.4. Example probe placement—notice the lack of probes on buildings' rooftops.

need them. And because the number of probes directly drove the generation and baking process times, we had to address the problem of game levels over-sampling.

In order to reduce the number of probes, we had to remove as many unnecessary probes automatically as possible—for instance, probes inside houses, in the ocean, or in unattainable areas. We decided to use the player and AI navigation mesh (navmesh) for that for a few reasons: it gave us a simple representation of our world, easy to query, but it also provided clues to where the player can and, most importantly, can't go.

We also wanted to avoid placing probes on the roofs. We used the navigation mesh in conjunction with another representation of our world called the ground-heights map (usually used for sound occlusion, it stores only the ground height; no roofs or platforms are included in this data). By computing the difference between the navmesh z position and the ground height position, we decided, under a certain threshold, whether to spawn the probe or not—see Figure 17.4 and Figure 17.5.

If included, the probe was spawned on the lowest z position of the navmesh. The xy position was decided by the regular grid. This gave us a 70% reduction of the number of probes spawned in our biggest game world, bringing it down to 30,000 probes.

Because of memory constraints, we couldn't keep all the data for the whole world loaded at the same time on consoles: we split it by sectors of 32×32 meters, aligned on the uniform grid. Therefore, the texture owned by a sector is 16×16 texels.

Figure 17.5. Example probe placement—regular grid.

Probes inside a sector could be moved, deleted, or added by artists to adjust the baking position if the automatic placement was problematic. At the export time, every texel of the deferred normalized irradiance probe (DNIP) texture was taking the closest probe available. During the game's postmortem, we were told that this feature was used very rarely: the original placement heuristic was robust enough.

17.3.2 Baking

For each probe, we needed to get irradiance value for four basis vectors. We didn't have any baking solution in our engine, and writing a dedicated ray tracer or renderer was out of question. We also wanted the lighting artists to be able to iterate directly on their computers (not necessarily DirectX 11 compatible at that point), so it had to be completely integrated inside our world editor.

Due to such constraints, we decided to use cube-map captures. It meant getting one G-buffer cube map and one shadow map for each time of day, lighting them, and integrating them to get the irradiance values. The normalized lighting was done at eight different times of day, with a plain white light, no weather effects enabled (rain, fog) and neutral but still artist-controllable ambient terms (to be able to still capture some bounces in the shadowed areas). To do the integration, for each basis and for each time of day, we computed a weighted integral of normalized irradiance responses against the basis.

The irradiance computation is very similar to that of [Elias 00]: for every single basis vector and for every cube-map texel, we project incoming radiance to diffuse the lighting contribution. To do this efficiently, we have a multiplier map that takes into account both Lambert's cosine law term and the hemicube's shape compensation. This weight map is normalized (the sum of all texel weights for a single basis is 1). Compensation is necessary because different cube-map texels corresponding to different positions subtend a different solid angle on a hemisphere. Once incoming radiance is multiplied by a bidirectional reflectance distribution function (BRDF) and normalization factors for a given basis, we can integrate it by simply adding all texel contributions together.

We faded the integrated radiance smoothly with distance. The reasoning for it was to avoid popping and aliasing artifacts that could happen because of a limited cube-map far plane (for optimization purposes)—in some cases, GI could suddenly appear. Then for every basis vector, we merged whole information from relevant cube-map faces and downscaled the result down to one pixel that represented our normalized irradiance at a given probe position or basis direction. All the data was then packed in our sector textures and added to our loading grid to be streamable at runtime.

Therefore, our first version directly used our renderer to generate each face of each cube map at each time of day independently, integrating the results on the CPU by locking the cube-map textures and integrating radiance in serial loops. Even with efficient probe number reduction like the one mentioned in Section 17.3.1, computing the data for around 30,000 probes for eight different times of day was a lengthy process: at 60 fps and 48 renders for every probe (6 faces × 8 times of day), it would take 400 minutes. This "quick and dirty" prototype generated data for the world in 12 hours. Most of the time was spent on the CPU and GPU synchronization and on the inefficient, serial irradiance integration. The synchronization problem was due to the fact that on PCs it is not uncommon for the GPU to be 2–3 frames behind the CPU and the command buffer being written due to driver scheduling and resource management. Also, sending and copying lots of data between GPU and CPU memory (needed for reading) is much slower than localized, GPU-only operations. Therefore, when we tried to lock the cube-map textures for CPU read-back in the naïve way (after every single cube-map face being rendered), we spent an order of magnitude higher times on synchronization and CPU computations than on the actual rendering. (See Figure 17.6.)

Therefore, the first step was to remove the CPU irradiance calculations part by processing all the downscaling and irradiance calculations on the GPU and reading back only final irradiance values on the CPU. This kind of operation is also trivially parallelizable (using many simple 2 × 2 down-sample steps) and is well suited for the GPU, making the whole operation faster than the CPU version.

But even when the whole algorithm was running on the GPU, we were still losing a lot of time on the CPU when locking the final result (1 lock per probe)

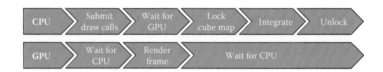

Figure 17.6. Diagram showing the first naïve implementation for the GPU-based baker. Work is done on a per-probe basis.

Figure 17.7. Overview of batched baking rendering pipeline. "Render Sector N" means drawing, lighting, and computing irradiance for each of the 16×16 probes in Sector N.

because the CPU was well ahead of the GPU. We decided to use a pool of textures and lock only when we knew the GPU actually wrote the data and it was ready to be transferred (we checked it using asynchronous GPU queries). Batching also helped: instead of locking texture for every probe, we locked once per sector—each probe was directly writing its data to its own texel inside the sector's texture. At that point, our entire baker was running asynchronously between CPU and GPU and was generating the whole map in around three hours. The GPU cost was still high, but we were mainly CPU traversal bound at that point. (See Figure 17.7.)

To cut some of the CPU cost, we wrote a new occlusion culling system that was much less accurate (it didn't matter for such short rendering distances), but simpler and faster. We used a simple custom traversal per sector (radial distance around the sector) and used also a reduced far-plane distance during the cube-map generation.

To reduce the GPU workload, we also generated only one shadow map per sector, instead of per probe. This helped reduce the GPU cost, as well as the CPU cost of traversing the scene for the shadow geometry pass each time for each time of day.

For each face of the cube map, we were generating the G-buffer only once. We could reuse it for each time of day, as material properties like albedo and normals don't change over time. We could light the cube maps per every keyframed time with the albedo, normal, and depth information we had, plus the sun and shadow-map direction at the requested time of day.

At the end, generating our biggest world was taking 8 minutes on an artist's computer. The baking was so fast that we provided a real-time baking mode. It was collecting the closest probes and computed lighting for them in the background. This way, artists could see the result of their work with GI almost

```
RenderSector
  Draw shadow maps containing sector for the eight times of day
  For each probe in sector
      For each of the six directions
          Render G-buffer centered on probe
          For each time of day
              Use sector shadow map for current time of day
              Perform lighting
                  For every basis
                      Compute texels irradiance BRDF contribution
                      Down-sample irradiance contribution until 1x1
```

Listing 17.1. Pseudocode used by the final GPU baker.

immediately, and it updated continuously when they moved meshes or changed lighting parameters.

Listing 17.1 summarizes the final GPU baker.

17.3.3 Debugging Tools

We also created a set of debugging tools for our algorithm and pipeline. The tools were aimed to help visualize the baking process by showing a normalized lighting cube map generated for each probe, the associated depth, the shadow map used, and also the runtime 2D texture used for the rendering later on. So by just selecting a probe, we could see all that information, debug the whole baking process, and pinpoint potential issues immediately. We had many display modes that showed probes placed in the world. Probes could be displayed showing either the stored, normalized data (not multiplied by the final sun color and intensity) or with the full final lighting on. We also provided a mode that showed which probe was selected for each sector texel.

In Figure 17.8, you can see the rendered data on the left and the sector boundaries in pink. Interesting information is shown by the green lines—they connected probes to additional points in the sector texture that didn't have a probe placed, and that probe was used to fill those texels to avoid any potential interpolation artifacts.

17.4 Runtime Details of Algorithm

17.4.1 Streaming

Each texture like the one in Figure 17.3 is embedded inside regular *entities*. These entities are owned by sectors of 32×32 meters, and the textures are streamed in like any other resource. They represent a subrectangle of the final textures that will be used during the final ambient lighting pass.

Figure 17.8. Implemented GI baking debugging tools. Top left inset, from left to right: the six faces of the normalized cube map for the current time of day, the associated depth for those faces, the current sector shadowmap, and the runtime heightmap texture (see Section 17.4.3).

Because all these texture are relatively lightweight (24 kB of VRAM per sector), the impact on the game streaming system was negligible and no additional effort was necessary to improve the loading times.

17.4.2   Resolved DNIP Textures

Having a varying number of textures at runtime (based on what is currently loaded) is not convenient to use for a unified ambient lighting pass: texture arrays are not available on Playstation 3 or Xbox 360, per-pixel dynamic branching is slow, and additional filtering work would be necessary for data between sectors. Therefore, we decided to generate an intermediate set of textures instead: the *resolved DNIP textures*.

These textures encode the irradiance in the same manner as the sector textures, but instead of storing normalized irradiance for multiple times of day, we store the final irradiance based on the current time of day and weather conditions. Figure 17.9 shows these resolved DNIP textures. This way, we have a fixed number of textures that cover the entire space around the camera: no additional work for filtering is needed.

Generating these resolve textures is done on the GPU. Figure 17.10 is a representation of the draw calls that are issued. Each square is a draw call; the one in yellow is currently being issued.

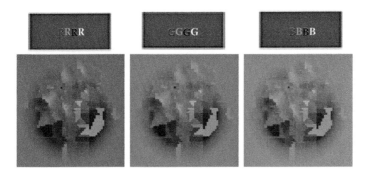

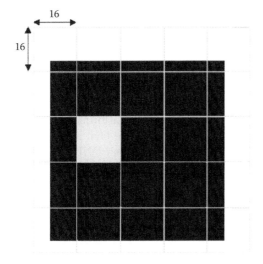

Figure 17.9. Resolved DNIP textures—the circle shape is a radial attenuation of the DNIP to hide popping when streaming data in or out.

Figure 17.10. Debug representation for the resolved DNIP textures: yellow square—single blitted sector; blue area—whole final irradiance texture; dashed squares—squares only partially blitted into final texture.

Each of these draw calls will interpolate the DNIP data from the two closest stored times of day, and multiply the result by the current lighting condition. Based on the distance to the camera, we fade out the DNIP contribution to a constant color. This allows us to stream in and out the DNIP data that is far away without any discontinuity. This shader is very cheap to evaluate (works on a configuration of three 128×128 render targets): less than 0.1 ms on Play-station 3.

Once these textures are generated, we use them during the ambient lighting pass.

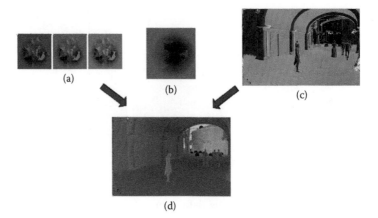

Figure 17.11. Visual summary of DNIP evaluation: (a) resolved DNIP textures, (b) world height-map data, (c) world-space normals buffer, and (d) final indirect sunlight GI contribution.

17.4.3 Ambient Lighting Pass

This pass works at full resolution on all platforms and needs to be as efficient as possible. The goal of this pass is to get the final ambient lighting color based on the pixel normal and position. The resolved DNIP textures contain the current ambient lighting in four directions. We compute the final color for the pixel in a similar manner as [Gilabert and Stefanov 12], but we precomputed the weights of each basis direction in a lookup cube texture: our profiling tools indicated that on a Sony Playstation 3, a better ALU:TEX ratio was achieved this way. Additionally, the packing used for the DNIP textures allows us to get the final color with three dot products per one texture read, because no swizzling is required inside the shader.

As mentioned before, the DNIP data is 2D only. During the resolve pass, we need to fade out the data vertically to a user-specified neutral color. This is done on the CPU by generating a dynamic texture based on height-map data. The difference between the current pixel height and the height stored in the dynamic texture is computed and scaled. This gives a factor to interpolate the DNIP data to a neutral value. Figure 17.11 is a visualization of the whole process. Figures 17.12 and 17.13 show how the final image is composited from different lighting contributions.

Jean-Francois St-Amour described our sky lighting occlusion factor (Figure 17.12(b)) where direct sky lighting gets an occlusion multiplier from a distance field called *world ambient occlusion* [St-Amour 13]. It consists of a low-resolution blurred top-down shadow map that is being sampled to get an estimated occluder height. (See Figure 17.14.)

Figure 17.12. Lighting composition: (a) direct sunlight, (b) direct sky lighting, (c) indirect sunlight (exaggerated), and (d) composed ambient lighting buffer.

Figure 17.13. Final composed image with direct sunlight and albedo.

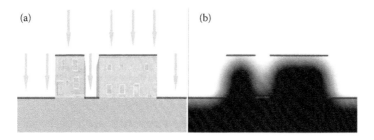

Figure 17.14. World ambient occlusion: (a) source top-down depth map and (b) blurred shadow map used for the runtime evaluation of the world ambient occlusion.

Figure 17.15. Examples of final images using DNIP in *Assassin's Creed 4*.

DNIP results are added to the sky lighting, giving the final ambient color.

On next-generation consoles and PCs, this ambient term gets multiplied by SSAO before being added to the direct lighting. On the previous generation of consoles, because of memory constraints, SSAO was multiplied at the end of the lighting pass (after sunlight and local lights). It was improper, but allowed us to alias some render targets and save a considerable amount of GPU memory.

17.5   Results and Discussion

17.5.1   Performance

The quality offered by the technique, associated with small performance impact at runtime, and the low overhead on production allowed us to ship it on all the maps in *Assassin's Creed 4: Black Flag*. Figure 17.15 shows the final achieved effect, composed with direct and sky lighting.

GPU Performance Cost	1.2 ms Fullscreen Pass 720p (Playstation 3)
Memory cost (probe data)	600 kB (VRAM only)
Memory cost (render targets)	56 kB
CPU cost	0.6 ms (amortized)
Num probes (non-optimized)	~ 110,000
Num probes (optimized)	~ 30,000, 1 probe per 2 meters
Full baking time for game world	8 minutes (GTX 680, one machine)

Table 17.1. Summary of the DNIP technique.

Table 17.1 gives a summary of the important data used by the DNIP technique. The GPU time indicates the total time taken by both the resolved DNIP textures generation and the ambient lighting pass. The 600 kB of VRAM is for a total of 25 DNIP textures of streamed sectors, which covers an area of 160×160 meters around the camera. The render targets are the resolved DNIP textures, which are 64×64 and cover an area of 128×128 meters around the camera.

17.5.2 Limitations and Future Extensions

Even if we are happy with the results we got in *Assassin's Creed 4*, removing support for current-generation consoles together with the additional processing power of Playstation 4 and Xbox One would allow for a lot of improvements.

Increasing the probe density in the X, Y, Z directions is the first easy solution. Having a layered approach like this would require some additional work on the resolve step of the algorithm, but it is definitely doable.

Used storage basis is not perfect, as we are losing any directional bounce coming from the sides and the ground color is bleeding to the sides. We tried changing the basis used by [Gilabert and Stefanov 12] to a six-axis cube basis. It was giving us definitely superior results, but was eventually dropped because of the performance and memory cost for Playstation 3 and Xbox 360. We decided to keep platform parity on such important topics as the lighting. On next-generation consoles, we could store lighting properly in 16-bit HDR formats. This way we could combine the DNIP data together with the sky lighting and achieve physically based sky occlusion.

Handling multiple light bounces was implemented, but dropped because of the increased baking time and the lack of HDR support in the engine. To do it, we were performing multiple passes of our algorithm iteratively (in the style of radiosity techniques). One-pass results were injected as additional indirect lighting into the second pass. Due to the linear properties of Lambertian lighting, it is mathematically correct. Unfortunately, for it to work properly, we would need to conserve energy to ensure that each additional pass does not add energy to the scene, but rather diffuses it—which was not the case because of our selected lighting basis (energy was lost in some directions but added in the direction of basis vectors).

Thanks to our baking algorithm running only on the GPU and not needing any special data structures, generating the indirect lighting in the runtime for the closest probes could also be another path to explore. This way we could support single- or multi-bounce indirect lighting from various light sources and occluded by dynamic objects, instead of just the key lighting.

Finally, having multiple volumes of GI would allow us to work at multiple content-dependent frequencies and help solve the potential light leaking problem that would happen in any game mixing indoors and outdoors. This was not a problem on *Assassin's Creed 4*, as it was a game based mostly on exteriors—in our case almost no system supported mixed interiors and exteriors, which was solved by game design and in data. All the interiors were already separate areas into which players were teleported instead of being real areas embedded in the world.

17.6   Acknowledgments

We would like to thank the whole *Assassin's Creed 4* team of rendering programmers, technical art directors, and lighting artists for inspiring ideas and talks about the algorithm and its optimizations. Special thanks go to Mickael Gilabert, author of "Deferred Radiance Transfer Volumes," for lots of valuable feedback and suggestions and to Sebastien Larrue, Danny Oros, and Virginie Cinq-Mars for testing and giving feedback and practical applications of our solution.

Bibliography

[Crassin 11] Cyril Crassin. "Gigavoxels", "GigaVoxels: A Voxel-Based Rendering Pipeline for Efficient Exploration of Large and Detailed Scenes." PhD thesis, Grenoble University, 2011.

[Elias 00] Hugo Elias. "Radiosity." http://freespace.virgin.net/hugo.elias/radiosity/radiosity.htm, 2000.

[Gilabert and Stefanov 12] Mickael Gilabert and Nikolay Stefanov. "Deferred Radiance Transfer Volumes." Presented at Game Developers Conference, San Francisco, CA, March 5–9, 2012.

[Kaplanyan 09] Anton Kaplanyan. "Light Propagation Volumes in CryEngine 3." SIGGRAPH Course: Advances in Real-Time Rendering in 3D Graphics and Games, SIGGRAPH 2009, New Orleans, LA, August 3, 2009.

[Mara et al. 14] M. Mara, M. McGuire, D. Nowrouzezahrai, and D. Luebke. "Fast Global Illumination Approximations on Deep G-Buffers." Technical Report NVR-2014-001, NVIDIA Corporation, June 16, 2014.

[McTaggart 04] Gary McTaggart. "Half Life 2/Valve Source Shading." *Direct 3D Tutorial*, http://http://www2.ati.com/developer/gdc/D3DTutorial10_Half-Life2_Shading.pdf, 2004.

[Ramamoorthi and Hanrahan 01] Ravi Ramamoorthi and Pat Hanrahan. "An Efficient Representation for Irradiance Environment Maps." In *Proceedings of the 28th Annual Conference on Computer Graphics and Interactive Techniques*, pp. 497–500. New York: ACM, 2001.

[Sloan et al. 02] Peter-Pike Sloan, Jan Kautz, and John Snyder. "Precomputed Radiance Transfer for Real-Time Rendering in Dynamic, Low-Frequency Lighting Environments." *Proc. SIGGRAPH '02: Transaction on Graphics* 21:3 (2002), 527–536.

[St-Amour 13] Jean-Francois St-Amour. "Rendering of Assassin's Creed 3." Presented at Game Developers Conference, San Francisco, CA, March 5–9, 2012.

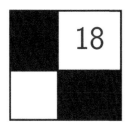

18

Volumetric Fog and Lighting
Bartłomiej Wroński

18.1 Introduction

This chapter presents *volumetric fog*, a technique developed at Ubisoft Montreal for Microsoft Xbox One, Sony Playstation 4, and PCs and used in *Assassin's Creed 4: Black Flag*. We propose a novel, real-time, analytical model for calculating various atmospheric phenomena. We address the problem of unifying and calculating in a coherent and optimal way various atmospheric effects related to atmospheric scattering, such as

- fog with varying participating media density,

- smoke and haze,

- crepuscular rays or light shafts,

- volumetric lighting and shadows.

This chapter provides a brief introduction to a light-scattering model that includes effects of in- and out-scattering and the Beer–Lambert law. We also describe how scattering can be computed and integrated numerically.

Volumetric fog supports light scattering coming from multiple light sources in a coherent and efficient manner. We include proper light shadowing (for volumetric shadows and light-shaft effects) and in-scattering of lighting coming from any complex ambient and global illumination models. The described technique uses compute shaders and data storage in volume textures. Unlike existing ray-marching solutions, our algorithm doesn't store information for a single depth value from a depth buffer but for all possible depth values for a given camera ray. Using volumetric storage, we are able to decouple multiple stages of atmospheric effects and calculate them in different resolutions. All phases of volumetric fog are independent of screen resolution, and due to use of trilinear filtering, the produced effect is free of edge artifacts.

The presented algorithm is compatible with many different shading models and rendering scenarios. It can be applied in deferred and forward shading models, doesn't require a depth prepass, and supports multiple layers of transparency at no additional cost. It can be computed asynchronously from regular scene geometric rendering on platforms that support such types of rendering (next-generation consoles, new APIs like AMD Mantle, and potentially DirectX 12).

18.2 Overview

Atmospheric scattering is a very important physical phenomenon describing interaction of light and various particles and aerosols in transporting media (like air, steam, smoke, or water). It is responsible for various visual effects and phenomena, like sky color, clouds, fog, volumetric shadows, light shafts, and "god rays."

Computer graphics research tries to reproduce those effects accurately. They not only increase realism of rendered scenes and help to establish visual distinction of distances and relations between objects, but also can be used to create a specific mood of a scene or even serve as special effects. Computer games and real-time rendering applications usually have to limit themselves to simplifications and approximations of the phenomena, including analytical exponential fog [Wenzel 06], image-based solutions [Sousa 08], artist-placed particles and billboards, or, recently, various modern ray-marching–based solutions [Tóth and Umenhoffer 09, Vos 14, Yusov 13].

All of those approaches have their limitations and disadvantages—but ray marching seemed most promising and we decided to base our approach on it. Still, typical 2D ray marching has number of disadvantages:

- Solutions like epipolar sampling [Yusov 13] improve the performance but limit algorithms to uniform participating media density and a single light source.

- The power of current GPUs allows us to calculate effect only in smaller-resolution buffers, which produces visual artifacts like jagged lines. More advanced up-sampling algorithms like bilateral up-sampling can miss some thin geometric features or introduce artifacts for high-contrast source images. Volumetric fog also operates on small-resolution volumes but uses 3D trilinear filtering to prevent edge artifacts from happening due to missing depth information in low-resolution image in 2D solutions.

- Most algorithm variations are not compatible with forward shading and multiple layers of transparent affected objects. A notable exception here is the solution used in *Killzone: Shadow Fall* [Vos 14], which uses low-resolution 3D volumes specifically for particle shading. Still, in this ap-

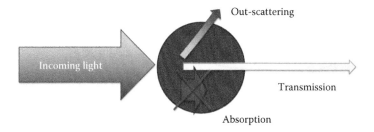

Figure 18.1. Process of atmospheric scattering.

proach, scattering effects for shaded solid objects are computed in an image-based manner.

Therefore, we decided to develop a novel solution that would overcome all those limitations, and we present the solution that we call *volumetric fog*. We used volumetric textures to transform the whole scattering problem into a 3D, easy-to-parallelize, filterable domain.

18.2.1   Atmospheric Scattering

The phenomenon of light scattering is caused by the interaction of photons with particles that form any transporting media. When light traverses any medium that isn't void, photons and light rays may collide with particles that create such a medium. On collision, they may either be diffused or absorbed (and turned into thermal energy). In optics, such a process is usually modeled statistically, and we can define the amount of energy that takes part in the following processes:

- transmittance,

- scattering,

- absorption.

As energy is always conserved, we can write that

$$\mathbf{L}_{\text{incoming}} = \mathbf{L}_{\text{transmitted}} + \mathbf{L}_{\text{absorbed}} + \mathbf{L}_{\text{scattered}}.$$

We can see these processes in Figure 18.1.

Depending on the particles that form the participating medium, the amount of light that takes part in those processes can be different. One example of scattering models is *Rayleigh scattering*. It is scattering of very small particles (like Earth's atmosphere air particles) and it responsible for the blue color of the sky. It is very isotropic and uniform but is wavelength dependent—scattering is stronger for shorter wavelengths and absorption is negligible.

18.3   Volumetric Fog Algorithm

Volumetric fog is an extension of existing ray-marching algorithms like in [Tóth and Umenhoffer 09]. However, by decoupling and splitting typical ray-marching steps and using intermediate storage, we aimed to solve the aforementioned disadvantages of classic 2D ray-marching solutions.

We based our algorithm on existing research on atmospheric scattering used in the CGI industry and movies [Wrennige et al. 10] and computer games algorithms using hardware volumetric 3D textures as an intermediate storage [Kaplanyan 09]. An article by Wrennige et al. describes how 3D textures and grids are used in the VFX industry to compute single- and multi-scattering effects and introduces a solution to scattering by numerical, iterative integration [Wrennige et al. 10]. We used a similar approach, but simplified it and adapted it to GPUs, real-time graphics, and pipelines used by in games. That article also mentions how to handle aliasing and subsampling problems that we faced. While we couldn't apply this part of CGI research directly due to prohibitive computational cost, it inspired our own solutions.

Volumetric fog requires DirectX 11+–level hardware (or OpenGL 4.3+) to work as it relies on compute shaders and random-access writes into volumetric textures using unordered access views.

18.3.1   The Algorithm Steps Overview

The algorithm consists of the following steps, run as separate passes:

1. estimating the density of participating media,

2. calculating in-scattered lighting,

3. ray marching,

4. applying the effect to shaded objects.

All passes compute volumetric information about scattering for the whole space within the camera frustum. We compute and store it for many steps or slices along sparse camera rays. Such information is stored in 3D textures.

18.3.2   Volumetric Texture Storage Format

For storage between multiple passes, volumetric fog uses view-frustum–aligned 3D volumetric textures. Depending on the target hardware platform, *Assassin's Creed 4* used 3D textures sized $190 \times 90 \times 128$ or $190 \times 90 \times 64$ texels. The X and Y dimensions are uniformly aligned with the main screen or viewport X and Y dimensions. The Z dimension is uniformly aligned with screen depth, but uses nonuniform, exponential depth slice distribution to an artist-defined range (in the case of *Assassin's Creed 4*, only 50–100 meters). Depending on

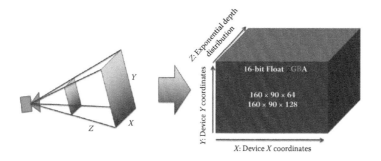

Figure 18.4. Mapping of a camera frustum to a 3D texture with volumetric intermediate storage data layout and format.

performance budgets and target hardware platforms (for example high-end PCs), used resolutions could be larger as the algorithm scales linearly in terms of used compute threads and the arithmetic logic unit (ALU).

We used two of such textures: one for in-scattered lighting at a given point and a density-related extinction coefficient and the second one to store final lookups for integrated in-scattering and transmittance. The used format for those two textures was a four-channel (RGBA) 16-bit floating point. The volumetric texture's layout can be seen in Figure 18.4.

The resolution of volumetric textures may seem very low in the X and Y dimensions, and it would be true with 2D ray-marching algorithms. To calculate information for low-resolution tiles, classic ray-marching approaches need to pick a depth value that is representative of the whole tile. Therefore, many depth values contained by this tile might not be represented at all. Algorithms like bilateral up-sampling [Shopf 09] try to fix it in the up-sampling process by checking adjacent tiles for similar values. However, this approach can fail in case of thin geometric features or complex geometry. Volumetric fog doesn't suffer from this problem because, for every 2D tile, we store scattering values for many depth slices. Even very small, 1-pixel wide objects on screen can get appropriate depth information. Figure 18.5 shows this comparison of 2D and 3D approaches in practice.

Still, even with better filtering schemes, small-resolution rendering can cause artifacts like under-sampling and flickering of higher-frequency signals. Sections 18.3.7 and 18.4.3 will describe our approach to fix those problems.

A significant disadvantage of such low volume resolution rendering is visual softness of the achieved effect, but it can be acceptable for many scenarios. In our case, it did fit our art direction, and in general it can approximate a "soft" multi-scattering effect that would normally have prohibitive calculation cost.

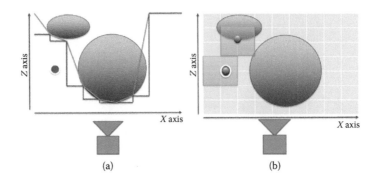

Figure 18.5. Flat XZ scene slice. (a) A smaller-resolution 2D image (black lines represent depth) causes lack of representation for a small object (black dot)—no adjacent tiles contain proper information. (b) All objects, even very small ones, get proper filtered information (3D bilinear filtering shown as green boxes).

18.3.3   Estimation of Participating Media Scattering Coefficients

To be able to calculate scattering coefficients and solve scattering, we need first to calculate participating medium density. Therefore, the first part of our algorithm computes the density of the participating medium at every 3D point corresponding to a volume texture texel and stores it in an intermediate volumetric texture.

In our algorithm implementation, we have support for varying densities of participating media. This allows not only for physically based density distributions, but also artist-authored and dynamically changing ones. Mie scattering is usually modeled using exponential height distributions due to the fact that aerosol particles are heavier than air and tend to gather near the ground. Exponential height density distribution is expressed using the equation

$$d(h) = d_0 \times e^{-hD},$$

where $d(h)$ is the calculated density for height h, d_0 is density at the reference level (literature usually specifies it as ground or sea level), and D is the scaling coefficient describing how fast the density attenuates. Coefficient D depends on the type of aerosols and particles, and in typical in-game rendering scenarios, it probably will be specified by the environment and lighting artists.

The second part of density estimation is purely art driven. We wanted to simulate clouds of dust or water particles, so we decided to use the animated, volumetric GPU shader implementation of Ken Perlin's noise function [Perlin 02, Green 05]. It is widely used in procedural rendering techniques as it has advantage of smoothness, lack of bilinear filtering artifacts, derivative continuity, and realistic results. We can see it in Figure 18.6. Perlin's improved noise can be combined in multiple octaves at varying frequencies to produce a fractal turbulence

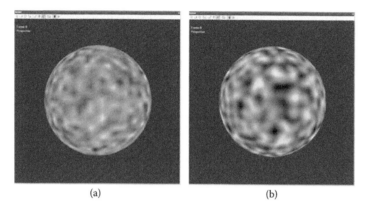

(a)   (b)

Figure 18.6. (a) Bilinear textured noise compared to (b) volumetric 3D improved Perlin noise [Green 05].

effect similar to clouds. We exposed animation tempo as an editable parameter but connected noise movement direction to the game world wind direction to make medium-density animation coherent with gameplay and particle wind. We tried using 2–3 octaves of noise to achieve a "cloudy" and fractal appearance of noise, but due to art direction preference decided to use only a single, simple octave of noise.

For *Assassin's Creed 4*, we didn't try any other density variation techniques, but we will describe them and ideas for extending controllability of effects in Section 18.4.4.

Due to exponential distribution of Z slices of volumetric texture, we must multiply the final estimated density by a slice length to get the amount of scattering that happens in given slice of space (more particles and more scattering in bigger or longer slices).

18.3.4   In-Scattered Light Calculation

Knowing the participating medium density, we were able to estimate scattering coefficients and calculate in-scattered lighting at every texel of the volumetric texture representing the camera frustum space covered by the volumetric fog effect.

We dispatched a compute shader launched in a 3D group one thread per volume texture texel and used unordered access views to access and write to volumetric texture and store such data. For every texel of our volumetric texture, we reconstructed its world position using corresponding world-space camera vectors. Using reconstructed position, it is possible to calculate shadowing and lighting for given point in space. The efficient and aliasing-free shadowing algorithm that we used for the sunlight will be explained in Section 18.3.7.

In a similar manner, we can calculate a list of dynamic lights (point- and spotlights) affecting the participating medium at a given point. In our case, we had a small number of lights affecting our scene in the camera frustum (between 0 and 4), so we were able to loop over all of them in negligible runtime cost. We performed regular light culling and added information about them to a constant buffer. Our compute shader simply looped over a uniform containing the number of lights and added contributions from them in every loop iteration. This allowed us to have proper, ordered influence of many local lights without any need for sorting.

Having lighting and shadowing information, we can simply multiply it by the scattering coefficient estimated from the participating medium density, the participating medium albedo, and a phase function for the given angle between light direction and the vector facing the camera. Whole computations performed per every texel in this pass of volumetric fog can be seen in HLSL pseudocode at Listing 18.1.

```
//World-space position of volumetric texture texel
float3 worldPosition
    = CalcWorldPositionFromCoords(dispatchThreadID.xyz);

//Thickness of slice -- non-constant due to exponential slice
//distribution
float layerThickness = ComputeLayerThickness(dispatchThreadID.z);

//Estimated density of participating medium at given point
float dustDensity = CalculateDensityFunction(worldPosition);

//Scattering coefficient
float scattering = g_VolumetricFogScatteringCoefficient * dustDensity
 * layerThickness;

//Absorption coefficient
float absorption = g_VolumetricFogAbsorptionCoefficient * dustDensity
 * layerThickness;

//Normalized view direction
float3 viewDirection = normalize(worldPosition - g_WorldEyePos.xyz);

float3 lighting = 0.0f;

// Lighting section BEGIN
// Adding all contributing lights radiance and multiplying it by
// a phase function -- volumetric fog equivalent of BRDFs

lighting += GetSunLightingRadiance(worldPosition)
    * GetPhaseFunction(viewDirection, g_SunDirection,
    g_VolumetricFogPhaseAnisotropy);

lighting += GetAmbientConvolvedWithPhaseFunction(worldPosition,
    viewDirection, g_VolumetricFogPhaseAnisotropy);

[loop]
for (int lightIndex = 0; lightIndex < g_LightsCount; ++lightIndex)
{
```

```
    float3 localLightDirection =
      GetLocalLightDirection(lightIndex, worldPosition);

    lighting += GetLocalLightRadiance(lightIndex, worldPosition)
      * GetPhaseFunction(viewDirection, localLightDirection,
      g_VolumetricFogPhaseAnisotropy);
}

// Lighting section END

// Finally, we apply some potentially non-white fog scattering albedo
color lighting *= g_FogAlbedo;

// Final in-scattering is product of outgoing radiance and scattering
// coefficients, while extinction is sum of scattering and absorption
float4 finalOutValue = float4(lighting * scattering, scattering
  + absorption);
```

Listing 18.1. Pseudocode for calculating in-scattering lighting, scattering, and absorption coefficients in compute shaders.

The last part of lighting in-scattering that helps to achieve scene realism is including ambient, sky, or indirect lighting. Ambient lighting can be a dominating part of scene lighting in many cases, when analytical lights are shadowed. Without it, the scene would be black in shadowed areas. In a similar way, if ambient lighting is not applied to in-scattering, the final scattering effect looks too dark (due to lighting out-scattering and extinction over the light path). Figure 18.7 shows a comparison of a scene with and without any ambient lighting.

The main difference between direct lighting and ambient lighting is that ambient lighting contains encoded information about incoming radiance from all possible directions. Different engines and games have different ambient terms—e.g., constant term, integrated cube sky lighting, or environment lighting containing global illumination. The main problem for calculating the in-scattering of ambient lighting is that most phase functions have only simple, directional, analytical forms, while ambient contribution is usually omnidirectional but nonuniform.

(a)   (b)

Figure 18.7. Effect of adding ambient lighting to volumetric fog in-scattering calculations: (a) Fog without sky lighting or GI = darkening, and (b) Fog with sky lighting and GI.

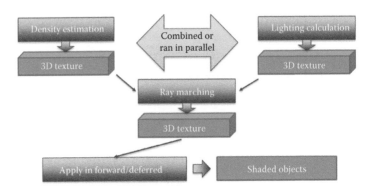

Figure 18.8. Volumetric fog algorithm steps.

In our case, ambient lighting was split into two parts. First, the indirect sunlight was stored and shaded using deferred normalized irradiance probes, described in the previous chapter [Huelin et al. 15]. We used a simple irradiance storage basis constructed from four fixed-direction basis vectors, so it was trivial to add their contribution to volumetric fog and calculate the appropriate phase function. The second part was the cube-map–based sky lighting (constructed in real time from a simple sky model) modulated by the precomputed sky visibility [St-Amour 13]. It was more difficult to add it properly to the fog due to its omnidirectional nature. Fortunately, when we calculated the cube-map representation using CPU and SPU jobs, we computed a second, simpler representation in spherical-harmonics basis as well. As described in Section 18.2.1, this orthonormal storage basis is very simple and often used to represent environment lighting [Green 03]. We used the Henyey–Greenstein phase function due to its very simple expansion to spherical harmonics and calculated its product integral with the sky lighting term in such form.

The optimization that we used in *Assassin's Creed 4* combines density estimation and lighting calculation passes together. As we can see in Figure 18.8, those passes are independent and can be run in serial, in parallel, or even combined. By combining, we were able to write out the values to a single RGBA texture—RGB contained information about in-scattered lighting, while alpha channel contained extinction coefficient (sum of scattering and absorption coefficients).

This way we avoided the cost of writing and reading memory and launching a new compute dispatch between those passes. We also reused many ALU computations—local texture-space coordinates, slice depth, and the texture voxel world position. Therefore, all computations related to in-scattering were performed locally and there was no need for an intermediate density buffer. It's worth noting though that in some cases it may be beneficial to split those passes—for example, if density is static, precomputed, or artist authored, or if we simply can calculate it in lower resolution (which often is the case). Splitting passes can lower effective register count and increase shader occupancy of them as well. It is also impossible to evaluate density in the lighting pass if some dynamic and nonprocedural density estimation techniques are used.

18.3.5 Ray Marching and Solving the Scattering Equation

The final *volumetric* step of our algorithm is an extension of typical ray-marching techniques [Tóth and Umenhoffer 09] that uses already computed values of light in-scattered into the view ray direction. Contrary to the previous pass, this pass is executed as a 2D group and operates serially, slice by slice. Our algorithm launches a 2D dispatch group of $X \times Y$ threads for a slice of our volumetric texture.

This compute shader pass marches along the view rays, accumulating scattering coefficients and the in-scattered lighting. It could be described as the following simple loop:

1. Read in-scattered lighting and extinction coefficients at slice N, starting with zero.

2. Add an extinction coefficient to the extinction accumulation register, and calculate transmittance from it using the Beer–Lambert law.

3. Apply transmittance to in-scattered lighting at a given slice, and add the result to the in-scattering accumulation RGB registers.

4. Write out to another volumetric texture at the same position RGB as the accumulated in-scattering and alpha of the transmittance value.

5. Increase N and proceed back to the Step 1.

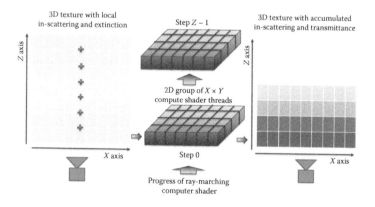

Figure 18.9. Scattering equation integration progress.

The pass progresses with this loop until all Z slices are processed. This process is illustrated in Figure 18.9.

A single step of this process accumulates both in-scattering color as well as the scattering extinction coefficients, which are applied in the Beer–Lambert law. This way, we can calculate transmittance for not only color but also the in-scattered lighting. Lighting in-scattered farther away from camera gets out-scattered by decreasing the transmittance function, just like the incoming radiance of shaded objects. Without it, with very long camera rays, in-scattering would improperly accumulate to infinity—instead, it asymptotically approaches some constant value. The entire code responsible for this is presented on Listing 18.2.

```
// One step of numerical solution to the light
// scattering equation
float4 AccumulateScattering(in float4 colorAndDensityFront,
in float4 colorAndDensityBack)
{
    // rgb = in-scattered light accumulated so far,
    // a = accumulated scattering coefficient
    float3 light = colorAndDensityFront.rgb + saturate(
        exp(-colorAndDensityFront.a)) * colorAndDensityBack.rgb;
    return float4(light.rgb,        colorAndDensityFront.a +
    colorAndDensityBack.a);}
}

// Writing out final scattering values}
void WriteOutput(in uint3 pos, in float4 colorAndDensity)
{
    // final value rgb = in-scattered light accumulated so far,
    // a = scene light transmittance
    float4 finalValue = float4(colorAndDensity.rgb,
        exp(-colorAndDensity.a));
    OutputTexture[pos].rgba = finalValue;
}

void RayMarchThroughVolume(uint3 dispatchThreadID)
{
    float4 currentSliceValue = InputTexture[uint3(dispatchThreadID.
    xy, 0)];

    WriteOutput(uint3(dispatchThreadID.xy, 0), currentSliceValue);

    for (uint z = 1; z < VOLUME{\_}DEPTH; z++)}
{
        uint3 volumePosition =
        uint3(dispatchThreadID.xy, z);}
        float4 nextValue = InputTexture[volumePosition];}
        currentSliceValue =}
            AccumulateScattering(currentSliceValue, nextValue);}
        WriteOutput(volumePosition, currentSliceValue);}
    }
}
```

Listing 18.2. Process of numerical integration of scattering equation.

```
// Read volumetric in-scattering and transmittance
float4 scatteringInformation = tex3D(VolumetricFogSampler,
positionInVolume);
float3 inScattering = scatteringInformation.rgb;
float transmittance = scatteringInformation.a;

// Apply to lit pixel
float3 finalPixelColor = pixelColorWithoutFog * transmittance.xxx
+ inScattering;
```

Listing 18.3. Manual blending for applying the volumetric fog effect.

18.3.6 Applying the Effect on Deferred- or Forward-Shaded Objects

Having scattering values written into a volumetric texture, we can express pixel color of a distant object as

$$\texttt{ShadedPixelColor} = \texttt{ShadedPixelColor} \times \texttt{Transmittance} + \texttt{InScattering},$$

where `InScattering` is described by the RGB value of a texel read from volumetric texture and `Transmittance` is in its alpha.

Because we store 3D information for many discrete points along the view ray (from camera position up to the effect range), it is trivial to apply the effect using trilinear filtering to any amount of deferred- or forward-shaded objects. In the case of deferred shading, we can read the value of the Z-buffer, and using it and the screen position of shaded pixel, we can apply either hardware blending (`Dest × SourceAlpha + Source`) or manual blending (Listing 18.3).

The sampler we are using is linear, so this way we get piecewise-linear approximation and interpolation of the in-scattering and transmittance functions. It is not exactly correct (piecewise-linear approximation of an exponential decay function), but the error is small enough, and even with the camera moving it produces smooth results.

For the deferred-shaded objects, this step can be combined together with a deferred lighting pass—as lighting gets very ALU heavy with physically based rendering techniques, this could become a free step due to latency hiding. Information for volumetric fog scattering can be read right at the beginning of the lighting shader (it doesn't depend on anything other than screen-space pixel position and depth value). It is not needed (there is no wait assembly instruction that could stall the execution) until writing the final color to the lighting buffer, so the whole texture fetch latency hides behind all the lights calculations.

For forward-lit objects, particles, and transparencies, we can apply scattering in the same way. The advantage of our algorithm is that we can have any number of layers of such objects (Figure 18.10) and don't need to pay any additional cost other than one sample from a volumetric texture and a fused multiplication–addition operation.

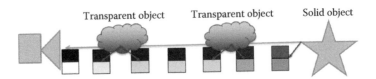

Figure 18.10. Multiple layers of opaque and transparent objects and trilinear 3D texture filtering.

18.3.7 Fighting Low-Resolution Under-Sampling Artifacts and Aliasing Problems

A common rendering problem is aliasing and under-sampling of geometric edges, shading, shadowing, and many other rendering pipeline elements. It happens when trying to sample complex, high-frequency signals in much lower resolution. While volumetric lighting in general is rather low frequency, the volumetric textures we used are so low resolution that some aliasing artifacts are inevitable.

In the case of *Assassin's Creed 4*, the main sources of volumetric fog aliasing were the shadow maps. Our rendering used four 1024×1024 shadow cascades that contained lots of very high-frequency animated details, like palm leaves. When the camera or those shadow-casting objects moved even slightly, the shadowing result, which was originally a binary function, changed a lot, causing unpleasant temporal artifacts. A common solution to any aliasing problem is super-sampling or low-pass filtering the source or target signal. A comparison of binary shadowing with frequencies in signals much higher than the Nyquist frequency and shadowing with proper low-pass filtering applied is shown in Figure 18.10. We applied such a solution and down-pass filtering to the shadowing function of volumetric lighting.

Our first attempt was using 32-tap percentage closer filtering (PCF) [Bunnell and Pellacini 04] of the shadowing test, but its performance was unacceptable for the real-time scenario and our budgets (a few-milliseconds filtering cost). We were noticing very high cache miss ratios due to large source shadow map resolution. We decided to look for other shadowing techniques that would allow us to down-sample shadow maps, do filtering in much cheaper 2D space, and potentially use some form of separable filtering on the signal.

There is ongoing research on the topic of better shadow-mapping techniques with different tradeoffs. There are already many existing shadowing algorithms that transform shadowing information from depth into some other domain and perform shadowing tests using some function that is lower frequency and filterable. Examples of those techniques are variance shadow mapping [Myers 07], convolution shadow maps [Annen et al. 07], exponential shadow maps [Annen et al. 08], transmittance function mapping [Delalandre et al. 11], and Fourier opacity mapping [Jansen and Bavoil 10].

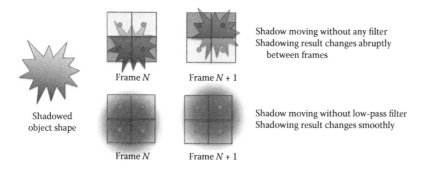

Shadow moving without any filter
Shadowing result changes abruptly
between frames

Shadow moving without low-pass filter
Shadowing result changes smoothly

Figure 18.11. Under-sampling and aliasing problems without a low-pass filter caused by small changes in the shadow map (top). Correct low-pass filtering helps to mitigate such problems (bottom).

We decided to use exponential shadow mapping [Annen et al. 07] due to its simplicity and low runtime and storage costs. It simplifies shadowing using exponential functions and allows us to perform shadow-map super-sampling, down-scaling, and separable filtering. To perform low-pass filtering, we transform the signal into the exponential domain and then do down-sampling four times for each shadow cascade—we end up with 256×256-sized textures. Then we perform separable Gaussian blur on those textures and end up with much lower frequency signal. The final shadowing test is trivial and is a smooth comparison ramp function of preconvolved values stored in shadow maps and an exponential function of the shadow-space depth of a shaded point in space.

The main disadvantage of exponential shadow maps that makes this algorithm not practical for most cases of regular rendering is the problem of *shadow leaking*. With exponential shadow maps, any fine-scale self-shadowing is impossible and shadows tend to be almost transparent on shadowed surfaces that are near the shadow casters. Shadows get harder farther away from shadow-casting objects, which is nonrealistic (the opposite effect should be visible) and is usually an unacceptable artifact. Fortunately in our case of volumetric shadows, self-shadowing is not really an issue because we perform shadowing tests not of real hard surface points but of the actual participating medium in between the surfaces. Therefore, shadow leaking and hardening artifacts were not visible and exponential shadow maps were good enough in our case.

18.4 Results and Discussion

Technique was implemented in *Assassin's Creed 4* for Microsoft Xbox One, Sony Playstation 4, and Microsoft Windows PC computers. We can see the achieved results (exaggerated, non-photorealistic rendering) in Figure 18.12.

Figure 18.12. Examples of volumetric fog in *Assassin's Creed 4*.

Our performance figures on Microsoft Xbox One are shown in Table 18.1. It is worth noting that we included in this table the cost of a separate fullscreen pass for effect application in deferred rendering—but in typical rendering scenarios this pass would be combined with deferred lighting. We also included the costs of shadow-map down-sampling and blurring—but those passes are not unique to the volumetric fog. They could be reused for particle shadowing or other low-frequency shadowing (translucent object shadowing), and this way the cost would be amortized among multiple parts of the rendering pipeline.

We are satisfied with the achieved results and performance and are already using it in many other projects. Still, it is possible to extend the algorithm and improve the quality and controllability, allowing us to achieve a slightly different visual effect and fit other rendering scenarios. It is also possible to improve performance for games with tighter frame budgets—like 60 fps first-person or racing games.

Total Cost	1.1 ms
Total cost without shadow-map operations and applying as a separate pass	*0.55 ms*
Shadow-map down-sample	0.163 ms
Shadow-map blur	0.177 ms
Lighting volume and calculating scattering	*0.43 ms*
Solving scattering equation	0.116 ms
Applying on screen	0.247 ms

Table 18.1. Algorithm performance numbers on Microsoft Xbox One.

The main area for future improvements is related to the low effect resolution. While most of the shadow aliasing is gone due to the described shadowing algorithm, aliasing from both density calculation and lighting could still be visible with extreme fog and scattering settings. Also, staircase bilinear filtering artifacts can be visible in some high-contrast areas. They come from piecewise linear approximation of bilinear filtering—which is only a C_0-continuous function.

Such strong scattering settings were never used in *Assassin's Creed 4*, so we didn't see those artifacts. However, this algorithm is now an important part of the Anvil game engine and its renderer and we discussed many potential improvements that could be relevant for other projects. We will propose them in the following subsections.

18.4.1 Potential Optimizations

Biggest cost of the algorithm is the in-scattering lighting and density estimation pass. It costs around 0.43 ms, even with very simple lighting models and only a few local lights. In the case of many lights, it could be important to accelerate this pass.

Because our volumetric lighting doesn't depend on the shaded onscreen scene geometry, only on the shadow maps, it is possible to reschedule it. With modern AMD GPU hardware and APIs like Mantle or next-generation console APIs, it is possible to use an *asynchronous compute* and launch the volumetric lighting in parallel with some other raster- and bandwidth-heavy passes.

We also didn't apply any early-out optimization to volumetric fog. Very often the algorithm also performed all calculations (density estimation, in-scattering calculation, and ray marching) for points behind the visible opaque objects. While it made the cost and timing of volumetric fog fixed (which can be desirable when creating frame time performance budgets), it was also a waste of GPU cycles. It is possible to use a hierarchical Z-buffer (which became quite common for forward and clustered lighting [Harada 12, Olsson et al. 12] or a hierarchical Z-buffer culling [Hill and Collin 11]) to reduce the number of unnecessary computations. By using such information, it is possible to perform an early-out exit in all algorithm passes and skip updating the fog texture volumes behind solid objects as this information won't be read and used for the shading of any currently visible object. It doesn't help in the worst case (when viewing distance is very large and the whole screen covers the full fog range), but in an average case (half of the screen is the ground plane or near objects), it could cut the algorithm cost by 30–50% by providing a significant reduction of both used bandwidth and ALU operations. It could also be used for better 3D light culling like in [Olsson et al. 12]. We didn't have hierarchical Z-buffer information available in our engine, and computing it would add some fixed cost, so we didn't try this optimization. On the other hand, relying on the depth buffer would mean that asynchronous compute optimization could not be applied (unless one has a depth prepass). Therefore, it is a tradeoff and its practical usage depends on the used engine, target platforms, and whole rendering pipeline.

18.4.2 Interleaved or Stochastic Sampling

In our implementation of volumetric fog, we used fixed sampling pattern, always sampling the center of the processed 3D texture texel. As literature proves [Tóth and Umenhoffer 09, Vos 14], it can be beneficial to use interleaved or stochastic sampling, alternating the sampling pattern between adjacent pixels and adding some jitter inside pixel cells (Figure 18.13). This way it is possible to reduce aliasing and ringing artifacts and trade them for increased noise. Noise is usually much easier to filter (it's a high-frequency component easily removed by low-pass filters), and the resulting image is more visually pleasant. We didn't try this approach in the shipped game, but it could be trivially extended into our solution—and the demo code for this chapter has it implemented in the most trivial form. It is possible to precompute some 3D sampling patterns that maximize sample variance in the neighborhood and are not biased and read them from a wrapped, low-resolution 3D texture. The process of jittered and stratified sampling and various possible sampling schemes are described very well in [Pharr and Humphreys 10]. It could work especially well to vary those patterns also in time with temporal super-sampling described in the next section.

18.4.3 Temporal Super-Sampling and Reprojection

One of rendering techniques that is gaining popularity is temporal super-sampling and antialiasing using temporal reprojection techniques. Temporal super-sampling and smoothing were used in *Assassin's Creed 4* for regular screen buffer antialiasing, but we also extended them easily to super-sample the screen-space ambient occlusion. As [Vos 14] and [Valient 14] showed in articles and presentations about *Killzone: Shadow Fall* technology, it can be used for many other effects, like screen-space reflections and volumetric lighting. In the case of a 2D image, temporal super-sampling and reprojection are quite difficult, as information for only

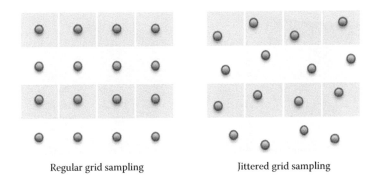

Regular grid sampling

Jittered grid sampling

Figure 18.13. Comparison of regular and jittered sampling patterns.

one layer of objects is stored (the depth buffer acts like a height field—we have no information for objects behind it). Therefore, when reprojecting a dynamic 2D scene, occlusion artifacts are inevitable and there is a need to reconstruct information for pixels that were not present in the previous frame (Figure 18.14).

In the case of volumetric reprojection, it is much easier, as we store information for whole 3D viewing frustum in volumetric textures, as well as for the space behind the shaded objects. Therefore, there are only two cases of improper data after volumetric reprojection:

1. data for space that was occupied by objects that moved away as shading changes,

2. data outside of the volume range.

We can see how much easier the reprojection is in a 3D case in Figure 18.15.

Reprojection itself stabilizes some motion flickering artifacts but isn't the solution for increasing image quality for a static scene or camera. A common

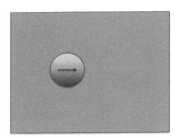

Frame *N*

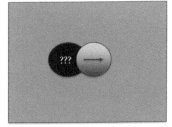

Frame *N* + 1, unknown pixels
Improper reconstruction data

Figure 18.14. Problems with 2D temporal reprojection of a dynamic scene.

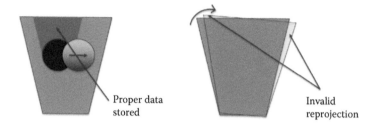

Figure 18.15. Volumetric reprojection (top view of the whole view volume).

technique used as temporal super-sampling is to introduce a temporal jitter—a variation between sampling points between frames. On its own, it would cause serious temporal artifacts like noise or image shaking, but in conjunction with the temporal reprojection and smoothing, it gives high-quality super-sampled images. We prototyped it after shipping *Assassin's Creed 4*, and we can see this technique in use in Figure 18.16. It shows how staircase artifacts appearing due to low resolution are fixed using temporal super-sampling with an accumulation buffer and many alternating, Poisson-distributed samples. We definitely aim to use this temporal super-sampling in future projects using volumetric fog.

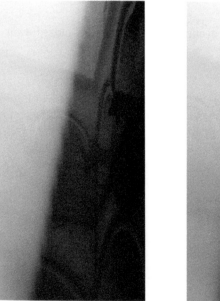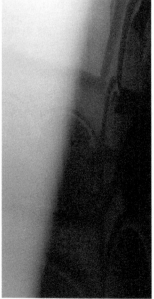

Figure 18.16. Fixing under-sampling and staircase artifacts in volumetric fog without (left) and with (right) temporal jittering and super-sampling.

18.4.4 Artist-Authored Variation of Participating Media Density

In our algorithm implementation, participating medium had a simple, procedurally modeled density using Perlin noise and simple exponential vertical attenuation (Section 18.3.3). We believe that it could be beneficial to add other ways of modeling scattering intensity and varying the participating medium density. We see two potential ways of increasing variety of scattering intensity:

1. baked-on levels and static,

2. dynamic and gameplay influence.

The first option could be useful especially for games with big and varied levels. Some parts of an environment contain lots of mist (plains and forests) or dust (interiors of uninhabited old buildings). Such areas would benefit from having different, larger scattering coefficients and a more pronounced scattering effect. Depending on the game type and level structure, it could be stored in various ways. For mainly outdoor, open-world games it could be stored as a simple, low-resolution 2D world texture with density painted on by artists. For interiors, artists and level designers could define them by adding analytical interior shapes.

Second, a dynamic way could utilize effects systems commonly used in games—particle systems, force fields, analytical dynamic shapes, etc. Effect artists know such tools very well and already use them for simulating scattering effects by alpha blending, so applying such tools in a physically based manner on volumetric fog effects should be easy for them. The article [Wrennige et al. 10] describes how it is possible to do this and counter common under-sampling and aliasing artifacts (used in high-quality, CGI and movie rendering). Regarding games, [Vos 14] describes the use of particles for the injection of scattering intensities based on an alpha particle into volumetric textures in an efficient way.

18.5 Acknowledgments

I would like to thank whole *Assassin's Creed 4* team of rendering programmers, technical art directors, and lighting artists for inspiring ideas and talks about the algorithm and its optimizations. Special thanks go to colleagues at Ubisoft Montreal who were working on similar topics for other games and shared their code and great ideas—Ulrich Haar, Stephen Hill, Lionel Berenguier, Typhaine Le Gallo, and Alexandre Lahaise.

Bibliography

[Annen et al. 07] Thomas Annen, Tom Mertens, Philippe Bekaert, Hans-Peter Seidel, and Jan Kautz. "Convolution Shadow Maps." In *Proceedings of the 18th Eurographics conference on Rendering Techniques*, pp. 51–60. Aire-la-Ville, Switzerland: Eurographics Association, 2007.

[Annen et al. 08] T. Annen, T. Mertens, H.-P. Siedel, E. Flerackers, and J. Kautz. "Exponential Shadow Maps." In *Graphics Interface 2008*, edited by L. Bartram and C. Shaw, pp. 155–161. Toronto: Canadian Human-Computer Communications Society, 2008.

[Bouthors et al. 06] Antoine Bouthors, Fabrice Neyret, and Sylvain Lefebvre. "Real-Time Realistic Illumination and Shading of Stratiform Clouds." Presented at Eurographics, Vienna, Austria, September 4–8, 2006.

[Bunnell and Pellacini 04] Michael Bunnell and Fabio Pellacini. "Shadow Map Antialiasing." In *GPU Gems*, edited by Randima Fernando, Chapter 11. Reading, MA: Addison-Wesley Professional, 2004.

[Delalandre et al. 11] Cyril Delalandre, Pascal Gautron, Jean-Eudes Marvie, and Guillaume François. "Transmittance Function Mapping." Presented at Symposium on Interactive 3D Graphics and Games, San Francisco, CA, February 18–20, 2011.

[Green 03] Robin Green. "Spherical Harmonic Lighting: The Gritty Details." Presented at Game Developers Conference, San Jose, CA, March 4–8, 2003.

[Green 05] Simon Green. "Implementing Improved Perlin Noise." In *GPU Gems 2*, edited by Matt Farr, pp. 409–416. Reading, MA: Addison-Wesley Professional, 2005.

[Harada 12] Takahiro Harada, Jay McKee, and Jason C. Yang. "Forward+: Bringing Deferred Lighting to the Next Level." Presented at Eurographics, Cagliari, Italy, May 13–18, 2012.

[Hill and Collin 11] Stephen Hill and Daniel Collin. "Practical, Dynamic Visibility for Games." In *GPU Pro 2: Advanced Rendering Technicques*, edited by Wolfgang Engel, pp. 329–347. Natick, MA: A K Peters, 2011.

[Huelin et al. 15] John Huelin, Benjamin Rouveyrol, and Bartłomiej Wroński, "Deferred Normalized Irradiance Probes." In *GPU Pro 6: Advanced Rendering Techniques*, edited by Wolfgang Engel, pp. 299–319. Boca Raton, FL: CRC Press, 2015.

[Jansen and Bavoil 10] Jon Jansen and Louis Bavoil. "Fourier Opacity Mapping." Presented at Symposium on Interactive 3D Graphics and Games, Bethesda, MD, February 19–20, 2010.

[Kaplanyan 09] Anton Kaplanyan. "Light Propagation Volumes in CryEngine 3." SIGGRAPH Course: Advances in Real-Time Rendering in 3D Graphics and Games, SIGGRAPH 2009, New Orleans, LA, August 3, 2009.

[Myers 07] Kevin Myers. "Variance Shadow Mapping." Technical report, NVIDIA, January 2007.

[Olsson et al. 12] Ola Olsson, Markus Billeter, and Ulf Assarsson. "Clustered Deferred and Forward Shading." In *Proceedings of the Nineteenth Eurographics Conference on Rendering*, pp. 87-96. Aire-la-Ville, Switzerland: Eurographics Association, 2012.

[Perlin 02] Ken Perlin. "Improving Noise." *ACM Trans. Graphics* 21:3 (2002), 681–682.

[Pharr and Humphreys 10] Matt Phar and Greg Humphreys. *Physically Based Rendering: From Theory to Implementation*, Second Edition. San Francisco: Morgan Kaufmann, 2010.

[Shopf 09] Jeremy Shoph. "Mixed Resolution Rendering." Presented at Game Developers Conference, San Francisco, CA, March 23–27, 2009.

[Sloan 08] Peter-Pike Sloan. "Stupid Spherical Harmonics (SH) Tricks." Presented at Game Developers Conference, San Francisco, CA, February 18–22, 2008.

[Sousa 08] Tiago Sousa. "Crysis Next Gen Effects." Presented at Game Developers Conference, San Francisco, CA, February 18–22, 2008.

[St-Amour 13] Jean-Francois St-Amour. "Rendering of Assassin's Creed 3." Presented at Game Developers Conference, San Francisco, CA, March 5–9, 2012.

[Tóth and Umenhoffer 09] Balázs Tóth, Tamás Umenhoffer, "Real-Time Volumetric Lighting in Participating Media." Presented at Eurographics, Munich, Germany, March 30–April 3, 2009.

[Valient 14] Michal Valient. "Taking *Killzone Shadow Fall* Image Quality into the Next Generation." Presented at Game Developers Conference, San Francisco, CA, March 17–21, 2014.

[Vos 14] Nathan Vos. "Volumetric Light Effects in *Killzone: Shadow Fall*." In *GPU Pro 5: Advanced Rendering Techniques*, edited by Wolfgang Engel, pp. 127–148. Boca Raton, FL: CRC Press, 2014.

[Wenzel 06] Carsten Wenzel. "Real-Time Atmospheric Effects in Games Revisited." Presented at SIGGRAPH, Boston, MA, July 30–August 3, 2006.

[Wrennige et al. 10] Magnus Wrenninge, Nafees Bin Zafar, Jeff Clifford, Gavin Graham, Devon Penney, Janne Kontkanen, Jerry Tessendorf, and Andrew Clinton. "Volumetric Methods in Visual Effects." SIGGRAPH Course, Los Angeles, CA, July 25–29, 2010.

[Yusov 13] Egor Yusov. "Practical Implementation of Light Scattering Effects Using Epipolar Sampling and 1D Min/Max Binary Trees." Presented at Game Developers Conference, San Francisco, CA, March 28–29, 2013.

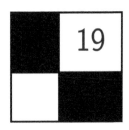

Physically Based Light Probe Generation on GPU

Ivan Spogreev

19.1 Introduction

As the quality and complexity of modern real-time lighting has steadily evolved, increasingly more and more advanced and optimal methods are required in order to hit performance targets. It is not merely enough nowadays to have a static ambient term or simple cube-map reflections to simulate indirect light. The environment needs to have lighting that fully matches the surroundings. The shading needs to not only handle and properly process direct lighting coming from the light source, but also lighting that bounces around the environment. Lighting received by a surface needs to be properly reflected toward the camera position as well. By generating and processing our lighting information entirely on the GPU, we were able to achieve dynamic, physically based environment lighting while staying well within our performance targets.

When we started working on *FIFA 15*, we decided that we require a physically based system that can dynamically update indirect lighting for the players on the pitch at runtime. The main goal was to generate the lighting information for the pitch at level load time. Because *FIFA* has a playable loading screen, there is significant latency and performance constraints on these lighting computations. When a player waits for the match to get started, the system cannot result in any frame drops or stuttering. This means that each step of the light-generation procedure needs to complete within a few milliseconds so we can completely render the rest of the frame. The second goal was to give the artist the ability to iterate on the lighting conditions without waiting for a pass of content pipeline to provide the relevant updates in lighting information. Under our approach, each time the artist would change a light direction, color value, or sky texture, he or she would immediately see an updated scene with the proper lighting. Finally, our technique also allowed us to include many area lights directly into the precalculated lighting information.

19.2   Light Probes Theory

Correctly lighting an object is a computationally intensive process. The light that propagates directly from a light source can bounce around the environment before it hits a given object. We will define the light that propagates directly from a light source as direct lighting, and the light that propagates as a result of bounces in the environment as indirect lighting. Direct lighting can be solved in a number of different ways depending on the light source type [Drobot 14] and is not covered in this chapter. Here we will focus on indirect lighting and how to calculate it.

To calculate all lighting coming from an environment we need to solve the general rendering equation:

$$L_o(\omega) = \int_\Omega \text{brdf}(\omega_i, \omega_o) \times L_i(\omega_i) \times (\omega_i \cdot n) d\omega_i, \qquad (19.1)$$

where ω_o is the direction of the outgoing light, ω_i is the negative direction of the incoming light, Ω is the unit hemisphere containing all possible values for ω_i, $L_i(\omega_i)$ is radiance coming from direction, and $\omega_i \cdot n$ is the dot product of the incoming direction and normal.

One can think about this integral as gathering all of the lighting information from all possible directions for a given surface point. When the incoming light from any particular direction hits a surface, we translate it to the reflected light toward the direction of the camera. The material function that defines how the light gets transformed and modulated is known as the bidirectional reflectance distribution function (BRDF). There are different types of BRDFs for various materials such as cloth, skin, hair, etc. In our work, we focused on dielectric and electric materials like plastic, metals, wood, concrete, and so on. For such materials, we treat light reflected directly off the surface differently than light refracted into it. Metals, in particular, have the property of absorbing all the refracted light. In contrast, dielectric materials absorb only a small fraction of the refracted light, and usually, after scattering inside the material, the light eventually finds its way back to out the surface and toward the viewer [Hoffman 12]. We define light resulting from scattering as *diffuse reflection* and differentiate it from *specular reflection*, which is light resulting from a pure surface reflection. Thus, the BRDF for such materials can be presented as a combination of the two BRDFs, diffuse and specular:

$$\text{BRDF} = \text{BRDF}_{\text{diffuse}} + \text{BRDF}_{\text{specular}}.$$

This is actually a common approach for representing a large variety of material types found in real-time applications such as video games [Hoffman 12].

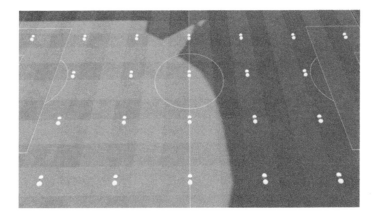

Figure 19.1. Light probes grid on a pitch.

Separating the integral in Equation (19.1) into two parts, we get

$$
\begin{aligned}
L_o(\omega_0) &= \int_\Omega \mathrm{brdf}(\omega_i, \omega_o) \times L_i(\omega_i) \times (\omega_i \cdot n) d\omega_i \\
&= \int_\Omega \mathrm{brdf}D(\omega_i, \omega_o) \times L_i(\omega_i) \times (\omega_i \cdot n) d\omega_i \qquad (19.2) \\
&\quad + \int_\Omega \mathrm{brdf}S(\omega_i, \omega_o) \times L_i(\omega_i) \times (\omega_i \cdot n) d\omega_i.
\end{aligned}
$$

In computer graphics, there are different methods to solve the rendering equation (e.g., path tracing and photon mapping), all of which require the tracing of many rays and performing heavy computations. This is simply not an option for games and real-time 3D graphics. So, instead of computing lighting every frame for every single shading point, we preintegrate it for some base variables and use the results later. Such precomputation should give us the quality we require with the real-time performance we need.

The composition of the preintegrated lighting information for a given position in space is commonly called a *light probe*. (See Figure 19.1.) Again, we introduce a separation. We define two light probes for both parts of the integral in Equation (19.2): diffuse light probes and specular light probes.

19.3 Generating Light Probes on the GPU

As described in the previous section, indirect lighting is light coming from the environment (as opposed to directly from the light source). Environment lighting for a given point in space can easily be represented by rendering the scene into a cube-map texture. For our application, *FIFA 15*, we must do this rendering during level load corresponding to our dynamic lighting conditions for each game match. When rendering into the cube map is complete, we run the preintegration step that will be described in the Sections 19.3.3, 19.3.4, and 19.3.5. After the preintegration step is done for one probe, we move to the next light probe and repeat the process. This process can incidentally increase the loading time of a level because we cannot render dynamic objects using the light probes without the completion of the preintegration step. It was thus important to make this process as performant as possible without making significant quality tradeoffs.

After a cube map gets generated, we need to solve the rendering integral in Equation (19.2). One well-known tool to generate the probes themselves is called CubeMapGen [Lagarde 12]. This tool can be used in the pipeline to generate the lighting information from an environment. It is open source, so it can be modified if need be. However, this tool uses the CPU to prefilter specular cube maps and takes a significant amount of time to process a high resolution environment map.

Because our goal was to generate the light probes in runtime during the level loading and we had graphics cycles to spare, a GPU solution appeared more favorable.

19.3.1 Generating Diffuse Light Probes from an Environment Map

First, we need to define our diffuse BRDF. We use the normalized Lambertian BRDF. It is very simple and easy to preintegrate and also matches the required visual quality:

$$\text{Lambertian BRDF} \quad = \quad \frac{1}{\pi}, \tag{19.3}$$

$$\int_{\Omega} \text{brdf} D(\omega_i, \omega_o) \times L_i(\omega_i) \times (\omega_i \cdot n) d\omega_i \quad = \quad \int_{\Omega} \frac{1}{\pi} \times L_i(\omega_i) \times (\omega_i \cdot n) d\omega_i.$$

The integral in Equation (19.3) depends on two vectors: normal and light direction. While the normal is constant per shading point, the incoming light (L_i) varies across the hemisphere. We treat each pixel in a cube map as a light source. Because the diffuse BRDF does not depend on the view direction, we integrate the rendering equation for every possible normal direction. We do this by integrating and projecting the rendering equation onto spherical harmonic coefficients [Ramamoorthi and Hanrahan 01] in real time using the GPU [King 05]. This method allows us to preintegrate the diffuse part of the integral in 0.5 ms on a GeForce GTX 760.

Spherical harmonics and their usage in real-time 3D graphics is out of the scope of this chapter. For more information, we recommend reading the great article from Peter-Pike Sloan: "Stupid Spherical Harmonics (SH) Tricks" [Sloan 08].

19.3.2   Generating Specular Light Probes from an Environment Map

Similar to diffuse light probe generation, we start by defining our specular BRDF. We use the Cook-Torrance BRDF [Cook and Torrance 81] shown in Equation (19.4) as the specular part with the normalized GGX [Walter et al. 07, Burley 12], and we use Equation (19.5) as the distribution function:

$$\text{Cook-Torrance specular BRDF} = \frac{D \times F \times G}{4 \times (V \cdot N) \times (N \cdot L)}, \tag{19.4}$$

where D is the microfacet distribution function, F is the Fresnel term, G is the geometric shadowing term, $(V \cdot N)$ is the dot product of the view and normal vectors, and $(N \cdot L)$ is the dot product of the normal and light vectors; and

$$\text{GGX } D(H) = \frac{a^2}{\pi(\cos(\theta_H)^2 \times (a^2 - 1) + 1)^2}, \tag{19.5}$$

where H is the half vector, $a = \text{roughness}^2$, and $\cos(\theta_H) = (N \cdot H)$.

Using the GGX function (Equation (19.5)) gives us good-looking specular highlights. The function can also be easily integrated (as will be seen later).

For more detailed information on choosing a distribution function, a Fresnel term ,and a masking term, please review the SIGGRAPH courses on physically based rendering [Hill and McAuley 12].

As with diffuse light probes, we need to preintegrate the specular integral. However, while the diffuse BRDF depends only on the normal and light directions, there are more variables in the specular BRDF. To simplify the BRDF for preintegration, we first assume that there are neither Fresnel effects (F) nor shadow masking (G) on the material. This removes the F and G terms from Equation (19.4). We integrate based on the reflected direction R—so for every direction, we store a preintegrated value in the cube map. Furthermore, different mip levels of the cube map correspond to different roughness values. The normal (N) is the only remaining unknown variable (L is the light direction). In order to simplify the integral further, we assume N is equal to V, which means that R is equal to V as well.

The specular BRDF for the preintegration is therefore

$$\text{brdfS}(\omega_i, \omega_o) = \frac{D}{4 \times (N \cdot L)}, \tag{19.6}$$

$$\int_\Omega \text{brdfS}(\omega_i, \omega_o) \times L_i(\omega_i) \times (\omega_i \cdot n)d\omega_i = \int_\Omega \frac{D}{4 \times (N \cdot L)} \times L_i(\omega_i) \times (\omega_i \cdot n)d\omega_i.$$

Note that $(N \cdot V) = 1$ since $N = V$, as mentioned above.

Assuming N is equal to V obviously produces error (for example, long highlights are lost at grazing angles). Furthermore, we also introduce inaccuracy

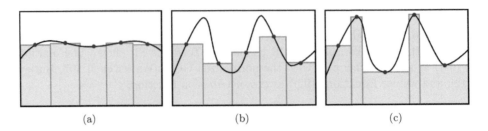

(a)   (b)   (c)

Figure 19.2. (a) When the function is regular, the Monte Carlo integration works well with a small number of samples. (b) When the function is irregular, it gets harder to estimate. (c) Importance sampling focuses on the difficult areas and gives us a better approximation.

by removing the F and G terms. At runtime, we compensate for this error by multiplying by a Fresnel term.

This derivation results in a prefiltering that is very similar to the *split-sum* method introduced by Brian Karis [Karis 13]. The difference is that by splitting the sum, they take into account the F and G terms, which produces more accurate results in the final runtime indirect lighting.

Monte Carlo importance sampling. To solve the integral from Equation (19.6), we use the Monte Carlo importance sampling method [Hammersley and Handscomb 64] shown in Equation (19.7):

$$\int_{\Omega} f(x)dx \approx \frac{1}{N} \sum_{i=1}^{N} \frac{f(X_i)}{p(X_i)}, \qquad (19.7)$$

where $p(x)$ is the probability distribution function (PDF).

One can think of importance sampling as trying to focus on the most "important" areas of the function. If one can imagine a function that is very smooth and regular (Figure 19.2(a)), then the sampling position would have little impact on the result. But when the function has local extremes (Figure 19.2(b)), it will be harder to estimate the integral correctly and many more samples will be needed. Importance sampling helps to capture samples whose values have a higher influence on the final result being computed (Figure 19.2(c)).

BRDF importance sampling. Using the BRDF shape as a PDF can result in a sample distribution that matches the integrand well. For example, with a mirror-like surface, it would make sense to focus on the directions around the reflection direction (Figure 19.3) as this would be the area where most of the visible light rays originate from.

In order to match the specular BRDF shape closely, we build the PDF based on the distribution function D and the cosine between the half vector H and the

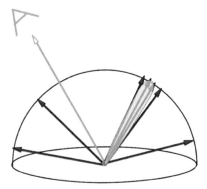

Figure 19.3. Illustration of the BRDF importance sampling. Most of the samples get generated toward the reflection vector, where the specular BRDF commonly has higher values.

normal N (Equation (19.8)) [Burley 12]. This is because D has the most effect on the BRDF's shape. The multiplication by the cosine term will help in further calculations:

$$\text{PDF}(H) = D(H) \times \cos(\theta_H). \tag{19.8}$$

The GGX microfacet distribution gives us the distribution of half vectors around the normal. The PDF (Equation (19.8)) is therefore defined in half-vector space. However, the integration step (Equation (19.6)) requires integrating the light direction against a specific view direction. Therefore, we need to convert the PDF from half-vector space to light space (from $\text{PDF}(H)$ to $\text{PDF}(L)$).

Per [Pharr and Humphreys 04], this PDF conversion is simply

$$\text{PDF}(L) = \frac{\text{PDF}(H)}{4\cos(\theta_H)}.$$

Because we can represent the half-vector in spherical coordinates ϕ, θ, we can also represent the PDF as a multiplication of $\text{PDF}(\phi)$ and $\text{PDF}(\theta)$ [Pharr and Humphreys 04]:

$$\text{PDF}(H) = \text{PDF}(\phi) \times \text{PDF}(\theta).$$

From Equation (19.8) and Equation (19.5), we can see that the $\text{PDF}(H)$ does not depend on the angle ϕ. So we can simply derive [Pharr and Humphreys 04] that $\text{PDF}(\phi)$ becomes constant with a value of $\frac{1}{2\pi}$:

$$\text{PDF}(\phi) = \frac{1}{2\pi}.$$

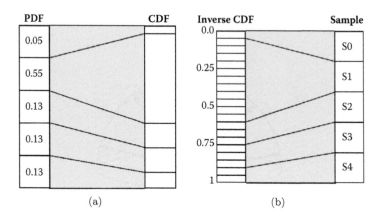

Figure 19.4. The illustration of the correlation between PDF and CDF. (a) The sample with the higher PDF value has more space on the CDF. (b) The inverse CDF maps the uniform distributed values to the samples. A given value on the $[0 : 1]$ interval has higher chance to get mapped to the sample S1.

Therefore,

$$\mathrm{PDF}_{(\theta)} = \frac{D(H) \times \cos(\theta_H)}{\mathrm{PDF}(\phi)} = \frac{2 \times a^2 \times \cos(\theta_H)}{(\cos(\theta_H)^2 \times (a^2 - 1) + 1)^2}.$$

By using the Monte Carlo importance sampling, with the $\mathrm{PDF}(H)$, we now have all we need to approximate the specular part of the rendering integral:

$$\int_\Omega \frac{D}{4 \times (n \cdot \omega_i)} \times L_i(\omega_i) \times (\omega_i \cdot n) d\omega_i \tag{19.9}$$

$$\approx \frac{1}{N} \sum_{i=1}^{N} \frac{D \times L_i(\omega_i) \times (\omega_i \cdot n)}{4 \times (n \cdot \omega_i) \times \mathrm{PDF}(\omega_i)} = \frac{1}{N} \sum_{i=1}^{N} L_i(\omega_i),$$

where N is the number of samples, ω_i is the sampling light direction, and $L_i(\omega_i)$ is the sampling color in direction ω_i.

The PDF only gives us the probability of a certain direction x. What we actually require is the inverse; we need to be able to generate samples based on a given probability. We start by computing a *cumulative distribution function* (CDF) for our PDF [Papoulis 84, pp. 92–94] (Equation (19.10)). For a value x, the CDF defines the uniformly distributed value ε on the $[0 : 1]$ interval in a proportion to $\mathrm{PDF}(x)$ [Papoulis 84, Pharr and Humphreys 04] (Figure 19.4(a)). While the CDF has a uniform unit probability distribution, it is actually the opposite of what we desire. To solve our problem, we simply need to calculate the inverse CDF (Figure 19.4(b)).

The following equations show how to calculate the CDFs ($\text{CDF}(\phi)$ and $\text{CDF}(\theta)$) for the PDF function derived from the original specular BRDF based on the formal definition (Equation (19.10)) of the CDF:

$$\text{CDF}(X) = \int \text{PDF}(x)dx, \tag{19.10}$$

$$\text{CDF}(\phi) = \int_0^\phi \frac{1}{2\pi}dx = \frac{1}{2\pi}\phi,$$

$$\text{CDF}(\theta) = \int_0^q \frac{2 \times a^2 \times x}{(x^2 \times (a^2 - 1) + 1)^2}dx = \frac{1 - q^2}{1 + q^2(a^2 - 1)},$$

where $q = \cos(\theta_H)$.

We now invert our CDF functions to produce mappings from uniform values ε_1 and ε_2 to the angles ϕ and θ, respectively:

$$\phi = \text{Inverse CDF}(\varepsilon_1) = \varepsilon_1 \times 2\pi, \tag{19.11}$$

$$\theta = \text{Inverse CDF}(\varepsilon_2) = \text{acos}\left(\sqrt{\frac{1 - \varepsilon_2}{1 + \varepsilon_{2(a^2-1)}}}\right). \tag{19.12}$$

Finally, we can now generate a direction (ϕ, θ) based on Equations (19.11) and (19.12) from uniformly distributed random values $(\varepsilon_1, \varepsilon_2)$ in $[0 : 1]$.

Putting all this together we get the code in Listing 19.1.

```
//e1, e2 is pair of two random values
//Roughness is the current roughness we are integrating for
//N is the normal
float3 ImportanceSampleGGX( float e1, float e2, float Roughness,
  float3 N )
{
    float a = Roughness * Roughness;

    //Calculate phi and cosine of theta using Equations (19.11)
    //and (19.12)
    float phi = 2 * PI * e1;
    float cos_theta = sqrt((1 - e2) / ( 1 + (a*a - 1) * e2 ));
    float sin_theta = sqrt( 1 - cos_theta * cos_theta);

    //Build a half vector
    float3 H;
    H.x = sin_theta * cos(phi);
    H.y = sin_theta * sin(phi);
    H.z = cos_theta;

    //Transform the vector from tangent space to world space
    float3 up = abs(N.z) < 0.999? float3(0,0,1): float3(1,0,0);
    float3 right = normalize( cross(up, N ) );
    float3 forward = cross( N, right);

    return right * H.x + forward * H.y + N * H.z;
}
```

```
//For the given Roughness and the View vector function
//samples the environment map using the BRDF importance sampling
//e1, e2 is pair of two random values
//totalWeight the number of the valid samples
float3 SampleBRDF(float e1, float e2, float Roughness, float3 V)
{
        float3 N = V;
        //Calculate the H vector using BRDF importance sampling
        float3 H = ImportanceSampleGGX(e1, e2 , Roughness, N );
        //Calculate the L vector using the standard reflection
        //equation
        float3 L = 2 * dot( V, H ) * H - V;

        float NoL = saturate( dot( N, L ) );

        float3 color = 0;
        //we skip the samples that are not in the same hemisphere
        //with the normal
        if( NoL > 0 )
        {
                        //Sample the cube map in the direction L
                        color += SampleTex(L).rgb;
        }

        return color;
}
```

Listing 19.1. BRDF importance sampling.

We use the Hammersley quasirandom low-discrepancy sequence [Niederreiter 92] to generate the uniformly distributed random values $\varepsilon_1, \varepsilon_2$ on the GPU (Listing 19.2).

Figure 19.5 shows some results. We preintegrate an environment map using 1024 samples per direction. The performance numbers for BRDF Importance Sampling preintegration on a GeForce GTX 760 are shown in Table 19.1 (timings are in milliseconds).

```
float radicalInverse (uint bits)
{
   bits = (bits << 16u) | (bits >> 16u);
   bits = ((bits & 0x55555555u) << 1u)|((bits & 0xAAAAAAAAu)>>1u);
   bits = ((bits & 0x33333333u) << 2u)|((bits & 0xCCCCCCCCu)>>2u);
   bits = ((bits & 0x0F0F0F0Fu) << 4u)|((bits & 0xF0F0F0F0u)>>4u);
   bits = ((bits & 0x00FF00FFu) << 8u)|((bits & 0xFF00FF00u)>>8u);
   return float(bits) * 2.3283064365386963e-10; // / 0x100000000
}

float2 Hammersley (uint i, uint N)
{
   return float2(float(i)/float(N), radicalInverse(i));
}
```

Listing 19.2. The Hammersley function generates a uniformly distributed quasirandom 2D point $(\varepsilon_1, \varepsilon_2)$.

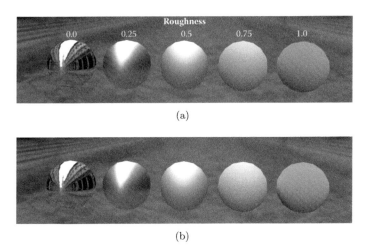

(a)

(b)

Figure 19.5. (a) The preintegrated specular BRDF for different roughness with 1024 samples per pixel. (b) The ground truth integration using 100,000 samples without the importance sampling.

Number of	Preintegrated Cube Map Face Size				
samples	128×128	64×64	32×32	16×16	8×8
64	2.8	0.8	0.2	0.04	0.02
128	6.2	1.6	0.5	0.1	0.08
512	25	6.5	1.7	0.4	0.3
1024	-	13.5	3	1	0.7
4096	-	53.8	15	5	3

Table 19.1. BRDF importance sampling preintegration on GTX 760.

The main problem with BRDF importance sampling (and importance sampling in general) is that a large number of samples are needed in order to reduce noise and get a smooth image (Figure 19.6). This problem gets even worse when

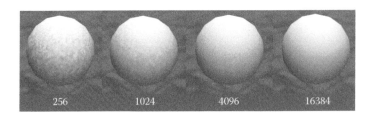

Figure 19.6. Number of samples and noise.

Figure 19.7. Dark environment map with few bright light sources using 1024 samples.

there are high-frequency details in the environment map (Figure 19.7). Some of our nighttime environments have area lights surrounded by dark regions (which introduces a lot of high-frequency details). Having such noisy prefiltered maps is a big issue. We needed some additional methods to help resolve this issue.

19.3.3 Prefiltered Environment Map

As mentioned above, thousands of samples are required for each pixel to keep the noise level low. It might take too much time even on the GPU to prefilter each probe for low roughness values (Table 19.1). We therefore use the following approach [Křivánek and Colbert 08] to reduce noise and keep the number of samples low.

The idea is simple: noise is created when there are high-frequency details in areas with relatively low values in the PDF. In order to combat that, we filter out the high-frequency details by creating a mip chain. This is in a similar vein to using a mip chain to avoid aliasing when down-sampling an image. For higher-probability samples, on the other hand, we still sample from the unfiltered image.

We proceed by using a ratio of the solid angle around a sample direction to the solid angle subtended by one pixel in the environment map [Křivánek and Colbert 08]. In the original paper, they found that biasing the mip level by 1 creates a less noisy result. However, in our case, we did not wish to bias in order to preserve detail for lower roughness. Therefore, we pick the starting mip based on the material roughness, as seen in Listing 19.3.

```
float pdf = a / pow(NoH*NoH * (a-1) + 1, 2);
float area = 2 * PI;

pdf = pdf * NoL / (4 * LoH);
float s_solidangle = 1.0 / (numBRDFSamples * pdf); //sample solid
                                                   //angle
float p_solidangle = area / (1.0 * mapW * mapH); //pixel solid angle
float base_mip = lerp(0,4, Roughness); // pick starting mip based
                                       // on roughness
float mipmapLevel = clamp(0.5 * log2(s_solidangle/ p_solidangle),
  base_mip, 5);
```

Listing 19.3. Choosing a mip level based on the sample PDF.

Figure 19.8. Source environment (left) and ground truth (right), with roughness 0.25 BRDF IS using 128 samples (middle left) and roughness 0.25 BRDF IS using 128 samples with prefiltering (middle right).

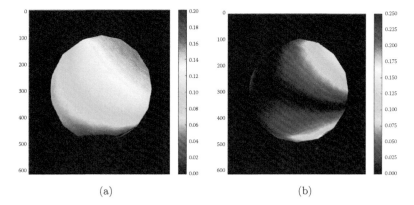

Figure 19.9. Error heat map of the final result using BRDF importance sampling with prefiltering: (a) a result using 128 samples, and (b) a result using 1024 samples.

Prefiltering the environment map solves most of the problems with noise. We found that it works well for daytime environments, where the energy is relatively similar in the local pixel neighborhood. However, for nighttime, although there is no noise in the result, the error is still higher due to the extremely high frequency details (Figure 19.8) that get excessively blurred. For example, a low-probability sample might get a lower energy value than it would have gotten in the ground truth (Figure 19.9).

We are thus faced with a problem. On one hand, if we don't prefilter the environment map, the result is too noisy. On the other hand, prefiltering produces high error with a low number of samples. So we added another technique for the preintegration of probes with high roughness values.

19.3.4   Environment Map Importance Sampling

Previously we discussed BRDF importance sampling where we use the PDF to match the behavior of the BRDF. But that might not always be the best sampling

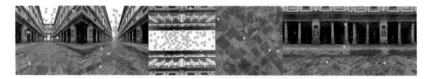

Figure 19.10. Sampling distribution.

Figure 19.11. Unwrapped environment map.

strategy. For example, consider the case of a dark room with very few bright light sources (or in *FIFA 15*'s case, a nighttime stadium with small but bright area light sources). Sampling based on the BRDF distribution might generate many samples that miss the light sources. This will create variance when the samples do hit the light source (especially if the samples had low probability). In that case, it would have been preferable to instead generate samples that tend to point toward light sources (i.e., pixels with high energy values). Environment map importance sampling [Colbert et al. 10] allows us to achieve exactly this. We use environment map importance sampling to focus the sample generation on areas with higher intensity (Figure 19.10).

First, we reduce the number of dimensions that we are working with to simplify calculations. Cube-map texture sampling is based on a 3D vector, yet it really only has a 2D dependency. We instead use spherical surface coordinates to represent a direction. We also need to map our sphere to a linear rectangular texture. In order to do that, we simply stack each cube map face one after the other (Figure 19.11).

In order to generate sample directions with proper probabilities, we need to define the PDF, CDF, and inverse CDF (similarly to the BRDF importance sampling). However, in this case, because the environment map is not analytical, we need to work with discrete versions of these functions.

We start with the PDF. We simply use the luminosity of each pixel as a basis for generating the PDF. This allows us to catch the "brightest" pixels in the image. We also need to define two types of PDFs: marginal and conditional (Figure 19.12). We use the marginal PDF to find which row of pixels we will sample from. The sum of the PDF for a given row is the probability that a random sample will fall within that row; this is the marginal PDF. Then we use the conditional PDF of this row to find which column the sample falls into. The

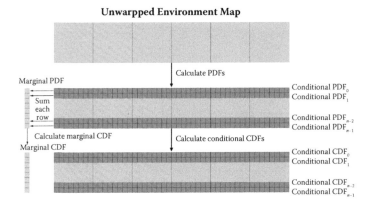

Figure 19.12. The structure of the marginal and conditional PDFs and CDFs. The conditional PDF and CDF are unique for each row and are represented as a 1D array for each row. However, there is only one marginal PDF and one marginal CDF for the image, which are also represented as 1D arrays.

conditional and marginal PDFs can be calculated using the following equations:

$$\text{conditional PDF}_{(i,j)} = \text{luminance}(i,j), \tag{19.13}$$

$$\text{marginal PDF}_j = \sum_{i=0}^{n} \text{luminance}(i,j). \tag{19.14}$$

For each type of PDF we define, there is a corresponding CDF: marginal and conditional CDFs. When a PDF is purely discrete, the CDF can be calculated as the sum of the PDF values from 0 to m for each location m [Pharr and Humphreys 04]:

$$\text{CDF}_m = \sum_{k=0}^{m} \text{PDF}_k. \tag{19.15}$$

The function that represents the summation of the rows' probabilities is the row-wise CDF for the image as a whole; this is the marginal CDF (Figure 19.12). The individual row PDFs are unique and each also has its own column-wise CDF, which is called the conditional CDF (Figure 19.12).

The simple example in Figure 19.13 demonstrates the behavior of the discrete CDF. Samples with high probabilities get mapped to a wide range on the Y axis. For example, if we randomly choose a $[0:1]$ value on the Y axis, the third sample will be picked with a probability of 0.7.

The inverse CDF is thus simply a mapping between a random $[0:1]$ value and its corresponding sample. Since by definition the CDF is a sorted array (Equation (19.15)), we can use a binary search to find the corresponding sample's index. In short the algorithm can be described as follows:

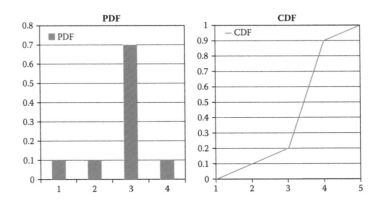

Figure 19.13. PDF and its corresponding CDF.

1. Generate a random number α in the range $[0:1]$.

2. Find an i where $\text{CDF}(i) \leq \alpha$.

3. Then, i is the resulting sample with $\text{PDF}(i)$.

Because we have the PDF, CDF, and inverse CDF, we can now generate the environment map samples. It is worth noting that since the samples' locations depend on neither the BRDF nor the shading point location and orientation, the samples can be pregenerated on the CPU. At the GPU stage, we simply integrate using those samples.

The final sample generation process can thus be described as follows:

1. For each pixel in each row of the map, calculate the PDF value using Equation (19.13).

2. For each j, sum the conditional PDF values and store them into marginal $\text{PDF}(j)$ (Equation (19.14)).

3. For each row, build the conditional CDF using Equation (19.15).

4. Build the marginal CDF using the marginal PDFs, using the Equation (19.15).

5. Pregenerate n samples on the CPU and pass them to the GPU.

Listing 19.4 shows the code that generates 128 samples using the stratified sampling method [Niederreiter 92]. We found that in our case 128 samples give the best results, given a required performance level.

Furthermore, we can improve the random sampling by stratifying the samples. Random 2D sampling might sometimes produce bad coverage (Figure 19.14). By

```
//Pregenerate 128 samples on CPU that we will pass to the GPU
for(int j = 0 ; j < 16; j++)
for(int i = 0 ; i < 8; i++)
{
    //Generate random values (e1,e2) using the stratified sampling
    //method
    float e1 = float(i) / 8.0f + randf() / 8.0f;
    float e2 = float(j) / 16.0f + randf() / 16.0f;

    //Find the row for the sample based on the conditional CDF
    int row = lower_bound(marginalCDF,e1);
    //Now, using our row, we find the correct column and therefore
    //sample
    int column = lower_bound(conditionalCDF[row], e2);

    //Get the PDF values of the sample for the further calculation
    //of the integral on the GPU
    float pdfRow = marginalPDF[row];
    float pdfColumn = conditionalPDF[row][column];

    //Save the sample position and PDF values in the array
    uint32_t index = i + 8*j;
    SamplesData[index*4 + 0] = row;
    SamplesData[index*4 + 1] = column;
    SamplesData[index*4 + 2] = pdfRow;
    SamplesData[index*4 + 3] = pdfColumn;
}
```

Listing 19.4. Generating samples based on environment PDF.

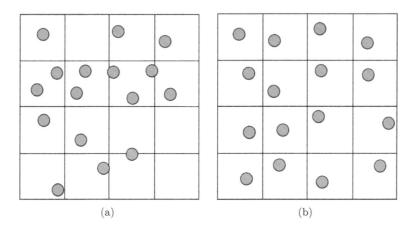

(a)   (b)

Figure 19.14. (a) Random samples might produce bad coverage. (b) Stratified sampling guarantees at least one sample in equally distributed areas.

stratifying the samples, we guarantee that we have at least one sample in equally distributed areas. This reduces the probability of sample "clumping" around a specific location.

We then have an array of samples that we pass on to the GPU. The GPU receives flattened (u, v) coordinates. In order to use those samples, we have to first convert (u, v) coordinates to direction vectors, and transform the PDF from the (u, v) distribution to a distribution over a solid angle [Pharr and Humphreys 04]. The PDF conversion can be derived from the environment map unwrapping where we have six cube-map faces in a row and each face has the field of view equal to $\frac{\pi}{2}$:

$$\text{solid angle PDF}_u = \text{PDF}_u \times 6 \times \frac{\pi}{2},$$

$$\text{solid angle PDF}_v = \text{PDF}_v \times \frac{\pi}{2}.$$

The final GPU code for the environment map importance sampling is shown in Listing 19.5.

```
//Calculate the outgoing radiance for the sample direction L
float3 envMapSample ( float Roughness, float2 uv, float3 L,
                      float3 N, float pdfV, float pdfU)
{
    //Cosine weight
    float NoL = saturate(dot(N, normalize(L)));
    float3 color = unwrapTex.Load( int3(uv.xy, 0 )).rgb;

    float3 V = N;
    float3 H = normalize(L+V);
    float D = GGX(Roughness, H, N);
    float brdf = D / (4*NoL);

    //Calculate the solid angle
    //dA (area of cube) = (6*2*2)/N^2
    //N is a face size
    //dw = dA / r^3 = dA * pow(x*x + y*y + z*z, -1.5)
    float dw = (6*4.0 / (CUBEMAP_SIZE*CUBEMAP_SIZE)) *
               pow(L.x*L.x + L.y*L.y + L.z*L.z, -1.5);

    //pdfV and pdfU is the PDFs for [0;1] range in a cube map face.
    //We need to convert them to a solid angle range.
    //Each face has HALF_PI fov and we have 6 faces.
    //Solid Angle PDFu (saPDFu) = PDFu * 6 * HALF_PI
    //Solid Angle PDFv (saPDFv) = PDFv * HALF_PI

    //E = brdf * color * NoL * dw / (saPDFu * saPDFv)

    return brdf * color * NoL * dw * / (pdfV * pdfU * 6 * PI * PI
        *0.5*0.5);
}

float3 SampleENV(int index, float Roughness, float3 N, float3 V)
{
    //Get the position of the sample
    float2 uv = samples[index].xy;

    //Get the PDF values of the current sample. Note that the final
    //PDF is pdfV* pdfU
    float pdfV = samples[index].z;
    float pdfU = samples[index].w;
```

```
        //Convert the uv sample position to a vector. We need this to
        //calculate the BRDF
        float3 L = normalize(uvToVector( uv ));
        //Sample the light coming from the direction L
        //and calculate the specular BRDF for this direction
        float3 envIS = envMapSample ( Roughness, uv, L, N, pdfV, pdfU);
        return envIS;
}

float3 PreintegrateSpecularLightProbe( float Roughness,
    int numENVSamples, float3 R )
{
        //For the preintegration, we assume that N=V=R
        float3 N = R;
        float3 V = R;

        float3 finalColor = 0;

        //Sample all of the pregenerated samples
        for(int i = 0; i < numENVSamples; i++)
        {
            finalColor += SampleENV(i, Roughness, N, V);
        }

        //The final color needs to be divided by the number of samples
        //based on the Monte Carlo importance sampling definition
        finalColor /= numENVSamples;

        return finalColor;
}
```

Listing 19.5. Environment map importance sampling.

Using this method helped us to reduce the error for the high roughness values in the nighttime lighting conditions (Figure 19.15). However, using environment map sampling alone isn't necessarily the best solution. Similarly to BRDF sampling, there can be situations where sampling purely based on the environment would generate a lot of noise (or "fireflies") (Figure 19.16). For example, this can occur if the environment samples do not follow the BRDF's specular lobe (much more likely in low roughness materials).

Because all of the samples are pre-generated on CPU, the preintegration computation time on the GPU for the high roughness values is less than 0.05 ms on a GTX 460.

19.3.5 Combining Both Importance Sampling Methods

We now have two independent methods that both work well in different situations (e.g., low roughness and/or high-frequency detail in the environment map). We would like to somehow combine both methods to have a solution that works well in most cases.

This is where multiple (or combined) importance sampling comes in. Multiple importance sampling allows us to combine two sampling techniques. The equation

Figure 19.15. Environment map importance sampling error for the roughness value 1 using 128 samples at the nighttime-specific lighting condition.

Figure 19.16. Specular light probe using environment map importance sampling. The first probe is black because it is a perfect mirror and none of the samples hit the reflection ray exactly.

for multiple importance sampling (or MIS) is as follows:

$$\frac{1}{n_f + n_g} \left(\sum_{i=1}^{n_f} \frac{f(X_i)g(X_i)w_f(X_i)}{p_f(X_i)} + \sum_{i=1}^{n_g} \frac{f(Y_i)g(Y_i)w_g(Y_i)}{p_g(Y_i)} \right),$$

where n_f is the number of samples taken from the p_f distribution method, n_g is the number of samples taken from p_g, and w_f and w_g are special weighting functions chosen such that the expected value of this estimator is the value of the integral $f(x)g(x)$ [Pharr and Humphreys 04]. In our case, p_f is the BRDF importance sampling distribution and p_g is the environment map importance sampling distribution.

For the weighing variables, w_f and w_g, we use the simplest possible method. We pick w_f to be n_f, and w_g to be n_g. We found that this method gives acceptable results for very low performance costs (as opposed to the balance heuristic; for example, [Pharr and Humphreys 04]).

As for the number of samples for each method, we simply use a hard-coded value that we achieved by trial and error (in our case, 64 for both methods). Fur-

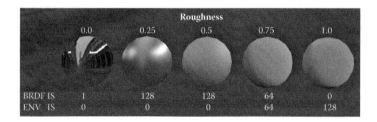

Figure 19.17. Number of samples in each method for a specular probe.

Figure 19.18. The ground truth render using 10,000 samples.

thermore, we only use environment map importance sampling when the roughness is greater than 0.7. With lower roughness values, BRDF importance sampling worked well alone. Figure 19.17 shows the number of samples for both methods with different roughness values.

Listing 19.6 demonstrates the final preintegration function that uses the combination of both methods.

Using the combined importance sampling gives us the required quality result within less than 2 ms of GPU time. (See Figure 19.18.)

19.4 Conclusion

Implementing combined importance sampling on the GPU gave us the ability to generate and prefilter the light probes during level loading. Each probe takes less than 2 ms to preintegrate. (This time does not include the time it takes to generate the environment map itself.) However, we split the light probe generation process across multiple frames in order to prevent frame drops.

Using environment importance sampling helps to reduce preintegration error in nighttime situations with small and bright area lights. It also helped keep the number of samples low in order to stay within performance restrictions. However, we found that BRDF importance sampling works well for the majority of cases. It is only during our specific case of nighttime lighting that BRDF importance sampling (with prefiltering) alone was not enough.

```
//Combined Importance Sampling for the specified roughness and the
//reflection vector R using numBRDFSamples for the BRDF IS
//and numENVSamples for the ENV IS
float3 PreintegrateSpecularLightProbe( float Roughness,
      int numENVSamples, int numBRDFSamples, float3 R )
{
    //For the preintegration we assume that N=V=R
    float3 N = normalize(R);
    float3 V = normalize(R);

    float3 finalColor = 0;
    float3 envColor = 0;
    float3 brdfColor = 0;

    //Solve the integral using environment importance sampling
    for(int i = 0; i < numENVSamples; i++)
    {
        envColor += SampleENV(i, Roughness, N, V);
    }
    //Solve the integral using BRDF importance sampling
    for(int i = 0; i < numBRDFSamples; i++)
    {
        //Generate the uniformly distributed random values using
        //Hammersley quasirandom low-discrepancy sequence
        //(Listing 19.2)
        float2 e1e2 = Hammersley( (i), numBRDFSamples );

        brdfColor += SampleBRDF(e1e2.x, e1e2.y, Roughness, N, V);
    }

    //Divide each results by the number of samples using to
    //compute it
    envColor /= numENVSamples;
    brdfColor /= numBRDFSamples;

    //Combine both method based on the number of samples using to
    //solve each of them
    float envColorWeight = numENVSamples / (numENVSamples +
                                                numBRDFSamples);
    float brdfColorWeight = numBRDFSamples/ (numENVSamples +
                                                numBRDFSamples);

    finalColor = envColor * envColorWeight +
                    brdfColor * brdfColorWeight;

    return finalColor;
}
```

Listing 19.6. Multiple (combined) importance sampling.

One positive side effect of having fast probe generation is quick feedback to the artist. The artist is able to iterate on the lighting setup and see the results almost instantaneously.

For future work, we would like to further optimize the shader code for specular probe generation. This would allow us to place even more probes in the level without affecting loading times.

19.5 Acknowledgments

I would like to express my gratitude to the people who supported me and proof-read this chapter: Peter McNeeley of EA Canada and Ramy El Garawany of Naughty Dog.

I would also like to thank the editors Michal Valient of Guerilla Games and Wolfgang Engel of Confetti FX.

Bibliography

[Burley 12] B. Burley. "Physically-Based Shading at Disney." Practical Physically Based Shading in Film and Game Production, SIGGRAPH Course, Los Angeles, CA, August 8, 2012.

[Colbert et al. 10] Mark Colbert, Simon Premože, and Guillaume François. "Importance Sampling for Production Rendering." SIGGRAPH Course, Los Angeles, CA, July 25–29, 2010.

[Cook and Torrance 81] R. Cook and K. Torrance. "A Reflectance Model for Computer Graphics." *Computer Graphics: Siggraph 1981 Proceedings* 15:3 (1981), 301–316.

[Drobot 14] Michal Drobot. "Physically Based Area Lights." In *GPU Pro 5: Advanced Rendering Techniques*, edited by Wolfgang Engel, pp. 67–100. Boca Raton, FL: CRC Press, 2014.

[Hammersley and Handscomb 64] J. M. Hammersley and D. C. Handscomb. *Monte Carlo Methods*, Methuen's Monographs on Applied Probability and Statistics. London: Methuen, 1964.

[Hoffman 12] N. Hoffman. "Background: Physics and Math of Shading." Practical Physically Based Shading in Film and Game Production, SIGGRAPH Course, Los Angeles, CA, August 8, 2012.

[Křivánek and Colbert 08] Jaroslav Křivánek and Mark Colbert. "Real-Time Shading with Filtered Importance Sampling." *Comp. Graph. Forum: Proc. of EGSR 2008*, 27:4 (20080, 1147–1154.

[Karis 13] Brian Karis. "Real Shading in Unreal Engine 4." SIGGRAPH Course, Anaheim, CA, July 21–25, 2013.

[King 05] Gary King. "Real-Time Computation of Dynamic Irradiance Environment Maps." In *GPU Gems 2*, edited by Matt Farr, pp. 167–176. Reading, MA: Addison-Wesley, 2005.

[Lagarde 12] Sébastien Lagarde. "AMD Cubemapgen for Physically Based Rendering." http://seblagarde.wordpress.com/2012/06/10/amd-cubemapgen-for-physically-based-rendering/, 2012.

[Niederreiter 92] Harald Niederreiter. *Random Number Generation and Quasi-Monte Carlo Methods.* Philadelphia: Society for Industrial and Applied Mathematics, 1992.

[Papoulis 84] A. Papoulis. *Probability, Random Variables, and Stochastic Processes*, Second Edition. New York: McGraw-Hill, 1984.

[Pharr and Humphreys 04] Matt Pharr and Greg Humphreys. *Physically Based Rendering: From Theory to Implementation.* San Francisco: Morgan Kaufmann, 2004.

[Ramamoorthi and Hanrahan 01] Ravi Ramamoorthi and Pat Hanrahan. "An Efficient Representation for Irradiance Environment Maps." In *Proceeding of SIGGRAPH*, pp. 497–500. New York: ACM, 2001.

[Hill and McAuley 12] Stephen Hill and Stephen McAuley, Organizers. "Practical Physically Based Shading in Film and Game Production," SIGGRAPH Course, Los Angeles, CA, August 5–9, 2012. (Available at http://blog.selfshadow.com/publications/s2012-shading-course/.)

[Sloan 08] Peter-Pike Sloan. "Stupid Spherical Harmonics (SH) Tricks." Presented at Game Developers Conference, San Francisco, CA, February 18–22, 2008.

[Walter et al. 07] Bruce Walter, Stephen R. Marschner, Hongsong Li, and Kenneth E. Torrance. "Microfacet Models for Refraction through Rough Surfaces." In *Proceedings of the Eurographics Symposium on Rendering*, pp. 195–206. Aire-la-Ville, Switzerland: Eurographics Association, 2007.

20

Real-Time Global Illumination Using Slices
Hugh Malan

20.1 Introduction

In this chapter, we'll present a method for implementing real-time single-bounce global illumination.

In recent years, several practical real-time global illumination techniques have been demonstrated. These have all been voxel-based scene databases.

The common theme of all these approaches is to initialize the data structure using the lit scene geometry. Then, a propagation or blurring step is applied, and after that the structure is ready for irradiance or reflection queries.

The Light Propagation Volumes (LPV) method [Kaplanyan and Dachs -bacher 10] uses a voxel array, where each voxel contains a first-order spherical harmonic representation of the irradiance. The array is initialized using reflective shadow maps; the propagation step is to iteratively transfer irradiance from each cell to its neighbors.

The voxel octrees algorithm [Crassin et al. 2011] converts the scene to an octree representation, where each leaf holds radiance. Non-leaf nodes are calculated to have the average of child node colors. Sharp reflections are computed by ray-tracing the octree and sampling the color from the leaf node hit; blurry reflections and irradiance are found by sampling a parent node, whose generation depends on blurriness.

The cascaded 3D volumes approach [Panteleev 2014] uses a sequence of 3D volumes. They are all the same dimension, but each one's side length doubles. The algorithm is comparable to the octree approach, but it can be updated and queried more efficiently.

Figure 20.1. Example of a single slice.

20.2 Algorithm Overview

Like the voxel approaches described in the introduction, our algorithm works by building a data structure using the lit scene geometry and then querying that structure to evaluate irradiance.

Here, the datastructure is a collection of *slices*. A slice is a scaled and deformed unit square, aligned to some surface of the scene (see Figure 20.1). During the initialization step, it captures the radiance of that part of the scene. It can then be queried to efficiently compute the irradiance due to the light emitted from that surface.

Slices are arranged in an array of distorted cuboids (called *cells*) that are fitted to the scene geometry; an example is shown in Figure 20.2.

To evaluate the irradiance for a particular location and surface normal, we begin by finding the cell containing that location. Then, the six slices making up the faces of that cell are queried to compute their irradiance. The six irradiance values are combined by summing them.

Like the LPV approach, we also need to propagate light from cuboid to cuboid, so a light emitted in one cuboid can illuminate geometry in another. This is done at slice initialization time by allowing light from nearby slices to contribute.

The rest of the chapter will be organized as follows. To begin with, we'll discuss how to efficiently compute irradiance due to an emissive flat surface.

Figure 20.2. Scene geometry with distorted cuboids (cells) fitted to it. The cuboid edges are shown with red lines; dimmer lines indicate hidden edges.

Then, we'll deal with the question of how to support multiple such surfaces, the motivation for the distorted-cuboid approach, and how to set up the array of cells to match the geometry for a given scene.

20.3 Approximating the Irradiance Due to an Emissive Plane

The irradiance at a point p with surface normal $\boldsymbol{n}$ is

$$E(p, \boldsymbol{n}) = \int_{H^+} L_i(p, \boldsymbol{\omega}) \cos \theta \; d\boldsymbol{\omega}, \tag{20.1}$$

where H^+ is the upper hemisphere above p centered on the direction $\boldsymbol{n}$, and $L_i(p, \boldsymbol{\omega})$ is the incoming radiance reaching p from the direction $\boldsymbol{\omega}$—where $\boldsymbol{\omega}$ can be in spherical polar coordinates as (θ, ϕ).

Imagine a plane at $z = 0$ that emits light, where the radiance is defined by a function $r(x, y)$. We're interested in finding an approximation to the function $E(p, \boldsymbol{n})$ that can be evaluated on the GPU in an efficient manner.

First, notice that evaluating irradiance can be expressed as a convolution of $r(x, y)$ with a kernel that depends on $\boldsymbol{n}$ and $|p_z|$, i.e., the distance from the plane:

$$E(p, \boldsymbol{n}) = \int_{x=-\infty}^{x=+\infty} \int_{y=-\infty}^{y=+\infty} r(x, y) W(x - p_x, y - p_y, -p_z, \boldsymbol{n}) dy \; dx,$$

where W is the convolution kernel

$$W(\Delta x, \Delta y, \Delta z, \boldsymbol{n}) = \frac{\max(0, (\Delta x, \Delta y, \Delta z) \cdot \boldsymbol{n})}{\left(\sqrt{(\Delta x^2 + \Delta y^2 + \Delta z^2)}\right)^3}.$$

Second, the kernel scales up with distance from the plane. If we sample a point k times farther from the plane, then the weighting function scales too:

$$W(\Delta x, \Delta y, k\Delta z, \boldsymbol{n}) = \frac{\max(0, (\Delta x, \Delta y, \Delta z) \cdot \boldsymbol{n})}{\left(\sqrt{(\Delta x^2 + \Delta y^2 + (k\Delta z)^2)}\right)^3}$$

$$= \frac{\max(0, k(\Delta x/k, \Delta y/k, \Delta z) \cdot \boldsymbol{n})}{\left(\sqrt{k^2((\Delta x/k)^2 + (\Delta y/k)^2 + \Delta z^2)}\right)^3}$$

$$= \frac{k \cdot \max(0, (\Delta x/k, \Delta y/k, \Delta z) \cdot \boldsymbol{n})}{k^3 \left(\sqrt{((\Delta x/k)^2 + (\Delta y/k)^2 + \Delta z^2)}\right)^3}$$

$$= \frac{W(\Delta x/k, \Delta y/k, \Delta z, \boldsymbol{n})}{k^2}.$$

So, the convolution kernel scales up in proportion to distance from the plane: for a point twice as far from the plane, the kernel is scaled up by a factor of 2 in the x and y directions.

This fact suggests that for a given $\boldsymbol{n}$, we could store the irradiance for the volume $(x, y, z) : x, y \epsilon [-s, +s], z \epsilon [0, t]$ in an image pyramid, where each level is twice as far from the plane as the previous level and half the resolution. If s is the distance to the first mip level, then

$$\text{distance from emissive plane to layer } m = s \cdot 2^m. \qquad (20.2)$$

The increase in texel size at each level corresponds to the increase in the convolution kernel size, so the fidelity can be expected to be consistent for all levels of the image pyramid.

This image pyramid can be implemented on the GPU by using a standard mipmapped texture, sampled using trilinear filtering.

For a given distance d from the emissive plane, the mipmap parameter is

$$\text{mipmap parameter} = \log_2\left(\frac{d}{s}\right) \qquad (20.3)$$

20.4   Building the Image Pyramid

Our approach was inspired by the summed-Gaussian approach used in "Advanced Techniques for Realistic Real-Time Skin Rendering" [d'Eon and Luebke 07]—a

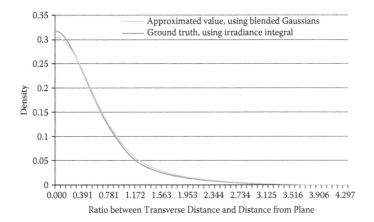

Figure 20.3. Irradiance contribution of a flat plane: cross section of the contribution of each point using the ideal irradiance integral and a paired-Gaussian approximation.

nonseparable function may be approximated by a weighted sum of a series of Gaussian blurs. Like that paper, we used just two Gaussian blurs.

The pair of blended Gaussian blurs were matched to the ideal convolution kernel by minimizing the least-squared error. If d is the distance from the emissive plane, here is the best-fit approximation:

g_0 = blurred radiance image using Gaussian blur with standard deviation $1.368d$;

g_1 = blurred radiance image using Gaussian blur with standard deviation $0.532d$;

approximate irradiance = $0.54g_0 + 0.46g_1$.   (20.4)

Figure 20.3 shows the comparison between the ideal and approximation.

The naive approach to generate the image pyramid is to consider each mipmap in turn, and for the implied distance from the plane, calculate the Gaussian blur radii, then blur and blend the radiance image correspondingly. Unfortunately, this leads to prohibitively large tap counts for more distant images.

The solution we used is to generate a second image pyramid from the radiance image as a preprocess—this image pyramid is like a mipchain; each layer is constructed by down-sampling the previous layer by a factor of 2 using a box filter.

Then, rather than blurring the full-resolution image, an appropriate mip level is chosen as input to the aforementioned Gaussian blur. The standard deviation of the Gaussian blur is specified in world units, so the number of taps will vary depending which mip level is chosen—though obviously the quality will degrade if the resolution and tap count are too low. This means the tap count for the Gaussian blur can be controlled, and it's possible to use even just 5–10 taps without substantial quality loss.

20.4.1 Putting It All Together

Given an emissive plane, begin by capturing the radiance and opacity in a texture map (R). The image pyramid for irradiance queries is generated from R as follows:

1. Generate a standard mipmap chain for the texture map R. Each mipmap is a half-size boxfiltered down-sample of the previous. Let R' be the resulting image pyramid. It contains radiance in RGB and opacity in A. The opacity value is not used for the irradiance pyramid generated here, but is required for the cell-to-cell propagation step described later in Section 20.8.

2. Allocate the irradiance image pyramid I. It will have the same dimensions and mipmap count as R'. Each mipmap corresponds to a certain distance from the emissive plane, defined by Equation (20.2).

3. For each mip level m of the image pyramid I, we generate the image as described by Equation (20.4).

For the current mip level, compute its distance from the emissive plane, and find the standard deviations of the two Gaussian blurs as a distance in world space. Find the two source mip levels to use as inputs for the blurs. (We found that evaluating the Gaussian out to two standard deviations and using five taps gave acceptable results.) Blur those two input images using the appropriate Gaussian functions, rescale the results so they're the same resolution, and blend the resulting two images to build the mipmap for I.

Note that because the image pyramid I contains RGB only, these image-processing steps can discard the alpha channel.

20.4.2 Sampling the Image Pyramid

With the image pyramid described, it's possible to query the irradiance. However, we're restricted to points that are directly above the planar region where the texture map R is defined. Also, the surface normal must be facing directly toward the emissive plane, as this is the assumption made for the image pyramid construction.

First, we find the relative position of the query point within the image pyramid volume, to obtain the (u, v) for sampling the pyramid. We compute the distance to the plane d. The mipmap we need to sample is determined by Equation (20.3). We sample the image pyramid with the computed (u, v) and mipmap parameter and the resulting value is the irradiance.

As it stands, the restrictions on surface normal and position make this method too limited to be useful. Here's how the restrictions may be lifted.

20.4.3 Supporting Arbitrary Normals

Consider the infinite plane at $z = 0$ radiating a constant color. Since the plane is infinite and radiance constant, the irradiance measured at a particular point will not vary if it's moved (without crossing the plane). The only thing that matters is what part of the visible hemisphere is covered by the emissive plane, and this is unaffected by movement. So in this case, the irradiance depends only on the surface normal.

Let E_0 be the irradiance measured at the point p_{xyz} with $p_z < 0$, facing directly toward the plane. Let E_1 be the irradiance measured at the same point with an arbitrary normal (n_{xyz}; assume it to be normalized). Then

$$\frac{E_1}{E_0} = \frac{1 + n_z}{2}. \tag{20.5}$$

We'll use the relationship from Equation (20.5) to attenuate the value sampled from the image pyramid, to support arbitrary query normals.

Proof: We're interested in computing the irradiance for a scene consisting only of a constant emissive plane. We may assume with no loss of generality that the sample point is at the origin, and the upper hemisphere over which we gather irradiance is $(0, 0, 1)$. The plane is initially at $z = -1$, with surface normal $(0, 0, 1)$; it is rotated around the x axis by the angle $\theta_{\max}$, where $\theta_{\max} \in [0, 180°]$. If $\theta_{\max}$ is $180°$, then the plane is above the origin with surface normal $(0, 0, -1)$, so the irradiance integral covers the full hemisphere as usual. But if $\theta_{\max} < 180°$, then areas on the hemisphere for which $\theta > \theta_{\max}$ correspond to rays that will miss the emissive plane. Therefore, the irradiance integral is restricted to directions in the range $[0, \theta_{\max}]$.

Figure 20.4 shows the situation. The grid represents the plane; it has been faded out in the middle so it doesn't obscure the rest of the diagram. The gray truncated hemisphere represents the set of directions that intersect the emissive plane.

The integral is identical to Equation (20.1), but expressed in spherical polar coordinates (ϕ and θ) and restricted to directions that intersect the emissive plane. For a given ϕ and θ, the z component is $\sin(\phi)\sin(\theta)$, which is equivalent to the $\cos(\theta)$ term in Equation (20.1). We also scale by $\sin(\phi)$ to compensate for the change in area near the poles. Suppose the constant color radiated by the plane is L_p. Then the integral is as follows:

$$\int_{\theta=0}^{\theta=\theta_{\max}} \int_{\phi=0}^{\phi=\pi} L_p \sin(\phi)\sin(\theta)\sin(\phi)d\phi d\theta$$

$$= L_p \int_{\theta=0}^{\theta=\theta_{\max}} \sin(\theta)d\theta \cdot \int_{\phi=0}^{\phi=\pi} \sin^2(\phi)d\phi$$

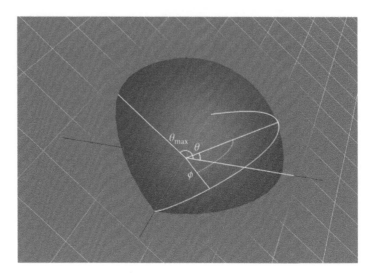

Figure 20.4. Integral variables.

$$= L_p \int_{\theta=0}^{\theta=\theta_{\max}} \sin(\theta) \cdot \frac{\pi}{2} = L_p[-\cos(\theta)]_0^{\theta_{\max}} \cdot \frac{\pi}{2}$$

$$= L_p([-\cos(\theta_{\max})] - [-\cos(0)]) \cdot \frac{\pi}{2} = L_p(1 - \cos(\theta_{\max})) \cdot \frac{\pi}{2}$$

$$= L_p \cdot \pi \cdot \frac{1 - \cos(\theta_{\max})}{2}$$

The irradiance E_0, when the surface normal points directly toward the plane, can be found by substituting $\theta_{\max} = \pi$. This gives $E_0 = L_p\pi$. The ratio E_1/E_0 is therefore

$$\frac{E_1}{E_0} = \frac{1 - \cos(\theta_{\max})}{2}.$$

Substituting $\cos(\theta_{\max}) = \boldsymbol{n} \cdot (0, 0, -1) = \boldsymbol{n}f_z$ gives Equation (20.5).   □

20.4.4   Sampling Outside the Depth Pyramid Volume

A reasonable approximation for irradiance outside the image pyramid volume is to clamp the sample point to the border of the image pyramid region, calculate irradiance from the image pyramid using the clamped location, and then scale down the resulting irradiance progressively as the query point moves farther from

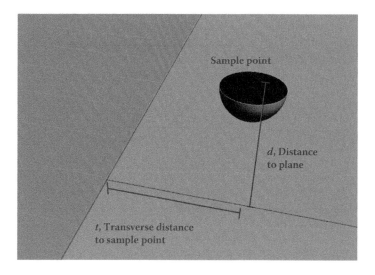

Figure 20.5. Sampling irradiance outside valid region.

the border, using

irradiance outside the valid region

$$= (\text{irradiance at the border}) \cdot \left(1 + \frac{d}{\sqrt{t^2 + d^2}}\right). \quad (20.6)$$

Figure 20.5 shows how the function is defined. The colored region on the left is the valid region, where the image pyramid is defined; we're considering it to be an infinite half-plane for simplicity. The hemisphere indicates the "upper hemisphere" (see Equation (20.1)) around which the irradiance for the sample point is gathered.

For a given sample point, with a surface normal pointing toward the emissive plane, we're interested in how much the valid region contributes to the irradiance. For points above the border, this will be exactly 50%. For points farther from the valid region, this value will tend to 0%.

Figure 20.6 shows a cross section of valid half-plane and irradiance hemisphere. There are strong similarities to the calculation of irradiance for a tilted plane described in Section 20.4.3: in both cases, the irradiance integral is restricted to a subset of the upper hemisphere, which can be expressed as the range $0 \leq \theta \leq \theta_{\max}$.

Making use of Equation (20.5) means finding the normalized vector to the edge of the valid region (s). Normalizing the vector $s = (t, d)$ gives

$$(t, d) \cdot \frac{1}{\sqrt{t^2 + d^2}}.$$

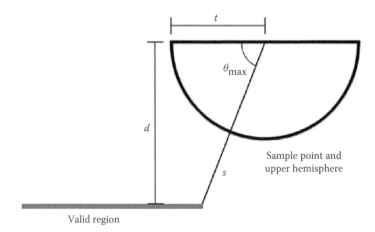

Figure 20.6. Cross section showing contribution of valid region.

Substituting the appropriate component into Equation (20.5) and simplifying it gives

$$\text{fractional contribution of the valid region} = 0.5 + \frac{d}{2\sqrt{t^2 + d^2}}. \qquad (20.7)$$

Dividing by 0.5, which is the value taken on the border, gives Equation (20.6). Figure 20.7 is a graph of Equation (20.7), showing how the fractional contribution to irradiance changes for points past the border. The reason for using the ratio t/d as an axis is that Equation (20.7) may be rewritten as a function of t/d.

20.4.5   Evaluating Irradiance Using the Image Pyramid

The image pyramid is sampled as follows. For the query point p, with normal n:

1. Find the relative position of p within the image pyramid volume, to obtain the (u, v) for sampling the pyramid. Compute d, the distance to the plane.

2. Find the mipmap parameter using Equation (20.3).

3. Sample the image pyramid using trilinear filtering, with the mipmap parameter calculated at the previous step. Clamp the (u, v) to the image pyramid region. Let c_{RGB} be the color sampled.

4. If the query point is not within the image pyramid volume, attenuate c_{RGB} using Equation (20.6).

5. Attenuate c_{RGB} based on surface normal using Equation (20.5).

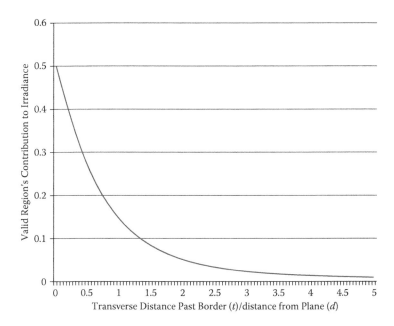

Figure 20.7. Contribution of the valid region to irradiance when sampling beyond the border.

20.4.6 Results

Before moving on, it's useful to compare the approximation that has been described, with the ground truth result.

Figure 20.8 shows the scene. The black square with the cyan circle is the emissive plane, at $y = 0$. We'll evaluate the irradiance at points on the transparent square, which are the points $-32 \leq x \leq +32$, $-64 \leq y \leq 0$, $z = 0$. For simplicity, the surface normal used for sampling is $n = (0, 1, 0)$, directly toward the emissive plane.

Figure 20.9 to Figure 20.11 show the resulting irradiance. Figure 20.9 shows the ground truth result where the indirect term at each point was evaluated using 16,000 importance-sampled rays. A lot of rays are needed because there's only a small bright region—even using 1000 rays per pixel gives noisy results.

Figure 20.10 shows the image-pyramid approximation described in this chapter. The image pyramid only covers a subset of this space: $-16 \leq x, y \leq +16$, between the yellow lines. Note that the values outside this region are still a good approximation because the trilinear sample is attenuated using Equation (20.6). For comparison, Figure 20.11 shows the standard boxfiltered mipchain without the Gaussian blurs or attenuation.

Figure 20.8. Emissive plane and sample area.

Figure 20.9. Ideal result—importance sampled using 16,000 rays.

Figure 20.10. Texture approximation. One trilinear filtered lookup from a 256 × 256 texture.

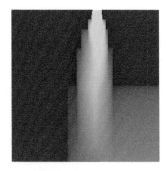

Figure 20.11. Comparison—trilinear lookup without Gaussian blurs or attenuation.

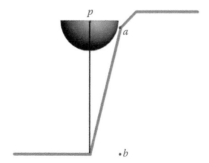

Figure 20.12. Extreme distortions cause significant approximation errors.

20.4.7 Limitations

It's tempting to try using the slice approach with arbitrary heightfields. Unfortunately, this can often give poor results: slices approximate the emissive surface as a flat plane and weight the contributions of each part of the emissive plane accordingly. With a heightfield, it's possible for there to be points quite close to our sample point, which means they should contribute significantly to irradiance—but with the slice approach, they have a very low contribution.

For instance, consider the situation shown in Figure 20.12. The green line is a cross section through a heightfield. Suppose we've distorted a slice to match it exactly, and use the slice to evaluate irradiance. The point p is the location where we'd like to sample irradiance; the semicircle indicates the hemisphere for the gather. The black line running vertically down from p to the heightfield shows the distance to the heightfield; this will be the distance used to calculate the mipmap parameter for the image pyramid lookup.

In Figure 20.12, point a is quite close to p, so it should contribute significantly to irradiance. However, the slice approximation will weight it as if it were at b.

So, if the shape of a slice is distorted too much, the quality of the approximation will suffer.

In conclusion, if we restrict the emissive surfaces to near-planar surfaces, then we can efficiently evaluate the indirect lighting contribution and, in addition, the steps to build the image pyramid are cheap enough to run in real time.

In the next sections of the chapter, we'll describe how to use this approach to support more general scenes.

20.5 Combining Multiple Slices

20.5.1 Irradiance Values May Be Combined Only If the Slices Do Not Occlude Each Other

The value sampled from the image pyramid is an RGB irradiance value.

Figure 20.13. Two emissive squares; one completely occludes the other when irradiance is gathered for the hemisphere indicated.

It's tempting to combine the irradiance values sampled from different slices. Unfortunately, the only way this can be reliably done is if the slices do not obscure each other.

Imagine two nearly coincident squares, one red and one blue, with their irradiance sampled, as shown in Figure 20.13. The red square does not contribute to the irradiance at all when they are combined; it's completely obscured by the blue square.

In this case, occlusion completely changes the result—and occlusion isn't accounted for with the slice approximation. However, it is possible to sum the irradiance and opacity sampled from two slices if they do not obscure each other at all. Recall the irradiance definition from, Equation (20.1):

$$E(p, \boldsymbol{n}) = \int_{H+} L_i(p, \boldsymbol{\omega}) \cos \theta \; d\boldsymbol{\omega},$$

where $L_i(p, \boldsymbol{\omega})$ is the incoming light falling on p from the direction $\boldsymbol{\omega}$. Define $L_i^A(p, \boldsymbol{\omega})$ to be the incoming light if there was only object A in the scene, and $L_i^B(p, \boldsymbol{\omega})$ similarly. These will give the RGB value $(0,0,0)$ for directions that don't hit the corresponding object.

If there are no p and $\boldsymbol{\omega}$ such that $L_i^A(p, \boldsymbol{\omega})$ and $L_i^B(p, \boldsymbol{\omega})$ are simultaneously nonzero—i.e., there is no sample position p and direction $\boldsymbol{\omega}$ from which one of the objects occludes the other—then $L_i(p, \boldsymbol{\omega}) = L_i^A(p, \boldsymbol{\omega}) + L_i^B(p, \boldsymbol{\omega})$. Then,

$$
\begin{aligned}
E(p, \boldsymbol{n}) &= \int_{H+} L_i(p, \boldsymbol{\omega}) \cos \theta \; d\boldsymbol{\omega} = \int_{H+} (L_i^A(p, \boldsymbol{\omega}) + L_i^B(p, \boldsymbol{\omega})) \cos \theta \; d\boldsymbol{\omega} \\
&= \int_{H+} L_i^A(p, \boldsymbol{\omega}) \cos \theta \; d\boldsymbol{\omega} + \int_{H+} L_i^B(p, \boldsymbol{\omega})) \cos \theta \; d\boldsymbol{\omega} \\
&= [\text{irradiance due to object } A] + [\text{iradiance due to object } B].
\end{aligned}
$$

So, we can sum the irradiance from different objects/slices if they never occlude each other.

However: the relation $L_i(p, \boldsymbol{\omega}) = L_i^A(p, \boldsymbol{\omega}) + L_i^B(p, \boldsymbol{\omega})$ will still be a reasonable approximation if the amount of overlap is low. If the amount of overlap is high—such as the above example where one object completely occludes another—then it will no longer hold.

20.5.2 An Array of Distorted Cubes

One way to construct a set of slices that never occlude each other is to arrange six slices as faces of a cube, and to allow only sampling from points within the cube. With this arrangement, we could accurately evaluate the irradiance within a cube using slices—but this is, of course, far too restrictive to be generally useful.

However, it's possible to stretch and skew the cube. The restriction that slices never occlude each other is equivalent to requiring that the shape remains convex. Secondly, there is the requirement that the slices not be too distorted from their original square shape—the greater the distortion, the more the irradiance approximation degrades.

A wide variety of shapes can be created that meet these two requirements: cuboids and extruded parallelograms are possible, as are more esoteric shapes created by nonlinear distortions, such as truncated square pyramids. It's even possible to allow a small amount of nonconvexity without the slice approximation failing (see the discussion on occlusion in the previous section) so transformations that lead to a slightly nonconvex result are still valid. An example is a bend or twist operation. Each of these distorted cubes is called a *cell*.

The next step is to fit the cells together. If a particular face is flat, then it could be shared with a neighboring cell: on the shared face, there would be two coincident slices, one associated with each neighbor.

It's possible to extend this even further to create a large group of cells that fill space with no overlaps. In this case, the process of evaluating irradiance is done by finding the cell that contains the query point, calculating the irradiance contributed by each of its six slices, and summing those six values.

Allowing an arbitrary arrangement of cells would be possible, but we imposed some restrictions to make the search for the cell containing the query point more efficient, as well as the transformation to slice space for evaluating irradiance.

20.6 Layered Heightfields

The approach we chose was to define a set of layered heightfields for each axis. For the x axis, we have $x = f_i(y, z)$, where the series of functions f_i define the heightfields; $0 \leq i \leq \boldsymbol{n}_x$. Figure 20.14 shows an example.

We also require that $f_i(y, z) < f_{i+1}(y, z)$ to enforce the layers to never intersect, and for each successive heightfield to be farther along the x axis. A similar series of functions g_j, h_k are defined for the y and z axes.

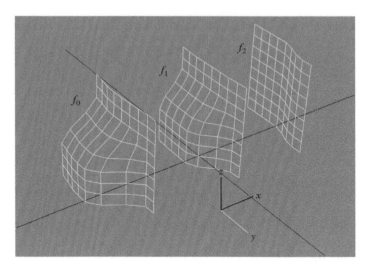

Figure 20.14. Layered heightfields for the x axis.

These heightfields define the split between neighboring cells. They produce a collection of cells that can be indexed using three integers (i, j, k), where $0 \leq i \leq n_x$, $0 \leq j \leq n_y$, and $0 \leq k \leq n_z$. The resulting arrangement of cells are like a distortion of an $n_x \times n_y \times n_z$ array of voxels.

The region covered by the cell (i, j, k) occupies the set of points $(f_i(y, z), g_j(x, z), h_k(x, y))$ where $x \in (i, i+1)$, $y \in (j, j+1)$, and $z \in (k, k+1)$.

Defining the distortion in this way does not allow arbitrary distortions to be represented. For instance, a twist distortion (like the "twirl" distortion in Adobe Photoshop) with an angle of more than 90 degrees cannot be expressed as a series of layered heightfields.

20.6.1   Mapping from World Space to Cell Space

The search for a containing cell is done on an axis-by-axis basis: for a given point (x, y, z), find the identifier (i, j, k) of the containing cell. The value of i is the value for which $f_i(y, z) \leq x < f_{i+1}(y, z)$; note that it's independent of j and k and may be done as a simple binary search within the series of heightfields. It specifically avoids the need for a volume texture lookup. (If the layered heightfields are constructed as described in Section 20.7, then the heightfields are restricted to a series of regular intervals, which simplifies the lookup substantially: the value of i can be found by querying two heightfields.) Values for j and k are computed in a similar fashion.

Secondly, we can find the relative position within the cell. This is the point (u, v, w), where $0 \leq u, v, w \leq 1$. It is found by the relative position between the boundary heightfields:

$$u = \frac{x - f_i(y, z)}{f_{i+1}(y, z) - f_i(y, z)},$$

$$v = \frac{y - g_j(x, z)}{g_{j+1}(x, z) - g_j(x, z)}, \quad (20.8)$$

$$w = \frac{z - h_k(x, y)}{h_{k+1}(x, y) - h_k(x, y)}.$$

The point (u, v, w) can be used directly for evaluating the slice irradiance. For example, to evaluate the contribution of the slice on the f_i side of the cell, the texture coordinate to sample the slice texture is (v, w), and the value u can be directly used to calculate the mipmap paramater (Equation (20.3)) if the distance to the first mipmap is also expressed in that space. The other five slices making up the cell can be evaluated in a similar way.

So at runtime, the full process of evaluating irradiance for a given point in world space involves these steps:

- Search the layered heightfields for each of the three axes to find the cell (i, j, k).

- Find the relative position (u, v, w) within the cell using Equation (20.9).

- Sample the image pyramid of each of the six slices associated with that cell.

- Scale and attenuate those six samples based on surface normal and distance outside border (if need be) to evaluate irradiance using Equations (20.4) and (20.5).

- Sum the resulting six irradiance values.

20.7 Slice Placement

For a given scene, we need a way to build the layered heightfields that divide up the space, and define the cells. The goal is for the cell faces to be coincident with scene geometry wherever possible.

The method we used is intended to be run offline, as a preprocess. It works as follows.

Let the number of slices for each axis be n_x, n_y, and n_z. Each axis will be processed in turn. For each axis, we'll generate the series of layered heightfields described earlier: i.e., for the x axis, the heightfields will be of the form $x_i = f_i(y, z)$, for integer i with $0 \leq i \leq n_x$; for the y axis, the heightfields will be of the form $y_j = g_j(x, z)$ for integer j with $0 \leq j \leq n_y$; and similar for the z axis. The collection of heightfields for a particular axis will never intersect each

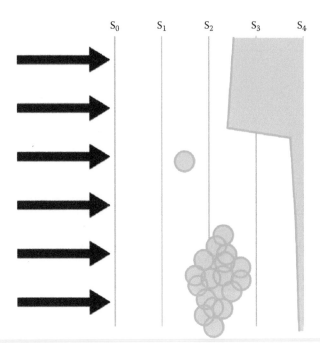

Figure 20.15. Scene divided into equal parts. The geometry is shown in green; the arrows on the left indicate the ray collection.

other—they'll form a series of layers. So $f_i(y, z) < f_{i+1}(y, z)$ always, with similar restrictions for the g and h series.

20.7.1   Generating the Defining Heightfields

The problem is to find a collection of layered heightfields for each axis that matches the significant surfaces of the scene.

This is the process to generate the $x = f_i(y, z)$ heightfield collection. This approach is repeated with obvious modifications to generate the y and z axis collections.

1. Find the scene extent: $(x_{min}, y_{min}, z_{min}) - (x_{max}, y_{max}, z_{max})$. Divide the scene into $\boldsymbol{n_x}$ equal-sized parts along the x axis, i.e., $\boldsymbol{n_x}$ subsets, each covering the region $(\boldsymbol{s_i}, y_{min}, z_{min}) - (\boldsymbol{s_{i+1}}, y_{max}, z_{max})$, where $\boldsymbol{s_0} = x_{min}, \boldsymbol{s_1} = x_{min} + k, \ldots, \boldsymbol{s_i} = x_{min} + ik, \ldots, \boldsymbol{s_{nx}} = x_{max}$.

2. Define a collection of rays in the direction $(1, 0, 0)$ that originate from a regular grid of points, i.e., (x, y, z) such that $x = x_{min}, y = y_{min} + p * (y_{max} - y_{min})/p_{max}$, and $z = z_{min} + q * (z_{max} - z_{min})/q_{max}$ for integer p, q. See Figure 20.15.

3. For each ray in turn, trace the ray through the scene, finding each of the surface intersections. Within each of the n_x subset spaces defined at step 1, find the front-facing intersection with the minimum x component, and the back-facing intersection with maximum x. (*Front-facing* means the surface the ray intersected has a surface normal whose x component is < 0—i.e., the ray hit the surface from the front. *Back-facing* means the opposite.) Let S_j be the resulting set of intersection points for ray j. Record the intersection by storing the ray parameter, i.e., the value p for which (ray origin) + (ray direction $\times p$) = intersection point. Figure 20.16 shows the relevant front- and back-faces for each scene subset.

4. We now assign a significance value to each of the points in S; S_j is $\{p_0, p_1, \ldots, p_{k_{max}}\}$, the ordered set of surface intersection points for ray j. Let the significance value of each point default to 0. For each k, if p_k is back-facing and p_{k+1} is front-facing, then the significance value is $|p_{k+1} - p_k|$; assign it to both p_k and p_{k+1}. Figure 20.17 shows red bars for each such interval. Note that there are no significance bars passing through the solid green regions, due to the check for back-face/front-face order. Ideally, the significance value would measure how often that surface point is seen. We're approximating this using the distance between that point and the point it is facing—this line segment is in open space, rather than within an object, so it's a space where the viewer may go, and the longer that line segment, the larger the open space is. Conversely, a surface that is hidden by another surface will be less significant.

5. Build a 2D table of value and weight for each scene subset. Within each of the n_x scene subsets, for each ray i we have up to two intersection points (a front-facing one and a back-facing one) and an associated significance value.

   Compute the pair $\{v * w, w\}$, where v is the sum of the ray parameters and w is the sum of the associated significance value for those intersection points— there will be zero, one, or two of them. Figure 20.18 shows the average positions.

   If there were no intersection points for the ray in this scene subset, let the pair be $\{0, 0\}$.

   Because the rays are defined to be a regular grid, indexed by the integers p and q (see Step 2) assign the pair $\{v, w\}$ to the table entry $T_i(p, q)$, where i indicates the scene subset.

6. Smooth and extrapolate the table associated with each of the scene subsets. Let $O(p, q)$ be the point at which the ray (p, q) originates. Then $T_i'(p, q) = \sum_{0 \le r \le p_{max}, 0 \le s \le q_{max}} T_i(r, s) \cdot c^{-|0(p,q)-o(r,s)|}$, where c is a constant controlling

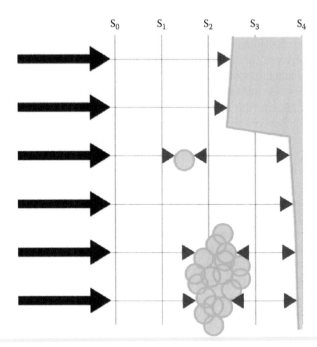

Figure 20.16. Red markers indicate front and back faces for each scene subset.

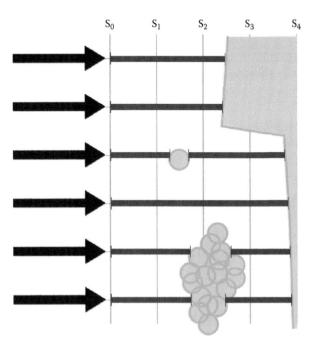

Figure 20.17. Red bars indicate significance.

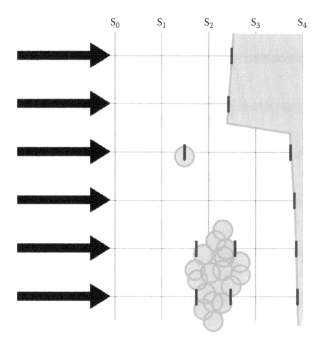

S_0 S_1 S_2 S_3 S_4

Figure 20.18. Average position of the intersection points in each scene subset.

the locality of the blur. Note that the values $T(p, q)$ are pairs of real values $\{a, b\}$; they are scaled and added like 2D vectors.

7. Output the heightfield. Define the 2D table U_i with the same dimensions as T_i'. $T_i'(p, q)$ is the pair $\{a, b\}$; the corresponding entry $U_i(p, q)$ is defined to be a/b. Note that b will be zero if and only if the b entry is zero for all entries in table T_i (see Figure 20.19). Note that the heightfields follow the scene geometry where possible, and there is no heightfield in the $s - s_1$ subset.

In short, assign a significance value to the relevant surface intersections in each scene subset, and perform a weighted blur that respects the significance factor to extrapolate and smooth out the heightfield. The parameter and significance pair is encoded as a homogenous value specifically to support this step.

The heightfield U_i will be contained within scene subset i, thereby meeting the requirement that the heightfields do not cross over.

Note that the input scene may well contain interpenetrating geometry—for example, a ray traveling through the scene may intersect several consecutive front-facing surfaces in a row. Also, there may be "open" or nonmanifold geometry—i.e., a ray passing completely through the scene may encounter a different number

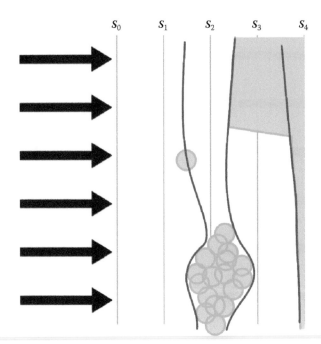

Figure 20.19. Final heightfield for each scene subset.

of front- and back-facing intersections. These problems are unavoidable when working with production scenes. The nearest front-face/last back-face logic in Step 3 is designed to support these situations.

20.7.2   Discussion

This approach works well for scenes which have strong axis-aligned features. That is, scenes where the main surfaces are roughly parallel to the xy, xz, and yz planes. Architectural scenes and game environments built out of prefabs usually meet this requirement.

Large curved surfaces run the risk of problems. If the surface needs to be represented by slices from more than one axis, parts of that surface may be missed (leading to light leakage) or have regions included in two slices (leading to too much indirect light).

These problem cases can usually be fixed by manually editing the distortion function to ensure that the surface always aligns with one and only one slice.

The slice placement step was intended to run offline, as a preprocess, to generate slice geometry that does not change at runtime.

Figure 20.20. Light propagating from one cell to another.

20.8 Propagating Irradiance

While the slice geometry does not change at runtime, the slice image pyramids are intended to be regenerated at runtime in response to lighting changes. Local lighting changes within a cell can be accommodated by recapturing the radiance for those slices and rebuilding the image pyramid as described in Section 20.4.

However, this doesn't allow light to have an effect outside the cell where it was emitted. To achieve this, we use a propagation step, analogous to the light propagation step described by [Kaplanyan and Dachsbacher 10]. For each step, each cell is considered in turn, and light within that cell is propagated to its neighbors. After enough steps, lighting changes will propagate throughout the array of cells.

Figure 20.20 shows a cross section through a collection of cells. The shape of the faces/slices are indicated by red lines—many have been omitted for clarity. We'll only consider some of the vertical slices, by the letters $a - c$. Light is emitted from the slice marked "source," as shown by the arrows.

Light is propagated from cell to cell in two ways. Firstly, it is propagated forward—from source to slice a, in the example image. This is done as follows: when regenerating slice a, the irradiance from *source* is sampled, scaled down by $(1 - \text{opacity})$, and added into the radiance of slice a, which is input for generating the image pyramids.

This definition means if a point on slice a is opaque, then the light from *source* will be blocked. If it's transparent, then the irradiance will be continuous—there will be no discontinuity or other artifact.

Secondly, it is propagated laterally—from *source* into slice b in Figure 20.20. This is done when generating the image pyramid for each slice by allowing the blurs to pick up color from neighboring slices, scaled by transparency of the intervening slices (c in the example case).

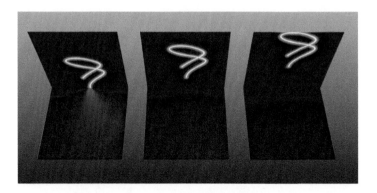

Figure 20.21. Light transport within a single cell.

Again, this definition means that if a slice is opaque, it will block the lateral flow of light. If a slice is transparent, then the light will flow laterally from cell to cell with no discontinuities or artifacts.

With this approach, the light will radiate outward in a plausible fashion, with no discontinuities at the cell borders.

20.9   Results

Figure 20.21 shows the simplest case. Light radiated from a wall is captured by a single slice. The floor plane samples that irradiance. The images demonstrate how the irradiance softens and widens with distance from the emissive surface. It also underlines that the emissive surface can radiate light in any pattern; it's not a point or line but a texture.

Figure 20.22 shows a scene with two cells separated by a perforated wall. This scene shows light propagation from cell to cell and how the attenuation is affected by the occluding wall. Note that the light that passes through the holes and falls on the floor gives a sharper pool of light for the hole near the floor. The farther hole gives a pool of light on the floor that's blurrier and farther from the wall.

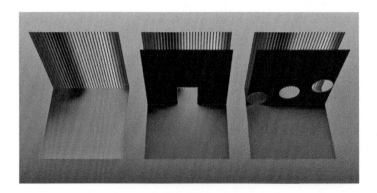

Figure 20.22. Light propagating from one cell to another, with attenuation.

Figure 20.23. Sample scene.

Figure 20.24. Example of changes possible at runtime.

Figure 20.23 shows a production scene where the irradiance is provided using slices. The inset image shows the direct lighting. The blue skylight was created by adding constant blue light into the transparent areas of the topmost layer. For this scene, the cells are roughly 5 m along each side, and each slice is 64×64 resolution.

Figure 20.24 illustrates the sort of changes possible at runtime: the lefthand image shows the a scene with a single light; on the right, a square hole has been cut out of the balcony and the roof above is now lit by bounce light. The slice shapes were not altered in any way: opening the hole in the balcony only changed the transparency of one of the slices, allowing light to propagate from the cell beneath the balcony to the cell above.

20.10 Conclusion

We have presented a method for efficiently evaluating irradiance from a flat surface using an image pyramid, and an efficient method for rebuilding the image pyramid at runtime.

The biggest weakness of this approach is the requirement that the scene be represented by a set of slices. If this requirement can't be met, there will be light leakage and other quality problems. While most architectural and man-made scenes can be adequately represented by slices, more organic environments are a challenge.

In addition, this method won't support dynamic objects moving through the scene. While it can support limited changes to the architecture (e.g., doors opening, a wall collapsing, a roof opening up), it isn't a solution for real-time irradiance effects due to characters moving through the scene.

In conclusion, this best use case for this approach is an architectural or other manmade scene that can be accurately represented by slices; where the lighting is dynamic, the effects of dynamic objects on irradiance is not significant, and the runtime changes to the scene geometry are limited (e.g., doors opening and closing). In this case, it will yield high-quality irradiance that updates in real time.

Bibliography

[Crassin et al. 2011] Cyril Crassin, Fabrice Neyret, Miguel Sainz, Simon Green, and Elmar Eisemann. "Interactive Indirect Illumination Using Voxel Cone Tracing." *Computer Graphics Forum: Proc. of Pacific Graphics 2011* 30:7 (2011), 1921–1930.

[d'Eon and Luebke 07] Eugene d'Eon and David Luebke. "Advanced Techniques for Realistic Real-Time Skin Rendering." In *GPU Gems 3*, edited by Hubert Nguyen, Chapter 14. Reading, MA: Addison-Wesley Professional, 2007. (Available online at http://http.developer.nvidia.com/GPUGems3/gpugems3_ch14.html.)

[Kaplanyan and Dachsbacher 10] Anton Kaplanyan and Carsten Dachsbacher. "Cascaded Light Propagation Volumes for Real-Time Indirect Illumination." In *Proceedings of the 2010 ACM SIGGRAPH Symposium on Interactive 3D Graphics and Games*, pp. 99–107. New York: ACM, 2010.

[Panteleev 2014] A. Panteleev. "Practical Real-Time Voxel-Based Global Illumination for Current GPUs." Presented at SIGGRAPH, Vancouver, CA, August 10–14, 2014. (Available at http://on-demand.gputechconf.com/gtc/2014/presentations/S4552-rt-voxel-based-global-illumination-gpus.pdf.)

21

Clustered Shading: Assigning Lights Using Conservative Rasterization in DirectX 12
Kevin Örtegren and Emil Persson

21.1 Introduction

Dynamic lights are a crucial part of making a virtual scene seem realistic and alive. Accurate lighting calculations are expensive and have been a major restriction in real-time applications. In recent years, many new lighting pipelines have been explored and used in games to increase the number of dynamic light sources per scene. This chapter presents a GPU-based variation of *practical clustered shading* [Persson and Olsson 13], which is a technique that improves on the currently popular *tiled shading* [Olsson and Assarsson 11, Swoboda 09, Balestra and Engstad 08, Andersson 09] by utilizing higher-dimensional tiles. The view frustum is divided into three-dimensional clusters instead of two-dimensional tiles and addresses the depth discontinuity problem present in the tiled shading technique. The main goal we aimed for was to explore the use of conservative rasterization to efficiently assign convex light shapes to clusters.

Clustered shading is a technique similar to tiled shading that performs a light culling step before the lighting stage when rendering a scene. The view frustum is divided into sub-frustums, which we call *clusters*, in three dimensions. The purpose of the light culling step is to insert all visible lights into the clusters that they intersect. When the light culling is done, the clusters contain information of which lights intersect them. It is then easy to fetch the light data from a cluster when shading a pixel by using the pixel's view-space position. The goal of the technique is to minimize the number of lighting calculations per pixel and to address some of the problems present in tiled shading. Tiled shading uses two-dimensional tiles and relies on a depth prepass to reduce the tiles in the z-dimension, whereas clustered shading has a fixed cluster structure in view space at all times.

(a) Conservative rasterization.   (b) Normal rasterization.

Figure 21.1. Difference between rasterization modes. Red cells represent the pixel shader invocations for the triangle.

Previous work on clustered shading first surfaced in 2012 [Olsson et al. 12] and have since spawned a few presentations and demos on the subject: Intel demo on forward clustered shading [Fauconneau 14], GDC15 presentation from AMD on tiled and clustered shading [Thomas 15], and a practical solution to clustered shading from Avalanche [Persson and Olsson 13]. As of writing this, there is one released game using clustered shading, namely *Forza Horizon 2* [Leadbetter 14].

21.2 Conservative Rasterization

The use of the rasterizer has traditionally been to generate pixels from primitives for drawing to the screen, but with programmable shaders there is nothing stopping the user from using it in other ways. The normal rasterization mode will rasterize a pixel if the pixel center is covered by a primitive. *Conservative rasterization* is an alternative rasterization mode where if any part of a primitive overlaps a pixel, that pixel is considered covered and is then rasterized. The difference between these modes is illustrated in Figure 21.1.

21.3 Implementation

This section will go through the different steps included in the light assignment algorithm as well as explain how the main data structure used for storing light and cluster data is created and managed, as it is an intricate part of the technique. An overview of the algorithm is listed below:

For each light type:

1. Shell pass: Find minimum and maximum depths in every tile for every light.

2. Fill pass: Use the minimum and maximum depths and fill indices into the light linked list.

The light assignment is complete when all light types have been processed and the light linked list can be used when shading geometry.

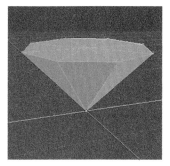
(a) A unit cone mesh with 10 vertices.

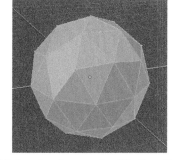
(b) A unit sphere mesh with 42 vertices.

Figure 21.2. Two example unit shapes created in Blender.

21.3.1 Light Shape Representation

Lights must have a shape representation to be able to be inserted into clusters. Approximating every light shape as an analytical sphere is the easiest and computationally cheapest approach, but it will be inaccurate for light shapes that are not sphere shaped. An analytic shape representation is suitable when performing general intersection calculations on the CPU or in, for example, a compute shader. Some shapes will, however, have a very complex analytical representation, which is why many techniques resort to using spheres.

The technique presented here uses the rasterizer and the traditional rendering shader pipeline, which is well suited to deal with high amounts of vertices. Shapes represented as vertex meshes are very simple and provide general representation models for all light shapes. The level of flexibility when working with vertex meshes is very high because the meshes can be created with variable detail.

Meshes are created as unit shapes, where vertices are constrained to -1 to 1 in the x-, y-, and z-directions. This is done to allow arbitrary scaling of the shape depending on the actual light size. Some light shapes may need to be altered at runtime to allow for more precise representations: for example, the unit cone will fit around a sphere-capped cone for a spot light, and thus the cap must be calculated in the vertex shader before light assignment. In the case of using low amounts of vertices for light shapes, the shapes could easily be created in code and also use very small vertex formats: for example, R8G8B8 is enough for the shapes in Figure 21.2.

21.3.2 Shell Pass

The *shell pass* is responsible for finding the clusters for a light shape that encompasses it in cluster space. The pass finds the near and far clusters for each tile for each light and stores them in an R8G8 render target for the following

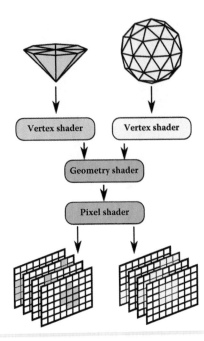

Figure 21.3. Illustration of the entire shell pass.

pass to fill the shell. The number of render targets for the shell pass correspond to the maximum number of visible lights for each light type. All render targets have the same size and format and are set up in a `Texture2DArray` for each light type. The sizes of the render targets are the same as the x- and y-dimensions of the cluster structure, otherwise known as the *tile dimension*. An overview illustration of the shell pass can be seen in Figure 21.3. The shell pass uses the traditional shader pipeline with conservative rasterization to ensure that the light meshes invoke all the pixels they touch. To activate conservative rasterization in DirectX 12, it is simply a matter of setting the `ConservativeRaster` flag to `D3D12_CONSERVATIVE_RASTERIZATION_MODE_ON` when creating a pipeline state object for the shader pipeline.

Vertex shader Each light type has its own custom vertex shader for translating, rotating, and scaling the light mesh to fit the actual light. This and the mesh are the only two things that have to be introduced when adding a new light type for the light assignment. The algorithm starts by issuing a `DrawIndexedInstanced` with the number of lights as the instance count. Also fed to the vertex shader is the actual light data containing position, color, and other light properties. The shader semantic `SV_InstanceID` is used in the vertex shader to extract the position, scale, and other properties to transform each vertex to the correct location in world space. Each vertex is sent to the geometry shader containing the view-space position and its light ID, which is the same as the previously mentioned SV_InstanceID.

Geometry shader The vertices will simply pass through the geometry shader where packed view positions for each vertex in the triangle primitive are appended to every vertex. The vertex view positions are flagged with nointerpolation as they have to remain correctly in the view space through the rasterizer. The most important task of the geometry shader is to select the correct render target as output for the pixel shader. This is done by writing a render target index to the SV_RenderTargetArrayIndex semantic in each vertex. SV_RenderTargetArrayIndex is only available through the geometry shader; this is a restriction of the current shading model and makes the use of the geometry shader a requirement. The geometry shader is unfortunately not an optimal path to take in the shader pipeline because it, besides selecting the render target index, adds unnecessary overhead.

Pixel shader The pixel shader performs most of the mathematics and does so for every triangle in every tile. Each pixel shader invocation corresponds to a tile, and in that tile the nearest or farthest cluster must be calculated and written for every light. When a pixel shader is run for a tile, it means that part of a triangle from a light shape mesh is inside that tile, and from that triangle part the minimum and maximum depths must be found. Depth can be directly translated into a Z-cluster using a depth distribution function, which is discussed in more detail in the next section.

All calculations are performed in view space because vertices outside a tile must be correctly represented; if calculations were performed in screen space, the vertices behind the near plane would be incorrectly transformed and become unusable. Tile boundaries are represented as four side planes that go through the camera origin $(0, 0, 0)$. Each pixel shader invocation handles one triangle at a time. To find the minimum and maximum depths for a triangle in a tile, three cases are used; see Figure 21.4. The three points that can be the minimum or maximum depths in a tile are as follows:

(a) Where a vertex edge intersects the tile boundary planes: Listing 21.1 shows the intersection function for finding the intersection distance from a vertex to a tile boundary plane. The distance is along the edge from vertex p0. Note that both N and D can be 0, in which case N / D would return NaN or, in the case of only D being 0, would return +/-INF. It is an optimization to not check for these cases, as the IEEE 754-2008 floating point specification in HLSL [Microsoft] states that

   1. the comparison NE, when either or both operands is NaN, returns TRUE;

   2. comparisons of any non-NaN value against +/-INF return the correct result.

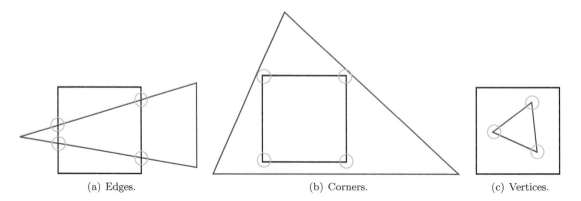

(a) Edges.   (b) Corners.   (c) Vertices.

Figure 21.4. The three cases of finding minimum and maximum depths on a triangle in a tile.

```
bool linesegment_vs_plane(float3 p0, float3 p1, float3 pn,out
                          float lerp_val)
{
    float3 u = p1 - p0;

    float D = dot(pn, u);
    float N = -dot(pn, p0);

    lerp_val = N / D;
    return !(lerp_val != saturate(lerp_val));
}
```

Listing 21.1. Vertex edge versus tile boundary plane intersection.

The second rule applies to the intrinsic function saturate. These two rules make sure that the function always returns the correct boolean.

(b) Where a triangle covers a tile corner: Finding the depth at a corner of a tile is simply a matter of performing four ray-versus-triangle intersections, one at each corner of the tile. The ray–triangle intersection function in Listing 21.2 is derived from [Möller and Trumbore 05].

(c) Where a vertex is completely inside a tile: The signed distance from a point to a plane in three dimensions is calculated by

$$D = \frac{ax_1 + by_1 + cz_1 + d}{\sqrt{a^2 + b^2 + c^2}},$$

where (a, b, c) is the normal vector of the plane and (x_1, y_1, z_1) is the point to which the distance is calculated. The variable d is defined as $d = -ax_0 -$

```
bool ray_vs_triangle(float3 ray_dir, float3 vert0, float3 vert1,
                     float3 vert2, out float z_pos)
{
  float3 e1 = vert1 - vert0;
  float3 e2 = vert2 - vert0;
  float3 q = cross(ray_dir, e2);
  float a = dot(e1, q);

  if(a > -0.000001f && a < 0.000001f)
    return false;

  float f = 1.0f / a;
  float u = f * dot(-vert0, q);

  if(u != saturate(u))
    return false;

  float3 r = cross(-vert0, e1);
  float v = f * dot(ray_dir, r);

  if(v < 0.0f || (u + v) > 1.0f)
    return false;

  z_pos = f * dot(e2, r) * ray_dir.z;

  return true;
}
```

Listing 21.2. Ray versus triangle intersection.

$by_0 - cz_0$, where (x_0, y_0, z_0) is a point on the plane. As all planes go through the origin in the view space, the variable d is eliminated; because the plane normals are length 1, the denominator is also eliminated. This leaves the function as $D = ax_1 + by_1 + cz_1$. Further simplification can be done by splitting the function into two separate functions: one for testing the side planes and one for testing the top and bottom planes. These functions are $D = ax_1 + cz_1$ and $D = by_1 + cz_1$, respectively, as the y-component of the plane normal is zero in the first case and the x-component is zero in the second case. By knowing the direction of the plane normals, the sign of the distance tells on which side of the plane the vertex is. See Listing 21.3 for HLSL code of these two functions.

When all three cases have been evaluated, the minimum and maximum depths for a tile have been determined and the result can be stored. The result is stored in a render target with the same size as the x- and y-dimensions of the cluster structure. When a triangle is run through a pixel shader, it can be either front facing or back facing. In the case of a triangle being front facing, the minimum depth will be stored, and in the back facing case, the maximum depth will be stored.

To save video memory, the depth values are first converted into Z-cluster space, which is what is used in the following pass. The render target uses the

```
bool is_in_xslice(float3 top_plane, float3 bottom_plane,
                  float3 vert_point)
{
  return (top_plane.y * vert_point.y + top_plane.z * vert_point.z
            >= 0.0f && bottom_plane.y * vert_point.y +
            bottom_plane.z * vert_point.z >= 0.0f);
}

bool is_in_yslice(float3 left_plane, float3 right_plane,
                  float3 vert_point)
{
  return (left_plane.x * vert_point.x + left_plane.z * vert_point.z
            >= 0.0f && right_plane.x * vert_point.x +
            right_plane.z * vert_point.z >= 0.0f );
}
```

Listing 21.3. Vertex point versus tile boundary planes intersection.

format `R8G8_UNORM`, which allows for the cluster structure to have up to 256 clusters in the z-dimension. As many triangles can be in the same tile for a light shape, it is important to find the minimum and maximum Z-clusters for all the triangles. This is done by writing the result to the render target using using a `MIN` rasterizer blend mode, which ensures that the smallest result is stored. To be able to use the same shader and the same blend mode for both front-facing and back-facing triangles, the HLSL system value `SV_IsFrontFace` is used to select in which color channel the result is stored. In the case of back-facing triangles, the result must be inverted to correctly blend using the MIN blend mode; the result is then inverted again in the next pass to retrieve the correct value. Figure 21.5 illustrates the found minimum and maximum depth points in a tile for a point light shape. A top-down illustration of the final result of the shell pass can be seen in Figure 21.6, where two point lights and a spot light have been processed, with the colored clusters representing the minimum and maximum Z-clusters for each tile and light.

21.3.3 Depth Distribution

The *depth distribution* determines how the Z-cluster planes are distributed along the z-axis in the view space. The depth distribution is represented as a function that takes a linear depth value as input and outputs the corresponding Z-cluster. Two functions have been evaluated in this implementation; one linear and one exponential. The linear distribution simply divides the z-axis into equally spaced slices while the exponential function is

$$Z = \log_2(d)\frac{1}{\log_2(f) - \log_2(n)}(c-1) + \left((1 - \log_2(n))\frac{1}{\log_2(f) - \log_2(n)}(c-1)\right),$$

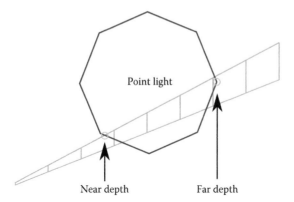

Figure 21.5. Top-down view of one tile and the found minimum and maximum depths for a point light mesh.

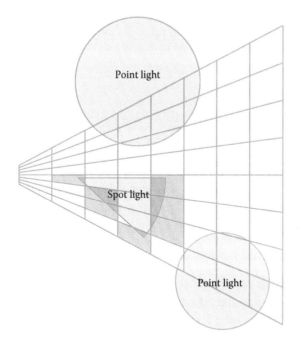

Figure 21.6. Two-dimensional top-down view of a shell pass.

where d is the view-space distance along the z-axis, f is the distance to the last z-plane, n is the distance to the second z-plane, and c is the number of clusters in the z-dimension. Note that most of these are constants and are not recalculated. Figure 21.7 shows the two functions in a graph with example values.

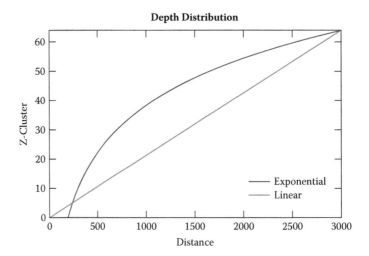

Figure 21.7. Graph of two distribution functions over an example depth of 3000 with 64 clusters in the z-dimension. The second z-slice of the exponential function is set to start at 200.

21.3.4   Fill Pass

The *fill pass* is a compute-shader-only pass with one purpose: to write the assigned lights into the light linked list, which is a linked list on the GPU derived from [Yang et al. 10].

Light linked list   A light linked list is a GPU-friendly data structure for storing and managing many index pointers to larger data. In the case of this algorithm, a fixed number of unique lights are active each frame, and hundreds of clusters can contain the same instance of a light. It would be wasteful to store the actual light data (position, color, etc.) in every cluster; instead, an index to the light data is stored. Light data can differ between light types and implementation, but in most cases they are larger than 64 bit, which is the size of the light linked list node. More specifically, the light linked list node contains three pieces of data: the pointer to the next node in the list, the pointer to the actual light data, and the light type. These can fit into either 64 bits or 32 bits, depending on the maximum amount of lights needed in the game. Examples of the data in a node are shown in Table 21.1. The 64-bit node has support for more lights than modern hardware can manage in real time, but the 32-bit node is at the limit of what could be viable in a modern game engine. A tradeoff has to be made between memory savings and the maximum number of supported lights. Note that in Table 21.1 the 32-bit node uses 2 bits for the light type and 10 bits for the light ID, which results in 4096 total lights. This can be switched around to

<table>
<tr><td colspan="3">(a)</td><td colspan="3">(b)</td></tr>
</table>

Data	Size	Max. Value	Data	Size	Max. Value
Light type	8 bits	256	Light type	2 bits	4
LightID	24 bits	16777216	LightID	10 bits	1024
Link	32 bits	4294967296	Link	20 bits	1048576

Table 21.1. Examples of (a) 64-bit and (b) 32-bit node layouts.

whatever fits the implementation best; for example, if only point lights and spot lights are used, the light type would only need 1 bit.

The data structures used to build the light linked list consists of three parts and can be seen in Figure 21.8. The start offset buffer is a Direct3D `ByteAddress-Buffer` with cells corresponding to each cluster. The elements are `uint32` and act as pointers into the linked node light list. Each cell in the start offset buffer points to the head node for a cluster. Simply following the head node in the linked list will go through all nodes for a given cluster. The light linked list is a large one-dimensional structured buffer containing the previously mentioned nodes. Each used node points to actual light data that can be fetched and used for shading.

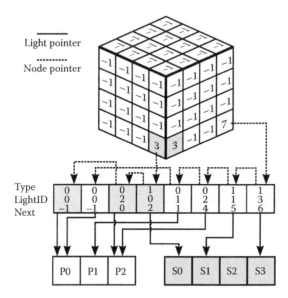

Figure 21.8. Illustration of the light linked list. The "Next" field is the index to the next node in the linked list; if a node is pointed to and has −1 as its next node, it means that it is the tail node and no more nodes are linked to that sequence. The three-dimensional structure contains a pointer from each cluster to the head node for that cluster. If a cluster is empty, there will be −1 in the corresponding cell. The types can be chosen per implementation, and in this case 0 stands for point lights and 1 stands for spot lights. For example, the cluster that points to node 7 touches lights P0, P1, P2, S1, and S3.

```
//This array has NUM_LIGHTS slices and contains the near and far
//Z-clusters for each tile.
Texture2DArray<float2> conservativeRTs : register(t0);

//Linked list of light IDs.
RWByteAddressBuffer StartOffsetBuffer : register(u0);
RWStructuredBuffer<LinkedLightID> LinkedLightList : register(u1);

[numthreads(TILESX, TILESY, 1)]
void main( uint3 thread_ID : SV_DispatchThreadID ){
  //Load near and far values (x is near and y is far).
  float2 near_and_far = conservativeRTs.Load(int4(thread_ID, 0));

  if(near_and_far.x == 1.0f && near_and_far.y == 1.0f)
    return;

  //Unpack to Z-cluster space([0,1] to [0,255]). Also handle
    //cases where no near or far clusters were written.
  uint near = (near_and_far.x == 1.0f) ? 0 :
      uint(near_and_far.x * 255.0f + 0.5f);
  uint far  = (near_and_far.y == 1.0f) ? (CLUSTERSZ - 1) :
      uint(((CLUSTERSZ - 1.0f) / 255.0f - near_and_far.y)
          * 255.0f + 0.5f);

  //Loop through near to far and fill the light linked list.
  uint offset_index_base = 4 * (thread_ID.x + CLUSTERSX *
                               thread_ID.y);
  uint offset_index_step = 4 * CLUSTERSX * CLUSTERSY;
  uint type = light_type;
  for(uint i = near; i <= far; ++i){
    uint index_count = LinkedLightList.IncrementCounter();
    uint start_offset_address = offset_index_base
                               + offset_index_step * i;

    uint prev_offset;
    StartOffsetBuffer.InterlockedExchange(start_offset_address,
                                   index_count, prev_offset);

    LinkedLightID linked_node;
    linked_node.lightID = (type << 24) | (thread_ID.z & 0xFFFFFF);
          //Light type is encoded in the last 8bit of the
          //node.lightID and lightID in the first 24bits.
    linked_node.link = prev_offset;

    LinkedLightList[index_count] = linked_node;
  }
}
```

Listing 21.4. The complete compute shader for the fill pass.

The last part is the actual light data storage that can be set up in multiple ways as long as it can be indexed using a uint32. In this implementation, the light data is stored in structured buffers. The complete compute shader is outlined in Listing 21.4.

When the fill pass is complete, the linked light list contains all information necessary to shade any geometry in the scene. An example of a completely assigned cluster structure is illustrated in Figure 21.9.

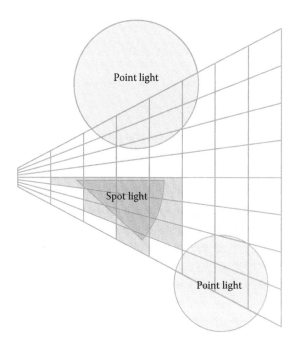

Figure 21.9. Two-dimensional top-down view of a fill pass.

21.4 Shading

The shading is done in the pixel shader by calculating in which cluster the pixel lies and getting the lights from that cluster. As the light types are stored sequentially in the light linked list, it is easy to loop through all lights without having to perform expensive branching. The pixel shader code is listed in Listing 21.5.

Finding out from which cluster the pixel should pull the lights is done by translating the screen-space x- and y-positions of the pixel into the cluster's x- and y-spaces. If the tile pixel size is a power of two, this can be done by a bit shift operation rather than using division. Finding the z-position of the cluster requires a depth value for the pixel, which could be sampled from a depth buffer in the case of deferred shading or could be the z-position of the interpolated geometry in the case of forward shading. The sampled depth is then translated into the Z-cluster space by applying the same depth distribution function used in the shell pass. Figure 21.10 shows what clusters are used for shading in an example scene using the assigned lights from Figure 21.9.

Each light type has its own `while` loop, and the `while` loops are in the reversed order from how the light types were assigned due to the the light linked list having its head pointing at the end of the linked sequence. For example, if point lights are assigned before spot lights, the spot lights will be before the point lights in

```
uint light_index = start_offset_buffer[clusterPos.x + CLUSTERSX *
   clusterPos.y + CLUSTERSX * CLUSTERSY * zcluster];

float3 outColor = float3(0,0,0);

LinkedLightID linked_light;

if(light_index != 0xFFFFFFFF)
{
  linked_light = light_linked_list[light_index];

  //Spot light
  while((linked_light.lightID >> 24) == 1)
  {
    uint lightID = (linked_light.lightID & 0xFFFFFF);

    outColor += SpotLightCalc(pos, norm, diff, spotLights[lightID]);

    light_index = linked_light.link;

    if(light_index == 0xFFFFFFFF)
      break;

    linked_light = light_linked_list[light_index];
  }

  //Point light
  while((linked_light.lightID >> 24) == 0)
  {
    uint lightID = (linked_light.lightID & 0xFFFFFF);

    outColor += PointLightCalc(pos, norm, diff, pointLights[lightID]);

    light_index = linked_light.link;

    if(light_index == 0xFFFFFFFF)
      break;

    linked_light = light_linked_list[light_index];
  }
}

  return float4(outColor, 1.0f);
```

Listing 21.5. Pixel shader code for going through the light linked list for shading a pixel.

the linked sequence. See Figure 21.8, where the node pointer arrows show how the linked list will be traversed.

21.5 Results and Analysis

This section will show results from the performed experiments and presents an analysis of performance, memory, number of assigned clusters, and depth distri-

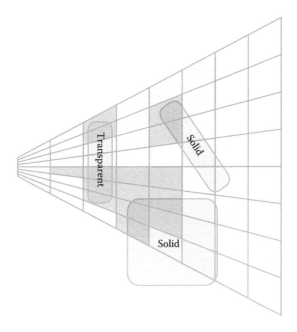

Figure 21.10. Two-dimensional top-down view of sampled clusters in a scene with objects. Note that transparent objects are shaded the same way as opaque objects. Colored clusters contain lights, and the blue clusters are used for shading the geometry.

bution in separate sections. The charts compare many different cluster structure setups, and in some of them the key legend describes the cluster structure dimensions and the depth distribution function used. The suffixes "-L" and "-E" mean linear and exponential, respectively. Performance is measured in milliseconds, and all measurements are done on the GPU.

The test scene is the CryTek Sponza Atrium with up to 4096 lights, and the test scenario is set up exactly as AMD's Forward+ demo [Harada et al. 13], which is also used as a comparison in the light assignment results. A screenshot of the test scene can be seen in Figure 21.11. All tests are performed on an NVIDIA GTX970 graphics card running DirectX 12 on Windows 10 build 10130. The resolution is 1536×768.

21.5.1 Performance

Apart from the performance inconsistencies between depth distribution functions, which are analysed in detail in Section 21.5.4, the performance results are consistent. A few observations can be made by examining Figures 21.12, 21.13 and 21.14: The shell pass remains constant in time when the x- and y-dimensions change, the fill pass increases in time when any of the three dimensions of the

Figure 21.11. CryTek Sponza Atrium test scene.

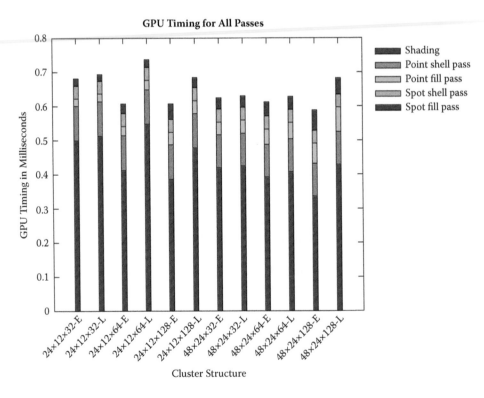

Figure 21.12. Total GPU timings in milliseconds split up into the different passes of the algorithm at 1024 lights. Lower is better.

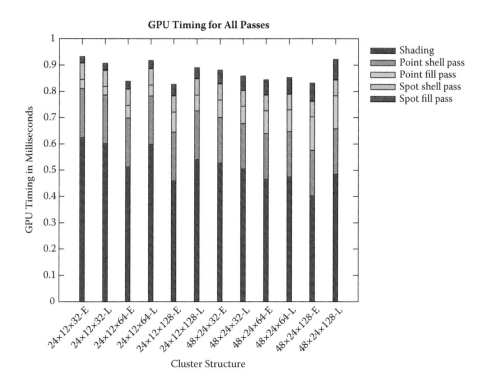

Figure 21.13. Total GPU timings in milliseconds split up into the different passes of the algorithm at 2048 lights. Lower is better.

cluster structure increases, and the total time increases close to linearly with regards to the number of lights.

The times for the two shell passes remain constant when going from 24×12 to 48×24 tiles, but there is a significant difference between them in time. The light shape mesh vertex count used for the respective shell passes are 42 and 10, which indicates that the pixel shader is not the bottleneck. This observation is further strengthened by the fact that going from 24×12 tiles to 48×24 will yield up to four times the number of pixel shader invocations for any number of triangles, which in turn means that the constant time for the shell passes is caused by the triangle processing and data transfer being the bottleneck. Packing data for transfer between shader stages has given the best performance increases when optimizing the shaders.

The fill pass suffers from bad scaling with being up to 6.5 times slower between $24 \times 12 \times 32$ and $48 \times 24 \times 128$ at 4096 lights; see Figure 21.14. As opposed to the pixel shader in the shell pass, which uses mostly ALU instructions, the fill pass writes a lot of data to the light linked list and becomes bandwidth intensive at a

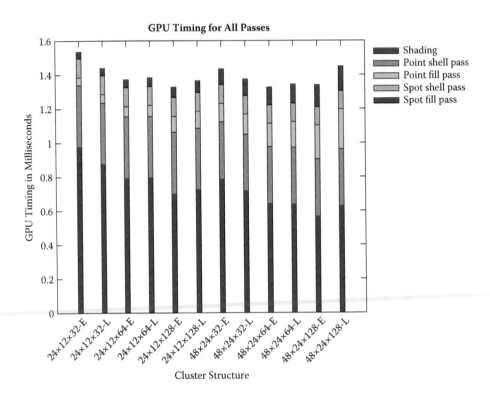

Figure 21.14. Total GPU timings in milliseconds split up into the different passes of the algorithm at 4096 lights. Lower is better.

large number of lights and clusters. The compute shader in the fill pass has low thread coherency and occupancy due to the shape of the cluster structure: lights close to the camera fill up most of their render targets while lights far away from the camera only fill a minimal part the their render targets. The compute shader will invoke threads for all texels, where empty texels cause an early exit for a thread. When using exponential depth, the lights close to the camera will be assigned to a large majority of the clusters. The shape and size of the lights also directly affects the thread coherency of the compute shader as lights that cover many clusters in the z-dimension will write more data as each thread writes data from the near to far clusters in each tile. This is also why the largest relative increases in time occur when adding more slices to the cluster structure. On top of those general observations, all the data writing is done by using atomic functions, which limits the level of parallel efficiency of the compute shader. The spot light fill pass goes from being one of the cheapest passes at a low cluster count to one of the most expensive passes at a high cluster count. The reason for having the fill

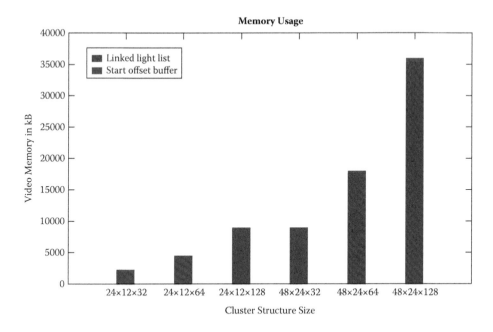

Figure 21.15. Video memory used by the cluster structure and light linked list at 4096 lights. Lower is better.

pass is because of the choice of data structure, the light linked list. The fill pass is decoupled from the shell pass and can be replaced by something else if another data structure is desired, this adds to the flexibility of the algorithm and could be a possible optimization. Another performance optimization possibility is to use fixed-size arrays for each cluster, but this will severely limit the number of lights as it would significantly increase the needed memory to store light pointers.

21.5.2 Memory

The memory model of this implementation is simple; it consists of the light linked list and the render targets for the lights. Figure 21.15 shows the memory used by the linked light list for the tested cluster structure sizes with 64-bit list nodes. The start offset buffer is always `numberOfClusters * 4` bytes large, and the light linked list is initialized to a safe size because it works like a pool of light pointers. In this case, the light linked list is `numberOfClusters * 8 * 30` bytes large; 30 is an arbitrarily chosen multiplier that provides a safe list size for this particular scenario. If the list size is not large enough, there will be lights missing at shading time. The missing lights will be noticeable: a light pointer could be missing from one cluster and correctly assigned to a neighbouring cluster, creating a hard edge at the tile border. Visually, missing light assignments will show up as darker

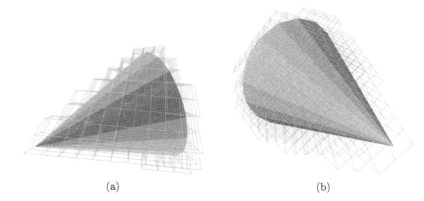

(a)   (b)

Figure 21.16. Clusters that were assigned to a spot light are visualized and viewed from two different angles. Perfect clustering with exponential depth distribution was captured from a medium distance at a clustered structure size of $24 \times 12 \times 64$.

blocks in the final shaded image. As can be seen in Figure 21.15, the actual linked list is a large majority of the memory usage at 4096 lights. Using a 32-bit node would only use half the memory of the linked list, but as previously shown in Table 21.1, only 1048576 linked nodes would fit at a 20-bit link size, which would limit the maximum cluster structure size depending on the concentration of lights in a scene.

The render target memory usage is not dependent on the cluster structure slice depth; it is dependent on the number of lights and the number of tiles. Each light needs `numberOfTiles * 2` bytes, and at 4096 lights with 24×12 tiles, this adds up to 2,359,296 bytes.

If memory is an issue, there is the alternative to use a 32-bit node in the light linked list and choosing an appropriate cluster structure size. Comparing the $24 \times 12 \times 128$ structure with 32-bit nodes to the $48 \times 24 \times 32$ structure with 64-bit nodes results in 6.87 MB and 18.2 MB, respectively. In this implementation, the $24 \times 12 \times 128$ structure even achieves better shading and light assignment times. This goes to show that knowing the use case of the application and choosing the right setup for this technique is important.

21.5.3   Light Assignment

Figure 21.16 shows a perfectly clustered spot light and how it fits in the cluster structure. Perfect clustering refers to the fact that a light shape is never assigned to clusters it does not intersect. Even with perfect clustering the shading pass will perform some unnecessary shading calculations due to parts of the clusters not being covered by the shape, as can be seen in the Figure 21.16. Smaller clusters will give less empty space for an assigned shape and give better shading times.

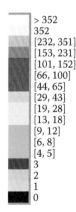

Figure 21.17. Weather radar colors corresponding to the number of lighting calculations.

(a) Clustered shading using $24 \times 12 \times 128$-E cluster structure.

(b) Tiled shading using 96×48 tiled structure.

Figure 21.18. Comparison between AMD's Forward+ tiled light culling demo using 2048 point lights and 2048 spot lights. Legend can be viewed in Figure 21.17.

The results from comparing AMD's Forward+ tiled light culling with the $24 \times 12 \times 128$-E cluster structure (following the legend in Figure 21.17) are demonstrated in Figures 21.18, 21.19, and 21.20. The colors correspond to the number of lighting calculations, where lower is better. AMD's tiled light culling implementations uses 96×48 tiles, using 6488064 bytes video memory and performing the light assignment in 0.6 ms on average. The $24 \times 12 \times 128$-E cluster structure uses a total of 8349696 bytes video memory including the 4096 render targets, as this comparison uses 2048 point lights and 2048 spot lights with the same light setup as AMD's demo. The clustered light assignment case takes 0.63 ms on average.

Figure 21.18 clearly shows that tiled light culling suffers from depth discontinuities and that at comparable performance the clustered light assignment performs better light assignment over all as well as having no depth discontinuities. The same is true when looking at the light types individually in Figures 21.19 and 21.20, but the spot light comparison also shows a significant reduction in

(a) Clustered shading using 24 × 12 × 128-E cluster structure.   (b) Tiled shading using 96 × 48 tiled structure.

Figure 21.19. Comparison between AMD's Forward+ tiled light culling demo using 2048 point lights and no spot lights. Legend can be viewed in Figure 21.17.

 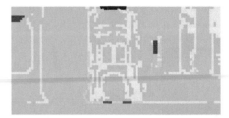

(a) Clustered shading using 24 × 12 × 128-E cluster structure.   (b) Tiled shading using 96 × 48 tiled structure.

Figure 21.20. Comparison between AMD's Forward+ tiled light culling demo using no point lights and 2048 spot lights. Legend can be viewed in Figure 21.17.

lighting calculations when using clustered light assignment. This proves both that approximating light types as spheres is detrimental to shading performance when using non-spherical light types and that using conservative rasterization with light meshes is efficient.

21.5.4 Depth Distribution

Figure 21.21 displays the negative side of having a perspective cluster structure with exponential depth distribution. Clusters far away will always be larger than the ones up close, and they will accumulate more lights, causing a large worst-case shading time for pixels in the red zone. Using a cluster structure with a large amount of clusters will mitigate the worst case, but the same ratio between worst and best case is still present. Using a linear depth distribution will reduce the worst case but at the same time increase the best case times. Figure 21.22 shows how linear depth distribution covers more empty space where the exponential depth distribution is very fine grained and follows the structure of the pillar. The small clusters are what create a very good best case, but as can

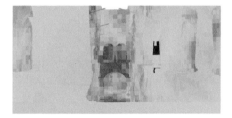

(a) 24 × 12 × 32 cluster structure.   (b) 48 × 24 × 128 cluster structure.

Figure 21.21. Two screen captures that show the number of lights used for shading each pixel. In this scene, 4096 lights are used: Green is 1 light, blue is 19 lights, and red is 38 or more lights. Values in between are interpolated colors.

(a) Linear depth distribution.   (b) Exponential depth distribution.

Figure 21.22. Two screen captures that show clusters close to the camera. Side view. Cluster structure size is 48 × 24 × 128.

be seen in Figure 21.23, the exponential depth distribution causes large clusters far from the camera as opposed to the linear distribution. Note that the depth distribution only affects the slice depth of the clusters, and even when increasing the number of cluster slices, making them thinner, the x- and y-size will remain the same. Increasing the number of slices will give better light assignment but will experience diminishing returns at a certain point due to the clusters still being large in the x- and y-dimensions and capturing many lights.

(a) Linear depth distribution.   (b) Exponential depth distribution.

Figure 21.23. Two screen captures that show clusters far from the camera. Top-down view. Cluster structure size is $48 \times 24 \times 128$.

Figure 21.12 shows that the exponential depth distribution, compared to linear depth distribution, results in better shading times in all cases. This is, however, not the case when looking at Figure 21.14, where both the $24 \times 12 \times 32$ and $24 \times 12 \times 64$ cluster structures have better shading times when using a linear depth distribution. This is caused by the fact that those cluster structures contain large clusters far away from the camera. This does not become an issue in a scene with few lights as the worst case large clusters only make up a minority of the shading cost. When a large amount of lights are used in the scene, the worst-case large clusters will be a majority of the shading cost. As can be seen in the cases where the clusters are smaller, the exponential depth distribution gives a better shading time.

There is a correlation between cluster shape and light assignment results where a cube-like cluster shape provides a good base shape. Looking at clusters structures $24 \times 12 \times 128$-E and $48 \times 24 \times 32$-E in Figure 21.14, where both contain the same amount of clusters, it is evident that the more cube-like clusters in $24 \times 12 \times 128$-E results in better performance. The performance increase gained when going from $24 \times 12 \times 128$-L to $24 \times 12 \times 128$-E is attributed to the exponential distribution creating cube-like clusters as opposed to the linear distribution, but 48x24x32-L does not benefit from going to $48 \times 24 \times 32$-E as the clusters will still have a dominant slice depth compared to the x- and y-dimensions.

21.6 Conclusion

This chapter has presented a novel technique for assigning arbitrarily shaped convex light types to clusters using conservative rasterization with good results and performance. The technique is not limited to clusters as many steps can be shared with a tiled shading implementation, nor is the technique limited to deferred shading. Using the technique to shade transparent object works without having to modify anything, and there is no requirement for a depth prepass.

Looking at the results in Section 21.5, it can be concluded that doing a finer clustering will be worthwhile as the shading pass becomes faster. Using costly shading models with many lights will increase the shading time significantly, while the light assignment will stay constant and be a minor part of the entire cost. With that said, there is a drawback of doing fine clustering: the memory usage. The total memory usage for the $48 \times 24 \times 128$ cluster structure at 4096 lights adds up to 45.4 MB, while the $24 \times 12 \times 64$ cluster structure uses 6.9 MB. The larger cluster structure achieves 28.3% better shading performance at a cost of using 6.6 times more memory.

As for finding the right cluster setup, the results have proven that cluster shape and size matters and that large and unevenly shaped clusters will be detrimental to the shading performance compared to cube-like clusters. Using an exponential depth distribution can help create cube-like clusters and gain some performance compared to linear depth distribution. However, if there are too few slices, the exponential structure will suffer from very large, far away clusters and provide worse light assignment.

Bibliography

[Andersson 09] Johan Andersson. "Parallel Graphics in Frostbite—Current and Future." Beyond Programmable Shading, SIGGRAPH Course, New Orleans, LA, August 3–7, 2009.

[Balestra and Engstad 08] Christophe Balestra and Pål-Kristian Engstad. "The Technology of Uncharted: Drake's Fortune." Game Developers Conference, San Francisco, CA, February 18–22, 2008.

[Fauconneau 14] Mark Fauconneau. "Forward Clustered Shading." https://software.intel.com/sites/default/files/managed/27/5e/Fast%20Foward%20Clustered%20Shading%20(siggraph%202014).pdf, 2014. Accessed May 20, 2015.

[Harada et al. 13] Takahiro Harada, Jay McKee, and Jason C. Yang. "Forward+: A Step Toward Film-Style Shading in Real Time." In *GPU Pro 4: Advanced Rendering Techniques*, edited by Wolfgang Engel, pp. 115–135. Boca Raton: A K Peters/CRC Press, 2013.

[Leadbetter 14] Richard Leadbetter. "The Making of Forza Horizon 2." http://www.eurogamer.net/articles/digitalfoundry-2014-the-making-of-forza-horizon-2, 2014. Accessed May 18, 2015.

[Microsoft] Microsoft. "Floating-Point Rules." https://msdn.microsoft.com/en-us/library/windows/desktop/jj218760(v=vs.85).aspx. Accessed May 18, 2015.

[Möller and Trumbore 05] Tomas Möller and Ben Trumbore. "Fast, Minimum Storage Ray/Triangle Intersection." In *ACM SIGGRAPH 2005 Courses*, article no. 7. New York: ACM, 2005.

[Olsson and Assarsson 11] Ola Olsson and Ulf Assarsson. "Tiled Shading." *Journal of Graphics, GPU, and Game Tools* 15:4 (2011), 235–251.

[Olsson et al. 12] Ola Olsson, Markus Billeter, and Ulf Assarsson. "Clustered Deferred and Forward Shading." In *Proceedings of the Fourth ACM SIGGRAPH/Eurographics Conference on High-Performance Graphics*, pp. 87–96. Aire-la-Ville, Switzerland: Eurographics Association, 2012.

[Persson and Olsson 13] Emil Persson and Ola Olsson. "Practical Clustered Deferred and Forward Shading." Advances in Real-Time Rendering in Games, SIGGRAPH Course, Anaheim, CA, July 23, 2013. Available online (http://s2013.siggraph.org/attendees/courses/session/advances-real-time-rendering-games-part-i).

[Swoboda 09] Matt Swoboda. "Deferred Lighting and Post Processing on Playstation 3." Game Developers Conference, San Francisco, CA, March 23–27, 2009.

[Thomas 15] Gareth Thomas. "Advanced Visual Effects with DirectX 11 and 12: Advancements in Tile-Based Compute Rendering." Game Developers Conference, San Francisco, CA, March 2–6, 2015. Available online (http://www.gdcvault.com/play/1021764/Advanced-Visual-Effects-With-DirectX).

[Yang et al. 10] Jason C. Yang, Justin Hensley, Holger Grün, and Nicolas Thibieroz. "Real-Time Concurrent Linked List Construction on the GPU." *Computer Graphics Forum* 29:4 (2010), 1297–1304.

22

Fine Pruned Tiled Light Lists
Morten S. Mikkelsen

22.1 Overview

In this chapter we present a new tiled lighting variant with a primary focus on optimization for the AMD Graphics Core Next (GCN) architecture. Our approach was used for the game *Rise of the Tomb Raider*. In particular, we leverage asynchronous compute by interleaving light list generation with rendering of shadow maps. Light list generation is done per tile in two steps within the same compute kernel. An initial coarse pass that generates a light list in local storage using simple screen-space AABB bounding volume intersection testing regardless of light type. The second step is fine pruning, which performs further testing on the coarse list by testing each pixel in the tile if the point in 3D space is inside the true shape of the light source.

Furthermore, we present an efficient hybrid solution between tiled deferred and tiled forward.

22.2 Introduction

Traditionally, real-time deferred lighting is done using alpha blending to accumulate lighting contributions one light at a time. The main big advantage is the ability to assign and apply lights specifically to pixels representing points in 3D space inside the light volume. With a basic forward-lit shading model, on the other hand, light lists are built on the CPU per mesh instance based on bounding volume intersection tests between the mesh instance and the light volumes. This approach often results in a significant overhead in light count to process per pixel, particularly for large meshes because the light list is shared for all pixels occupied on screen by the mesh instance.

Recently, since the introduction of DirectX 11, compute-based tiled lighting has become a popular alternative to deferred lighting. Tiled lighting works by representing the frame buffer as an $n \times m$ grid of tiles where the tiles are of a fixed resolution. The GPU is used to generate a list of indices per tile containing

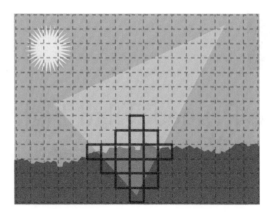

Figure 22.1. The screen separated into tiles. A spot light is shown intersecting with the foreground. This light is added to the light list of every tile containing a valid intersection, which is indicated here with a solid tile boundary.

references to the lights overlapping screen boundaries of a tile. A lighting pass pulls the light list from the tile containing the currently processed pixel (see Figure 22.1).

This is a high-level overview of how a basic tiled lighting scheme works in compute:

1. Per tile

    (a) For each tile find a minimum and a maximum depth in the depth buffer.

    (b) Each thread checks a disjoint subset of lights by bounding sphere against tile bounds.

    (c) Indices to lights intersecting the tile are stored in local data storage (LDS).

    (d) Final list is available to all threads for further processing.

Recently several proposed methods for tiled lighting have emerged such as AMD's Forward+ Tiled Lighting [Harada et al. 12], which is primarily aimed at moving away from traditional deferred lighting in order to leverage EQAA. This method partitions tiles evenly by depth into cells, thus making it a 3D grid of light lists $n \times m \times l$. Culling is performed by testing the bounding sphere of the light against the side planes of the tile frustum and the near and far plane of the cells. Another known variant is Insomniacs' Light Linked List [Bezrati 14], which proposes a solution where the footprint of the light lists is reduced/managed using linked lists on the GPU. Another variant is Clustered Deferred and Forward

Shading [Olsson et al. 12], which reduces tile occupancy further by clustering. This achieves a more ideal partitioning of tiles into cells.

Among main advantages of tiled lighting are the following:

1. Tiled deferred lighting is single pass since each pixel is lit simply by looping over the lights referenced by the list stored in the corresponding tile. This makes the approach more resilient to overlapping lights than traditional deferred lighting because the data in the G-buffer is only pulled once and because the resulting color is only written to the frame buffer once.

2. Unlike traditional deferred lighting, there exists a forward variant when using tiled lighting. The reason is that as we draw the polygonal meshes, we can pull the same light list in-process from the tile containing the pixel being shaded.

3. A less commonly known advantage to using tiled lighting is that the light list generation is an ideal candidate for asynchronous compute, which allows us to interleave this processing with unrelated graphics work earlier in the frame update.

Previous methods such as [Harada et al. 12] and [Olsson et al. 12] have excess lights in the per tile light lists because these are built based on a simple bounding spheres intersection test. Additional redundancy exists with all previous techniques because the cells contain significant amounts of unoccupied space. In AAA games many of our lights are not spheres, and in fact, we must support several light shapes such as cones, capsules, and boxes with different features. Building lists based on bounding volumes and partitioned tile bounds alone leaves much redundancy in the light lists compared to the final list we end up with when fine pruning.

We found that by writing a lean dedicated compute shader to perform fine pruning, we were able to achieve significant gains due to the more complex shader used for lighting not having to deal with the redundant lights in the list. Furthermore, the separation between light list building and actual lighting allowed us to run the list building in asynchronous compute during rendering of shadow maps, which in practice gives us fine pruned lists for free.

Furthermore, our approach is a hybrid between tiled deferred and tiled forward lighting. This allows us to light the majority of pixels by a deferred approach using a narrow G-buffer, which is more hardware efficient, and then deviate from this for cases where we need a material-specific lighting model by using tiled forward.

22.3 Our Method

Previous papers on tiled lighting such as [Harada et al. 12] and [Olsson et al. 12] are particularly aimed at processing high quantities of sphere lights. The numbers quoted are in the 1–2 thousand range. Furthermore, these papers describe algorithms that are designed to handle scenarios where the lights have a relatively optimal distribution in space. While our method is also capable of handling high numbers of lights, we found we generally have no more than 40–120 lights inside the camera frustum in our real world levels. In our case we found that we often have fewer very large lights that occupy the same space. Many of our lights are large spot lights that are narrow to achieve a good distribution of pixels in the shadow map. The bounding sphere is a bad representation in this case. Ultimately, without additional culling, our light lists would contain high numbers of lights, several of which do not affect any of the actual tile pixels.

In every frame we receive a set of lights that have been classified visible (inside the camera frustum) by the cell and portal system. For each tile on the screen, we generate a *fine pruned light list*. Each light is included only if at least one pixel in the tile represents a point in 3D space that is inside the light volume. Testing all pixels in a tile against all visible lights is prohibitively expensive. To solve this, we first build a *coarse light list* containing lights whose screen-space axis aligned bounding box (AABB) intersects the tile boundary. The tile boundary is trivially defined by its xy-region on the screen and minimum and maximum depths in the depth buffer within tile region. We determine, on the GPU, the screen-space AABB around each visible light.

The process is described below in pseudo-code.

1. Per camera

   (a) On the CPU find lights that intersect the camera frustum.

   (b) Sort this set of lights by shape.

   (c) On the GPU find the tight screen-space AABB per light source regardless of shape. This is done by finding the intersection volume between the camera and a convex hull for the light. We further constrain the AABB using a bounding sphere of the light.

2. Per 16×16 pixel tile

   (a) For each tile find a minimum and a maximum depth in the depth buffer.

   (b) Each compute thread tests the intersection of a disjoint subset of lights by an AABB against tile bounds.

   (c) Indices to lights intersecting the tile are stored in LDS. We refer to this as the *coarse list*.

   (d) In the same kernel loop over the coarse list of lights.

       i. Each thread tests four pixels of the tile depth buffer to see if these are inside the true shape of the light.

      ii. The status of the test is stored in a bit field maintained by each thread where each bit represents the corresponding coarse light.

    (e) Perform a bitwise OR of all bit fields into a single bit field and use it to generate a *fine pruned light list*.

The distinction between fine pruning and performing an early out during lighting is, in concept, subtle. However, the difference is significant for two reasons. First, the shader associated with lighting consumes more resources relative to a lean shader dedicated to culling, which, as we describe in the next section, has implications on performance. Second, by using asynchronous compute, we can absorb most of the cost of fine pruning, which includes the cost of looping through redundant lights.

22.4   Implementation Details

In the following we are targeting the AMD GCN architecture specifically, though the practices are generally good for any modern-day GPU. A modern GPU core hides latency by shuffling through jobs. We will refer to these cores as a CU (compute unit). All work is packaged into wavefronts. Whether it is compute, vertex shading, pixel shading, etc., each CU can harbor up to 40 wavefronts, and each wavefront represents 64 threads. These threads run in lock-step similar to how SSE4 is 4 wide running in lock-step. The pool of resources such as registers and local store LDS are shared on each CU, which implies that the more you consume these, the fewer jobs get to occupy each CU, which means the GPU's ability to hide latencies deteriorates dramatically.

As it turns out, the rendering of shadow maps and generation of fine pruned light lists are a great match. According to our timings, shadow map rendering generally takes 2–4 ms in our game. Furthermore, it is a process that generates very few wavefronts of work and relies primarily on the primitive scan converter and trafficking of data. The reason for this is that shadow map rendering is a depth-only pass, which means no actual pixel shading CU work is generated for opaque meshes. Generating fine pruned light lists, on the other hand, is primarily propagating ALU-heavy wavefronts. This allows us to absorb most of the time spent on generating the lists using asynchronous compute.

Let us describe the algorithm steps in detail. First, Step 1(a) is to gather all visible lights in the frame. We do this using a typical cell and portal system on the CPU.

In Step 1(b) we sort, on the CPU, the visible lights by their type of shape. This allows us to process the lights using a fixed sequence of loops where each loop is dedicated to a specific light type. This is particularly important in the context of tiled forward lighting since in this case the 64 pixels being processed in a wavefront do often not exist in the same tile. Because the 64 threads run in lock-step, a divergence in execution path is inefficient. Having sorted the lights by type maximizes the likelihood that all threads are in alignment execution path-wise. In our case sphere/capsule is one type/execution path, cone/wedge is a type, and box is the final type.

Next, in Step 1(c) we find the screen-space AABB for each light in the visible set. As input each light source is represented by an oriented bounding box (OBB) with a nonuniform scale at the top four vertices, which allows us to represent narrow spot lights and wedges better. To determine the AABB for the light, we find the point set to the intersection volume between the camera frustum and the convex bounding volume. This is done by frustum clipping the quads of the scaled OBB and using the final point set of each resulting fan to update the AABB. Any of the eight points of the camera frustum that are inside the convex bounding volume must also be applied to the fitting of the AABB. Last, we determine the AABB around the bounding sphere of the light and then store the intersection between this and the already established AABB as the final result. It should be noted that though this is a lot of processing, it is done once per camera and *not per tile*. This work can be done on the CPU but we do it on the GPU as an asynchronous compute shader.

In Step 2 the work of generating the final per-tile light list is performed, and we describe the various components to it in the following. All the parts within Step 2 are performed on a per-tile level within one compute kernel. Since the tile size is 16×16 pixels, the dispatch of the kernel is executed using the following threadgroup counts: (width + 15)/16, (height + 15)/16, and 1. The kernel is declared as a single wavefront threadgroup: $64 \times 1 \times 1$.

First, in Step 2(a) we must establish the screen-space AABB associated with the tile being operated on by the threadgroup. Each of the 64 threads reads four individual depths of the tile and establish the minimum and maximum of the four samples. Next, the collective minimum and maximum of the tile is established using `InterlockedMin()` and `InterlockedMax()`, which are HLSL intrinsic functions.

In Steps 2(b)–(c) we perform the initial coarse pruning test. Each of the visible lights will have its screen-space AABB tested for intersection against the AABB of the tile regardless of the true light shape. Each thread handles a disjoint subset of lights and thus performs `numVisibleLights`/64 iterations. Furthermore, using a single wavefront threadgroup allows us to preserve the order of the lights passing the coarse test because the 64 threads run in lock-step. The resulting coarse list of indices to lights is stored in LDS.

It is worth noting that the screen-space AABB corresponds to a sheared sub-frustum in the camera space, as shown in Figure 22.2. In [Harada et al. 12] and [Olsson et al. 12] tiled lighting is implemented such that the bounding sphere around each light is tested against the frustum planes associated with each tile. However, we can do the same test faster when we already know the screen-space AABB for each light. This also allows for a tighter fit than a bounding sphere around certain light types, such as a spot light, which allows us to spend less

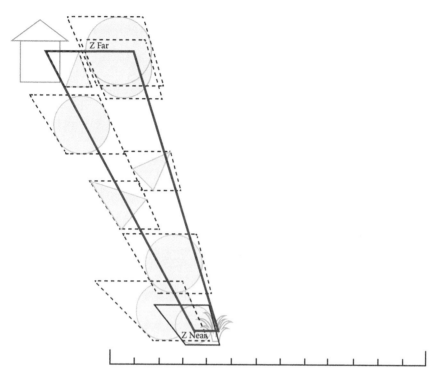

Figure 22.2. The sheared frustum associated with a tile from the frontmost pixel to the one farthest away. In this case there are six sphere lights and three spot lights. All nine lights pass the coarse intersection test but only one passes the fine pruned intersection test.

time on fine pruning. Potentially using AABB for the test also leads to a lower register count since we no longer need to keep six frustum planes for the tile in registers during iteration through the lights.

Finally, in Steps 2(d)–(e) we perform fine pruning. The fine pruned light list is a subset of the coarse light list. Each pixel in the tile is tested to see if the corresponding point in 3D space is inside the true shape of the light volume. Lights that contain one or more such points are put in the fine pruned light list. Each thread is responsible for testing 2×2 pixels of the 16×16 tile (1×1 for half-resolution lighting), and each thread maintains a record in the form of a 64-bit mask where each bit is enabled if the volume of the corresponding light contains at least one of the four points managed by the thread. Once we have processed all coarse lights in this manner, we finally determine the collective 64-bit mask by using the HLSL intrinsic `InterlockedOr()`. The resulting bit mask is used to remove redundancies from the coarse light list and write the final fine pruned list to memory. The effect of fine pruning is shown in Figure 22.2.

A CU has both vector and scalar registers. For a vector register VGPR, every thread has an individual dword, which gives a total footprint of 256 bytes per register. A scalar register SGPR is a dword that is shared for all threads with a total of 4 bytes per register. As mentioned at the beginning of this section, a high consumption of resources by a shader has a negative impact on performance. A shader used for lighting often consumes a relatively high amount of vector registers due to the overall complexity in code. If we can ensure during lighting that every thread of a wavefront represents a pixel in the same tile and thus pulls the same light list, then the attributes of the light such as color, position, fall-off, etc. can be pulled into SGPRs instead of VGPRs. It is easy to organize the treads accordingly in a compute shader; however, as will be discussed in the next section, we are using a full-screen stencil tested pixel shader for the final deferred lighting pass. This means that we are no longer in direct control of how the wavefronts are packaged. For a full-screen primitive we can ensure that the pixel shader wavefronts are fully packaged as 8×8 pixels by calling `SetScanConverterModeControl(false, false)` on the pixel shader used for deferred tiled lighting at initialization time. In addition to this, we must also run the pass after high stencil testing but before the low stencil test to maintain the execution in blocks of 8×8. Finally, we must inform the shader compiler to pull the attributes as scalar as opposed to vector. This is done by using the HLSL intrinsic `__XB_MakeUniform()` wherever we pull data from the tile.

For us this resulted in a drop from 76 to 52 in VGPRs and up to about a 1.3-ms reduction in execution time. In comparison, our kernel for generating fine pruned light lists consumes only 28 VGPRs, which as expected is much less.

The API calls mentioned above are for Xbox One only, though we suspect the equivalent API calls exist for Playstation 4 as well. No equivalent exists in the generic DirectX 11 API, though, so in this case there are two options: Either settle for vector registers on this platform, which preserves the stencil optimize, or alternatively implement the deferred lighting as a compute shader. In the latter case we would read the stencil as a texture look-up in the compute shader and perform the stencil test manually to avoid lighting the pixel twice.

22.5   Engine Integration

In order to achieve greater flexibility in shaders, it has become common to use a wide G-buffer to allow storage of more parameters. However, this consumes larger amounts of memory and puts a significant strain on the bus. It was an early decision that our game must run at 1920×1080; to achieve this, we decided to use a prepass deferred implementation, which is described in [Engel 09], with a narrow G-buffer. Our G-buffer contains a depth buffer and normal and specular power in signed R8G8B8A8 format. The sign bit of the specular power is used to indicate whether Fresnel is to be enabled or disabled on the specular reflection. The lean footprint allows us to leverage fast ESRAM on Xbox One.

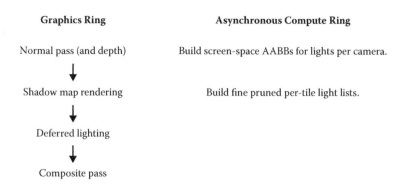

Figure 22.3. Our primary stages running on the main command buffer (left) and our asynchronous compute work (right). Generation of AABBs is interleaved with the normal-depth pass, and generation of fine pruned per-tile light lists is interleaved with rendering of the shadow maps.

The stages of our prepass rendering pipeline are shown on the left side of Figure 22.3. The geometry is rendered to the screen twice. The first time is the normal-depth pass that creates the G-buffer as depth, with world-space normal and specular power. The second time the geometry is rendered to the screen is the composite pass, which is the last stage. This stage does the shading and folds in the lighting. Rendering of shadow maps comes after the normal-depth pass, while generation of per-tile light lists is scheduled to run at the same time as an asynchronous compute job. The next stage is deferred lighting, which runs as a full-screen pass. Each pixel is lit by accumulating contributions from lights stored in the list associated with the tile to which the pixel belongs. We write the final diffuse and specular results to separate render targets, which allows us to modulate these by different textures during the final composite pass.

To achieve custom lighting on certain materials such as eyes, skin, and cloth, we use tiled forward lighting. In this case the lighting is done in-process during the composite pass by pulling and processing the light list for the tile similar to how we do this during deferred lighting. This presents a problem since we will pay the cost of lighting the pixel both deferred and forward. To solve this problem, we mark every pixel in the stencil buffer that is lit as tiled forward. During deferred lighting, we skip such pixels by using stencil testing.

In regards to the format of the per-tile light list, it can be stored in a number of ways. The obvious option is one buffer for the whole screen where each tile consumes some fixed number of 8-bit or 16-bit entries for the light indices. Using 8 bits will only allow for 256 lights on screen, and 16 bits give more range than we need. To achieve a more compact footprint, we chose to store the list as blocks of R10G10B10A2_UINT, where the 10-bit components each store an index to a light and the 2-bit component tells us how many of the three indices are active. We store eight such blocks per tile, which results in a final limit of 24 lights per tile after fine pruning. As previously mentioned, we allow up to 64 lights in the coarse list while in LDS. The total footprint for eight such blocks is 32 bytes per tile and thus 1 bit per pixel on screen. Note that 10-bit indices indicate a limit of 1024 lights intersecting the camera frustum per frame.

In our implementation we use separate light lists for direct lights and probe lights, each with a limit of 24 per tile. It is important to note that the light list generation is executed *once only*. This is possible since up to 64 fine pruned lights may exist temporarily on the compute side during the execution of Step 2(e). Subsequently, in this step we separate these in LDS according to their designated light list.

As mentioned in the introduction, it is common for a tiled lighting implementation to partition the tile farther along depth into cells, as is done in [Olsson et al. 12]. This grows the footprint further because each cell stores a separate list of lights. A different problem with this strategy during deferred lighting is that each thread may pull the list of lights from a different cell than other threads in the wavefront. This forces us to pull the attributes of the lights into vector registers instead of scalar registers, which as mentioned in the previous section reduces our ability to populate more wavefronts per CU, which reduces our ability to hide latency on the GPU. Ultimately, we found that the act of fine pruning our lists of lights removes most redundancies in practice, which negates the need for partitioning into cells. This is also indicated in Figure 22.2 and evident from the heat map in the next section.

One limitation when using our method is that the generated lists only work for opaque surfaces that write to a depth buffer. In our case the majority of transparencies are particle effects with many stacked layers occupying the same local space. We concluded that we could not afford to light these per pixel as it would be too costly, and we decided to light these using vertex lighting.

For regular mesh-based transparencies, we decided to use traditional forward lighting where light lists are built on the CPU for each mesh based on a bounding volume intersection. Since our transparent surfaces are sorted on a per-material basis, these are not large meshes and thus do not benefit as much from tiled light lists. Additionally, we support *light groups*, which allow artists to manually remove specific lights from the light lists of traditionally forward-lit objects. This feature allows them to prune the list to the most essential set of lights that intersect the transparent surface.

22.6   Results

In this section we show an interior scene running at 1920×1080 with and without fine pruning. Figure 22.4 shows the results of coarse culling. The coarse list generation takes 0.5 ms and runs asynchronously. Figure 22.5 shows the results

Figure 22.4. Number of lights per tile after coarse culling.

after fine pruning, which costs 1.7 ms in list generation. The cost is however well hidden because of asynchronous compute. The heat map in Figure 22.6 indicates the occupancy of lights per tile in Figures 22.4 and 22.5. We can see that the light counts without fine pruning are significantly higher in almost every tile. As expected, we see a significant drop in execution time of deferred lighting, dropping from 5.4 ms to 1.4 ms with fine pruning enabled.

22.7 Conclusion

We have demonstrated a new tiled lighting variant that performs light list generation per tile in two steps within the same compute kernel. The initial coarse pass generates a light list in local storage based on simple screen-space AABB bounding volume intersection testing regardless of light type. The second step is fine pruning, which performs further testing on the coarse list by testing each pixel in the tile if the corresponding point in 3D space is inside the true shape of the light source. Lights that contain one or more such points are put in the fine pruned list, which is written to memory. We have found that in practice this process reduces the light count per tile significantly.

On the AMD GCN architecture a depth-only pass of opaque meshes generates very little work for the GPU cores. We take advantage of this fact by using asynchronous compute to hide most of the combined cost of the coarse and the fine pruning steps by interleaving this work with the rendering of shadow maps, which gives no redundancy light lists for free.

Figure 22.5. Number of lights per tile after fine pruning.

0   1   2   3   4   6   8   11   15   19   24

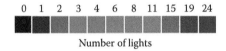

Number of lights

Figure 22.6. Color heatmap with number of lights per tile.

While supporting multiple light types, the final footprint for the light list is 1 bit per pixel with a maximum number of 24 fine pruned lights per tile.

Finally, an efficient hybrid between tiled deferred and tiled forward is presented where tiled deferred lighting is done as a stencil tested full-screen pass to avoid lighting twice for pixels that are lit by tiled forward materials. To further accelerate tiled forward, we keep the light list sorted by type in a fixed order. This allows us to maximize the chance that all pixels in a wavefront are processing lights in the same light loop.

22.8 Acknowledgments

Thank you to editor Michal Valient for his support in the development of this chapter and for his reviews. Additionally, thank you to Manchor Ko and Kasper H. Nielsen for proofreading the chapter. I would also like to thank Paul Houx at Nixxes for his excellent work and collaboration on integrating this method into the foundation engine at Crystal Dynamics. And finally, thanks go to Scott Krotz for his support and help getting asynchronous compute to work properly.

Bibliography

[Bezrati 14] Abdul Bezrati. "Real-Time Lighting via Light Linked List." Paper presented at SIGGRAPH, Vancouver, Canada, August 12–14, 2014.

[Engel 09] Wolfgang Engel. "The Light Pre-Pass Renderer: Renderer Design for Efficient Support of Multiple Lights." SIGGRAPH Course: Advances in Real-Time Rendering in 3D Graphics and Games, New Orleans, LA, August 3, 2009.

[Harada et al. 12] Takahiro Harada, Jay McKee, and Jason C. Yang. "Forward+: Bringing Deferred Lighting to the Next Level." Eurographics Short Paper, Cagliari, Italy, May 13–18, 2012.

[Olsson et al. 12] Ola Olsson, Markus Billeter, and Ulf Assarsson. "Clustered Deferred and Forward Shading." Paper presented at High Performance Graphics, Paris, France, June 25–27, 2012.

Deferred Attribute Interpolation Shading

Christoph Schied and Carsten Dachsbacher

23.1 Introduction

Deferred shading is a popular technique in real-time rendering. In contrast to a traditional rendering pipeline, deferred shading is split into two phases. First, the geometry is sampled and stored in the geometry buffer, which serves as input for the second phase where the shading is computed. Thereby, the complexity for shading is decoupled from the geometric complexity, and furthermore advanced geometry-aware screen-space techniques may be employed. However, deferred shading does not play well with multi-sample antialiasing. Multi-sample antialiasing samples the visibility of a primitive at several subpixel positions, however the shading is only evaluated once inside a pixel per primitive. Deferred shading samples the geometric attributes, and the shading is deferred into a second phase where the correspondence between primitives and visibility samples is lost, which makes it hard to avoid redundant shading. Furthermore, the geometry buffer can become prohibitively large in case of high screen resolutions and high visibility sampling because each sample needs to store all attributes.

In this chapter based on our publication [Schied and Dachsbacher 15], we present a technique to dramatically reduce the memory consumption of deferred shading in the aforementioned setting. Unlike deferred shading, our method samples solely visibility in the geometry phase and defers the attribute interpolation and material evaluation to the shading phase. This allows us to store the data needed for shading at per-triangle instead of per-sample frequency. Compared to a G-buffer sample, storing a triangle uses more memory, but since in practice most triangles will cover several pixels, the cost is amortized across several visibility samples, which leads to a significant reduction in the overall memory cost. Visible triangles are identified in the geometry phase and stored in the triangle buffer. The geometry buffer is replaced by a visibility buffer [Burns and Hunt 13],

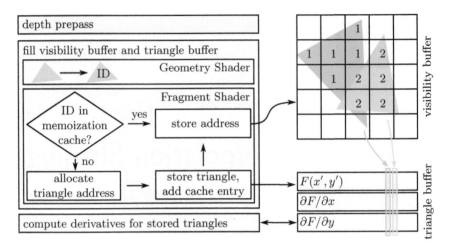

Figure 23.1. The first phase of our algorithm that samples the visibility of triangles. A depth prepass is performed to ensure that in the second geometry pass only visible triangles will generate fragment shader invocations. In the second pass, each triangle is first assigned an ID that is used in the fragment shader as a lookup into the memoization cache that stores mappings between triangle IDs and physical addresses. In case the cache does not contain the mapping yet, a new entry is allocated in the triangle buffer, the triangle is stored, and the new address is added to the cache. Finally, for each triangle the screen-space partial derivatives, needed for attribute interpolation, are computed in a separate pass.

which stores references in the triangle buffer. To enable efficient attribute interpolation during shading, triangles are represented using partial derivatives of the attributes.

23.2 Algorithm

Similar to deferred shading, the drawing of a frame is split into two phases. In the first phase all visible triangles are determined and stored in the triangle buffer. (See Figure 23.1.) Furthermore the visibility buffer is populated with references to these triangles. In the second phase the triangle attributes are interpolated and the shading is computed. Our method stores visible triangles after vertex transformations have been applied. Therefore, vertex transformations do not need to be carried out during the shading phase, and furthermore this makes our method compatible with the use of tessellation shaders. Compared to deferred shading, we introduce the cut in the pipeline at an earlier stage, i.e., before attribute interpolation and material evaluation. The following sections describe the attribute interpolation as well as the two rendering phases in more detail.

23.2.1 Attribute Interpolation Using Partial Derivatives

Interpolation of vertex attributes a_i with respect to a triangle is commonly done by barycentric weighting of all attributes. The barycentric coordinates λ_i of a point (x, y) with respect to a triangle with points $p_i = (u_i, v_i)$ can be computed as a ratio of areas by

$$
\begin{aligned}
\lambda_1(x, y) &= \frac{(v_2 - v_3)(x - u_3) + (u_3 - u_2)(y - v_3)}{D}, \\
\lambda_2(x, y) &= \frac{(v_3 - v_1)(x - u_3) + (u_1 - u_3)(y - v_3)}{D}, \\
\lambda_3(x, y) &= 1 - \lambda_1(x, y) - \lambda_2(x, y),
\end{aligned}
\tag{23.1}
$$

where $D = \det(p_3 - p_2, p_1 - p_2)$. The interpolated attribute is then determined as

$$
\tilde{a}(x, y) = \sum_{i=1}^{3} \lambda_i(x, y) \cdot a_i .
\tag{23.2}
$$

Because $\lambda_i(x, y)$ is linear in the x- and y-directions, the partial derivatives with respect to x, y are constant, and Equation (23.2) can be reformulated as

$$
\begin{aligned}
\tilde{a}(x, y) &= a_{x'y'} + (x - x') \sum_i \frac{\partial \lambda_i}{\partial x} \cdot a_i + (y - y') \sum_i \frac{\partial \lambda_i}{\partial y} \cdot a_i \\
&= a_{x'y'} + (x - x') \frac{\partial a}{\partial x} + (y - y') \frac{\partial a}{\partial y},
\end{aligned}
\tag{23.3}
$$

assuming that the attribute $a_{x'y'}$ is known for an arbitrary sample point (x', y'). (See Figure 23.2.)

For projected triangles defined in four-dimensional homogenous coordinates with the vertices (x_i, y_i, z_i, w_i), a perspective correction needs to be applied when interpolating attributes. This correction is done by interpolating a_i/w_i and $1/w_i$ linearly in the screen space and dividing the interpolants afterward. This leads to an interpolation scheme defined as $a(x, y) = (\sum \lambda_i a_i/w_i)/(\sum \lambda_i/w_i)$. Reformulating this expression similar to Equation (23.3) leads to

$$
a(x, y) = \frac{\frac{a_{x'y'}}{w_{x'y'}} + (x - x')\frac{\partial a/w}{\partial x} + (y - y')\frac{\partial a/w}{\partial y}}{\frac{1}{w_{x'y'}} + (x - x')\frac{\partial 1/w}{\partial x} + (y - y')\frac{\partial 1/w}{\partial y}}.
\tag{23.4}
$$

Assuming that the triangle has been clipped and projected to the screen, the partial derivatives of the attributes can be computed as

$$
\frac{\partial a/w}{\partial x} = \sum_i \frac{\partial \lambda_i}{\partial x} \cdot \frac{a_i}{w_i}, \qquad \frac{\partial a/w}{\partial y} = \sum_i \frac{\partial \lambda_i}{\partial y} \cdot \frac{a_i}{w_i},
\tag{23.5}
$$

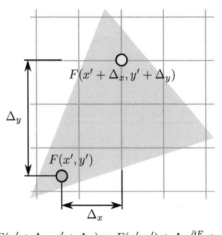

$$F(x' + \Delta_x, y' + \Delta_y) = F(x', y') + \Delta_x \tfrac{\partial F}{\partial x} + \Delta_y \tfrac{\partial F}{\partial y}$$

Figure 23.2. A sample of the attribute is stored at a sample point (green). The attribute can be interpolated at an arbitrary position (yellow) by weighting the partial derivatives in the x- and y-directions by their respective screen-space distances Δ_x and Δ_y.

whereas the partial derivatives of the barycentric coordinates are derived from Equation (23.1) as

$$\frac{\partial \lambda_1}{\partial x} = \frac{y_2 - y_3}{D}, \quad \frac{\partial \lambda_2}{\partial x} = \frac{y_3 - y_1}{D}, \quad \frac{\partial \lambda_3}{\partial x} = \frac{y_1 - y_2}{D},$$

$$\frac{\partial \lambda_1}{\partial y} = \frac{x_3 - x_2}{D}, \quad \frac{\partial \lambda_2}{\partial y} = \frac{x_1 - x_3}{D}, \quad \frac{\partial \lambda_3}{\partial y} = \frac{x_2 - x_1}{D}. \tag{23.6}$$

23.2.2   Visibility Sampling Phase

The first phase employs two geometry passes to identify and store visible triangles. A depth prepass is performed that constrains the fragment shader execution in the second pass to visible surfaces. Therefore, we can use the fragment shader in the second geometry pass to store visible triangles. Since it is our goal to share the triangle data across several visibility samples, we need to ensure that triangles are uniquely stored. Additionally, the address of the stored triangle needs to be communicated to all fragment shader invocations, which store the address in the visibility buffer. We assign each triangle a unique ID and use a memoization cache that stores mappings between triangle IDs and physical addresses. This allows each fragment shader invocation to query the cache if the triangle is already stored, and thereby get the physical address of the triangle. If a requested triangle ID is not found in the cache, one invocation is selected to allocate space in the triangle buffer and to store the ID-to-address mapping in the cache. Finally, the triangle is stored by the same invocation in the triangle buffer. All invocations store the physical address in the visibility buffer.

23.2.3 Shading Phase

Because the geometry pass only samples visibility and does not capture the geometric attributes per visibility sample, these attributes need to be interpolated in the shading phase. A compute pass is used to determine the partial derivatives needed to interpolate attributes, as described in Section 23.2.1 for each visible triangle.

During shading the visible triangles can be determined per pixel using a lookup into the visibility buffer. The precomputed data needed for interpolation is loaded, the attributes are interpolated according to Equation (23.4), and finally the materials are evaluated.

23.2.4 Multi-rate Shading

Shading contributes a large part to the computational costs for rendering a frame and becomes increasingly expensive with growing screen resolutions. Since not all components of the shading signal are high frequency (such as, for example, indirect illumination, which is particularly costly to evaluate), such components can be sampled at reduced frequency. Our pipeline allows us to create shading samples that reference a primitive and store a screen-space position. These shading samples are referenced by an additional render target in the visibility buffer and are evaluated in a compute pass prior to shading. In the shading phase the results of the evaluated shading samples are combined with the full shading-rate signal. While it would be possible to achieve arbitrary shading-rates using a similar approach as proposed by Liktor et al. [Liktor and Dachsbacher 12], we use a simplified approach that relies on inter-thread communication inside of a shading quad.

23.3 Implementation

The following section explains our implementation that makes use of the OpenGL 4.5 API.

23.3.1 Visibility Sampling Phase

At first the depth buffer is populated with front-most surfaces by performing a depth prepass. Setting the depth test in the second geometry pass to GL_EQUAL allows us to perform alpha-clipping in the depth prepass and thus to ignore alpha in the second geometry pass. In the second pass the geometry shader is used to pass all vertices of the triangle through to the fragment shader. When using tessellation shaders, each triangle needs to be assigned a unique ID; otherwise, the language built-in variable `gl_PrimitiveID` may be used. To assign a unique ID, an atomic counter is incremented and passed through to the fragment shader. We use frustum culling in the geometry shader, which can be implemented efficiently using bit operations to reduce the number of atomic counter operations.

Early depth testing has to be enabled in the fragment shader to ensure that the fragment shader is executed for visible fragments only:

```
layout(early_fragment_tests) in;
```

In the fragment shader a lookup into the memoization cache is performed to get the physical address of the stored triangle. The return value of the lookup function tells if the triangle needs to be stored by the current invocation. Our implementation of the memoization cache closely follows the implementation by Liktor et al. [Liktor and Dachsbacher 12]. It is explained in depth in Section 23.3.2.

The fragment shader stores all vertices of the triangle in the triangle buffer, whereas in a later pass the vertices are overwritten by their partial derivatives, since the original vertex data is not needed anymore during shading. To reduce storage costs when storing the vertices, normal vectors are encoded to 32 Bit using a octahedral encoding [Cigolle et al. 14]. In the beginning of the triangle struct we store a material ID what enables the use of multiple storage formats.

23.3.2 Memoization Cache

Our implementation of the memoization cache (refer to Listing 23.1) closely follows the implementation by Liktor et al. [Liktor and Dachsbacher 12]. The image buffer `locks` stores a lock for each cache bucket, where each entry can be either `LOCKED` or `UNLOCKED`. Furthermore, the `cache` image buffer stores two cache entries, each represented by a triangle ID and the corresponding address. Invalid addresses are represented by negative values. When an ID is found in a cache bucket, the found address is stored in the address variable. The return value of the function denotes if a new slot was allocated and therefore the data has to be stored by the current invocation. In the case that the cache does not contain the desired entry, a `imageAtomicExchange` operation is issued to gain exclusive access to the cache bucket. When exclusive access is granted, a new address is allocated and stored alongside the ID in the cache bucket. Older entries are removed in a FIFO manner. This strategy is reasonable because it is to be expected that fragment shader invocations are scheduled according to the rasterization order. For the same reason, a simple modulus hash-function works well with monotonically increasing triangle IDs. When the fragment shader invocation fails to gain access to the cache bucket, it waits a limited amount of time for the bucket to be unlocked and reloads the entry.

Graphics cards execute several threads in lock-step whereby diverging branches are always taken by all threads and the results are masked out accordingly af-

```
 1 layout(rgba32ui) coherent volatile restrict uimageBuffer cache;
 2 layout(r32ui)    coherent volatile restrict uimageBuffer locks;
 3
 4 bool lookup_memoization_cache(
 5   int id, int hash_mod, int triangle_size, out int address)
 6 {
 7   bool store_sample = false;
 8   int hash = id & hash_mod;
 9   uvec4 b = imageLoad(cache, hash);
10   address = get_address_from_bucket(id, b);
11   for(int k = 0; address < 0 && k < 1024; k++) {
12     // ID not found in cache, make several attempts.
13     uint lock = imageAtomicExchange(locks, hash, LOCKED);
14     if(lock == UNLOCKED) {
15       // Gain exclusive access to the bucket.
16       b = imageLoad(cache, hash);
17       address = get_address_from_bucket(id, b);
18       if(address < 0) {
19         // Allocate new storage.
20         address = int(atomicAdd(ctr_ssid[1], triangle_size));
21         b.zw = b.xy; // Update bucket FIFO.
22         b.xy = uvec2(id, address);
23         imageStore(cache, hash, b);
24         store_sample = true;
25       }
26       imageStore(locks, hash, uvec4(UNLOCKED));
27     }
28     // Use if(expr){} if(!expr){} construct to explicitly
29     // sequence the branches.
30     if(lock == LOCKED) {
31       for(int i = 0; i < 128 && lock == LOCKED; i++)
32         lock = imageLoad(locks, hash).r;
33       b = imageLoad(cache, hash);
34       address = get_address_from_bucket(id, b);
35     }
36   }
37   if(address < 0) { // Cache lookup failed, store redundantly.
38     address = int(atomicAdd(ctr_ssid[1], triangle_size));
39     store_sample = true;
40   }
41   return store_sample;
42 }
```

Listing 23.1. The memoization cache uses several `imageBuffers` to store locks as well as cache entries. An access to the cache bucket determines if the cache contains the requested ID. If it is not found, all invocations concurrently try to acquire exclusive access to the cache where the winner is allowed to allocate memory. All other invocations repeatedly poll the cache to retrieve the updated cache entry.

terward. Since an `if-else` statement does not carry any notions about the first executed branch in case of divergence, this statement must be explicitly sequenced by dividing it into two disjunct statements when it contains side effects that require explicit ordering. This is important when implementing the memoization cache because invocations should be waiting for the updated cache buckets strictly following the update step; otherwise, deadlocks might occur.

```
 1 void compute_attribute_derivatives(
 2    in Triangle triangle, out TriangleDerivatives d)
 3 {
 4    mat3x4 pos; mat3x2 tex_coord; mat3 normal;
 5    for(int i = 0; i < 3; i++) {
 6       pos[i]       = P * vec4(triangle.positions[i], 1.0);
 7       normal[i]    = triangle.normals[i];
 8       tex_coord[i] = triangle.tex_coords[i];
 9    }
10    // Clip triangle against all frustum planes.
11    for(int i = 0; i < 3; i++) {
12       shrink_triangle(pos, tex_coord, normal, i, true);
13       shrink_triangle(pos, tex_coord, normal, i, false);
14    }
15    vec3 one_over_w = 1.0 / vec3(pos[0].w, pos[1].w, pos[2].w);
16    vec2 pos_scr[3]; // projected vertices
17    for(int i = 0; i < 3; i++) {
18       pos_scr[i]    = pos[i].xy * one_over_w[i];
19       tex_coord[i] *= one_over_w[i];
20       normal[i]    *= one_over_w[i];
21    }
22    vec3 db_dx, db_dy; // Gradient barycentric coordinates x/y
23    compute_barycentric_derivatives(pos_scr, db_dx, db_dy);
24    // Compute derivatives in x/y for all attributes.
25    d.d_normal_dx = normal * db_dx;
26    d.d_normal_dy = normal * db_dy;
27    d.d_tex_dx    = tex_coord * db_dx;
28    d.d_tex_dy    = tex_coord * db_dy;
29    d.d_w_dx      = dot(one_over_w, db_dx);
30    d.d_w_dy      = dot(one_over_w, db_dy);
31    // Compute attributes shifted to (0,0).
32    vec2 o = -pos_scr[0];
33    d.one_by_w_fixed = one_over_w[0]
34                     + o.x * d.d_w_dx + o.y * d.d_w_dy;
35    d.tex_coord_fixed = tex_coord[0]
36                     + o.x * d.d_tex_dx + o.y * d.d_tex_dy;
37    d.normal_fixed = normal[0];
38                     + o.x * d.d_normal_dx + o.y * d.d_normal_dy;
39 }
```

Listing 23.2. Derivatives are computed according to Equation (23.5). First, the stored triangles are transformed into clip space and consecutively clipped against all view planes, which allows us to project them to the screen. The derivatives of the barycentric coordinates are computed according to Equation (23.1) to compute the partial derivatives for all attributes. Finally, the sample point of the attribute is extrapolated to the center of the screen to make the storage of the sample point's coordinate redundant.

23.3.3 Computing Partial Derivatives of Triangle Attributes

For the attribute interpolation, the partial derivatives need to be computed for each triangle. (Refer to Listing 23.2.) In theory it would be possible to compute the derivatives using the fragment shader built-in dFdx,dFdy functions. However, the numerical precision is not sufficient, and therefore the derivatives need to be

```
 1 void shrink_triangle(inout mat3x4 pos,  // Positions in clip space
 2                      inout mat3x2 tex,          // Texture coordinates
 3                      inout mat3   normal,       // Normals
 4                      const int axis, const bool is_min) // Clip plane
 5 {
 6   const int V0 = 1, V1 = 2, V2 = 4;
 7   uint clipmask = 0;
 8   if(is_min) {
 9     clipmask |= pos[0][axis] < -pos[0].w ? V0 : 0;
10     clipmask |= pos[1][axis] < -pos[1].w ? V1 : 0;
11     clipmask |= pos[2][axis] < -pos[2].w ? V2 : 0;
12   } else {
13     clipmask |= pos[0][axis] >  pos[0].w ? V0 : 0;
14     clipmask |= pos[1][axis] >  pos[1].w ? V1 : 0;
15     clipmask |= pos[2][axis] >  pos[2].w ? V2 : 0;
16   }
17   float a, b1, b2;
18 // Push the vertex on the edge from->to.
19 #define PUSH_VERTEX(from, to)                                       \
20     b1 = is_min ? pos[to  ][axis] : -pos[to  ][axis]; \
21     b2 = is_min ? pos[from][axis] : -pos[from][axis]; \
22     a = (pos[to].w + b1)                              \
23         / (pos[to].w - pos[from].w + b1 - b2);        \
24     pos[from]    = mix(pos[to],    pos[from],    a);  \
25     tex[from]    = mix(tex[to],    tex[from],    a);  \
26     normal[from] = mix(normal[to], normal[from], a);
27
28     // Only two vertices may be outside; otherwise,
29     // the triangle would not be visible.
30     switch(clipmask) {
31     case V2|V0: PUSH_VERTEX(2, 1);
32     case V0:    PUSH_VERTEX(0, 1); break;
33     case V0|V1: PUSH_VERTEX(0, 2);
34     case V1:    PUSH_VERTEX(1, 2); break;
35     case V1|V2: PUSH_VERTEX(1, 0);
36     case V2:    PUSH_VERTEX(2, 0); break;
37     }
38 }
```

Listing 23.3. Shrinking a triangle to make it fit into the frustum. First, a bitmask is computed that indicates for each vertex if it is outside with respect to the current clip plane. This bitmask is used to determine which of the edges alongside the respective vertices are pushed.

computed manually in a separate pass after visibility of the triangles has been established.

For computing the partial derivatives of the attributes as described in Section 23.2.1, the triangles need to be projected to the screen, which necessitates clipping against the view frustum. Our implementation uses homogenous clipping, however we do not create additional triangles since the derivatives are identical for all resulting clipped triangles.

A bitmask is computed (refer to Listing 23.3) that stores per vertex if it is outside with respect to the current clip plane. Since this computation considers only visible triangles, at most two vertices may be outside with respect to a single clip plane. The bitmask is used to determine which vertices need to be pushed, and furthermore the corresponding triangle edge to the vertex lying inside the frustum is found. The intersection of the edge with the clip plane is computed, and the vertex is moved to the intersection point.

23.3.4   Shading

Attributes are interpolated according to Equation (23.3). By storing a material ID in the first field of the triangle struct, different materials and triangle storage formats can be identified. Akin to deferred shading, the world-space position could be reconstructed from the depth buffer; however, we reconstruct the world-space position from the $1/w$ attribute, allowing us to reconstruct the attribute precisely for arbitrary screen positions. First, the position $p_{\mathrm{NDC}} = (x, y, z, 1)_{\mathrm{NDC}}^{T}$ is computed from the screen-space coordinate; z_{NDC} is computed from the w-component as $z_{\mathrm{NDC}} = P_{34}/w - P_{33}$, where P is the projection matrix. The world-space position p thus can be computed as $p = w \cdot (PV)^{-1} p_{\mathrm{NDC}}$ with V as the view matrix.

For the shading the materials need to be evaluated. We use OpenGLs bindless texture mechanism for random access to the resources needed by the materials. A gradient is needed for the texture access to ensure proper texture filtering, which can be computed by interpolating the attribute offset to the neighboring pixel and by computing the difference to the attribute at the shaded pixel. We do not store the tangent space as an additional attribute but rather compute the tangent using screen-space derivatives [Schueler 07].

23.3.5   Linked List of Visibility Samples

Since, for most pixels, only a small number of different triangles is referenced, it is more memory efficient to dynamically allocate memory for a linked list and to reference that linked list using a per-pixel head pointer. Each linked list element stores a pointer to the next list element as well as a reference to the triangle. The coverage mask reported in the fragment shader is used to determine if a pixel is fully covered by the current triangle. The depth prepass ensures that correct coverage information is determined; however, the coverage information needs to take the depth test into account. The following code fragment shows how to determine the correct number of covered samples:

```
#extension GL_ARB_post_depth_coverage : require
layout(post_depth_coverage) in;
uint num_samples_covered = bitCount(gl_SampleMaskIn[0]);
```

In the case of full coverage, the head pointer is used to directly encode the triangle reference, which is indicated using a special bit in the head pointer. Otherwise,

```
 1  #extension GL_NV_shader_thread_group: enable
 2  uint sid = 0; // Shading sample address
 3  if((gl_ThreadInWarpNV & 3) == 0) // One thread allocates memory.
 4    sid = atomicCounterIncrement(ctr_shading_samples);
 5  // Communicate to all invocations.
 6  uint sid_sw = floatBitsToUint(
 7        quadSwizzle0NV(uintBitsToFloat(sid)));
 8  if(sid_sw == 0) { // Fails when there are helper-invocations.
 9    if(sid == 0) // Allocate shading samples for all invocations.
10      sid = atomicCounterIncrement(ctr_shading_samples);
11    store_shading_sample(sid);
12  } else if((gl_ThreadInWarpNV & 0x03) == 0) {
13    sid = sid_sw;
14    store_shading_sample(sid);
15  } else { // Communication worked, do not need to store.
16    sid = sid_sw;
17  }
```

Listing 23.4. Multi-rate shading samples are created in the fragment shader by a specific invocation that then tries to broadcast this address to all invocations in the shading quad. If the broadcast fails, each invocation creates a shading sample, which might happen if there are helper-invocations.

the linked list is build similar to *order independent transparency* techniques by allocating samples using an atomic counter and performing an atomic exchange operation on the list head pointer. Alongside the triangle address, the number of covered samples is stored to allow for correct weighting of the samples in the shading phase.

23.3.6 Multi-rate Shading

Our multi-rate shading approach requires shading samples to be spawned that are referenced by the visibility buffer. Each of the shading samples stores a reference to the triangle to be shaded, as well as the screen-space coordinate to enable attribute interpolation. Our approach uses inter-shading-quad communication to determine which fragment shader invocation creates the shading sample and to communicate the address of the sample to all four invocations. Listing 23.4 shows our approach to communicate the shading sample address. First, one invocation allocates memory and tries to communicate the address to all other invocations in the quad. Next, all invocations check if the communication succeeded, as it might fail in case there are helper-invocations inside the shading quad. If the communication of the sample failed, each invocation creates a separate shading sample.

We issue a compute pass for all samples and compress the computed shading into the LogLuv [Larson 98] representation. The compressed result replaces the input needed for shading in-place. In the final shading phase, these samples are read by looking up the visibility buffer and are combined with the full shading.

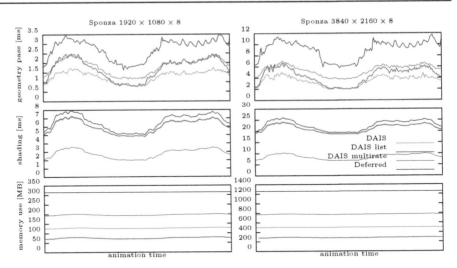

Figure 23.3. Timings and total memory usage for an animation in the Sponza scene. The geometry pass corresponds to the visibility sampling phase and includes the depth prepass. The memory consumption includes all buffers needed for shading. Note the varying y-axis scaling.

23.4   Results

We compare the performance characteristics and memory consumption of three versions of our algorithm to a standard deferred shading implementation. *DAIS* uses a standard multi-sample render target, whereas *DAIS list* employs a per-pixel linked list of visibility samples. Furthermore, we test our multi-rate shading implementation that reduces the shading rate for indirect illumination evaluated using reflective shadow maps [Dachsbacher and Stamminger 05] to 50%. Our deferred shading implementation uses a G-buffer format of 20 bytes per visibility sample.

Figure 23.3 shows our measurements for a camera animation in the Sponza scene, which has 262,267 triangles. Furthermore, we performed the measurements (refer to Figure 23.4) using the San Miguel scene, which has 8,145,860 triangles. On the Sponza scene our method is consistently able to outperform deferred shading while at the same time significantly reducing the storage consumption. Due to the large number of triangles, the San Miguel scene stresses our method, which is not able to meet the performance of deferred shading at a resolution of $1920 \times 1080 \times 8$; however, our method is able to outperform deferred shading at the higher screen resolution.

We furthermore evaluated our method using tessellation shaders (refer to Figure 23.5) to spawn equally-sized triangles in screen space on the Sponza scene. The performance characteristics are similar to the San Miguel scene as shown in Figure 23.4.

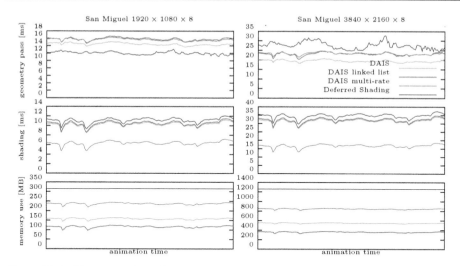

Figure 23.4. Timings and total memory usage for an animation in the San Miguel scene. The geometry pass corresponds to the visibility sampling phase and includes the depth prepass. The memory consumption includes all buffers needed for shading. Note the varying y-axis scaling.

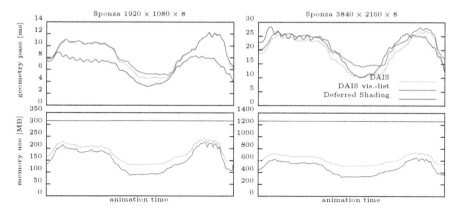

Figure 23.5. Timings and total memory usage for an animation in the Sponza scene. A tessellation shader was used to create triangles with approximately equal screen-space size, generating up to 13 and 26 million triangles for the resolutions of $1920 \times 1080 \times 8$ and $3840 \times 2160 \times 8$, respectively.

23.5   Conclusion

In this chapter we presented a memory-efficient deferred shading algorithm that makes the usage of multi-sample antialiasing in conjunction with high screen resolutions viable. Storing data per triangle instead of per visibility sample significantly reduces the memory usage and allows us to employ caches efficiently, which makes the method faster and more memory efficient compared to deferred shading. The visibility buffer is of low entropy since many visibility samples store the same reference, which allows the GPU to effectively apply transparent memory compression to further reduce the memory bandwidth usage.

Bibliography

[Burns and Hunt 13] Christopher A. Burns and Warren A. Hunt. "The Visibility Buffer: A Cache-Friendly Approach to Deferred Shading." *Journal of Computer Graphics Techniques (JCGT)* 2:2 (2013), 55–69. Available online (http://jcgt.org/published/0002/02/04/).

[Cigolle et al. 14] Zina H. Cigolle, Sam Donow, Daniel Evangelakos, Michael Mara, Morgan McGuire, and Quirin Meyer. "A Survey of Efficient Representations for Independent Unit Vectors." *Journal of Computer Graphics Techniques (JCGT)* 3:2 (2014), 1–30. Available online (http://jcgt.org/published/0003/02/01/).

[Dachsbacher and Stamminger 05] Carsten Dachsbacher and Marc Stamminger. "Reflective Shadow Maps." In *Proceedings of the 2005 Symposium on Interactive 3D Graphics and Games, I3D '05*, pp. 203–231. New York: ACM, 2005.

[Larson 98] Gregory Ward Larson. "LogLuv Encoding for Full-Gamut, High-Dynamic Range Images." *Journal of Graphics Tools* 3:1 (1998), 15–31.

[Liktor and Dachsbacher 12] Gábor Liktor and Carsten Dachsbacher. "Decoupled Deferred Shading for Hardware Rasterization." In *Proceedings of the ACM SIGGRAPH Symposium on Interactive 3D Graphics and Games*, pp. 143–150. New York: ACM, 2012.

[Schied and Dachsbacher 15] Christoph Schied and Carsten Dachsbacher. "Deferred Attribute Interpolation for Memory-Efficient Deferred Shading." In *Proceedings of the 7th Conference on High-Performance Graphics*, pp. 1–5. New York: ACM, 2015.

[Schueler 07] Christian Schueler. "Normal Mapping without Pre-Computed Tangents." In *ShaderX5: Advanced Rendering Techniques*, edited by Wolfgang F Engel. Boston: Charles River Media, 2007.

24

Real-Time Volumetric Cloudscapes

Andrew Schneider

24.1 Overview

Real-time volumetric clouds in games usually pay for fast performance with a reduction in quality. The most successful approaches are limited to low-altitude fluffy and translucent stratus-type clouds. We propose a volumetric solution that can fill a sky with evolving and realistic results that depict high-altitude cirrus clouds and all of the major low-level cloud types, including thick, billowy cumu-

Figure 24.1. Several cloudscapes that were drawn in real time for the game *Horizon: Zero Dawn*.

lus clouds. Additionally, our approach approximates several volumetric lighting effects that have not yet been present in real-time cloud rendering solutions. And finally, this solution performs well enough in memory and on the GPU to be included in a AAA console game. (See Figure 24.1.)

24.2   Introduction

The standard solutions for rendering clouds in AAA console games involve assets of some kind, either 2D billboards, polar sky dome images, or volumetric libraries that are instanced at render time. For games that require a constantly changing sky and allow the player to cover vast distances, such as open world, the benefits of highly detailed assets are overshadowed by the cost of storing and accessing data for multiple camera angles, times of day, and lighting conditions. Additionally, the simulation of cloud system evolution is limited to tricks or fakes such as rotating the sky dome or distorting images using 2D noise.

Numerous techniques for procedural cloud systems do not rely on assets. Several good examples are freely available on ShaderToy.com, such as "Clouds" [Quilez 13]. Evolution studios used middleware called TrueSky to deliver impressive atmospheric weather effects for the game *Drive Club* [Simul 13].

Yet, there are several limitations with these approaches:

- They all only describe low-altitude stratus clouds and not the puffy and billowy stratocumulus or cumulus clouds.

- Current volumetric methods do not implement realistic lighting effects that are specific to clouds.

- Real-time volumetric clouds are often quite expensive in terms of performance and memory and are not really worth the quality of the results produced.

For the game *Horizon: Zero Dawn*, we have developed a new solution that addresses these problems. We submit new algorithms for modeling, lighting, and rendering, which deliver realistic and evolving results while staying within a memory budget of 20 MB and a performance target of 2 ms.

24.3   Cloud Modeling

Figure 24.2 shows the various cloud types and their height ranges. There are two layers that we render volumetrically: the low stratus clouds, which exist between 1.5 km and 4 km, and the cumulonimbus clouds, which span the entire lower atmosphere from 1 km to 8 km. The alto and cirro class clouds are usually very thin in height and can be rendered for less expense with a 2D texture lookup.

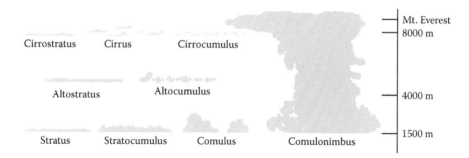

Figure 24.2. A map of the major cloud types.

As the day progresses and the sun heats the earth, water vapor rises from the surface and travels through these layers of atmosphere. Each layer has its own wind direction and temperature. As the vapor travels higher in the atmosphere, the temperature decreases. As temperature decreases the vapor condenses into water or ice around particles of dust it encounters. (Sometimes this comes back down as rain or snow.) The great deal of instability in the flow of this vapor introduces turbulence. As clouds rise, they tend to make billowing shapes. As they diffuse, they stretch and dissipate like fog [Clausse and Facy 61].

Clouds are really amazing examples of fluid dynamics in action, and modeling this behavior requires that the designer approach clouds in a way that approximates the underlying physics involved. With these concepts in mind, we define several techniques that will be used in our ray march to model clouds.

Sections 24.3.1 through 24.3.3 detail some concepts that are used to model clouds and Section 24.3.4 explains how they are all used together.

24.3.1 Modified Fractal Brownian Motion

The standard approach for modeling volumetric cloud systems in real time involves using a ray march with a technique called *fractal Brownian motion*, or FBM for short [Mandelbrot and van Ness 68]. (See Figure 24.3.) FBM is the sum of a series of octaves of noise, each with higher frequency and lower amplitude.

Perlin noise [Perlin 85] is commonly used for this purpose. While this is a reliable model for producing the fog-like shapes of stratus clouds, it fails to describe the round, billowy shapes in cumulus clouds or give them an implied sense of motion as seen in Figure 24.4.

Perlin noise can be flipped over in the middle of its range to create some puffy shapes, but because it is just one flavor of noise, it still lacks the packed cauliflower pattern seen in clouds. Figure 24.5 shows Perlin noise, the result of `abs(Perlin * 2 + 1)`, and photographic reference of the fractal billowing pattern found in clouds.

Figure 24.3. Procedural clouds generated with a ray march and an FBM noise.

Figure 24.4. Photographic reference showing round billowing shapes, similar to puffs of smoke from a factory vent.

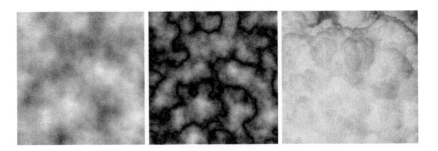

Figure 24.5. Seven-octave Perlin noise (left), Perlin noise made to look "puffy" (center), and photographic reference of the packed cauliflower shapes in clouds (right).

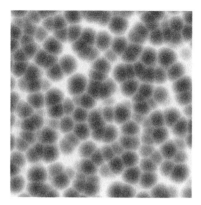

Figure 24.6. Worley noise.

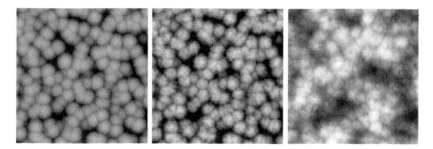

Figure 24.7. Inverted Worley noise (left), FBM composed of Worley noise (center), and Perlin-Worley noise (right).

Another flavor of noise, Worley noise, was introduced in 1996 by Steven Worley [Worley 96] and is often used in rendering caustics and water effects, as seen in Figure 24.6.

If inverted and used in a FBM, Worley noise approximates a nice fractal billowing pattern. It can also be used to add detail to the low-density regions of the low-frequency Perlin noise. (See Figure 24.7, left and center.) We do this by remapping the Perlin noise using the Worley noise FBM as the minimum value from the original range.

```
OldMin = Worley_FBM
PerlinWorley = NewMin + (((Perlin - OldMin) / (OldMax - OldMin))
    * (NewMax - NewMin))
```

This method of combining the two noise types adds a bit of billowing to the connectedness produced in Perlin noise and produces a much more natural result.

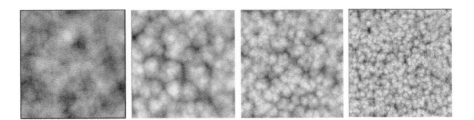

Figure 24.8. A slice of the low-frequency noise's RGBA channels. The first slice is Perin-Worley noise. The last three are Worley noises at increasing frequencies. (Resolution: 128^3.)

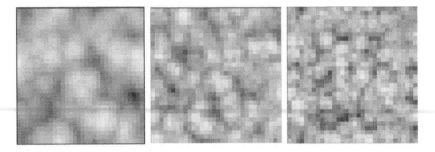

Figure 24.9. From left to right, a slice of the high-frequency noise's RGB channels and Worley noise at increasing frequencies. (Resolution: 32^3.)

We refer to this as our low frequency Perlin-Worley noise and it is the basis for our modeling approach. (See Figure 24.7, right.)

Instead of building the FBM using one texture read per octave, we precompile the FBM so we only have to read two textures. Figure 24.8 shows our first 3D texture, which is made of the Perlin-Worley noise FBM and three octaves of Worley noise FBM's. Figure 24.9 shows our second 3D texture, which consists of three more octaves of Worley noise.

The first 3D texture defines our base cloud shape. The second is of higher frequency and is used to erode the edges of the base cloud shape and add detail, as explained further in Section 24.3.4.

24.3.2 Density-Height Functions

Previous work in this area creates a specific cloud type by biasing or scaling the cloud density value, based on height [Quilez 13].

This function is used to bias or scale the noise signal and produce a cloud. This has limited the types of clouds seen in other work to one type because the maximum height of the clouds never changes.

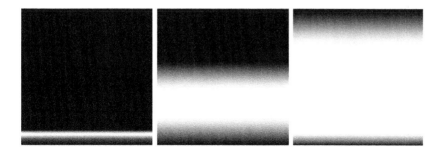

Figure 24.10. The gradients produced by three density height functions to represent stratus (left), cumulus (center), and cumulonimbus (right) clouds.

Figure 24.11. Results of three functions used to represent stratus (left), cumulus (center), and cumulonimbus (right) clouds.

We extend this approach by using three such functions, one for each of the three major low-level cloud types: stratus, stratocumulus, and cumulus. Figure 24.10 shows the gradient functions we used. Figure 24.11 shows the results of using these functions to change cloud density over height.

At runtime we compute a weighted sum of the three functions. We vary the weighting using a weather texture to add more or less of each cloud type—details are in the next section.

24.3.3 Weather Texture

For our purposes we want to know three things at any point in the domain of our cloud system:

1. Cloud coverage: The percentage of cloud coverage in the sky.

2. Precipitation: The chance that the clouds overhead will produce rain.

3. Cloud type: A value of 0.0 indicates stratus, 0.5 indicates stratocumulus, and 1.0 indicates cumulus clouds.

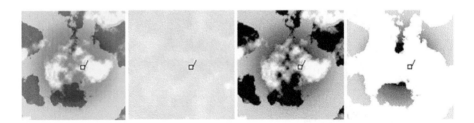

Figure 24.12. Weather texture (left), then (from left to right) coverage signal (red), precipitation signal (green), and cloud type signal (blue).

These attributes can all be expressed as a probability between zero and one, which makes them easy to work with and to preview in a 2D texture. This buffer can be sampled to get a value for each attribute at any point in world space.

Figure 24.12 breaks the weather map for this scene down into its components. The scale of this map is $60,000 \times 60,000$ meters, and the arrows indicate camera direction.

In reality, rain clouds are always present where it is raining. To model this behavior, we bias cloud type to cumulonimbus and cloud coverage to at least 70% where the chance of rain is 100%.

Additionally, we allow the artist to override the weather texture to produce art-directed skies for cutscenes or other directed experiences [Schneider 15, slide 47].

24.3.4   Cloud Sampler

Having established the components of the cloud density function, we will now move on to the cloud model.

Like all other volumetric cloud solutions to date, we use a ray march. A ray march takes steps through a domain and samples density values for use in lighting and density calculations. These data are used to build the final image of the volumetric subject. Our cloud density sample function does most of the work of interpreting the sample position and the weather data to give us the density value of a cloud at a given point.

Before we start working in the function, we calculate a normalized scalar value that represents the height of the current sample position in the cloud layer. This will be used in the last part of the modeling process.

```
// Fractional value for sample position in the cloud layer.
float GetHeightFractionForPoint(float3 inPosition,
                                float2 inCloudMinMax)
{
    // Get global fractional position in cloud zone.
    float height_fraction = (inPosition.z - inCloudMinMax.x ) /
```

```
                                    (inCloudMinMax.y - inCloudMinMax.x);

    return saturate(height_fraction);
}
```

We also define a remapping function to map values from one range to another, to be used when combining noises to make our clouds.

```
// Utility function that maps a value from one range to another.
float Remap(float original_value, float original_min,
            float original_max, float new_min, float new_max)
{
    return new_min + (((original_value - original_min) /
            (original_max - original_min)) * (new_max - new_min))
}
```

The first step of our sampling algorithm is to build a basic cloud shape out of the low-frequency Perlin-Worley noise in our first 3D texture. The process is as follows:

1. The first step is to retrieve the four low-frequency noise values required to build a basic cloud shape. We sample the first 3D texture, containing low-frequency octaves.

2. We will use the first channel, which contains the Perlin-Worley noise, to establish our base cloud shape.

3. Though the basic Perlin-Worley noise provides a reasonable cloud density function, it lacks the detail of a realistic cloud. We use a remapping function to add the three other low-frequency noises to the edges of the Perlin-Worley noise. This method of combining noises prevents the interior of the Perlin-Worley cloud shape from becoming non-homogenous and also ensures that we only add detail in the areas that we can see.

4. To determine the type of cloud we are drawing, we compute our density height function based on the cloud type attribute from our weather texture.

5. Next, we multiply the base cloud shape by the density height function to create the correct type of cloud according to the weather data.

Here is how it looks in code:

```
float SampleCloudDensity(float3 p, float3 weather_data)
{
    // Read the low-frequency Perlin-Worley and Worley noises.
    float4 low_frequency_noises = tex3Dlod(Cloud3DNoiseTextureA,
        Cloud3DNoiseSamplerA, float4 (p, mip_level) ).rgba;

    // Build an FBM out of  the low frequency Worley noises
```

Figure 24.13. The low-frequency "base" cloud shape.

```
// that can be used to add detail to the low-frequency
// Perlin-Worley noise.
float low_freq_FBM = ( low_frequency_noises.g * 0.625 )
                   + ( low_frequency_noises.b * 0.25 )
                   + ( low_frequency_noises.a * 0.125 );

// define the base cloud shape by dilating it with the
// low-frequency FBM made of Worley noise.
float base_cloud = Remap( low_frequency_noises.r, -
    ( 1.0 -  low_freq_FBM), 1.0, 0.0, 1.0 );

// Get the density-height gradient using the density height
// function explained in Section 24.3.2.
float density_height_gradient =
    GetDensityHeightGradientForPoint( p, weather_data );

// Apply the height function to the base cloud shape.
base_cloud *=  density_height_gradient;
```

At this point we have something that already resembles a cloud, albeit a low-detail one (Figure 24.13).

Next, we apply the cloud coverage attribute from the weather texture to ensure that we can control how much the clouds cover the sky. This step involves two operations:

1. To make the clouds realistically grow as we animate the coverage attribute, we expand the base cloud shape that was produced by the previous steps using the cloud coverage attribute in the remapping function.

2. To ensure that density increases with coverage in an aesthetically pleasing way, we multiply this result by the cloud coverage attribute.

Figure 24.14. The "base" cloud shape with coverage applied.

Here is how it looks in code:

```
// Cloud coverage is stored in weather_data's red channel.
float cloud_coverage = weather_data.r;

// Use remap to apply the cloud coverage attribute.
float base_cloud_with_coverage  = Remap(base_cloud,
    cloud_coverage, 1.0, 0.0, 1.0);
// Multiply the result by the cloud coverage attribute so
// that smaller clouds are lighter and more aesthetically
// pleasing.
base_cloud_with_coverage *= cloud_coverage;
```

The result of these steps is shown in Figure 24.14. The base cloud is still low detail but it is beginning to look more like a system than a field of noise.

Next, we finish off the cloud by adding realistic detail ranging from small billows created by instabilities in the rising water vapor to wispy distortions caused by atmospheric turbulence (see examples in Figure 24.15).

We model these effects using three steps:

1. We use animated curl noise to distort the sample coordinate at the bottom of the clouds, simulating the effect of turbulence when we sample the high-frequency 3D texture using the distorted sample coordinates.

2. We build an FBM out of the high-frequency Worley noises in order to add detail to the edges of the cloud.

3. We contract the base cloud shape using the high-frequency FBM. At the base of the cloud, we invert the Worley noise to produce wispy shapes in

Figure 24.15. Photographic reference of billowy shapes and wispy shapes created by atmospheric turbulence.

this region. Contracting with Worley noise at the top produces billowing detail.

Here is how it looks in code:

```
// Add some turbulence to bottoms of clouds.
p.xy += curl_noise.xy * (1.0 - height_fraction);

// Sample high-frequency noises.
float3 high_frequency_noises = tex3Dlod(Cloud3DNoiseTextureB,
    Cloud3DNoiseSamplerB,  float4 (p * 0.1, mip_level) ).rgb;

// Build-high frequency Worley noise FBM.
float high_freq_FBM = ( high_frequency_noises.r * 0.625 )
                    + ( high_frequency_noises.g * 0.25 )
                    + ( high_frequency_noises.b * 0.125 );

// Get the height_fraction for use with blending noise types
// over height.
float height_fraction  = GetHeightFractionForPoint(p,
                                        inCloudMinMax);

// Transition from wispy shapes to billowy shapes over height.
float high_freq_noise_modifier = mix(high_freq_FBM,
        1.0 - high_freq_FBM, saturate(height_fraction * 10.0));

// Erode the base cloud shape with the distorted
```

Figure 24.16. The final cloud shape.

```
    // high-frequency Worley noises.
    float final_cloud = Remap(base_cloud_with_coverage,
        high_freq_noise_modifier * 0.2 , 1.0, 0.0, 1.0);

    return final_cloud;
}
```

The result of these steps is shown in Figure 24.16. This series of operations is the framework that our sampler uses to create cloudscapes in the ray march, but we take additional steps to add that implied sense of motion that traditional noise-based solutions for cloudscapes lack.

To simulate the shearing effect as a cloud rises from one atmosphere layer to another, we offset the sample position in the wind direction over altitude. Additionally, both 3D texture samples are offset in the wind direction and slightly upward over time, but at different speeds. Giving each noise its own speed produces a more realistic look to the motion of the clouds. In a time lapse, the clouds appear to grow upward.

```
    // Wind settings.
    float3 wind_direction = float3(1.0, 0.0, 0.0);
    float cloud_speed = 10.0;

    // cloud_top offset pushes the tops of the clouds along
    // this wind direction by this many units.
    float cloud_top_offset = 500.0;

    // Skew in wind direction.
    p += height_fraction * wind_direction * cloud_top_offset;
```

Figure 24.17. Sample cloudscapes, captured on the Playstation 4.

```
// Animate clouds in wind direction and add a small upward
// bias to the wind direction.
p+= (wind_direction + float3(0.0, 0.1, 0.0)  ) * time
    * cloud_speed;
```

This code must be located before any 3D texture samples in the `CloudDensity-Sample()` function.

24.3.5 Results

Some volumetric cloudscapes created using different weather settings are illustrated in Figure 24.17.

This modeling approach allows us to sculpt numerous unique cloudscapes. When a rain signal approaches the camera along the wind direction, it gives the effect of an approaching storm front [Schneider 15, slide 43–44].

24.4 Cloud Lighting

Volumetric cloud lighting is a very well researched area of computer graphics. Unfortunately for game developers, the best results come from taking high numbers of samples. This means that we have to find ways to approximate the complicated and expensive processes that take place when producing film-quality clouds.

Figure 24.18. Photographic reference of directional scattering (left), the silver lining effect (center), and the dark edges effect (right).

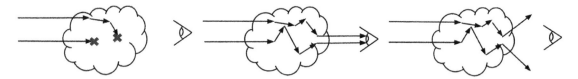

Figure 24.19. Examples of three light behaviors in a cloud: absorption (left), in-scattering (center), and out-scattering (right).

There are three effects in particular for which our approach solves with approximations: the multiple scattering and directional lighting in clouds, the silver lining effect when we look toward the sun, and the dark edges on clouds when we look away from the sun. Figure 24.18 shows photographic references of these three effects.

24.4.1 Volumetric Scattering

When light enters a cloud, the majority of the light rays spend their time refracting through water droplets and ice inside of the cloud before scattering toward our eyes [Van De Hulst 57]. There are three things that can happen to a photon entering a cloud (see also Figure 24.19):

1. It can be absorbed by water or non-participating particles in the cloud such as dust; this is *extinction* or *absorption*.

2. It can exit the cloud toward the eye; this is *in-scattering*.

3. It could exit the cloud traveling away from the eye; this is *out-scattering*.

Beer's law is a standard method for approximating the probability of each of these three outcomes.

24.4.2 Beer's Law

Originally conceived of as a tool for chemical analysis, Beer's law models the attenuation of light as it passes through a material [Beer 52]. (See Figure 24.20.)

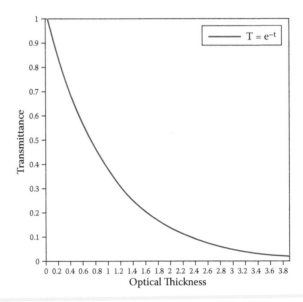

Figure 24.20. Beer's law: Transmittance as a function of optical depth.

In the case of volumetrics, it can be used to reliably calculate transmittance based on optical thickness [Wrenninge 13].

If our participating media are non-homogenous, like clouds, we must accumulate optical thickness along the light ray using a ray march. This model has been used extensively in film visual effects, and it forms the foundation of our lighting model.

Here is how it is implemented in code:

```
light_energy = exp( - density_samples_along_light_ray );
```

24.4.3   Henyey-Greenstein Phase Function

In clouds, there is a higher probability of light scattering forward [Pharr and Humphreys 10]. This is responsible for the silver lining in clouds. (See Figure 24.21.)

In 1941, the Henyey-Greenstein phase function was developed to mimic the angular dependence of light scattering by small particles, which was used to describe scattering of light by interstellar dust clouds [Henyey and Greenstein 41]. In volumetric rendering the function is used to model the probability of light scattering within participating media. We use a single Henyey-Greenstein phase function with an eccentricity (directional component) g of 0.2, to make sure that

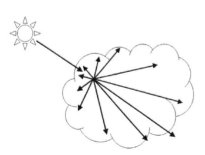 

Figure 24.21. Illustration of forward scattering of light in a cloud (left), and photographic reference of the silver lining effect (right).

more light in our clouds scatters forward:

$$p_{\text{HG}}(\theta, g) = \frac{1}{4\pi} \frac{1 - g^2}{1 + g^2 - 2g \cos(\theta)^{3/2}}.$$

And here is how it looks implemented in code:

```
float HenyeyGreenstein(float3 inLightVector, float3 inViewVector,
                       float inG)
{
    float cos_angle = dot(normalize(inLightVector),
                          normalize(inViewVector));
    return ((1.0 - inG * inG) / pow((1.0 + inG * inG -
        2.0 * inG * cos_angle), 3.0 / 2.0)) / 4.0 * 3.1415;
}
```

The results are shown in Figure 24.22.

Figure 24.22. Clouds without the Henyey-Greenstein phase function (left), and clouds with the Henyey-Greenstein phase function (right).

Figure 24.23. A diagram showing the 180-degree view angle where the dark edge effect is apparent (left), and photographic reference of the dark edge effect (right).

24.4.4   In-Scattering Probability Function (Powdered Sugar Effect)

Beer's law is an extinction model, meaning that it is concerned with how light energy attenuates over depth. This fails to approximate an important lighting effect related to in-scattering on the sun-facing sides of clouds. This effect presents itself as dark edges on clouds when a view ray approaches the direction of the light ray. There is a similar effect in piles of powdered sugar, the source of our nickname for this effect. See Figure 24.23 for an illustration.

This effect is most apparent in round, dense regions of clouds, so much so that the creases between each bulge appear brighter than the bulge itself, which is closer to the sun. These results would appear to be the exact opposite of what Beer's law models.

Recall that in-scattering is an effect in which light rays inside a cloud bounce around until they become parallel and then exit the cloud and travel to our eyes. This phenomenon even occurs when we look at a sunlit side of a cloud (Figure 24.24).

Also recall that more light scatters forward, along the original light ray direction, due to forward scattering. However, a relatively large optical depth must exist for there to be a reasonable chance for a photon to turn 180 degrees. Paths around the edge of the cloud won't pass through a sufficiently large optical depth to turn a noticeable fraction of the photons completely around. Paths that do have an optical depth large enough to turn a photon 180 degrees are almost always well inside the cloud, so Beer's law extinction will kill this contribution before it leaves the cloud toward our eye. Crevices and cracks are an exception; they provide a window into the interior of the cloud volume where there are photon paths with relatively large optical depths, allowing a low-density shortcut for photons to escape, making the crevices brighter than the surrounding bulges.

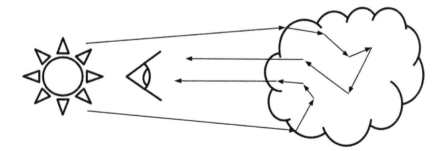

Figure 24.24. An illustration of in-scattering producing a 180-degree turn in the incoming light rays.

We chose to express this phenomenon as a probability. Imagine you are looking at one of these bulgy regions on a cloud at the same angle as a group of light rays coming from the sun behind you (Figure 24.25).

If we sample a point just below the surface on one of the bulges and compare it to a point at the same depth in one of the crevices, the point in the crevice will have more potential cloud material that can contribute to in-scattering (Figure 24.26). In terms of probability, the crease should be brighter.

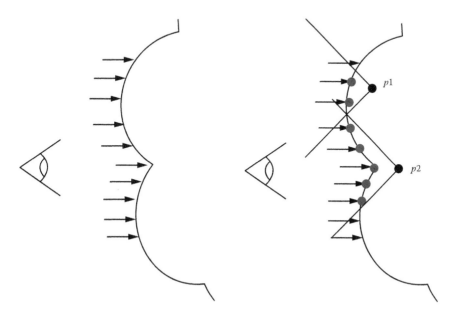

Figure 24.25. Light hitting bulges on a cloud.

Figure 24.26. Illustration showing higher in-scatter potential for the creases.

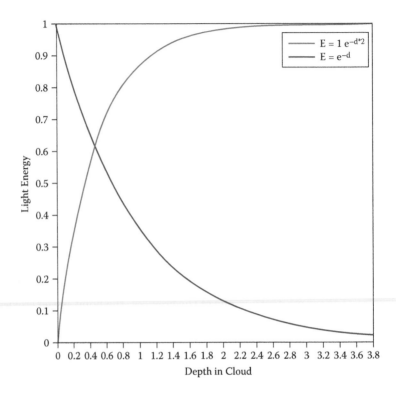

Figure 24.27. Beer's law compared to our approximation for the powdered sugar effect.

Using this thought experiment as a guide, we propose a new function to account for this effect. Because this result is effectively the opposite of Beer's law, we represent it as an inverse of the original function (Figure 24.27).

For our purposes this is an accurate enough approximation of this phenomenon, which does not require any additional sampling.

We combine the two functions into a new function: Beer's-Powder. Note that we multiply the entire result by 2, to bring it closer to the original normalized range (Figure 24.28).

Here is how it is implemented in code:

```
powder_sugar_effect  = 1.0 -  exp( - light_samples * 2.0 );
beers_law = exp( - light_samples );
light_energy = 2.0 * beers_law * powder_sugar_effect;
```

Some results both from an isolated test case and from our solution in-game are shown in Figure 24.29.

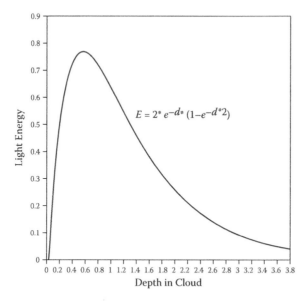

Figure 24.28. The combined Beer's-Powder function.

Figure 24.29. Lighting model without our function (top left) and with our function (top right). In-game results without our function (bottom left) and with our function (top right).

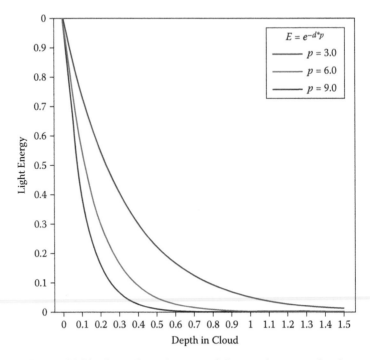

Figure 24.30. Several results using different absorption levels.

24.4.5   Rain Clouds

Our system also models the darker bases of rain clouds. Rain clouds are darker than other low-level clouds because the water droplets have condensed so much that most of the light gets absorbed before reaching our eye.

So, since we already have a precipitation attribute for the point that we are sampling, we can use it to artificially "thicken" the cloud material. This task is easily accomplished by increasing the sampled density that goes into the Beer's-Powder function; see Figure 24.30. The variable p stands for precipitation.

Figure 24.31 shows some results.

Figure 24.31. Rain clouds with (left) and without (right) increased light absorption.

24.4.6   Lighting Model Summary

In review, our lighting model is a combination of four components:

1. Beer's law (August Beer, 1852),

2. Henyey-Greenstein phase function (Henyey and Greenstein, 1941),

3. in-scattering probability function (powdered sugar effect),

4. rain cloud absorption gain.

With E as light energy, d as the density sampled for lighting, p as the absorption multiplier for rain, g as our eccentricity in light direction, and θ as the angle between the view and light rays, we can describe our lighting model in full:

$$E = 2.0 \times e^{-dp} \times \left(1 - e^{-2d}\right) \times \frac{1}{4\pi} \frac{1 - g^2}{1 + g^2 - 2g\cos(\theta)^{3/2}}.$$

24.5   Cloud Rendering

Choosing where to sample data to build the image is very important for performance and image quality. Our approach tries to limit expensive work to situations where it could potentially be required.

24.5.1   Spherical Atmosphere

The first part of rendering with a ray march is deciding where to start. When the viewer is located on a seemingly "flat" surface such as the ocean, the curvature of the Earth clearly causes clouds to descend into the horizon. This is because the Earth is round and cloud layers are spherical rather than planar. (See Figure 24.32.)

In order to reproduce this feature, our ray march takes place in a 3.5 km thick spherical shell starting at 1.5 km above the surface of the Earth. We use a sphere intersection test to determine the start and end points for our ray march. As we look toward the horizon, the ray length increases considerably, which requires that we increase the number of potential samples. Directly above the player, we take as many as 64 steps and at the horizon we take as many as 128 steps. There are several optimizations in our ray-march loop, allowing it to exit early, so the average sample count is much lower than this.

24.5.2   Ray March Optimizations

Instead of evaluating the full cloud density function every time, we only evaluate the low-frequency part of the cloud density function until we are close to a cloud. Recall that our density function uses low-detail Perlin-Worley noise to establish

Figure 24.32. Spherical atmosphere.

the base shape of our clouds and higher frequencies of Worley noise, which it applies as an erosion from the edges of this base cloud shape. Evaluating just the low-frequency part of the density function means one 3D texture is read instead of two, which is a substantial bandwidth and instruction count savings. Figure 24.33 illustrates the step through empty air using "cheap" samples and then the switch to expensive samples when close to a cloud. Once several samples return zero, we return to the "cheap" sample.

To implement this in code, we start with a `cloud_test` value of zero and accumulate density in a loop using a boolean value of `true` for our sampler. As long as the `cloud_test` is 0.0, we continue on our march searching for the cloud boundary. Once we get a nonzero value, we suppress the march integration for that step and proceed using the full cloud density sample. After six consecutive full cloud density samples that return 0.0, we switch back to the cloud boundary search. These steps ensure that we have exited the cloud boundary and do not trigger extra work.

Figure 24.33. Cloud boundary detection (left), and full samples inside of the cloud boundary (right).

```
float density = 0.0;
float cloud_test = 0.0;
int zero_density_sample_count = 0;

// Start the main ray-march loop.
for (int i = 0; i <sample_count; i++)
{
    // cloud_test starts as zero so we always evaluate the
    // second case from the beginning.
    if(cloud_test > 0.0)
    {
        // Sample density the expensive way by setting the
        // last parameter to false, indicating a full sample.
        float sampled_density = SampleCloudDensity(p,
            weather_data, mip_level, false);

         // If we just samples a zero, increment the counter.
         if( sampled_density = 0.0)
         {
            zero_density_sample_count ++;
         }
        // If we are doing an expensive sample that is still
        // potentially in the cloud:
        if(zero_density_sample_count != 6)
        {
            density += sampled_density;
            p += step;
        } // If not, then set cloud_test to zero so that we go
          // back to the cheap sample case.
        else
        {
            cloud_test = 0.0;
            zero_density_sample_count = 0;
        }
    }
    else
    {
        // Sample density the cheap way, only using the
        // low-frequency noise.
```

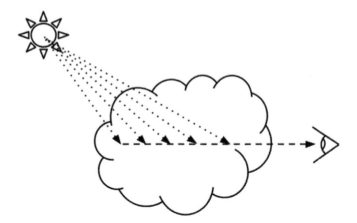

Figure 24.34. A light ray march for each view ray-march step.

```
cloud_test = SampleCloudDensity(p, weather_data,
                                mip_level, true);
if( cloud_test == 0.0)
{
    p += step;
}
        }
    }
}
```

This algorithm cuts the number of 3D texture calls in half for the best case, where we are marching through empty sky.

To calculate the lighting, more samples need to be taken toward the light at each ray-march step. The sum of these samples is used in the lighting model and then attenuated by the current sum of density along the view ray for each view ray-march step. Figure 24.34 illustrates a basic light sample integration march within a ray march.

Because we are targeting for use in a game engine that is supporting many other GPU intensive tasks, we are limited to no more than six samples per ray-march step.

One way to reduce the number of light samples is to execute them only when the ray march steps inside of a cloud. This is an important optimization because light samples are extremely costly. There is no change in the visual result with this optimization.

```
...
            density += sampled_density;
            if( sampled_density != 0.0)
            {
                // SampleCloudDensityAlongRay just walks in the
                // given direction from the start point and takes
```

```
                    // X number of lighting samples.
                    density_along_light_ray =
                        SampleCloudDensityAlongRay(p)
                }
                p += step;
    ...
```

24.5.3   Cone-Sampled Lighting

The obvious way to find the amount of sun illumination is by measuring the transmittance of the cloud between the query point and the sun. However, the light at any point in a cloud is greatly affected by the light in regions around it in the direction of the light source. Think of it as a funnel of light energy that culminates at our sample position. To make sure that the Beer's law portion of our lighting model is being influenced in this way, we take our six light samples in a cone that spreads out toward the light source, thus weighting the Beer's law attenuation function by including neighboring regions of the cloud. See Figure 24.35.

Banding artifacts present themselves immediately because of the low number of samples. The cone sampling helps break up the banding a bit, but to smooth it out further, we sample our densities at a lower mip level.

To calculate the cone offset, we used a kernel of six noise results between $-(1, 1, 1)$ and $+(1, 1, 1)$ and gradually increased its magnitude as we march away from our sample position. If the accumulated density along the view march has surpassed a threshold value where its light contribution can be more generalized (we used 0.3), we switch our samples to the low-detail mode to further optimize the light march. There is very little visual difference at this threshold.

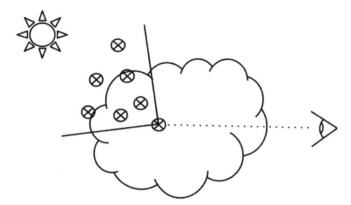

Figure 24.35. A cone-shaped sample area for the light ray-march samples.

```
static float3 noise_kernel[] =
{
... some noise vectors...
}

// How wide to make the cone.
float cone_spread_multplier = length(light_step);

// A function to gather density in a cone for use with
// lighting clouds.
float SampleCloudDensityAlongCone(p, ray_direction)
{
    float density_along_cone = 0.0;

    // Lighting ray-march loop.
    for(int i=0; i<=6; i++)
    {
        // Add the current step offset to the sample position.
        p += light_step + ( cone_spread_multiplier *
                            noise_kernel[i] * float(i) );
        if( density_along_view_cone < 0.3)
        {
            // Sample cloud density the expensive way.
            density_along_cone += SampleCloudDensity(p,
                        weather_data, mip_level + 1, false);
        }
        else
        {
            // Sample cloud density the cheap way, using only
            // one level of noise.
            density_along_cone += SampleCloudDensity(p,
                        weather_data, mip_level + 1, true);
        }
    }
}
```

Additionally, to account for shadows cast from distant clouds onto the part of the cloud for which we are calculating lighting, we take one long distance sample at a distance of three times the length of the cone. (See Figure 24.36.)

Figure 24.36. Long distance light sample combined with the cone samples.

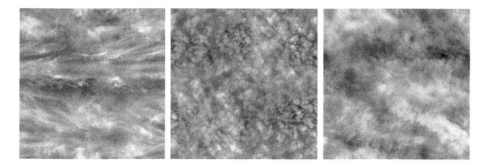

Figure 24.37. Several alto and cirrus cloud textures used instead of a ray march.

24.5.4   High Altitude Clouds

Our approach only renders low-level clouds volumetrically. High-altitude clouds are represented with scrolling textures. However, in order to integrate them with the volumetric clouds, they are sampled at the end of the ray march. The cost of this texture read is negligible for a 512^2 texture with three channels. We animate them in a wind direction that is different from the wind direction in our weather system to simulate different wind directions in different cloud layers. (See Figure 24.37.)

24.5.5   Results

A sequence of lighting results that illustrates a changing time of day is illustrated in Figure 24.38.

24.6   Conclusion and Future Work

This approach produces realistic, evolving cloudscapes for all times of day and completely replaces our asset-based approaches to clouds. It also means that the memory usage for our entire sky is limited to the cost of a few textures that total 20 MB instead of hundreds of megabytes for multiple sky domes and billboards for varying weather conditions and times of day. Performance on the GPU is roughly 20 ms, but when we build our image using temporal reprojection, that number reduces to 2 ms [Schneider 15, slide 91–93].

The in-scattering probability function was based on a thought experiment, but we are researching this further. We plan to use the brute-force approach used by Magnus Wrenninge [Wrenninge 15], which produces the dark edges naturally, to gather data points along the light ray and develop a function that fits these data more precisely.

Figure 24.38. Time lapse of a cloudscape, captured from the Playstation 4.

24.7 Acknowledgments

I would like to thank Nathan Vos, Michal Valient, Elco Vossers, and Hugh Malan for assistance with our development challenges. I would also like to thank Jan-Bart van Beek, Marijn Giesbertz, and Maarten van der Gaag for their assistance in accomplishing our look goals for this project.

Additionally, I would like to personally thank colleagues whose work has greatly influenced this: Trevor Thomson, Matthew Wilson, and Magnus Wrenninge.

Bibliography

[Beer 52] A. Beer. "Bestimmung der Absorption des rothen Lichts in farbigen Flüssigkeiten" (Determination of the Absorption of Red Light in Colored Liquids). *Annalen der Physik und Chemie* 86 (1852), 78–88.

[Clausse and Facy 61] R. Clausse and L. Facy. *The Clouds*. London: Evergreen Books, LTD., 1961.

[Henyey and Greenstein 41] L. G. Henyey and J. L. Greenstein. "Diffuse Radiation in the Galaxy." *Astrophysical Journal* 93 (1941), pp. 78–83.

[Mandelbrot and van Ness 68] B. Mandelbrot and J. W. van Ness. "Fractional Brownian Motions, Fractional Noises and Applications." *SIAM Review* 10:4 (1968), 422–437.

[Perlin 85] K. Perlin. "An Image Synthesizer." In *Proceedings of the 12th Annual Conference on Computer Graphics and Interactive Techniques*, pp. 287–296. New York: ACM Press, 1985.

[Pharr and Humphreys 10] M. Pharr and G. Humphreys. *Physically Based Rendering: From Theory to Implementation.* Boston: Morgan Kaufmann, 2010.

[Quilez 13] I. Quilez. "Clouds." *Shadertoy.com*, https://www.shadertoy.com/view/xslgrr, 2013.

[Schneider 15] A. Schneider. "The Real-Time Volumetric Cloudscapes Of Horizon: Zero Dawn." Paper presented at ACM SIGGRAPH, Los Angeles, CA, August 26, 2015.

[Simul 13] Simul. "TrueSKY." http://simul.co/truesky/, 2013.

[Van De Hulst 57] H. Van De Hulst. *Light Scattering by Small Particles.* New York: Dover Publications, 1957.

[Worley 96] Steven S. Worley. "A Cellular Texture Basis Function." In *Proceedings of the 23rd Annual Conference on Computer Graphics and Interactive Techniques*, pp. 291–294. New York: ACM Press, 1996.

[Wrenninge 13] M. Wrenninge. *Production Volume Rendering: Design and Implementation.* Boca Raton, FL: CRC Press, 2013.

[Wrenninge 15] M. Wrenninge. "Art-Directable Multiple Volumetric Scattering." In *ACM SIGGRAPH 2015 Talks*, Article no. 24. New York: ACM Press, 2015.

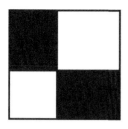

About the Contributors

Abdul Bezrati is a senior engine programmer at Insomniac Games studio in Burbank, California. He is passionate about finding new real-time rendering techniques and sharing them with other game developers.

Carsten Dachsbacher is a full professor at the Karlsruhe Institute of Technology. His research focuses on real-time computer graphics, global illumination, scientific visualization, and perceptual rendering, on which he published articles at various conferences and journals including SIGGRAPH, IEEE VIS, EG, and EGSR. He has been a tutorial speaker at SIGGRAPH, Eurographics, and the Game Developers Conference.

Péter Dancsik received his MS in technical informatics in 2009 from the Budapest University of Technology and Economics. During his graduate work he researched real-time ray tracing on the GPU. His interests include real-time rendering and GPU programming.

Michal Drobot is a principal rendering engineer at Infinity Ward, Activision. He most recently helped design and optimize the 3D renderer in *Far Cry 4* at Ubisoft Montreal. Prior to that, he worked at Guerrilla Games, designing and optimizing the rendering pipeline for the Playstation 4 launch title *Killzone: Shadow Fall*. He likes sharing his work at conferences as well as spending time writing publications about art and technology. He finds fast and pretty pixels exciting.

Elmar Eisemann is a professor at Delft University of Technology (TU Delft), heading the Computer Graphics and Visualization Group. Before, he was an associated professor at Telecom ParisTech (until 2012) and a senior scientist heading a research group in the Cluster of Excellence (Saarland University / MPI Informatik) (until 2009). His interests include real-time and perceptual rendering, alternative representations, shadow algorithms, global illumination, and GPU acceleration techniques. He coauthored the book *Real-Time Shadows* and participated in various committees and editorial boards. He was local organizer of EGSR 2010, EGSR 2012, and HPG 2012, as well as co-paper chair for HPG2015, and he was honored with the Eurographics Young Researcher Award in 2011.

Wolfgang Engel is the CEO of Confetti (www.conffx.com), a think tank for advanced real-time graphics for the game and movie industry. Previously he worked for more than four years in Rockstar's core technology group as the lead graphics programmer. His game credits can be found at http://www.mobygames.com/developer/sheet/view/developerId,158706/. He is the editor of the *ShaderX* and *GPU Pro* book series, the author of many articles, and a regular speaker at computer graphics conferences worldwide. He is also a DirectX MVP (since 2006), teaches at UCSD, and is active in several advisory boards throughout the industry. You can find him on twitter at @wolfgangengel.

Thorsten Grosch is a junior professor of computational visualistics at the University of Magdeburg, Germany. Prior to this appointment he worked as a postdoctoral fellow at MPI Informatik in Saarbruecken. Thorsten received his PhD at the University of Koblenz-Landau; his main research interest is in both the areas of physically accurate and real-time global illumination.

Holger Gruen ventured into creating real-time 3D technology over 20 years ago writing fast software rasterizers. Since then he has worked for games middleware vendors, game developers, simulation companies, and independent hardware vendors in various engineering roles. In his current role as a developer technology engineer at NVIDIA, he works with games developers to get the best out of NVIDIA's GPUs.

Ralf Habel is a postdoctoral researcher at the Institute of Computer Graphics and Algorithms of the Vienna University of Technology, where he received his PhD in 2009. He studied theoretical physics and computer graphics at the University of Stuttgart and the Georgia Institute of Technology. His current research interests are real-time rendering, precomputed lighting and transfer, and computational photography.

John Huelin is a graphics programmer at Ubisoft Montreal, where he has worked mostly on the *Assassin's Creed* games developing and optimizing a variety of 3D technologies. He earned his master's degree in computer science at University of Technology of Belfort-Montbeliard (UTBM), where he focused on image and 3D.

Anton Kaplanyan is a Lead Researcher at Crytek. During the development of Crysis 2 and CryEngine 3 he was responsible for research on graphics and porting of CryEngine 2 to the current generation of consoles. Currently he is busy working on the next iteration of the engine to keep pushing both DX11 and next-gen console technology. Additionally he has been working on his PhD thesis within Karlsruhe University since 2009. Prior to joining Crytek he received his MS in computer science at Moscow University of Electronic Engineering, Russia, in early 2007.

Oliver Klehm is a PhD student in the computer graphics group at the Max Planck Institute (MPI) for Informatics. In 2011 he received an MSc from the Hasso-Plattner-Institut, Potsdam, Germany. His research interests include interactive global illumination and visibility algorithms, as well as general-purpose GPU programming. In addition to an algorithmic focus, he is also interested in designing complex software that incorporates sets of different algorithms.

Jason Lacroix has been involved in the games industry since 2000 and has worked for a wide range of companies including Artificial Mind and Movement (now bEhavior Interactive), Electronic Arts, Factor 5, and Crystal Dynamics. He has spent the last 9 years working on low level rendering code and shader programming for a variety of systems, including PC, Xbox/360, PS2/PS3, and GameCube/Wii. He is currently employed at Crystal Dynamics where he heads the rendering efforts for the Tomb Raider team.

Hugh Malan is a principle tech programmer at Guerrilla Games. Previously, he worked for CCP on Dust 514, and before that at Realtime Worlds, as graphics lead on *Crackdown*. He developed the "Realworldz" real-time procedurally-generated planet demo for 3Dlabs. He has an MSc in computer graphics from Otago University, New Zealand, and a BSc in physics with honors in mathematics from Victoria University, New Zealand.

Timothy Martin works as a graphics programmer at Confetti Inc.

Oliver Mattausch is currently employed as a post doctorate in the VMML Lab of the University of Zurich, working on processing and visualizing large datasets. Previously he worked as a computer graphics researcher at the Vienna University of Technology and at the University of Tokyo/ERATO. He received his MSc in 2004 and his PhD in 2010 from Vienna University of Technology. His research interests are real-time rendering, visibility and shadows, global illumination, and geometry processing.

Morten S. Mikkelsen has had graphics as his hobby for more than a quarter of a century and has been an industry professional for 16 years. He was with IO-Interactive for seven years and with the ICE team at Naughty Dog for almost five years. More recently, he was the lead/principal graphics programmer on *Rise of the Tomb Raider*. He has a double major in mathematics and computer science from the University of Copenhagen and a master's in computer science. Today he is a director of graphics at Unity Technologies Lab in San Francisco.

Anders Nilsson is a software engineer at Illuminate Labs, working on precomputed lighting for games. He is an obsessive graphics coder with a MSc in engineering mathematics from Lund University.

Kevin Örtegren is a junior graphics programmer in the core technology team at Guerrilla Games, where he works on the rendering engine that brings the world of *Horizon: Zero Dawn* to life on the Playstation 4. Kevin started out his graphics programming career by pursuing a master's degree in games and software development at Blekinge Institute of Technology, where he wrote his master's thesis at Avalanche Studios.

Emil Persson is the Head of Research at Avalanche Studios, where he is conducting forward-looking research, with the aim to be relevant and practical for game development, as well as setting the future direction for the Avalanche Engine. Previously, he was an ISV Engineer in the Developer Relations team at ATI/AMD. He assisted tier-one game developers with the latest rendering techniques, identifying performance problems and applying optimizations. He also made major contributions to SDK samples and technical documentation.

Tobias Ritschel is a postdoctoral researcher at the CG Group, Télécom ParisTech (CNRS). He received his PhD in computer science at the Max-Planck-Institut Informatik, in Saarbrücken, Germany, in 2009 and was awarded the Eurographics Dissertation Prize at Eurographics 2011. His research interests include interactive global illumination rendering, GPU programming, perception, and GPU geometry processing.

Benjamin Rouveyrol has been working in the game industry for the past ten years, working on the *Far Cry* and *Assassin's Creed* series. He is currently working at Ubisoft Montreal on *Rainbow Six Siege*, making pixel faster and prettier.

Daniel Scherzer is currently a post-doctoral research fellow at the Max-Planck Institute for Informatics, Saarbrücken. He also gives lectures at the Vienna University of Technology and the FH Hagenberg. He previously worked at the Ludwig Boltzmann Institute for Archaeological Prospection and Virtual Archaeology and as an assistant professor at the Institute of Computer Graphics and Algorithms of the Vienna University of Technology, where he received an MSc in 2005, an MSocEcSc in 2008, and a PhD in 2009. His current research interests include temporal coherence methods, shadow algorithms, modeling and level-of-detail approaches for real-time rendering. He has authored and co-authored several papers in these fields.

Christoph Schied is a scientific researcher at the computer graphics group at Karlsruhe Institute of Technology (KIT), working on his PhD. He received his diploma with honors from Ulm University in 2013. His research interests include real-time rendering pipelines, antialiasing, and global illumination.

Andrew Schneider is the Principal FX Artist at Guerrilla Games in Amsterdam. In addition to developing effects solutions, his focus is developing the real-time volumetric cloud system for *Horizon: Zero Dawn*. He has presented this work at SIGGRAPH 2015 as part of the "Advances in Real-Time Rendering" course. Previously, he was a Senior FX Technical Director at Blue Sky animation studios in Greenwich, Connecticut, where his focus was developing the volumetrics pipeline, SmogVox, for use with rendering fluid effects, billion+ fine particle renders, and clouds. This work was presented as production talks at SIGGRAPH 2011, 2012, and 2013. He completed his bachelor's degree in computer art and visual effects at the Savannah College of Art and Design in 2005.

Hans-Peter Seidel is the scientific director and chair of the computer graphics group at the Max Planck Institute (MPI) for Informatics and a professor of computer science at Saarland University, Saarbrücken, Germany. He is cochair of the Max Planck Center for Visual Computing and Communication (MPC-VCC) (since 2003), and he is the scientific coordinator of the Cluster of Excellence on Multimodal Computing and Interaction (M2CI) that was established by the German Research Foundation (DFG) within the framework of the German Excellence Initiative in 2007. In addition, Seidel is a member of the Governance Board of the newly established Intel Visual Computing Institue (IVCI) (since 2009).

Ivan Spogreev is a rendering software engineer at EA Canada working on *FIFA* for Xbox One, Playstation 4, and PC. He started his career in the game industry in 2007 and has always been passionate about 3D graphics technology and visuals. He has previously worked at Ubisoft and HB Studios on various projects including *Madden*, *Assassin's Creed 2*, and *Splinter Cell: Conviction*. His main focus is making games look as realistic as possible.

László Szécsi is an associate professor at the Technical University in Budapest, Hungary. He gives lectures in programming, computer graphics, and computer game development. His research revolves around global illumination, real-time rendering techniques, and the combination of the two. László has published numerous scientific papers and has been a regular contributor to the *ShaderX* book series.

Nicolas Thibieroz has spent all of his professional life working in developer relations for graphics hardware companies. He taught himself programming from an early age as a result of his fascination for the first wave of "real-time" 3D games such as *Ultima Underworld*. After living in Paris for 22 years, he decided to pursue his studies in England where he obtained a Bachelor of Electronic Engineering in 1996. Not put off by the English weather, Nicolas chose to stay and joined PowerVR Technologies to eventually lead the developer relations group, supporting game developers on a variety of platforms and contributing to SDK content. He then transitioned to ATI Technologies and AMD Corporation, where he is now managing the worldwide ISV Gaming Engineering group.

Yasin Uludag works as a rendering software engineer at EA DICE.

Michael Wimmer is an associate professor at the Institute of Computer Graphics and Algorithms of the Vienna University of Technology, where he received an MSc in 1997 and a PhD in 2001. His current research interests are real-time rendering, computer games, real-time visualization of urban environments, point-based rendering, and procedural modeling. He has coauthored many papers in these fields, was papers cochair of EGSR 2008 and of Pacific Graphics 2012, and is associate editor of the journal *Computers & Graphics*.

Bartłomiej Wroński is a senior staff programmer at Sony Computer Entertainment America. He started his career at the Polish game development studio CD Projekt RED in Warsaw, working as an engine and graphics programmer for *The Witcher 2* and later leading the technical side of the porting process for *The Witcher 2: Enhanced Edition* for Xbox 360. After conducting R&D activities and developing new rendering and lighting techniques for upcoming titles *The Witcher 3: Wild Hunt* and *Cyberpunk 2077*, he joined the Ubisoft Montreal studio. He worked there on next-generation visual effects for critically acclaimed AAA video game titles including *Assassin's Creed IV: Black Flag* and *Far Cry 4*. Recently, Bart joined Sony Computer Entertainment America at the Santa Monica Studio to continue his work on novel real-time algorithms for the Sony Playstation console platform. He runs a graphics- and photography-oriented blog at www.bartwronski.com. His hobbies include digital and film photography, electronic music synthesis and sound processing, strength sports, and traveling.

Chris Wyman is an assistant professor in the Computer Science Department at the University of Iowa. His research interests focus on interactive global illumination techniques, specular materials, and participating media.

Jason Yang has been involved in the games industry since 2000, and he has worked for a wide range of companies including Artificial Mind and Movement (now bEhavior Interactive), Electronic Arts, Factor 5, and Crystal Dynamics. He has spent the last 11 years working on low-level rendering code and shader programming for a variety of systems, including PC, Xbox/360/One, PS2/PS3/PS4, and GameCube/Wii. He is currently employed at Crystal Dynamics where he heads the rendering efforts for the *Tomb Raider* team.

Egor Yusov is a graphics software engineer in Visual Computing Engineering group at Intel, where he has worked on a variety of 3D technologies including deformable terrain and physically based water rendering, shadows, and post-process effects. He received his PhD in computer science from Nizhny Novgorod State Technical University, Russia, in 2011. His research interests include real-time visualization and rendering, data compression, GPU-based algorithms, and shader programming.

Printed and bound by CPI Group (UK) Ltd, Croydon, CR0 4YY

17/10/2024

01775698-0001